Y0-BZB-532

ARTS
AMERICA

ARTS AMERICA

Enjoying the Best Art Museums, Theater, Classical Music, Opera, Jazz, Dance, Film, and Summer Festivals in America

Executive Editor
Jeffrey Compton

Associate Editors
Norma Foote, Sean Kent, Brooke Pierce

Contributing Editors
Kathleya Afanador, Dance; Patrick Allen, Classical Music;
Tiffany DuMouchelle, Classical Music; Kara Mason, Visual Arts;
Alex Riccomini, Visual Arts; Mark Sanderlin, Jazz; Melissa Somosky, Film;
John Broughton, go-artsamerica.com

Huntington Press • Las Vegas, Nevada

ARTS AMERICA

Enjoying the Best Art Museums, Theater, Classical Music, Opera, Jazz, Dance, Film, and Summer Festivals in America

Published by
Huntington Press
3665 Procyon St.
Las Vegas, NV 89103
Phone (702) 252-0655
e-mail: books@huntingtonpress.com

Copyright ©2009, Jeffrey Compton and Norma Foote

Associate Editors:
Norma Foote, Sean Kent, Brooke Pierce

Contributing Editors:
Kathleya Afanador, Dance
Patrick Allen, Classical Music
Tiffany DuMouchelle, Classical Music
Kara Mason, Visual Arts
Alex Riccomini, Visual Arts
Mark Sanderlin, Jazz
Melissa Somosky, Film

John Broughton, go-artsamerica.com

ISBN: 978-1-935396-35-2

Cover Photos: ©iStockPhoto: jeancliclac, sbayram; Wikimedia Commons: Dejeuner-canotiers (PD-old); Broadway-Plakate (Martin Dürrschnabel); Disney Concert Hall (Carol M. Highsmith); Janusz-Olejniczak (Adam Bielawski); Jill Merk (arts-america logo)

Inside Images: ©iStockPhoto: kickstand (New York), tacojim (Chicago), egdigital (Los Angeles), goldenangel (San Francisco), jmoor17 (Washington, D.C.), nano (Philadelphia), photoquest7 (Seattle); Wikimedia Commons: Austin from Congress Bridge-daylight (Daniel Mayer); Jill Merk (arts icons)

Design & Production: Laurie Shaw

All information provided in *Arts America* is deemed reliable but is not guaranteed and should be independently verified. For additional updates visit: go-artsamerica.com.

All rights reserved. No part of this publication may be translated, reproduced, or transmitted in any form or by any means, electronic or mechanical, including photocopying and recording, or by any information storage and retrieval system, without the express written permission of the copyright owner.

DEDICATION

To two Arts Angels—
William H. Compton Jr. (1945–2007)
Adam Fine (1969–2008)

ACKNOWLEDGMENTS

Arts America is a team effort—and this team has a lot of boosters. First thanks go to our Huntington Press editors Deke Castleman and Heidi Christ for making us sound considerably more interesting than we actually are. I also send warm kudos to publisher Anthony Curtis for his consistent down-to-earth encouragement, not to mention assuming the risk in publishing our dream. And this dream would have been a nightmare except for the outstanding efforts of Huntington's graphics artist Laurie Shaw. She brings an entire new meaning to the word "patience."

To the staffs of New Dramatists and the Center for Fiction for providing team meeting space in New York City and to the El Cortez for giving me Las Vegas office space (my other home) at an unbelievable rate.

A nice bouquet goes to Diana Price for her helpful comments regarding the manuscript and her 25 years of arts camaraderie.

Thanks to Bob Dancer, Howard Simpson, and Robert Page for providing interesting insights. Also thanks to our genre editors Kathleya Afanador, Patrick Allen, Tiffany DuMouchelle, Kara Mason, Alex Riccomini, Mark Sanderlin, and Melissa Somosky.

A salute to John Broughton for his assistance in mapping out our cyberspace future and explaining it in terms that both the editors and Jill Merk (our wonderful Web designer) could understand.

And finally, thanks to associate editors Norma Foote, Sean Kent, and Brooke Pierce for their invaluable assistance, advice, hard work—and good company. I hope that you enjoyed the ride.

CONTENTS

WHY ARTS AMERICA?

by Jeffrey Compton, Executive Editor

Judy lives about 30 minutes by train from Chicago. A schoolteacher by trade and a pianist by hobby, she makes a resolution every year that she'll enjoy more classical-music concerts, but she never manages to get it together. Whenever she has the time, she does not have the money and whenever she has the money …

Primarily due to Steve's career, he, Kathryn, and their two children live in a small town in Oklahoma. They love the town and their neighbors; they especially like the schools. But the cultural life is very limited. Steve and Kathryn have never investigated the museums, theater, or opera in nearby Dallas. Instead, they blow their wad on two annual weekend trips to New York City.

Cindy lives in Brooklyn—and recently lost her fashion-design job due to downsizing. She's trying to make ends meet freelancing, but doesn't know if she'll ever be able to enjoy the arts in New York again.

A home contractor from Los Angeles, Joe barely graduated high school. As a favor to his new girlfriend, he attended a performance of Handel's *Messiah*—and really enjoyed it. Now he wants to explore the world of classical music (and visit an art museum), but doesn't have a clue where to begin.

Randy is on the road two weeks of every month—and he gets little advance warning as to where he'll be next. He loves theater and classical music, but because he doesn't have time to do research, he usually ends up at the nearest multiplex seeing the same movie playing two blocks from his house.

Sound familiar? Maybe you know these people. We certainly do.

We, the editors of *Arts America*, range in age from 20 to 65 and hail from

Texas, California, Washington, D.C., and New York City. We're all passionate about the cultural arts in America. We like to visit museums and attend performances and concerts (as well as late-night jazz joints) everywhere we go. Neither our time nor our funds are unlimited, so we've learned how to quickly check out what's available and how to get best for the least. We also love to share our discoveries with friends—and it's for these friends (and hopefully many more) that we created this book.

It's wonderful to be an art lover in America. Our country's sheer size, its large, educated, and prosperous population, and diverse geographical and cultural history all combine to create a tremendous artistic smorgasbord. The United States offers many of the best museums, theaters, orchestras, operas, and dance the world has ever known. Jazz is an American invention; Hollywood is the film capital of the world. While we encourage everyone to travel internationally as much as possible, an American doesn't have to go to Europe to fully appreciate the cultural arts. There is much in his own backyard—or at least within 100 miles—to discover and at a much cheaper price than running off to London or Paris.

Why *Arts America*? It's out hope that by reducing, if not eliminating entirely, some of the most common barriers—lack of time, lack of money, or lack of knowledge—we'll increase the number of positive cultural-art experiences in your lives as well as our own. Some people are happy to go to a museum or see a show or concert once a month. Others like to go three times a week. Whatever works for you is fine as long as you're having a good time and, with luck, a stimulating experience for minimal inconvenience and money.

HOW WAS *ARTS AMERICA* COMPILED?

Over the past several years, Norma Foote and I have not only enjoyed the fruits of our cultural-arts research, but have also passed along tons of tips to all of our friends (or whomever we're sitting next to on the plane). Several happy recipients of our information and advice have mentioned that we should write a book, especially as no similar source is currently available on the bookstore shelves.

In late 2008 we got serious. Norma and I began compiling a list of all the major theater, opera, dance, and classical-music groups, as well as the non-profit museums, in the country. Using an admittedly quick-and-dirty point system, we selected which cities to explore in this book, including the five urban areas (New York, Chicago, Los Angeles, San Francisco, and Washington, D.C.) that are true world-class cultural-arts destinations. In every city we cover, we added information on jazz venues, art movie houses, and multi-art venues.

We would have liked to include many more of our favorite destinations, but size restrictions left out such intriguing places as Anchorage, Austin, Birmingham, Buffalo, Charleston (SC), Cincinnati, Columbia (SC), Columbus, Detroit, Ft. Wayne, Honolulu, Indianapolis, Jacksonville, Little Rock, Louisville, Memphis, Milwaukee, New Orleans, Oklahoma City, Phoenix, the Portlands (ME and OR), Princeton, Providence, Raleigh, Reno, Richmond, San Antonio, Santa Barbara, Santa Fe, Sacramento, Salt Lake City, Savannah, St. Louis, Tampa/St. Pete, Tucson, Tulsa, and Wichita—all of which have cultural-arts scenes well worth your time and money to explore. (Note: These cities will be covered on our website at go-artsamerica.com.)

The next step was to assemble the best talent possible to research and compile all the necessary information, then write it up in a way that conveys the excitement these arts institutions and performance groups deserve. On that score, the muses were kind and I can confidently say that the best descriptions were written by neither myself nor Norma Foote, but by one of our other talented editors: Kathleya Afanador, Patrick Allen, Kara Mason, Tiffany DuMouchelle, Sean Kent, Brooke Pierce, Alex Riccomini, Mark Sanderlin, and Melissa Somosky. I'm also blessed that the best Internet expert I know, John Broughton, has also been a good friend for 40 years.

All information submitted by the editors was checked twice, the second recheck just weeks before publication. With human error as well as the effects of the recession, we assume that there are some minor inaccuracies, not to mention a few outright errors. For those we apologize, and promise that when we find out about any error, we'll post a correction on our website.

The primary goal of *Arts America* is to pass along both the passion and the practical, or, put another way, *why* you should enjoy the arts and *how* to enjoy the arts. So make us happy—and *enjoy the arts in America*!

SAVING MONEY AND ENJOYING THE ARTS—AT THE SAME TIME

America likes good entertainment. The stock market, car purchases, and home construction may be down, but movie sales are up. Broadway's 2008–2009 season was a banner year—offering the theater-goer a total of 75 different shows. Many cultural-arts institutions are struggling due to cuts in endowments as well as corporate and government funding, but attendance appears to be more than holding its own. This is a good thing. An artist needs an audience to create and maintain great art.

Whatever the economy, lots of people always want to experience more things cultural, but don't think they can afford it. They read about $20 museum admissions and $200 Broadway tickets and quickly conclude that American culture and their pocketbook don't jibe.

Our quick response to this: Wrong.

Yes, you can drop a couple of C-notes to see the best theater, classical music, jazz, and dance, but you don't have to. You can pay full admission price at every museum you visit, but you don't have to. You can pay $10 every time you want to watch a movie, but you don't have to.

Over the last few decades, tickets and other related costs have increased significantly, but so has the number of available discounts and other cost-cutting methods. In addition, the Internet makes it simple to learn about these discounts and to take full advantage of them.

THE GROUND RULES

Before we start, let's cover some ground rules.

You can't see everything. Nor should you try—you'll just feel overwhelmed. As long as what you're seeing (or hearing) is worthwhile, in your opinion, that's all that matters. You're out to have a good time, not to increase your "most-concerts-attended" cocktail-party chatter. If following our advice allows you to enjoy twelve arts activities a year instead of six, we'll add you to our win column.

Do not spend more than you can afford. Every city we discuss in the upcoming chapters offers excellent art choices for less than $30 (especially when you factor in various discounts). Have a budget and stick to it; you can do a whole year of wonderful things (even in New York) for the $450 you didn't spend on *Jersey Boys* tickets.

Do not equate size and price with quality. Three years ago, two of us saw a very small production of *Guys and Dolls* in North Hollywood for $15 a ticket. The theater held 80 people and the sets were minimal. But the acting, singing, and costumes were first-rate. It was the best production of the Frank Loesser classic we ever saw, far better than the recent Broadway revival at $75 a ticket (and those were bought at discount). A lot of good art happens in small places.

Never avoid a cultural offering because you feel that you don't understand enough about it. Most performances or exhibitions require little or no background to enjoy them and if you want to learn more before you go, a lot of inexpensive resources (which we discuss) are available. If after a few tries, you decide some cultural happenings aren't your thing, that's fine, but at least you're making this determination based on experience, not fear or ignorance.

Maintain a current art-news network. Knowing what's available as soon as you can is three-fourths of the battle. Under each city we list a few sources for current information, including newspapers, websites, and magazines. These suggestions are strictly jumping-off points; with very little effort you'll find many others (especially blogs) that may be better suited to your particular needs and interests.

MUSEUM DISCOUNTS

Four years ago, the rebuilt Museum of Modern Art (MoMA) in New York City opened to much fanfare, much praise, and a $20 admission fee, which has since been happily paid by scores of unquestioning visitors. Those in the know pay far less using a variety of discounts, such as the following, that can be found at most museums.

FREE DAYS

Almost every non-profit museum in the world offers free access one day (or part of one day) a week. And because free days differ from venue to venue, you can visit one museum for free on Tuesday, another on Wednesday, a third on Thursday, and so on. Be aware, however, that this is also the best-known museum discount, so expect crowds and long lines, especially if there's a major exhibition. Our advice is to go as early as possible on a free day.

SENIORS/STUDENTS

If you're a full-time student or over the age of sixty (sometimes less), check to see if the museum offers any admission discounts, as well as any other special programs that may be available.

BANK OF AMERICA'S "MUSEUMS ON US"

Do you have a Bank of America credit card, ATM card, or check with your name imprinted on it? If yes, then thanks to B of A's Museums on Us program, you have free admission the first weekend of every month to more than 100 museums across America, including the Metropolitan Museum of Art, the Art Institute of Chicago, the De Young Museum in San Francisco, and the Los Angeles County Museum of Art. For a full list go to museums. bankofamerica.com.

MUSEUM MEMBERSHIP

Do you visit a particular museum at least three times a year? If so, it's probably in your best interest to become a member by making a small (sometimes as little as $35 a year) donation to the museum. Besides supporting a vital institution and getting a tax deduction, you'll soon find that membership has its privileges. The most important are free admission to the museum for one year and information (newsletters and email) regarding upcoming events. Other privileges usually include a gift-shop discount (which can be a godsend near the holidays), free or discounted audio guides, and free or discounted admission to any concert or film programs the museum provides.

Members of the Isabella Gardner Museum in Boston, for example, receive discounted admission to the museum concert series, the longest-running museum music program in the nation, held in the Gardner's intimate and atmospheric Tapestry Room gallery. MoMA members receive free admission to the extensive film screenings held in the movie theaters located in the museum's basement.

To address the needs of a wider (and younger) audience, some museums have member-only family days (usually on Saturdays) or increasingly popular social mixers held on Friday nights.

At the higher levels ($100+), museum members are frequently granted special viewing hours and invitations to exhibition openings, educational programs, and other special events. Several museums offer discounted memberships to students and seniors, while those in the larger cities provide special plans to anyone living 200 or more miles away.

RECIPROCAL MUSEUM MEMBERSHIP

Are you already a member of your hometown museum? If so, contact its membership office or check the website for reciprocal privileges at other museums across the country. Higher-level members of the Metropolitan Museum of Art can avoid paying admission to the Boston Museum of Fine Arts, the Wadsworth Atheneum in New Haven, and the Los Angeles County Museum of Art. For some museums, such as the Newark Museum, the reciprocal museum network is an important factor in maintaining a membership.

Reciprocal memberships aren't limited to art institutions. If you belong to any type of non-profit museum (health, science, natural history, planetarium), botanical garden, aquarium or zoo, you may already have reciprocal privileges that can save you serious dollars when you travel.

OTHER TYPES OF MUSEUM DISCOUNTS

Group Discounts—You don't have to be a member of a large recognized group to get a group discount. Many museums give them to any group of six people who call ahead and all arrive at the same time.

Organization Memberships—The two most common membership discounts are AAA and Public Television, but there are others, such as the local Chamber of Commerce or a city club. If you belong to any of these groups, obtain a recent copy of their brochures or check out their websites for a list of available local discounts. AAA members should develop a habit of asking about discounts almost every time they spend money.

Employer—Larger companies often obtain local-museum discounts for their employees, especially if the company is a donor. It doesn't hurt to ask.

Union—Many unions (especially entertainment and arts related, but others as well) offer museum discounts to members.

Industry Related (AAM)—If you work for or actively volunteer at any non-profit museum, check to see if it's a member of the American Association of Museums and can assist you in obtaining an individual membership, which is good for free admission and major discounts at museums across the country.

THE BEST TIP

If someone, no matter where he or she lives, asked us for the best *Arts America* tip, our answer would be simple: Go to the websites of your favorite museums, theaters, dance groups, etc., and sign up for free email alerts. More and more non-profit and for-profit organizations are seeing the huge advantages of email marketing. Email is cheaper and greener than snail mail and it's instantaneous. A theater offering discount tickets to a slow-selling matinée now uses email to get the word out. Museums hosting inexpensive events or special showings are turning more and more to email and only email.

Initially, don't sign up for email from more than a dozen organizations or you'll be overwhelmed. Also, learn the features and capabilities of your email program, especially regarding junk-mail management and message sorting.

Coupons—Just like commercial business, many museums distribute discount coupons at local hotels, in magazines, or in the popular *Entertainment* annual coupon book.

Pay-What-You-Can Admission—New York museums built on city-owned land (including the Metropolitan Museum of Art and the Museum of Natural History) may ask for a "suggested admission," but are required to accept whatever a person can pay. What should you do? Pay what you can! If you're broke, pay only half or a third, but if you can afford full board, pay that, remembering that we want great institutions to remain accessible and affordable.

No admission—The world-class Cleveland Museum of Art has never charged an admission fee (except for special exhibitions) and recently other museums have also dropped the door tax, including the Baltimore Museum of Art and the nearby Walters Art Museum. In this way, these museums can get more people through the door, thus getting more money from individual members and foundations. We hope this trend continues.

PERFORMANCE DISCOUNTS

Theater and concert tickets cost considerably more than museum admissions. However, considerably more discount opportunities are also available—from small reductions to completely free tickets—if you're willing to do a little homework.

SUBSCRIPTIONS

If you frequent a theater, opera company, or dance ensemble that you would like to attend more often, you should strongly consider subscribing. The overall discount is often considerable for the best seats and even more if you don't mind making little sacrifices in seating and attending on week nights. More important, the subscription process forces you to make decisions as to what you want to see and when to see it. This means you'll actually be in the seats instead of just "thinking about it."

Types of Subscriptions—Subscriptions may be for a full or partial season. Venues that host many different types of performances might have one subscription aimed at classical music fans, another aimed at ballet lovers, one with children's programming, etc. Student and senior subscriptions are offered at even greater discounts. You may even find subscriptions for couples, for a parent and child, and for patrons with a hearing disability (ensuring that your tickets will be for special signed performances).

Subscription Setup—In the old days, you'd subscribe to specific performances, all chosen in advance, receive the tickets in the mail, and go through hell if you had to make a change. While some groups still work that way, many have made it much easier to change your seats. Other groups now send their subscribers flyers for each show, giving information about the performance and the different ways to reserve your tickets. Another variation is a partial subscription, which allows you

VISITING GALLERIES AND AUCTION PREVIEWS

Just because you're not in the market for a million-dollar masterpiece (or even a thousand-dollar masterpiece) doesn't mean you shouldn't visit art galleries or attend art-auction previews. Most of the walk-ins at any gallery don't buy anything, but the gallery prefers any traffic to no traffic. In most cities, galleries hang out together in neighborhoods, such as Chelsea in New York and River North in Chicago, so look up a couple in newspapers and on the Web, then spend an afternoon wandering from one to another. If you happen to like a particular gallery, sign the guestbook or leave a card with your e-mail address. You might be invited to the next opening party.

As interest and value run hand in hand, art auction houses actively market their previews. Nothing raises the bids faster than a bunch of folks taking time out of their lives to admire something. The best way to find out about auction previews is to check out the website of the auction houses in your area or where you plan to visit and sign up for their emails.

to pay a fixed fee or take out a membership, then order all your tickets at a discount on a show by show basis.

Additional Subscription Benefits—Subscribers are usually given a discount on extra single tickets, as well as priority seating, opportunities to buy tickets to special events in advance of the general public, and admission into talkbacks, parties, and other happenings. They will often get discounts to other local arts companies, as well as parking and restaurant discounts.

To Renew or Not To Renew?—If you've purchased a subscription in the past and have gotten enjoyment out of it (and have missed no more than one performance), definitely renew. Was the last season a turkey? First, decide if it was one show or an overall decrease in quality. If the group has a good track record, continue to subscribe, especially if the one objectionable show was just an experiment gone bad (it happens). The main reason we would consider not renewing a subscription is we missed more than one performance in the past and expect the same circumstances in the future. It may be because of travel or job demands, or the theater has an inconvenient or inflexible policy regarding subscribers switching performances.

MEMBERSHIP

Membership is kind of a cousin to subscription. Some arts organizations use the terms interchangeably, so if you become a member, you automatically get a season subscription. But for the most part, organizations, especially the larger ones, differentiate them. A subscription ensures that you have a ticket to each performance in the season, but a membership is just a way of supporting the organization, sometimes with a donation of as little as $25. Usually, there are different levels to membership and the more you donate, the more benefits you receive. Basic perks often include a newsletter subscription and your name listed in the performance program or quarterly newsletter, but as you get higher up the donation ladder, those benefits include more discounts and free tickets, as well as invitations to opening-night parties or even receptions with the cast.

Many of the larger non-profit performance venues (Lincoln Center, Carnegie Hall, Los Angeles Music Center) offer membership programs worth investigating, especially if you already frequent the place. For example, at the basic level, Carnegie Hall members receive access to half-price tickets to several concerts every month and invites to dress rehearsals.

SPECIAL-DAY PERFORMANCE DISCOUNTS

If you only go to a concert or show on Friday or Saturday night, you'll probably pay full board, but a few scheduling maneuvers can mean big savings.

Dress Rehearsals—Thirty years ago it was common for a theater company or orchestra to "paper" the final dress rehearsal in order to have a small friendly audience for the cast to play to. Today, dress-rehearsal tickets are sold as "almost regular" performances (albeit at a very large discount) or given away free to members and senior and student groups.

In our experience, most theater dress rehearsals are run as if it's the first performance of the show. The action isn't stopped unless there's a major problem with a performer. However, classical-music-concert dress rehearsals are usually very informal (we've seen people reading a newspaper during them) and can vary widely in what's presented. Some dress rehearsals offer the complete concert; others are the orchestra practicing one movement of a symphony. Either way can be fun!

Previews—Remember the days when a Broadway show ran two previews, then had an early-evening opening night so the critics could make their deadlines? Sorry, long gone. Not only Broadway, but many regional theaters do at least three weeks of previews, including a press week, before opening night. This is the main reason that theater reviews have lost almost all sense of spontaneity. Not only are preview performances cheaper to attend, it can be a lot of fun to pre-guess the critics.

There is, of course, one major downside to attending a preview: You could be seeing a bomb that you would have otherwise avoided after the notices came out. For us, however, that has been a very rare experience. In fact, Jeffrey Compton was glad he saw two of Broadway's most recent short-run musical disasters: *Glory Days* and *The Story of My Life*. However, a couple of early-preview performances have been spoiled by a sound problem or a set not moving, which was easily fixed before the next performance. For that reason, we recommend avoiding the first two or three previews.

Weekdays—Tuesday is the slowest night for any performance week. Wednesday is next, followed by Thursday. And unless the show is a complete sell-out, tickets are usually cheaper and available if you go at these times. Note: If you do go during the week, especially Tuesdays, double-check curtain times, which are frequently earlier than Friday or Saturday. On Broadway, weekday evenings aren't cheaper, though discounts are far more abundant, but Wednesday matinées are often priced a bit lower than other performances.

EMAIL DISCOUNTS

Direct—Nothing is cheaper or quicker than email and almost every form of cultural-arts performance group uses email to distribute discount information (usually via discount codes) to their current shows. You don't have to be a member or subscriber, though you frequently get better-quality email if you are; just visit the website and see where you can sign up for emails.

Through Third Parties—Many towns (especially, as you might guess, New York) have organizations, usually ticket agencies, that regularly send out discount notices on shows.

DISCOUNT WEBSITES

Half-Price and Deep Discount—Although Broadway's well-known half-price TKTS booth isn't online yet, many other cities have half-price ticketing services that allow you to purchase day-of-show tickets online or sometimes even days in advance. In addition, websites like Goldstar.com offer significant discounts on tickets to performance events in several cities. Just get on the email list to learn about their offerings in advance. New Yorkers who qualify for TDF membership can use the extensive website (see "New York City Discounts").

Discount Codes—Why more people don't use discount codes, we'll never know. They're much more convenient than any half-price booth, because you can use them to get your tickets well in advance and from the comfort of your home. Sites like Playbill.com and TheaterMania.com allow you to access these codes by signing up for free, or you can find many of them at BroadwayBox.com. Discount codes are distributed in numerous other ways too, including snail-mail flyers and Telecharge e-mails. And here's a tip: Take the code to the box office and buy your tickets in person if you want to save on service and handling fees.

GOOGLING YOUR WAY AROUND

Learning a new public transporation system can save you money, but it can also cost you valuable time. The Internet to the rescue! Some cities, such as San Francisco, have centralized public-transit planners (transit. 511.org) for their metropolitan areas. If one doesn't exist (or you can't find one for your needs), we recommend Google Maps, which requires only a few quick steps. Once you're in the application, enter the address of your destination. Then click the "Get Directions" link (upper left) and enter the address where you'll be starting from. Finally, change the mode from "By Car" (the default) to "By Public Transit" and click "Get Directions." More and more cities are being added to this system every day, so check back frequently to see if your destination (or hometown) is included.

Papering Services—"Papering" is mostly a New York thing right now (though L.A. is coming on), but it's probably the best way to see a maximum of performances for a minimum of cost. With Theater Extras, for instance, you pay an annual membership fee of $99, then only a $4-per-ticket service charge for any event you see through the year. Each day you can log in to the database and see that tickets are available for different Off-Off Broadway shows and performance events, as well as tickets for some Off-Broadway and even the occasional Broadway show.

Resale—When people can't use their already-purchased tickets, they often sell them on websites such as Craigslist, eBay, and Stubhub; to entice buyers, they often sell the tickets for less than face value. Beware, though: Frequently, the people selling tickets on these sites are actually brokers. Summertime in New York City brings a cottage industry of folks willing to stand in line for free Shakespeare in the Park tickets, then sell them online for $30–$150 a pop, depending on how popular the particular show is.

DAY-OF-THE-SHOW DISCOUNTS

What, you want to go today and still get a good deal on tickets? Don't despair, you have some options.

Half-Price Ticket Windows—New York has three, Boston has two, and they're popping up in many other cities across the country. Out-of-towners who just want the experience of a live show, but aren't picky about which one, gravitate toward these booths, which sell half-price tickets on the day of performance. In-the-know locals also love them, as a way to get a cheap culture fix. Don't go expecting to find any "hot-ticket" shows or concerts here, since the specialty is under-sold performances. But don't let the fact that these shows aren't smash hits deter you, either. We've seen numerous gems this way, many of them better than some of the overpriced and over-praised sell-out shows.

Rush/Lotteries—In the beginning, Rush tickets, usually $20 front-row seats, were sold on the basis of first-come first-served. But to prevent kids from spending the night on the sidewalk and scalpers from snapping up too many of these cheap tickets, most shows that offer Rush tickets now distribute them in a lottery held at the theater a few hours prior to curtain. Prices are usually $20–$30 and often must be paid in cash right away if you win. Policies vary slightly depending on the show, so always check at the box office or online (Playbill.com keeps an updated list of Rush info) in advance.

Coupons—Though it isn't as simple as clipping coupons for groceries, coupons for performing-arts companies can at times be found at hotels, in local magazines, in the *Entertainment* coupon books, and inside programs for other local arts events.

Seniors/Students—Student and senior discount policies vary considerably depending on the venue or show, but most offer them, so inquire at the box office or check the website. Student ticket discounts tend to be greater than senior discounts. Sometimes these discounts are available in advance and sometimes they are designated as Rush (you can get them only on the day of performance). Unfortunately, seniors are usually left out in the cold when it comes to getting discounts for Broadway shows and national tours.

OTHER DISCOUNTS

Group Sales—Group discounts are probably the most common discount of all. Every arts organization likes to have a guaranteed full house, so they're always willing to offer a discount to groups. The average minimum to qualify for a group discount is 10 people, but the number may be less (for a venue that has trouble filling seats) or more (15–20 for a popular venue or show). And the more people you add to your party, the bigger the discount gets. If you're able to regularly put together a sizable group to see a show, you'll soon find yourself being contacted by shows or organizations in advance offering you even better deals.

Ushering—If you're willing to work a little for it, you can get free admission to all kinds of venues by serving as an usher. Many organizations, particularly the smaller non-profits, let you sign up for a designated performance, show up an hour before curtain, stuff some programs, help people to their seats, and clean up a bit afterwards; as a reward you enjoy the show for free. Some organizations put their ushers through a more formal process in which they attend an orientation and are expected to usher on a semi-regular basis.

Standing Room—If the show is sold out, it may sell standing-room "seats" in the back of the theater. Of course, policies and the quality of the view vary from venue to venue.

Affiliate Discounts—As with museums, you might be able to get discounted tickets through your PBS membership or other groups you belong to.

Employer—Big companies or major institutions, including schools, often acquire discounts on behalf of their employees or students (this is especially common for organizations that the company has donated to).

Union—Members of some unions, particularly those that serve people in the arts and entertainment industries (e.g., Actors Equity, Screen Actors Guild, Writers Guild, etc.), are sometimes eligible for discounts. In New York City, freelancers billing more than $10,000 a year can join the Freelancer's Union, which offers a variety of arts-related discounts.

Industry-Related—Does your dance group, chorus, or orchestra be-

THE BEST SEATS?

Some folks aren't happy unless they're sitting mid-orchestra, especially if they might run into someone they know. Others are willing to sit anywhere for the right price, as long as they can see (for theater and dance) or hear (for musical events). Norma Foote is just under five feet, so balcony seats are better for her, while at six-two, Jeffrey Compton prefers a seat on the aisle. One thing they both do, though, is note the layout of almost every theater they frequent, so they can take advantage of the best seating deals.

For example, the last few rows of the orchestra at Avery Fisher Hall at Lincoln Center (home of the New York Philharmonic) are not only the cheapest in the auditorium, they get every note. The top row in the American Airlines mezzanine has excellent sight lines and the best prices, as do the farthest rows in the Mark Taper Forum in Los Angeles. The Carnegie Hall balcony, however, is cramped, at the top of four long flights of stairs, has a terrifyingly steep pitch, and the restrooms are a floor below.

long to a national service organization (such as Dance/USA, America Orchestra League, Chorus America, or Opera America)? Check to see if you're entitled to any discounts, especially if you're visiting another city. This applies to board members as well as performers.

Credit-Card Discounts—American Express and Visa Signature card holders are often eligible for certain performance-related advantages, such as getting in on advance ticket sales. This is nice, but it doesn't mean there's a discount involved. However, rewards points and special offers available through these cards can sometimes equal free or discounted tickets.

FILM DISCOUNTS

Either because films are so popular with the mainstream or movie tickets are already fairly inexpensive relative to, say, opera tickets, movie-theater owners seem reluctant to offer discounts. However, we've discovered several ways to get your flick fix (plus a little free popcorn) at a discount.

Free Screenings—Anywhere from a few weeks to several months prior to the official release of a movie, it may be screened in several cities to test audience reaction or give critics a chance to view it. Free tickets are handed out to people on the street in order to fill up seats. Passes are often distributed outside cineplexes during the day or when movie screenings let out.

Once you've attended one, you can usually get on an email or call list to be invited to future screenings. Also try signing up at a website like USAAudiences.com. The catch is that some of these screenings are in the afternoon or early evening before the nine-to-fivers get off work. Furthermore, attendees cannot be involved in the media or film industry.

Free Passes—Local entertainment weeklies or magazines like *Time Out New York* give out free passes through regular drawings all the time. Usually, you just have to go to a Web address and submit your email/contact info to be considered. Radio stations often give out passes to listeners who call in at the right time or can answer a special quiz question.

Matinées and Off-Peak Hours—Most movie theaters sell tickets for a few dollars less in the afternoon when they have a harder time filling seats. AMC Theaters sell tickets to morning showings (Friday thru Sunday and on holidays) for half-price.

Discounts for Students, Seniors, and Kids—Many theaters offer discounts for seniors, students with valid ID, and for children.

Special Weekday Deals—Check with your local movie houses to see if they offer any bargains on slow days. Tuesdays are most often targeted as "bargain" days, but some theaters discount prices on other weekdays as well.

Second-Run Movie Houses—Often referred to as "dollar theaters" (though prices can vary anywhere between 50 cents and a few bucks), these second-run theaters are a good way to see a flick on the big screen without paying big prices, as long as you're willing to wait a couple months after a movie's theatrical release.

Coupons—Coupons for movies are hard to come by, but you can often find them in the *Entertainment* coupon books.

Rewards Cards—Check to see if your favorite movie chain or theater offers a rewards card. AMC's MovieWatcher card and Regal's Crown Club reward customers primarily with free popcorn and drinks, but if you rack up enough points, you can qualify for free or discount movie tickets as well.

Memberships—Some smaller "art-house" movie theaters have membership programs good for significant discounts on tickets, plus admission to member-only events and other perks. A few large arts organizations, such as the Brooklyn Academy of Music or the Museum of Modern Art, offer small theaters for movie screenings; membership at BAM or just a one-day admission ticket to the MoMA will get you free and discounted admission to many films.

WHAT TO DO WITH TICKETS YOU CANNOT USE?

Three months ago you purchased two tickets to the ballet, but a week before the curtain goes up, you find out that your pregnant niece is suddenly getting married that weekend. What do you do?

The first thing is to contact the organization that sold you the tickets and find out what your options are. Even though the tickets say non-refundable non-exchangeable, most theaters know that they're in the goodwill business and will try to help you. When William Compton Jr. died in Los Angeles, he had more than $1,200 worth of unused tickets. Jeffrey had to contact more than a dozen theaters, but all of them (with the sole exception of the Pasadena Playhouse) agreed to credit a full refund back to Bill's credit cards.

Subscribers and members can usually call the organization and arrange to go on a different night, or attend to the entire process over the Internet.

If the theater won't take back your tickets, you can try to sell or give them to your friends or to the general public on eBay, Craigslist or a site like StubHub using Paypal to collect the funds. As with all Internet transactions, use common sense and read the help sections of the various sites to make sure that you understand your protections . You can also post a sign at work, around your apartment or condo complex, or at the gym.

Night of the show and still no takers? Consider going to the theater and selling the tickets by the door. If you can before you go, contact the theater or check the website to see if the show is sold out. That will help you determine how much to ask. In most cities, selling personal tickets for a profit isn't a crime, so you don't have to be super discreet about it. Just go to the theater 60–90 minutes before curtain and hold the two tickets where everybody can see them. Have the seat numbers and locations written down on a separate piece of paper so someone can check to see where the seats are without handling the tickets. Most importantly, agree to the price before turning over the tickets—and it does not hurt to see the money first. Of course, if you're at your niece's wedding, you might have to find someone who can sell your tickets at the theater for you, preferably someone you trust.

Finally, if you can't trade the tickets in or don't want to deal with a stranger-related sale, find out if they can be donated back to the theater or venue (which has to be non-profit) for a tax deduction. At least you can get a portion of your money back, and some organizations even credit the donation toward membership privileges.

NO HOMEWORK REQUIRED!

There are many ways to prepare for a cultural event. Some people like to read as much as they can about it, so they know what to expect. Other people enjoy trying new things and don't want a review of what they'll be seeing; they're happy going into the concert, play, opera, or museum without any preparation. Either approach (or something down the middle) is a matter of choice. There is no right or wrong.

One way of learning about a visual or performing art is very simple. Just go to an event and decide if it's something that you enjoy doing. Two parts of the learning experience when you see a play or listen to music or watch dance are your reactions to the specific piece and the overall art form. If you liked a symphony, go back again to enjoy another classical event. Or go out and try something totally different. While some people like to have a lot of alternatives they're interested in, others concentrate on just one or two genres and discover all they can find within those choices.

Do you need a great deal of arts-related knowledge to appreciate a museum visit, symphony, jazz concert, or Broadway musical? The answer is based on what we mean by "appreciate." None of the arts requires background to enjoy them, but to better understand what the artists are communicating, a little knowledge of both the art and the specific work can be helpful.

Why is Mozart a genius? Why are *Oklahoma* and *Citizen Kane* considered milestones? Who were the Impressionists? What is bebop? Who are the two bums waiting for in *Waiting for Godot* (which, by the way, is still under dispute!)? Researching the answers to these types of questions before you go can enhance the experience.

Does that mean you need to have substantial knowledge or do a required amount of specific homework before each performance or activity to enjoy yourself? Of course not.

Sometime in our lives, we may have passed on the opportunity to try something new when a lack of specific information made us uncomfortable about the experience. However, skipping a trip to a hometown championship football game because we don't understand what a safety is or can't differentiate between a tight-end and a fullback is a waste of a good time. Not only would we miss out on some fun, but attendance would probably increase our appreciation and knowledge of the game.

In 1975, Jeffrey Compton was touring Europe with a good friend who let Jeffrey plan the entire two-month trip, except for three days that the friend, now a professional musician, wanted to spend in Montreux, Switzerland, attending the legendary jazz festival. At that time Jeffrey had never listened to a jazz recording, but to preserve the camaraderie of the trip, he reluctantly went along—and over the course of two days saw live performances by Ella Fitzgerald, Count Basie, Dizzy Gillespie, and dozens of other jazz greats. A love affair was born that weekend that is still going strong.

Thirty years later, Jeffrey persuaded his brother Bill to attend an Edvard Munch (*The Scream*) retrospective at the MoMA on what would be his brother's last trip to his beloved New York City. Although Bill "didn't understand art" and avoided museums, he went along—and was overwhelmed by both the power of the work and what he learned about Munch himself. He spoke of it for months afterward.

No matter how much you know about the arts, at times you'll have no choice but to see a work cold. It's often amazing how much you learn when you watch and listen. Your concentration alone enriches the art.

LEARNING AS YOU GO

All of us have attended an exhibition or performance unprepared, but in almost every instance, we could have taken advantage of resources that cost little in time and money. Most of these resources are provided by the arts institutions themselves, either at the performance, exhibition, or through the website. Like all things in this world, quality varies greatly, but considering the investment involved, they're almost always worth looking into.

Museum Website—Almost all museums now create special pages on their site for current and upcoming exhibitions, including short discussions of the artists and period, plus a few high-resolution photographs of some of the works you'll see. It usually takes only 15 minutes to go through the entire presentation. While you're there, you can check out sections devoted to past related exhibitions, especially if they're relevant to what you're about to see.

Museum Audio Tour—Earphones have become de rigueur at almost every major art exhibition, allowing attendees to learn details about some or all of the pieces shown. The audio tour is either included in the price of the exhibition or the museum charges extra for this service, unless you're a museum member. Sometimes the commentaries are wonderfully insightful and add to your knowledge and enjoyment of the exhibit, but all too frequently the audio commentary becomes background noise full of "who-cares" details. We know many patrons who avoid using them altogether, in favor of relying on the information (next to the picture or written on the wall) or prior research. Or if time permits, they'll walk through the show once to see everything, then pick up the audio-tour equipment for a second look at specific works. Many museums are now using iPod technology for their tours, which allows iPod owners to selectively listen to the tour on equipment they're familiar with.

Podcasts—Informational podcasts created/hosted by either the museum staff or third-party guides can be downloaded to your iPod, iPhone, or home personal computer. Quality can vary, but most podcasts are free and can be found on the museum's website, or by searching Google and/or YouTube.

Tours/Lectures—A guided tour of a museum for a specific exhibition or an introduction to the entire museum can be great fun. Conducted by either a member of the museum staff or a docent (a qualified volunteer), the tours can help you see and learn about the highlights of an exhibition quickly. A plus: It's always interesting to see how other visitors on the tour are reacting to the art through their expressions and questions.

As with audio tours, museum policies vary on tours. Smaller museums tend to put them into the price of admission, while larger ones offer both free and paid tours. It's the same with lectures; the always-running audio may be free, but a specific lecture by a visiting expert has a charge (especially if you're not a member).

Performance-Related Websites—One positive trend in music and theater is the increasing number of performance groups putting program notes on their websites a week or so before the event. It's much easier to read it at home—in bigger type—than just before the performance or standing in the restroom line at intermission. The website may also offer additional notes from the director or other artistic professionals, or even audio/video highlights of the show. And all of it's free.

Preview Mailings—Subscribers and patrons, as well as those who give the group their email addresses, frequently receive extensive background information through the mail or over the Web. While it can be very helpful, these mailings are occasionally overwritten by the press department and include mandatory interviews with the stars, all of whom say that this is the most interesting project with which they've ever been involved.

Professional Reviews—Music and theater critics are a dying breed as more and more cash-strapped newspapers cut their arts staff to reduce overhead. Still, a review can be very helpful (especially if it persuades you to see something) as long as you take it as one, albeit informed, opinion. No one critic should prevent you from seeing a show. However, you should

SAVING ON ...

It was tough, but you managed to scrape together the dough for those tickets. Now you can just enjoy the show without thinking anymore about money, right? Wrong. What about getting to the theater? What about dinner? What about drinks afterwards? And what if your date wants a treat at intermission?

Sometimes it seems like the expenses for a simple night out never end. But if you're smart, you can keep the evening within your budget.

First, see if you can get to the venue via public transportation. Theaters and music halls tend to be in well-trafficked areas near subway stations and bus stops. If you can't find any transportation info on the venue's website, call and ask. If you're driving, find out if any free parking is nearby. Sometimes if you're willing to walk a bit, a cheaper lot is a little farther from the theater. You might also be able to find a spot on the street if you arrive early. Some garages offer discounts on evening and weekend parking, so inquire at the garages or hunt around online for coupons.

As for dinner, don't feel like you absolutely have to eat out before attending a performance, and you should never try to combine true gourmet dining and entertainment in one evening. Theater and concert regulars know that this just isn't feasible and settle for many pre-show meals at home. If your only option is to grab a bite out, consider getting a sandwich at a deli or dropping in at a favorite fast-food joint. On a date or a special occasion, look for places that have good prix-fixe deals; res-

question dropping dollars on anything receiving universal pans. The best way to get a complete set of opinions is to type the name of the show followed by the name of the theater (or theater group) and the word "review" into Google and see what comes up. Well-written art-exhibition reviews can be especially helpful to read in preparation for a museum visit.

Blogs—Is there anyone who doesn't have one? For better or for worse, arts blogs are replacing professional music, film, and theater reviews and, much more than their print counterparts, quality can vary greatly. While some are very well-written, we really don't know the background of who's writing the reviews and if he or she has any personal or professional conflicts or biases. Treat blog reviews as you would the word-of-mouth comments from friends. If they've given you a good tip before, listen a little more closely. Otherwise take it with a large grain of salt.

... THE EVENING EXTRAS

taurants right by the theater often do. (Note: If you really enjoy going out before or after a show, try to patronize the same places instead of jumping around. Regular customers, especially those who tip well, are frequently offered special deals.)

Need an intermission sweet-tooth fix? Whatever you do, don't pay for the over-priced concessions the theater sells (unless it's a smaller theater, where they may be more reasonably priced). We advise dropping by a convenience store before the show and stocking your purse with M&Ms or other snacks for your intermission treat. If you've got a big enough bag, bring a water bottle from home, too. But be sure to put everything away before the curtain goes back up. No one wants to hear you slowly unwrapping your crinkly Snickers wrapper and gnawing on a candy bar during the performance.

Want a drink or nosh after the show? Check your program to see if it advertises special deals. Theaters frequently make deals with local establishments that offer discounted drinks if you present your ticket stub. (Note: Ignore the "Celebrity Choice" column in New York Playbills, which is all advertiser PR.) If no deals are forthcoming and you're with a good friend with whom you just want to chat, there's no harm in finding the nearest pizza place and getting a cheap soda and a table where you can share your thoughts on the performance. After all, the whole point of enjoying the arts is inspiration and communication, not fancy food and high-priced drinks.

Pre- (or Post-) Performance Lecture—Classical-music groups (especially the larger symphonies) as well as jazz and dance presenters now offer free talks before the concerts. Their primary value is that you see the performance immediately afterwards and thus will benefit from the information and opinions of the presenter (frequently the conductor or artistic director). Theater groups (and some film societies) tend to do post-performance talks, which allow the actors to participate. If you have twenty minutes to kill after a show, stick around; you'll always hear something interesting.

Program—Programs are the old standby for on-the-spot background, and the variance is fascinating. Some programs (the Boston Symphony is a good example) are written at a Ph.D. level. Others can be tremendously effective at getting across key points. At the bottom are those that contain nothing but the actors thanking their mothers, teachers, lovers, and God. If you haven't prepared at all for the show, read as much of the program as you can beforehand or take it home to enjoy later.

FOR EVEN MORE KNOWLEDGE AND ENJOYMENT

Over the past year, we've asked our editors (and bugged our in-the-know friends) to turn us onto their opinions of the best books, DVDs, CDs, and websites available to learn more about the arts. In all cases we purchased the items and reviewed them personally—and in almost every instance, we agreed with the recommendations.

This is by no measure a complete list. It's just to get you started.

ALL GENRES—THE TEACHING COMPANY

Founded in 1990 by Thomas M. Rollins, former Chief Counsel of the United States Senate Committee on Labor and Human Resources and a graduate of Harvard Law School, the Teaching Company offers more than 260 courses in every major field of academic study, including classical music, musical theater, jazz, and art history. All are taught by "renowned" college professors and are available on either CD or DVD, usually with extensive printed materials.

We reviewed several of these courses and while all of them imparted considerable and valuable information, like many of the professors we had in college, some of presenters had very quirky speaking habits that became quite distracting. Cost can also be a factor, as some sets run upwards of $250, but almost all of them go on sale sometime during the year. Before purchasing any, you may want to check to see if they're available from your local public library. (Note: The series done on the Metropolitan Museum of Art is outstanding.)

BEGGING A FREE TICKET

Almost all steady theater devotees and concert-goers have been in the situation where a spouse or date has cancelled on them—maybe three days before or maybe at the last minute. But they still want to see the show anyway. They've checked with all their friends and no one is interested, so out of kindness or a desire not to have an empty seat next to them, they offer the ticket on the free section of Craigslist or go to the theater to see if anyone wants it.

If you want to be the lucky recipient of that ticket, here are some suggestions. When answering a Craigslist free ad, tell as much about yourself as possible, including your gender, approximate age, and why you want to see the show. You might even send a picture. Don't include your phone number or mailing address; your email address is enough. It's probably a good idea to say upfront if you're married or in a relationship, so the other party doesn't begin with the wrong agenda. If you get a positive response, which should also have a photograph, agree to meet in front of the theater no less than 20 minutes before the show.

Trying to get a free ticket the night of the show? Tip one: Have a good clean appearance. No one wants to spend two hours sitting next to a bum. Tip two: Stand in front of the theater and ask, "Does anyone have a free ticket they aren't using?" Make sure you say "free," so everyone knows the score. If people there are selling tickets (usually holding them up in their hand), politely say, "I can't afford to pay for the ticket, but if you can't sell it, I'd be glad to have it." Be friendly and don't ask anyone more than once. Most importantly, don't become a pest. Due to complaints, several of the larger venues (including Lincoln Center) are cracking down on insistent ticket begging. You want to see the show, not spend the evening at Night Court!

VISUAL ARTS

Books—*The Art Book* (Phaidon) is a huge general guide to 500 painters and sculptors, ranging from medieval to current, and offers a great overview/introduction to those with a general or beginning interest in art. We also recommend Phaidon's heavier and more expensive *30,000 Years of Art*.

DVDs—It's still a hoot to see a cloistered nun in full habit explaining a Lucian Freud frontal male nude, but the various Sister Wendy's collections are an excellent beginning guide to visual art, especially her *Story of Painting* series. Also recommended is *Civilization: The Complete Series* by Kenneth Clark.

THEATER

Books—Although written more than 40 years ago, *The Season* by William Goldman is still relevant—and extremely entertaining. *Not Since Carrie* by Ken Mandelbaum and *Second Act Trouble* by Steven Suskin offer insight-

---

CUTTING DOWN ON TRAVEL COSTS

While this may be the only book about enjoying the arts in America, hundreds of excellent guidebooks can help you save on travel costs in every city we discuss. Here, Norma and Jeff pass along a few tips that work for them.

They rarely stay in hotels, preferring to rent private homes or apartments, almost all of which they find on Craigslist. For the price of one medium-priced hotel room (sans taxes), they get a multi-bedroom apartment or house with a full kitchen, laundry facilities, and several nice places to write. The writing of this book began on a porch in southern Vermont overlooking the Berkshires and ended in a Los Angeles garden cabana.

The next concern is food, so Norma usually asks the locals, including the landlord, for tips on where to shop; a large supermarket with good prices is usually nearby. They keep an eye out for sales and at checkout ask if they have to join the supermarket club to take advantage of special deals. Some run the sale through a house account, while others make customers fill out a form and take a card, but either way Norma and Jeff usually save 10%-20%. They don't use Costco or Sam's Club, as the quantities are too large for two people on a short trip.

Many cities don't require a car. If Jeffrey and Norma do rent one, Jeffrey makes a reservation as soon as he can, using both multi-company car-rental sites and sites for the individual companies, then double checks the prices every two weeks up until the day before they pick up the car. Frequently, a better deal shows up. If you go this route, avoid pre-paid reservations through Hotwire et al.; you can't change them. Also, check with your credit-card company to see if they offer upgraded car-rental protection. For example, Jeffrey gets an excellent collision policy from American Express that's $20 per trip versus $15 a day from the rental company.

If you tend to use only one or two airlines (or Amtrak), take the time to learn in depth how their frequent-customer programs work, to the point where you know more about them than club personnel. Also find the credit cards that give you the most miles per dollar spent, especially if you pay off your cards every month and don't have to worry about the interest rate.

ful and funny discussions of famous musical bombs. For a real memory-lane trip, pick up a copy of a *Theater World*, an annual publication that has come out every year since 1945, or for more recent seasons, *Playbill Broadway Yearbook*. *Broadway Musicals: The 101 Greatest Shows of All Time* has great pictures and interesting stories and looks good on the coffee table.

CD—David Timson's *The History of Theater* is an informative introduction to drama, especially when read by Derek Jacobi.

DVDs—*Broadway: The American Musical*, a six-hour PBS special, and *Broadway's Lost Treasures Collection,* clips of performances done at the Tony Awards, are both recommended.

Websites—For news, check out playbill.com; for gossip and blogs, go to broadwayworld.com and talkinbroadway.com/allthatchat; and for history, visit the Internet Broadway Database, ibdb.com.

CLASSICAL MUSIC

Books—Any or all of the three classical music books published by National Public Radio (NPR) is a good start: *The NPR Classical Music Companion: An Essential Guide for Enlightened Listening; The NPR Listener's Encyclopedia of Classical Music;* and *NPR Guide to Building A Classical Music Library*. For more on Choral Works check out *Choral Masterworks: A Listener's Guide* by Michael Steinberg, containing 47 essays on the major choral-orchestral works of 28 composers, from J.S. Bach to John Adams.

CD—Need a break from listening to classical music, but still want to remain in the muse? Get and play *Richard Fawkes' History of Classical Music*, read by Robert Powell.

DVDs—Two good choices, both with the incomparable Lenny Bernstein: *Young People's Concerts—New York Philharmonic* and *The Unanswered Question—Six Talks at Harvard*.

OPERA

Book—*First Night at the Opera* is a very readable mix of performance stories, personalities, and gossip.

CD—Also by Richard Fawkes and also read by Robert Powell (see above) is *History of the Opera*.

JAZZ

Books—The recently published *Moving to Higher Ground— How Jazz Can Change Your Life* by Wynton Marsalis is a joy to read, especially when complemented with the more informational *History of Jazz* by Ted Gioia or *What Jazz Is: An Insider's Guide to Understanding and Listening to Jazz* by Jonny King. Autobiography fans should check out *Miles* (Miles Davis); biography fans might want to read *Coltrane—The Story of Sound* by Ben Ratliff.

DVDs—*Jazz–A Film* by Ken Burns is 19 hours long and spends too much time on Armstrong and Ellington and too little time on more modern artists, but it's still the most enjoyable way to learn about jazz. Also check out the new *Jazz Icon* box sets featuring live performances of the greats.

Websites—All About Jazz (allaboutjazz.com) is just that—news, reviews, background stories and forums. Down Beat Magazine website (downbeat.com) is another good choice.

APPRECIATING CHORAL MUSIC ...

[Editor's Note: Robert Page is the Paul Mellon Professor of Music at Carnegie Mellon Universtity and the Music Director Emeritus at the Mendelssohn Choir of Pittsburgh.]

So you want to attend a choral concert? Be careful, for you can easily (and often) get sonically screwed.

There's a well-spread rumor that all choruses are alike—just a gang of people singing, much like a sing-along at a bar or Sunday morning church choir. It really ain't so! I have to admit that "everyone can sing"; the Being put the same sort of vocal folds in the throats of every human (and some animals). But learning really to sing, and not just sing, is the important difference. A concert by a choral ensemble of trained, versatile, educated singers is a thrill no other music ensemble can match. But a concert by a choral ensemble of people who "just love to sing" doesn't make it.

So the question arises: What makes a quality choir or chorus? The expertise of the individual singer in a choral ensemble is the bottom line. Some people have the idea that a trained singer cannot possibly match the sound (called "blend") of another voice. Wrong. A quality chorus has singers who sing more than one way. Professional singers don't change the music to accommodate their own inadequacies, but have the ability to adjust their vocal technique to fit the music. Palestrina isn't sung like Verdi; Josquin isn't the same as Brahms; Schubert is different from Sondheim.

I suggest that two types of choral concerts can attract you. One is the large-scale work, usually chorus and orchestra, with the chorus numbering around 80 to 100 voices. Attend a large symphonic choir, or orchestra and chorus, performing *Carmina Burana* by Carl Orff—exciting, earthy, primitive—and you'll probably want to dance. Alternatively, take in the sheer operatic spectacle of the Verdi *Requiem* or the Prokofiev *Alexander*

FILM

Books—There are a lot of choices, from annually updated guides to coffee-table books, but *Awake in the Dark: The Best by Roger Ebert* is a good place to start. Theater-restoration fans will enjoy *Cinema Treasures: A New Look at Classic Movie Theaters* by Ross Melnick and Andreas Fuchs. It's first a meticulously researched survey of the eras of movie exhibition and second

... BY ROBERT PAGE

Nevsky or the Mahler Second (*Resurrection*) or Eighth (*Symphony of a Thousand*) symphonies or the Berlioz *Requiem* (with four brass bands surrounding you, stereophonic to the nth degree!). The pacific and contemplative side of this combination of choral/orchestral works include the touching *Stabat Mater* by Antonin Dvorak and (after the opening declaration) the last part of Chichester Psalms of Leonard Bernstein—12 of the most gorgeous measures of music ever written.

The second type of choral concert is that of the chamber ensemble. Even the most knowledgeable choral buff may not recognize some of the composers. Many of the works presented by chamber choruses are written by living composers, contrasting with the larger works where almost all the composers are dead. But if you identify a chorus (preferably a professional, not amateur) that programs works of Eric Whitacre, Edie Hill, Libby Larsen, Nancy Galbraith, Morten Lauridsen, or Paulus, buy the ticket. You won't be disappointed. I might add that there are beautiful and exciting chamber-size works written by some dead composers (but not dead for too long), such as Samuel Barber (*Reincarnations*), Francis Poulenc (any of the dozens of pieces), Aaron Copland (particularly *In the Beginning*), Paul Hindemith (yep, gorgeous settings of the Rilke texts), and Benjamin Britten (*Hymn to St. Cecilia*).

To enjoy any choral concert, have your "listening ears on," as Judge Judy says. Don't just hear, but listen. The singer is communicating words that touch the heart, enrich the spirit, churn the blood, expand the soul. But you have to be ready to absorb the text as much as the beautiful sounds that carry the text. A choral concert differs from the instrumental concert in that there's a special message that the choral concert is communicating and a specific reaction on the part of the audience is the goal. In an instrumental concert situation, the listener can choose his/her own inner scenario based on the music being played.

a series of capsule descriptions of 30 notable examples of those cinema treasures still operating.

DVDs—The best collection of films (and film history) available is *Essential Art House—50 Years of Janus Films*. Beautifully packaged with a 200-page guide, this 50-DVD collection offers the 50 greatest "Art House" films, from *Alexander Nevsky* and *The Seventh Seal* to *Jules and Jim, M, Pygmalion, The 39 Steps*, and much more. It's pricey at $700 (though you can get it for considerably less if you look around), but worth every penny.

DANCE

Books—Though some may find it a bit too much like a textbook, *Ballet and Modern Dance* by Susan Au is still the best introductory book in the field. *Speaking of Dance: 12 Contemporary Choreographers* and their Craft by Joyce Morgenroth is both informative and entertaining, especially if you want to learn more about Merce Cunningham, Bill T. Jones, and others.

DVDs—*Martha Graham–An American Original in Performance* contains more than 90 minutes with the Modern Dance originator. *Also check out Balanchine and Bill T. Jones—Dancing to the Promised Land.*

All information provided in *Arts America* is deemed reliable, but isn't guaranteed and should be independently verified. For additional updates visit: go-artsamerica.com.

NEW YORK

uch can be said, good and bad, about the New York art scene. The edgy days of the '30s-'40s and the truly experimental '60s are in the past and the Big Apple gets more commercial and expensive every year. But the city still dominates the American (and world) cultural-arts arena like no other. The best in art, from *Portrait of Adele Bock-Bauer* to *Oklahoma*, originates in or finds its way to New York City.

ARTS INFO

PUBLICATIONS

New York Times (nytimes.com)—Excellent feature coverage of all the arts; the reviewers (unjustly perhaps) still have the power to make or break many shows.

TimeOut New York (newyork.timeout.com)—Subscribe for super cheap and have an abundance of NYC events listings (many of them free) at your fingertips each week. Also offers excellent reviews.

Village Voice (villagevoice.com)—New York City's premiere alternative paper isn't as edgy as it used to be, but it's still a great resource for arts lovers—and it's free.

New York Post (nypost.com)—Check out the Wednesday and Friday editions for Michael Riedel's newsy (and very dishy) column. It can also be read at nypost.com/entertainment/columnists/riedel.htm.

WEBSITES

Club Free Time (clubfreetime.com/new_york.asp)—An excellent and encyclopedic listing of all the free events (walks, lectures, concerts, theater, etc.) going on in New York. Plus, the Club sponsors special high-quality low-price events for its members, who pay only $20 a year.

Playbill Online (playbill.com)—The best site for up-to-the-minute theater news and a great resource for insider info, such as weekly grosses and job listings.

Playbill Arts (playbillarts.com)—Covers classical music, opera, dance, and jazz.

TheaterMania (theatermania.com)—Articles, reviews, and comprehensive listings that include many music, dance, and comedy shows, in addition to the Broadway and Off-Broadway listings.

Talkin' Broadway (talkinbroadway.com)—Reviews, columns, and a special board where you can sell (or request) theater tickets and merchandise, but what people really come here for is the dish on the "All That Chat" forum, which features many posters from the theater industry.

Broadway World (broadwayworld.com)—The lively message board here is more youth-oriented and less moderated than "All That Chat"; the site is also loaded with features, press releases, and photos and video.

BROADCAST

"On Stage" (NY 1) features theater-related news, interviews, and reviews, but you must be a Time Warner subscriber to receive it.

"Theatre Talk" (Multiple PBS stations) concentrates primarily on interviews and is co-hosted by Susan Haskins and the irrepressible Michael Riedel.

"Broadway Beat" is a Manhattan public-access show (viewable online at broadwaybeat.com) that covers rehearsals, show openings, and special NYC theater events.

DISCOUNTS

Theater and concert ticket prices in New York City are probably among the highest in the nation, thanks to large visitor and business-account demographics. To make up for it (and thus allow for a local audience), New York has an abundance of discount methods and schemes that you don't find in many other cities.

PAPERING SERVICES

New York's "papering services" perform a dual role: Theaters can get additional bodies into their seats (a big boost for the artists on stage) and the members can get good seats at very little cost. Most frequently, the shows offered are at the very beginning (and/or the very end) of their run, but we're consistently surprised by the quality of the offerings. Among the many Broadway performances we saw through papering services was *Who's Afraid of Virginia Woolf* just five hours before Bill Irwin (George) won the Tony Award for Best Actor in a Play. They also offer extensive and excellent classical music, dance, and jazz/cabaret events. We have friends who only see shows that they can get through a papering service and they consider their cultural lives quite fulfilling.

There are currently four papering services in New York City:

• **Audience Extras** (audienceextras.com): Annual membership fee is $85, plus an initial deposit of $30 to start your Personal Reserve Fund. Each ticket is charged off your fund at $3.50. Very user-friendly site.

• **Play-by-Play** (play-by-play.com): Annual fee is $107, plus $3.50 per ticket.

• **TheaterMania** (theatermania.com/gold): Annual fee is $89 and there are no additional fees for tickets. While this is the cheapest arrangement, we find that they have the least selection.

• **Theater Extras** (theaterextras.com): Annual fee is $99 plus a $4 per ticket charge. The relative new kid on the papering-service block, Theater Extras not only has the best inventory, it consistently sends out emails telling members about the latest offerings.

If money is tight, join Theater Extras; however, many folks do sign-up for all four. And one final word on papering services: Unlike other sources of tickets, papering services have little tolerance for no-shows. Warm bodies are their business and if you don't show up, they lose out. Repeated no-showing may cause the service to cut off your membership, so if you have a good reason not to go, then notify them immediately. If you don't have a good reason, then go to the show and have a good time.

THEATRE DEVELOPMENT FUND (tdf.org)

One of the major sources of theater, dance, and concert tickets for in-the-know New Yorkers, TDF operates the TKTS windows in Manhattan (see below), as well as an online ticket-discount service for their membership. The online service is extremely user-friendly (except that you don't know where your seats are until you get to the theater) and the overall ticket inventory and prices are excellent. The trick is obtaining a TDF membership; you must be one of the following: full-time student, full-time teacher, union member, retiree, civil-service employee, staff member of a not-for-profit organization, performing-arts professional, or a member of the armed forces or clergy. Upon application you have to prove eligibility, but once you're in you're in! When Jeffrey and Norma came to New York, Norma was able to join TDF, thanks to her teaching background, and Jeffrey had no problem obtaining tickets on her account (using his credit card). He was later able to get his own membership through the Freelancers Union. TDF also sells Off-Off-Broadway vouchers in sets of four for $36. Although you don't have to be a member to obtain them, it's not always clear which theaters are accepting them on any given night.

HALF-PRICE ONLINE SERVICES

While New York City offers a variety of very cheap tickets (see above), the half-price online deals can be meager. Unlike similar services in other cities, you can't obtain half-price tickets from the TKTS service online; you have to go to one of its booths (see below). Also, the Goldstar's New York section (goldstar.com) doesn't have anywhere near the selection found in Chicago or Los Angeles or even Boston. Worth a free look, but you may be disappointed.

TICKET DISCOUNT SITES (playbill.com; broadwaybox.com; theatermania. com; schooltix.com; seasonofsavings.com)

Perhaps the most reliable sources for obtaining discounted Broadway tickets (as well as tickets to other performance events) on a specific date, including seat numbers, are these five websites, all featuring 15%–50% discounts (which computes to less when you add all the service fees). The best time to hit any of these sites is before the reviews come out, especially for musicals. Tickets for plays can usually be obtained anytime, except for well-reviewed star-studded limited runs. Each of these sites offers free email notification announcing new shows and/or new discounts.

Ticket Central (ticketcentral.com) and Smart Tix (smarttix.com) are good sources for Off and Off-Off Broadway tickets and discounts, especially if you sign up for their email services; plus, Ticket Central has a special site for Student Discounts (ticketcentral.com/student). We've also found several members-only sites that offer the same discounts as the above, but for a small fee. Avoid them!

SPECIALIZED DISCOUNT SITES

Playbill's sister site Playbill Arts (playbillarts.com) offers some discounts on classical music, opera, dance, and jazz. Dancelink (set up through nycity center.com) is an email club devoted strictly to dance.

OTHER NEW YORK CITY DISCOUNTS

Audience Rewards (audiencerewards.com)—Recently established by the Broadway League, this loyalty program awards points when you purchase your tickets (from the theaters, not through TDF or papering services) that can be redeemed for tickets, collectables, CDs, etc. As with most loyalty programs (airline miles, casino players clubs), Audience Rewards isn't that impressive on the surface, but those who take the time to really learn the system can shave more than a few dollars off their annual budget. For example, Amtrak Guest Reward points (earned on a Chase MasterCard) can currently be transferred to Audience Rewards and the site has a variety of Broadway tickets at various attainable point levels. Membership is free.

High 5 (high5tix.org)—Dedicated to making the arts affordable for teens, High 5 provides $5 tickets to hundreds of New York's dance, music, theater, film, and museum events year-round. Plus, each teen can purchase one additional $5 ticket, so they can be accompanied by one adult, or another teen or pre-teen. Teens don't have to be from New York, but they must have proof of age or school enrollment (a report card will do).

Hiptix (hiptix.com)—Providing discounted tickets to Roundabout Theatre shows for patrons 18–35.

School Theatre Ticket Program (schooltix.com)—This respected Times Square organization provides discount coupons to musicals and plays on and off Broadway, events at Lincoln Center, and other events in New York City. It also assists school groups of 20 or more in getting good seats at the best price.

ART MUSEUMS

ASIA SOCIETY AND MUSEUM
725 Park Avenue (at 70th Street)
212-517-2742 • asiasociety.org

Public Transportation: Excellent (convenient to 6 and F subway lines and MTA buses).
Handicapped Accessibility: Good
Hours: Tuesday–Sunday 11 a.m.–6 p.m., with extended evening hours on Friday until 9 p.m. (except July 4 through Labor Day), closed Monday.
Admission: Regular admission is $10, seniors $7, students $5, members free, children under 16 free; groups of 20 or more adults discounted admis-

sion and personalized tour-planning assistance. Admission is free to all on Fridays from 6 to 9 p.m. (free Fridays suspended July 4 to Labor Day).

Tours: Free

Audio Tours: Free cell-phone audio tour is included in the price of admission.

Membership: $65 individual membership fee entitles members to unlimited free admission, invitations to members-only exhibition previews and other events, and additional discounts on merchandise. Teacher membership $50. Discounted $40 membership available to students, seniors (65+), and associates (those living in the United States beyond a 150-mile radius of New York City).

Other Benefits: The Asia Circle ($150/annual) is for museum patrons 21–40 and hosts events designed exclusively for its members, spanning the areas of arts, culture, business, politics, current affairs, and social issues.

From the Editors: Established by John D. Rockefeller III in 1956, this museum specializes in the art of south, southeast and east Asia (especially Japan). In 2000, the museum was reconfigured and expanded to include a skylit garden court.

BROOKLYN MUSEUM
200 Eastern Parkway, Brooklyn
718-638-5000 • brooklynmuseum.org

Public Transportation: Very good (2 or 3 subway line to Eastern Parkway/Brooklyn Museum B71, B41, B69, B48 buses).

Handicapped Accessibility: Good

Hours: Saturday 11 a.m.–6 p.m., Sunday 11 a.m.–6 p.m., Wednesday–Friday 10 a.m.–5 p.m., closed Monday and Tuesday. First Saturday of each month 11 a.m.–11 p.m.

Admission: $8 (suggested donation), students and seniors $4 (suggested donation), children under 12 free. On the Brooklyn Museum's Target First Saturdays, visitors enjoy free art and entertainment each month 5–11 p.m.

Tours: Free and led by museum guides (schedules vary).

Membership: Individual membership fee of $55 entitles members to free unlimited general admission for one , invitations to members-only preview receptions, free parking during members-only events, and discounts at museum shops. Adults (62+), artists, educators, and students save $10 on individual membership dues. The $150 Contributor membership gets you reciprocal admission to other museums.

From the Editors: An excellent facility forced to play second fiddle to its more glamorous Central Park sister, the Brooklyn Museum has a comprehensive collection of European and American paintings and sculptures, plus an outstanding (and well-explained) Egyptian collection. Check out the *The Dinner Party* by Judy Chicago, a massive ceremonial banquet arranged on a triangular table commemorating important women from history, or join the party each month on Target's First Saturdays when thousands of New Yorkers from all five boroughs enjoy free programs of art and entertainment from 5 to 11 p.m.

COOPER-HEWITT NATIONAL DESIGN MUSEUM
2 East 91st Street (at Fifth Avenue)
212-849-8351 • cooperhewitt.org

Public Transportation: Excellent (routes include the Lexington Avenue 4, 5, and 6 subways and Fifth and Madison Avenue buses).

Handicapped Accessibility: Good

Hours: Monday–Friday 10 a.m.–5 p.m., Saturday 10 a.m.–6 p.m., Sunday noon–6 p.m.; garden entrance on 90th Street open May–September (weather permitting).

Admission: $15, students and seniors with ID $10, Smithsonian Institution members and children under 12 free.

Tours: Free daily tours last approximately 45 minutes. All tours begin in the Great Hall on the main level of the museum.

Membership: Individual membership is $75 annually and entitles members to unlimited free admission for one person to the National Design Museum and Arthur Ross Terrace and Garden, invitations to exclusive members' exhibition previews, programs and events, and access to the Design Resource Center, including Drue Heinz Study Center for Drawings and Prints, Henry Luce Study Room for American Art, Doris and Henry Dreyfuss Memorial Study Center, and the National Design Museum's Design Archives. It also includes discounts on parking and purchases at selected Manhattan design establishments and a subscription to *Smithsonian* magazine. Also offered is a national/international membership of $55/annual for individuals living beyond a 150-mile radius of New York City, which includes all benefits of individual membership. Student and senior memberships are offered at $50.

From the Editors: The Cooper-Hewitt National Design Museum has been housed in the landmark Andrew Carnegie Mansion on Fifth Avenue since 1976. Built between 1899 and 1902, the 64-room house is an impressive object of historical design itself, the perfect building to house the only collection in the nation devoted exclusively to historic and contemporary design. With a permanent collection that includes everything from wall coverings and textiles to product design and decorative arts, the museum is a must-stop along Museum Mile for design aficionados and the design-curious. A great destination for families, current exhibitions include such child-friendly exhibits as Wall Stories: Children's Wallpaper and Books, featuring works from the permanent collection that explore the relationship between wallpaper and books created for children since the 1870s.

Programming at the museum is particularly hands-on and educational, including events such as the Teen Design Fair, internships for high-school students, and a master's program affiliated with Parson's The New School for Design. But for those just interested in a world-wide journey through historic and contemporary design, treasures are found within these walls.

And while you're there, ask about one of the most intriguing (and controversial) pieces in the collection—an unsigned drawing, *Design for a Candelabrum*, purchased in 1942 and identified some 60 years later as drawn by the hand of Michelangelo.

FRICK COLLECTION AND FRICK ART REFERENCE LIBRARY
1 East 70th Street
212-288-0700 • frick.org

Public Transportation: Very good (6 subway local to 68th Street, M1–M4 bus).

Handicapped Accessibility: Good

Museum Hours: Tuesday–Saturday 10 a.m.–6 p.m., Sunday 11 a.m.–5 p.m., closed Mondays and holidays.

Library Hours: Monday–Friday 10 a.m.–5 p.m., Saturday 9:30 a.m.–1 p.m., closed Sunday, holiday weekends, Saturdays in June and July, and throughout August. (Note: First-time researchers must bring a photo ID and arrive before 3 p.m. on weekdays or 11 a.m. on Saturdays.)

Admission: Regular admission $15, seniors (62+) $10, students with valid identification $5; Sunday pay what you wish 11 a.m.–1 p.m.; group discounts should be made by telephone at least two weeks in advance at 212-288-0700 or by e-mail to groupvisits@frick.org.

Tours: Free—A 22-minute audio-visual program titled "The Frick Collection: An Introduction" is shown in the Music Room every hour on the half-hour from 10:30 a.m. to 4:30 p.m.

Audio Tours: Free

Membership: Individual membership is $60 annually and includes unlimited free admission for one person for one year, discounts on purchases at the Museum Shop, a subscription to the members' magazine, and an invitation to the new-members' reception. Discount memberships for students are $25; Non-Resident membership is $40 (member must reside beyond 100 miles from New York City).

Other Benefits: Contributing Friend membership ($200/annual) gets you reciprocal admission to other museums. Sustaining Friend membership ($600/annual) gets you special visiting privileges and invitations to opening parties.

From the Editors: The Frick Collection is housed in the neo-Classical mansion built by Henry Clay Frick in 1913–14. Set back from Fifth Avenue by an elevated garden and guarded by three large magnolia trees, the estate is an art sanctuary. Inside are 16 galleries filled with masterpieces of Western painting, sculpture, and decorative art, including portraits by Rembrandt and Valésquez, exceptional 18th-century French furniture and Sévres porcelain, and the masterworks of Bellini, El Greco, Holbein, and Titian. For those with a special interest, the Frick Collection recently gained a bequest of 25 clocks and 14 watches dating 1500 to 1830. This small but immaculate collection is a quirky break—if you need it—from the staggering collection of big names (Corot, Degas, Goya, Turner, Vermeer, Whistler; the list goes on) that line the galleries. Note that the museum is not very family-friendly; in fact, it doesn't admit children under 10 and children under 16 must be accompanied by an adult.

SOLOMON R. GUGGENHEIM MUSEUM
1071 Fifth Avenue (at 89th Street)
212-423-3500 • guggenheim.org

Public Transportation: Very good (close to subway 4, 5, or 6 and MTA buses).

Handicapped Accessibility: Good, except for the High Gallery, at the top of the first ramp and only accessible by two low stairs.

Hours: Saturday–Wednesday 10 a.m.–5:45 p.m., Friday 10 a.m.–7:45 p.m., closed Thursday.

Admission: Regular admission $18, students and seniors (65+) with valid ID $15, children under 12 free, discounts available for groups of 10 or more; on Friday evenings beginning at 5:45 p.m., the museum hosts pay what you wish, in which admission is by donation. The last tickets are issued at 7:15 p.m. These tickets are not free and cannot be purchased in advance.

Tours: Free; schedules are subject to change. For daily schedules, consult the electronic signboard near the admissions desk. Gallery Guides are arts professionals available throughout the museum during all open hours to discuss the art on view, the Frank Lloyd Wright building, and the history of the Guggenheim.

Audio Tours: Free

Membership: Individual membership is $75 annually and entitles members to free unlimited admission for one to all Guggenheim museums (New York, Venice, Berlin, Bilbao), the ability to bypass ticket lines, invitations to exclusive members-only exhibition previews, free admission for one at Art After Dark: First Friday events (regular price $20), and a free subscription to *Guggenheim* magazine. A 15% discount is available on membership for students, seniors, and artists at the individual member level.

Other Benefits: Young Collectors' Council individual membership ($500/annual) and Fellow Associate membership ($250/annual) allow you reciprocal admission to other museums.

From the Editors: Museum Mile's gem, the Solomon R. Guggenheim Museum building is an artwork in and of itself. The famous spiraling design by Frank Lloyd Wright has endured for 40 years and was recently unveiled once again after an exhaustive exterior restoration. Inside, you'll find works from the collection—Beuys, Chagall, Kandinsky, Klee, Monet, Twombly—generally housed in the tower galleries, while one central exhibit sprawls from the ground floor up the spiraling rotunda. Recent exhibitions of note have included Catherine Opie's mid-career retrospective of explosive portraits and meditative landscapes and Chinese artist Cai-Guo Qiang's rotunda exhibition Cait Guo Qiang: I Want to Believe, featuring his installations, unique gunpowder paintings, and videos.

Programming includes free events such as Just Drop In, a program for families to explore galleries with an educator who leads creative and interactive projects. The basement floor of the museum opened to the public in 2001 as the Sackler Center for Arts Education and features studio art, computer and multimedia labs, an exhibition gallery, resource center, and theater where current exhibition–related programming takes place every day.

HISPANIC SOCIETY OF AMERICA MUSEUM AND LIBRARY
Audubon Terrace, Broadway (between 155th and 156th Streets)
212-926-2234 • hispanicsociety.org

Public Transportation: Excellent (1 subway line to Broadway and 157th Street and bus access).

Handicapped Accessibility: Poor
Hours: Tuesday–Saturday 10 a.m.–4:30 p.m., Sunday 1–4 p.m., closed Monday.
Admission: Free
Tours: Free 45-minute tours of the building and collections are given by museum curators or the education department at 2 p.m. on Saturdays.
Membership: Membership is $50 annually. Benefits include invitations to receptions, exhibition openings, advance announcements of all upcoming programs and events, and access to "friends-only" tours with lectures by curators and conservators on the collections and special exhibitions.

From the Editors: This little-known collection located on the Audubon Terrace features art and artifacts from Spain (including several El Grecos and Goyas), Latin America, and the Philippines.

JACQUES MARCHAIS MUSEUM OF TIBETAN ART
388 Lighthouse Avenue, Staten Island
718-987-3500 • tibetanmuseum.org

Public Transportation: Fair/Poor (accessible from S74 bus, but requires transfer from S.I. Ferry terminal and 10-minute walk).
Handicapped Accessibility: Good
Hours: Wednesday–Sunday 1–5 p.m., closed Monday and Tuesday.
Admission: $5, students and seniors (50+) $3.
Membership: Individual membership is $25 annually and includes free unlimited admission to the museum, invitations to special events, and discounts on special museum programs and merchandise. Student and senior membership is $20.

From the Editors: Tibetan art is displayed in a beautiful Staten Island hillside setting resembling a Tibetan temple and monastery. His Holiness the Dalai Lama blessed the temple during his visit in 1991.

JEWISH MUSEUM OF NEW YORK
1109 Fifth Avenue (at 92nd Street)
212-423-3200 • thejewishmuseum.org

Public Transportation: Very good (convenient to 4, 5, or 6 subway to 86th Street/Lexington Avenue and bus lines).
Handicapped Accessibility: Good

Hours: Saturday–Wednesday 11 a.m.–5:45 p.m., Thursday 11 a.m.–8 p.m., closed Friday.

Admission: $12, seniors $10, students $7.50.

Free Day: Saturday

Tours: Free 45-minute tours, led by museum-trained docents, meet in the museum lobby at scheduled times listed on the museum website. Audio tours are also free.

Membership: Individual membership is $75 annually. Benefits include personalized membership card, unlimited free admission for one adult, invitations for two to special members-only previews of new exhibitions, and discounts at local restaurants and parking garages. Membership is 100% tax deductible. Discounted membership ($55/annual) available for students, seniors, and out-of-town patrons.

Other Benefits: A $250 membership entitles patrons to receive membership reciprocity at numerous other museums nationwide.

From the Editors: The Jewish Museum contains permanent and temporary collections of art by Jewish artists or featuring Jewish subjects, including a large collection of Jewish ceremonial objects.

METROPOLITAN MUSEUM OF ART (The Met)
1000 Fifth Avenue (at 82nd Street)
212-708-9400 • www.metmuseum.org

Public Transportation: Good (convenient to 4, 5, 6 subway lines and cross-town buses).

Handicapped Accessibility: Good (accessible to wheelchair users via the street-level entrance at Fifth Avenue and 81st Street or the museum parking garage at Fifth and 80th).

Hours: Tuesday–Thursday 9:30 a.m.–5:30 p.m., Friday and Saturday 9:30 a.m.–9 p.m., Sunday 9:30 a.m.–5:30 p.m., closed Monday (except some Monday holidays).

Admission: Suggested $20, seniors (65+) $15, students $10, members free, children under 12 free. Fee includes same-day admission to the main building and the Cloisters. No extra charge for entrance to special exhibitions. Group discounts on parties of 10 or more. School groups from within NYC are free.

Guided Tours: Free; gallery talks and guided tours do not require tickets or reservations. These programs usually last one hour and are geared toward an adult audience.

Audio Tours: General public $7, members $6, groups of 14 or fewer $6 each, groups of 15 or more $4 each, children under 12 $5. Audio guide play-ers are free for visitors who are blind, partially sighted, or hard of hearing, and for New York City high school students with valid ID.

Membership: Met Net is the basic level of membership for visitors who live within a 200-mile radius of the museum. $60/annual includes free admission, one-time use of the trustees' dining room overlooking Central Park for Friday or Saturday dinner or weekend brunch, Met screen savers, online audio features for selected special exhibitions and the permanent collection, members-only offers in the online Met Store, 10% discount on museum merchandise, and discounts on audio guides.

Other Benefits: Sustaining members ($500/annual) receive reciprocal membership to 14 other major art museums across the country. Individual members ($95/annual) get invitations for two to selected previews of two special exhibitions.

From the Editors: The Metropolitan Museum of Art is perhaps the most iconic art museum in New York City; nestled among the greenery of Central Park, this enormous collection of art from around the world is a must-see. Due to the imposing size and breadth of its artwork, it's best for visitors to pick one area, special exhibition, or event on which to focus. For locals, it's a place to wander into again and again, whether you have an afternoon to let yourself get lost deep inside the permanent-collection gal-leries or you need a special place to duck into from the rain. With admission prices set at suggested amounts, this museum is open to anyone at a pay-what-you-can rate.

Programming for adults includes screenings of feature films and videos related to special exhibitions and the permanent collection, and the popu-lar Concerts & Lectures series (in its 55th year), which present free lectures in conjunction with special exhibitions, the permanent collection, and other related topics.

Extensive programming for children and families includes family ori-entations (one-hour slide introductions to select special exhibitions), Story Time at the Met podcast episodes that present legends, myths, and other stories related to works of art in the museum's collection, and thematic gal-lery tours and creative art activities.

Recent exhibitions have included a retrospective of the Italian painter Giorgio Morandi and a selection of work from the permanent collection titled Provocative Visions: Race and Identity, but don't miss the rich perma-nent-collection galleries where the Egyptian, Greek and Roman, and Native American art are housed. In addition, the newly formed Young Members group is dedicated to the specific interests of members ages 21–35 from any membership level.

THE MORGAN LIBRARY & MUSEUM
225 Madison Avenue (at 36th Street)
212-685-0008 • themorgan.org

Public Transportation: Excellent (convenient to 4, 5, 6, 7, B, D, F, and Q subway, PATH, and bus).
Handicapped Accessibility: Good
Hours: Tuesday–Thursday 10:30 a.m.–5 p.m., Friday 10:30 a.m.–9 p.m., Saturday 10 a.m.–6 p.m., Sunday 11 a.m.–6 p.m.
Admission: $12; students, seniors, and children under 16 $8, children under 12 free; admission free on Friday 7–9 p.m.
Tours: Free exhibition and historical tours are available each day.
Membership: Introductory membership is $75. Benefits include unlimited free admission, an invitation to one private members' viewing for a major exhibition and discounts at the Morgan shop.

From the Editors: Recently expanded and renovated, the Morgan has a collection of rare books, illuminated manuscripts, and more than 10,000 prints, including works by Degas, Rubens, and Gainsborough.

MUSEUM OF MODERN ART (MoMA)
11 West 53 Street (between 5th and 6th Avenues)
212-708-9400 • moma.org

Public Transportation: Very good (convenient to E, V, B, and D subway and bus).
Handicapped Accessibility: Good
Hours: Wednesday–Sunday 10:30 a.m.–5:30 p.m., Friday 10:30 a.m.–8 p.m., closed Tuesday.
Admission: $20, seniors (65+ with ID) $16, students (full-time with current ID) $12, children (16 and under) free, group discounts available, everyone free 4–8 p.m. on Friday evenings.
Tours: Free
Audio Tours: Free. The museum offers six distinctive audio programs: Special Exhibitions, Modern Voices, Modern Kids, Visual Descriptions, Red Studio Teen Podcast, and Think Modern: Adult and Academic Programs Audio Archive. There are several ways to enjoy the audio programs: on a portable player; via free MoMA WiFi access using your iPhone, iPodTouch, or other wireless device, or by downloading individual MP3 files to your desktop or MP3 player at home. You can also subscribe to MoMA audio podcasts and receive new updates automatically.

Membership: Individual $75/annual. Benefits include membership card(s) granting unlimited free admission, privileged access when visiting, including bypassing ticketing lines, unlimited cardholder entry to MoMA's film screenings, advance ticketing privileges, and complimentary cardholder admission to P.S. 1 Contemporary Art Center, including the annual Warm-Up summer music series.

Special Membership for Seniors or Non-Residents: National/international $60 (for individuals more than 150 miles outside of New York City).

Special Young Adult Membership: Student membership is $50/annual (available for full-time students enrolled at an accredited high school, college, university, or art school).

From the Editors: The Museum of Modern Art's newly re-designed building (by architect Yoshio Taniguchi) opened in November 2004. Situated in midtown Manhattan near Rockefeller Center and across the street from the American Folk Art Museum, the building uses imaginative materials, a creative application of light, and modern spaces to house its permanent collection and touring exhibitions. You'll find everything from mass-produced industrial objects from the mid-19th century to the present, displayed in the Architecture and Design galleries, to such masterpieces of modern art as Vincent Van Gogh's *The Starry Night* (perhaps the museum's most popular holding).

Special exhibitions, such as the recent Richard Serra retrospective, make use of the building's outdoor sculpture garden, where weekend crowds can spread out a bit.

Adult programming includes a heavy schedule of film screenings, lectures, and symposia, not to mention the adult programming for the younger set—it's not unusual to find M.I.A. performing at the annual Party in the Garden. Family programs run the age gamut, with events such as Tours for Fours (for children age four and their adult companions), family art workshops, and Watch This! Films for Tweens.

Although the museum does offer free admission on Friday evenings, the ticket line often stretches around the block, and while a lively crowd is great in the garden, it can make for difficult viewing of the museum's more staggeringly famous artworks from Cézanne, Dali, Monet, Picasso, Pollack, Warhol, et al. Another universal crowd-pleaser can be found suspended above the escalators—be sure not to miss Arthur Young's Bell-47D1 helicopter, one of 3,000 of its kind manufactured between 1946 and 1973.

NEUE GALLERY
1048 Fifth Avenue
718-987-3500 · neuegalerie.org

Public Transportation: Very good (Short walk to 4, 5, or 6 subway at 86th Street or by bus).
Handicapped Accessibility: Good
Hours: Thursday–Monday, 11 a.m.–6 p.m. (closed Tuesday and Wednesday).
Admission: $15, students/seniors $10. Children under 12 not admitted; children 12–16 must be accompanied by an adult.
Tours: Acoustiguide audio tours are included with admission. Free public tours take place Saturday and Sunday at 2 p.m.
Membership: Individual membership begins at $275 and includes free entry to all lectures, concerts and exhibition receptions.

From the Editors: The newest addition to New York City's Museum Mile opened in November 2001. Specializing in early 20th-century German and Austrian art (assembled primarily by cosmetics-fortune heir and well-regarded art collector Ronald S. Lauder), the Neue Gallerie features work by Egon Schiele, Oskar Kokoschka, Paul Klee, and Wassily Kandinsky, among others. Also on display is Gustav Klimt's *Portrait of Adele Bloch-Bauer* purchased by Lauder in 2006 for $135 million—making it the most expensive painting ever sold.

In addition to the gallery, the museum has a design shop, bookstore, and two well-regarded Viennese cafés: the comfortable Café Fledermaus; and the more formal Café Sabarsky, which is open till 9 p.m. Thursday–Sunday and occasionally offers cabaret entertainment in addition to its excellent Austrian-Hungarian cuisine.

NEW MUSEUM OF CONTEMPORARY ART
235 Bowery
212-219-1222 • newmuseum.org

Public Transportation: Excellent (convenient to F & V subway's 2nd Avenue, Lower East Side station).
Handicapped Accessibility: Good
Hours: Wednesday noon–6 p.m., Thursday and Friday noon–9 p.m., Saturday and Sunday noon–6 p.m., closed Monday and Tuesday.
Admission: General admission $12, seniors $10, students $8, 18 and under and members free.

Tours: Free daily tours Wednesday and Thursday 2 p.m., Friday 2 and 7 p.m., Saturday and Sunday 2 and 4 p.m.

Membership: Individual $60, dual/family $100, student/artist/senior/teacher $35; all include free admission and discounts to special events. Deluxe members ($400) receive opening-reception invitations and reciprocal membership to more than 20 contemporary-art institutions.

From the Editors: Housed in an exciting new space in the Bowery (named one of the architectural seven wonders by Condé Nast *Traveler*), the New Museum of Contemporary Art exhibits works of under-recognized artists from around the world.

RUBIN MUSEUM OF ART (RMA)
150 West 17th Street
212-620-5000 • rmanyc.org

Public Transportation: Excellent (take 1 subway to 18th St. or 2, 3, F, L, V lines to 14th Street).

Handicapped Accessibility: Good

Hours: Monday 11 a.m.–5 p.m., Wednesday 11 a.m.–7 p.m., Thursday 11 a.m.–5 p.m., Friday 11 a.m.–10 p.m., Saturday and Sunday 11 a.m.–6 p.m., closed Tuesday.

Admission: $10, seniors/students/artists (with valid ID) $7, neighbors in zip codes 10011 and 10001 (with valid ID) $7, college students $2, children under 12 free, members free. Gallery admission is free to all every Friday 7–10 p.m. and free to seniors (65+) on the first Monday of every month.

Membership: Individual $55, artist/neighbor/senior/student $35, dual/family $75, including free admission, invitations for two to select previews and other events, and discounts on lectures, performances, and films.

From the Editors: Dedicated to the art of the Himalayas and surrounding regions, the Rubin Museum of Art opened its doors in October 2004. Located in a former Barneys in Chelsea, the building boasts 25,000 square feet of exhibition space, while preserving the original six-story spiral staircase (famously featured in "Sex and the City"). More than 1,000 objects are displayed, including paintings, sculpture, and textiles, as well as ritual objects from the 2nd to 20th centuries. The RMA also hosts national and international exhibitions to advance the study and appreciation of Himalayan arts and culture.

WHITNEY MUSEUM OF AMERICAN ART
945 Madison Avenue (at 75th Street)
212-570-3600 • whitney.org

Public Transportation: Very good (6 subway to 77th Street M1, M2, M3, M4 buses).

Handicapped Accessibility: Good

Hours: Wednesday–Thursday 11 a.m.–6 p.m., Friday 1–9 p.m. (6–9 p.m. pay what you wish admission), Saturday and Sunday 11 a.m.–6 p.m., closed Monday and Tuesday.

Admission: Regular admission is $15, seniors (62+) and students with valid ID $10, NYC public-school students with valid student ID and children under 12 free. Group discounts are available (maximum 30). New York City public schools, CUNY and Columbia University groups are free, but a reservation is required.

Tours: Free docent-led Gallery Tours through the museum's current exhibitions are offered each day. Tour schedules are available at the Information and Membership desk in the museum lobby and are posted in front of the elevators.

Membership: Individual membership is $75 annually. This fee includes unlimited free admission for one to the museum's galleries and film programs, invitations for two to members-only preview days and morning viewing hours with breakfast, and an invitation for two to an opening cocktail reception of a major exhibition and the ability to bypass the admission lines. Artist, student, and senior memberships are $40 (includes all Individual-level benefits, with the exception of invitations to one opening cocktail reception).

From the Editors: If you can time your visit to the Whitney Museum of American Art during its annual and biennial exhibitions, you'll take in the tradition it's held since 1932 to showcase recent contemporary art from the most important living and working artists of the time. Over the decades, the Whitney has purchased many works for its collection from young and relatively unknown artists to spotlight in these exhibitions and add to the museum's collection of masterpieces by Stuart Davis, Jasper Johns, and more recently, Louise Bourgeois and Matthew Ritchie.

Gertrude Vanderbilt Whitney originally opened her museum to the public on W. 8th Street with 700 pieces from her personal collection. Now housed in the Marcel Breuer-designed five-story building (with two underground levels), the collection has amassed more than 18,000 works of contemporary art by the likes of O'Keefe, Pollack, and Warhol.

Rich programming for all ages illuminates the exhibitions and collection, with a wide range of activities, including Family Fun Art Workshops ($10/family), Youth Insights programs (paid after-school opportunities for 10th–12th grade students), and a large range of free programs for seniors in collaboration with community senior centers. Whitney After Hours occurs every Friday evening 6–9 p.m. during pay-what-you-wish admission and includes live performances, artists appearances, and educational events for adults.

OTHER MUSEUMS OF INTEREST

AMERICAN MUSEUM OF NATURAL HISTORY (AMNH)
Central Park West and 79th Street
212-769-5100 • amnh.org

Public Transportation: Very good (via the B and C subways and numerous MTA bus routes).
Handicapped Accessibility: Good
Hours: Daily 10 a.m.–5:45 p.m., closed Thanksgiving and Christmas.
Admission: $15, students and seniors with ID $11, children (2–12) $8.50. Member children and adults are free. All admissions prices are suggested, rather than obligatory.
Basic Tour: Free
Membership: Individual membership $70, includes unlimited complimentary general-admission and special-exhibition tickets for one; unlimited discounts on the Space Show and IMAX presentations for one; a one-year subscription to *Natural History* magazine and *Rotunda*, the member's newsletter; discounts in the shops and restaurant and on programs; opportunities to participate in special tours, programs, and workshops for members only; and invitations to special exhibition previews for yourself and a guest. $55 of the membership cost is tax deductible and $10 of your dues are allocated to *Natural History* magazine. Dual ($90) and family ($115) memberships are also offered.

From the Editors: The Museum of Natural History is a world-class attraction. With exhibitions that include a recyclable skating rink, butterfly conservatory, the IMAX film *Wild Ocean*, and *SonicVision*, a digitally animated music show, this creative and evolving museum is sure to entertain anyone and everyone with an interest in why the world is the way it is. The hands-on technology-forward attitude makes it a prime spot for families; the museum even offers A Night at the Museum sleepover for eight- to twelve-year-olds! While the admission charge is on the higher end, so is the entertainment level and when in New York, you simply cannot pass up a visit to the Museum of Natural History.

CLOISTERS MUSEUM AND GARDENS
99 Margaret Corbin Drive
212-923-3700 • metmuseum.org/Works_of_Art/the_cloisters

Public Transportation: Good (A Train to 190th St., then a short walk or M4 bus; M4 bus also goes door-to-door from the Metropolitan Museum of Art to the Cloisters).

Handicapped Accessibility: Limited

Hours: March–October Tuesday–Sunday 9:30 a.m.–5:15 p.m.; November–February Tuesday–Sunday 9:30 a.m.–4:45 p.m.; closed Monday, New Year's Day, Thanksgiving, and Christmas.

Admission: $20, seniors (65+) $15, students $10, members free, children under 12 accompanied by an adult free. Note: Anyone paying admission to either the Met or the Cloisters gets same-day admission to both; hang on to your admission button.

Tours: Free garden tours are offered every Tuesday–Sunday at 1 p.m. from May–October.

Membership: See Metropolitan Museum of Art.

From the Editors: Part of the Metropolitan Museum of Art, the Cloisters Museum and Gardens is a beautifully recreated monastery impressively perched over the Hudson River in Fort Tyron Park (extreme northern Manhattan). A work of medieval art itself, the Cloisters has many exquisite treasures and is well worth the trip uptown.

LOUIS ARMSTRONG HOUSE MUSEUM
34–56 107th Street, Corona
718-478-8274 • louisarmstronghouse.org

Public Transportation: Good (easily accessible via the 7 subway).

Handicapped Accessibility: Fair (The entire ground floor, which includes the Welcome Center, museum store, exhibit area, and restrooms is wheelchair-accessible. The historic house tour, however, requires the ability to climb two sets of steep stairs and to stand for 40 minutes. Visitors unable to take the tour receive a virtual tour instead.)

Hours: Tuesday–Friday 10 a.m.–5 p.m., Saturday and Sunday noon–5 p.m., closed Monday.

Admission: $8, seniors (65+), students and children $6, larger groups $6 per person, members and children under four free.

Basic Tour: Required and included in price of admission.

Audio Tour: Virtual tours are available and included in the price of admission.

Membership: Individual membership is $45 and all members receive the following benefits: free admission to the museum, a 10% discount on museum store purchases, a subscription to Dippermouth News (the museum newsletter), and invitations to members-only events. Discounted senior, student, neighbor, and family memberships are also available.

From the Editors: Louis and Lucille Armstrong lived in this modest house from 1943 until his death in 1971. Operated as a historic house by the City University of New York's Queens College, the museum also archives Armstrong's writings, books, recordings, and other memorabilia, as well as maintains an active concert schedule.

NEW YORK HISTORICAL SOCIETY
170 Central Park West (between 76th & 77th Streets)
212-873-3400 • nyhistory.org

Public Transportation: Good (readily accessible via the B and C subway and MTA bus).

Handicapped Accessibility: Good

Hours: Open to the general public Tuesday–Saturday 10 a.m.–6 p.m.; Sunday 11 a.m.–5:45 p.m.

Admission: $10, seniors (65+) and educators $7, students $6; members, researchers, and children 12 and under accompanied by an adult free .

Free Day: Friday 6–8 p.m.

Audio Tour: Podcasts only.

Membership: Individual membership ($55) includes unlimited free admission to the galleries and library (bypassing admission lines), a calendar of events, reduced admission to all public programs, 10% discount at the store and for online and café purchases, 20% discount on books at public book signings, invitations to member-only events, and a personalized membership card and membership in the Empire State Museums Reciprocal Program, which includes discount admission to many historical societies and museums nationwide. A discounted student/senior/educator membership ($40) is also available among other varied membership options.

From the Editors: Located across from the Natural History Museum, this marble palace features a collection of 19th-century paintings, including several Audubon watercolors.

THE NEW YORK PUBLIC LIBRARY (NYPL)
Humanities & Social Sciences Library/Main Building
Fifth Avenue and 42nd Street
212-930-0830 • nypl.org

Public Transportation: Good (readily accessible via the B and C subway and MTA bus).

Handicapped Accessibility: Good

Hours: Sunday 1–5 p.m., Monday, Thursday–Saturday 11 a.m.–6 p.m.; Tuesday and Wednesday 11 a.m.– 7:30 p.m.

Admission: Free

Basic Tour: Free one-hour tours are offered Tuesday–Saturday at 11 a.m. and 2 p.m. (departing from Astor Hall).

Membership: Associate membership ($25) includes a 10% discount at the Library Shop at Fifth Avenue & 42nd Street or online, 10% off prints from the NYPL Digital Gallery, and a personalized membership card. At the Friend level ($40), members receive additional benefits, including preferred shopping times at the Library Shop with an additional discount, an invitation for two to attend the gala holiday open house in December, a year's subscription to the Library's magazine, *Bookmark*, invitations to Friends-only exhibition previews and lectures, a 33% savings and waived service charge on LIVE from the NYPL tickets.

From the Editors: One of the iconic architectural edifices in America, this 1911 Beaux Arts masterwork should be a requirement for any tourist. The New York Public Library houses an astounding 2,800,000 pictures, 6,000,000 books, and 12,000,000 manuscripts. As one of the only truly quiet niches in New York City, time spent in the library is time treasured.

Walking through the bronze doors into Astor Hall as well as taking in special exhibitions and the breathtaking periodical room, one cannot help but be moved by the experience of it all. Be sure to bring a good read to the Rose Main Reading Room, whose length spans nearly two full city blocks. Even if you just stop by to get out of the hustle of the city, missing the unique and historic New York Public Library would be a shame.

☹ THEATER ☺

BROADWAY

Venues: 40 legitimate theaters located near Times Square (42nd and 7th Avenue).

Public Transportation: Yes (all)

Handicapped Accessibility: Good (all)

Performances/Programs: Standard Broadway performance schedule is Tuesday–Sunday (though a few shows have Monday performances).

Ticket Prices: Range from $20 to $140, with discounts including student Rush, general Rush, and Standing Room Only; some of the non-profits have special programs for young professionals or 35-and-unders. Though they're not classified as discounts, some theaters have rear-mezzanine or stage seats at much lower than regular prices. Wednesday matinée performances are sometimes priced a bit lower than other performances. (Note: Tickets for shows at all theaters, except Roundabout Theatre Company's American Airlines Theatre and Studio 54, can be purchased through Ticketmaster or Telecharge.)

Subscriptions: Only the non-profit theaters (Roundabout Theatre Company, Manhattan Theatre Club) offer subscriptions.

From the Editors: What is Broadway? Broadway is the general term for roughly 40 legitimate theaters, almost all of which are situated in the vicinity of Times Square and contain between 500 and 2,000 seats each. (Any theater with 100 to 499 is designated as an Off-Broadway venue; fewer than 100 categorizes it as Off-Off-Broadway.) Very few Broadway theaters are actually on the street called Broadway; most are on the "side" streets from West 41st up to West 54th.

Broadway isn't just for musicals. Many plays are also produced in Broadway theaters, but they tend not to run as long as musicals and they're never as popular with visitors.

Broadway is almost exclusively for commercial theatrical productions; however, a few non-profit theater companies produce shows in Broadway theaters, including the Manhattan Theatre Club and the Roundabout Theatre Company. Shows coming from non-profit theaters outside New York (Steppenwolf's *August: Osage County*) or even from non-profit Off-Broadway theaters (New York Public Theater's *Hair*) are usually done as commercial productions when they arrive on Broadway.

Each year, dozens of new shows open on Broadway. Some play "lim-

THE LOWDOWN ...

For many theater lovers visiting New York City, a trip to the TKTS discount booth in Times Square is a necessity. Despite the long lines that frequently form at this bustling spot, tourists and locals looking for same-day entertainment bargains patiently line up to enjoy up to 50% off on tickets for numerous Broadway and Off-Broadway productions, as well as other specially discounted events.

Since opening in 1973, the Times Square TKTS booth (run by the not-for-profit Theatre Development Fund) has offered discounted theater tickets and in recent years has expanded its services to include on-line offers that can be accessed from the comfort of home several days or weeks in advance of the show. Using codes provided by TDF through Telecharge or Ticketmaster, you can purchase low-cost tickets in advance for many of the same productions offered at the booth.

TDF also runs two other centrally located TKTS booths in NYC, one in lower Manhattan at the South Street Seaport, the other at a Jay Street and Myrtle Avenue location in the heart of downtown Brooklyn. Note: Be aware that online discounts are not as generous as those found at the TKTS booth.

Despite the added convenience of online discounts, the experience of visiting the TKTS booth is a singular one, and last-minute offerings from in-demand productions can become available at any time during the booth's hours of operation. Even though major hit shows playing at high capacity will not be available through TDF, on average up to 85% of the shows running on Broadway in any given week will offer discounted tickets through the organization.

Before you set out, check out the TDF's recently redesigned website, which tells you how often a particular play or musical is available "at the window." You can also sign up for daily email updates if you plan on us-ing the TKTS booth on a regular basis.

Try to arrive at the booth approximately one hour before it opens to get first crack at the shows offered that day. TKTS opens at 10 a.m. on matinée days and at 3 p.m. on days with evening performances only. If you can't get to the TKTS booth early, don't worry! Ticket supplies are replenished throughout the day, so even as late as 7 or 7:30 p.m., there's availability. Choices may be limited, but lines are much shorter at this time and it's always worth it to investigate what's being offered.

The booth also has two "plays-only" windows to accommodate cus-tomers seeking non-musical entertainment. If your preference is a straight play, this line moves very quickly and will save you time.

In addition to the cost of the tickets, TKTS applies a $4 surcharge

... ON TKTS

per ticket for all purchases. Also remember that even though the Times Square TKTS location (finally) accepts credit cards, the other locations accept cash or traveler's checks only.

Although you won't be able to select your exact seats, TKTS patrons are frequently offered different seating options for specific productions at varying prices.

The TKTS booth is not a great option if you have your heart set on seeing this season's hot musical hit, but it can be a reliable source for quality theater at a reasonable price.

TIMES SQUARE

Location: Under the red steps in Father Duffy Square; Broadway and 47th Street.

Hours: For evening performances Monday–Saturday 3 p.m.–8 p.m., Sunday 3 p.m. until a half-hour before the latest curtain time being sold. For matinée performances Wednesday and Saturday 10 a.m.–2 p.m. (Note: No evening tickets are sold from 10 a.m. to 2 p.m. at Times Square.) Sunday 11 a.m.–3 p.m.

Public Transportation: Excellent (easily accessible by 1, 2, 3, 4, 5, 6, N, R, W, A, and C subways to Times Square).

SOUTH STREET SEAPORT

Location: Corner of Front and John Streets, at 199 Water Street.

Hours: For same-evening and next-day matinée performances Monday–Saturday 11 a.m.–6 p.m., Sunday 11 a.m.–4 p.m. Note: Matinée tickets are only sold on the day before at TKTS Seaport.

Public Transportation: Very good (easily accessible via subway lines J, M, Z, 2, 3, 4, 5 to Fulton Street or the A, C line to Broadway-Nassau, as well as M15 bus).

DOWNTOWN BROOKLYN

Location: 1 MetroTech Center at the corner of Jay Street and Myrtle Avenue.

Hours: For same-evening and next-day matinée performances Tuesday–Saturday 11 a.m.–6 p.m. Note: Matinée tickets are only sold on the day before at TKTS Brooklyn.

Public Transportation: Very good (easily accessible via subway lines A, C, and F to Jay Street-Borough Hall; M, R, 2, 3, 4, and 5 to Court Street-Borough Hall; and M and R to Lawrence Street, as well as multiple MTA bus lines).

ited engagements" that aren't scheduled to last more than a few months. Most shows are designated as "open runs," meaning that they can close in a few weeks or last 20 years, depending on how strong audience demand is. (Note: Many shows intended for an open run initially advertise as a limited engagement to stimulate sales.)

Almost all Broadway show tickets are sold through either Ticketmaster or Telecharge or can be purchased directly at the theater's box office. The standard Broadway performance schedule is Tuesday at 7 p.m., Wednesday through Saturday at 8 p.m., with 2 p.m. matinées on Wednesday and Saturday and 3 p.m. matinées on Sunday, but there are also many exceptions. Ticket prices can be as low as $20 for a student Rush or Standing Room Only ticket or as high as $120 for a center-orchestra seat at a popular show (special "premium seats" can cost three times that amount).

BROADWAY TICKET STRATEGIES ...

You're coming to New York City for a three-day trip next month and during your time in the city you'd really like to see three Broadway shows. **Show A** is a popular musical, **Show B** is a recently opened straight play that got very good reviews, and **Show C** will be in previews.

How should you go about buying tickets?

If you're visiting over Thanksgiving weekend or the week between Christmas and New Year's, consider booking all tickets well ahead of time. You may have to pay full price (but only full price, not a scalper's fee), but you'll have your tickets in hand. During any other time of the year, however, business at most shows allows you to use less-than-full-price options.

Before you go, research how popular the shows you want to see are. Go to broadwayworld.com and click on "Grosses." This will give you ticket-sales information regarding the last two weeks of almost every Broadway show. If you click on a specific show, you get several weeks more—and in greater detail.

Now let's examine the ticket availability and pricing options for each show:

Show A is steadily selling 95% of its seats every week. More important, the average price per ticket for this production is more than $110, which doesn't allow a lot of room for discounting. Tickets to this show, especially on a weekend, will have to be purchased well in advance. You

MAJOR NON-PROFIT THEATER COMPANIES

ATLANTIC THEATER COMPANY
212-691-5919 • atlantictheater.org

Venues: Linda Gross Theater, 336 West 20th Street; Atlantic Stage 2, 330 West 16th Street.
Public Transportation: Good
Handicapped Accessibility: Good
Performances/Programs: Performance schedule is Tuesday–Sunday.
Ticket Prices: Single tickets $35–$55, group discounts available.
Subscriptions/Membership: All-in-One membership $182 (one ticket to each production and all Atlantic readings); an individual membership

... FOR OUT-OF-TOWNERS

may even have to obtain premium seats ($300+) through Ticketmaster or an independent ticket broker to get in at all. If you're on a budget (and you should be), maybe you should hold off on seeing this show at the moment. Unless it's on a specific limited run (this season's *Hamlet* with Jude Law, for example), this show will be around a long time and tickets will be available for considerably less.

Show B (the straight play) is playing to 75% capacity with the average ticket price at around $52. Tickets will probably be available to this show at one of the TKTS windows during your stay. If it's really important that you see this show or you notice that business has been steadily increasing over the last few weeks (last season's *God of Carnage*), then go through playbill.com or broadwaybox.com and purchase advance tickets with a discount code.

As for **Show C**, almost every show in previews sells tickets through the TKTS window, unless it's a musical that had strong out-of-town notices, a play with a top box-office movie star, or is based on a successful London production. At the very least, **Show C** should be available using an online discount code.

A final piece of advice: Don't fill every possible "show" slot in your schedule before you come to town. A little breathing room should be built into your theater schedule in case you decide to do something totally different or simply take a break.

$55 allows you to purchase $25 tickets to each main-stage show, discount-ed tickets to Stage 2 and Atlantic for Kids production, and readings are free. Member benefits include ticket exchanges and guest ticket discounts.

From the Editors: The Atlantic Theater Company is like the East Coast home base for indie Hollywood. With its two stages ensconced in a nonde-script part of town well outside the theater district, the Atlantic has a scruffy outside-the-mainstream feel, yet this is the place where Woody Allen goes when he writes a new play or wants to take a shot at stage directing. Anoth-er film writer/director, Ethan Coen, has tried his hand at playwriting here and independent movie actors like Giancarlo Esposito, Felicity Huffman, and Isiah Whitlock Jr. are among the Atlantic's regular acting ensemble.

None of this is surprising, considering that the Atlantic was founded by William H. Macy and David Mamet, two stage-and-screen pros. They creat-ed the company in 1985 with the motto, "The story of a play and the intent of its playwright are at the core of the creative process."

Although the Atlantic Theater Company favors harder-edged works by such playwrights as Martin MCDonagh and Harold Pinter, it has a soft side too. Atlantic For Kids is the children's theater series, which presents family plays every season and, believe it or not, even Mamet has penned a few! Education is a crucial part of Atlantic's mission, which it has realized through the Atlantic Acting School, a private conservatory and New York University undergrad program that emphasizes a technique first devel-oped by Mamet and Macy.

CHERRY LANE THEATER
38 Commerce Street
212-989-2020 • cherrylanetheatre.org

Public Transportation: Good
Handicapped Accessibility: Good
Performances/Programs: Performance schedule varies.
Ticket Prices: Tickets start at $10.
Subscriptions: Cherry Pass $99 (tickets for two mainstage and three mentor projects), Premium membership $250 (house seats to opening nights), Cherry Picker membership $180 (four mainstage tix and four Men-tor Projects), Mentor Project membership $45 (one ticket for all three Men-tor Project plays, discounts on Late Night and special events, free readings). Subscriber benefits include invites to cast party and free ticket exchanges. Discount membership for educators.

From the Editors: If there were an award for Most Picturesque Location of a theater, the Cherry Lane would win hands down. This old playhouse, built out of a box factory, is nestled on the incongruously named Commerce Street, a beautiful leafy little lane in the West Village. Opened in 1924, the Cherry Lane was on the ground floor of the most significant alternative theater movements of the 20th century, producing Odets, Pirandello, and Saroyan in the '40s, Samuel Beckett, John Cage, and even a play by Pablo Picasso in the '50s, and Edward Albee, Jean Genet, Harold Pinter, and Ionesco in the '60s.

Cherry Lane's days as the epicenter of the downtown theater scene are long over, but it does still maintain a devotion to cultivating new artists and new voices. The theater's pride and joy is the Mentor Project, a wonderful development program that each year pairs three beginning playwrights with experienced ones like Michael Weller, Marsha Norman, Tony Kushner, and Alfred Uhry. The elder writer gives guidance to the "newbie" as he or she works on a play that's given a showcase production by Cherry Lane at the end of the season.

ENCORES! GREAT AMERICAN MUSICALS IN CONCERT
City Center, 131 West 55th Street
212-581-1212 • nycitycenter.org/content/stage/encores.aspx

Public Transportation: Good
Handicapped Accessibility: Good
Performances/Programs: Performance schedule is Wednesday–Sunday.
Ticket Prices: Single tickets are $25–$110, tickets sometimes available on TDF.

From the Editors: It's a sign of Encores' success and longevity that it has already begun to outrun its mission. Launched in 1994 as a staged concert series dedicated to presenting in their full glory the original scores of seldom-produced musicals, Encores! spent its early years reviving shows like Rodgers & Hammerstein's *Allegro*, Cole Porter's *Out of This World*, and Irving Berlin's *Call Me Madam*—musicals with marvelous scores and books that don't usually stand up well in a full production. But as time has gone on, Encores! has resorted to perennial favorites like *Bye Bye Birdie* and *Hair*.

Whatever they do, though, they always do with style, bringing in a huge orchestra, casting top-notch performers, and even charging playwrights like David Ives and Terrence McNally with the task of "editing" the book (usually read script-in-hand by the cast). In many cases, Encores! Productions, such as *The Apple Tree*, *Wonderful Town*, *Gypsy*, and most famously *Chicago* have gone on to open-ended Broadway runs, but if you want to see Encores! at City Center, be sure to get your tickets quickly. And if you go for the cheap seats in the rear gallery, be forewarned: It's a long long way from the stage!

LINCOLN CENTER THEATER
150 West 65th Street
212-239-6200 • lct.org

Public Transportation: Excellent
Handicapped Accessibility: Good
Performances/Programs: Performance schedule is Tuesday–Sunday.
Ticket Prices: Single tickets are $65–$125, $20 student tickets sometimes available, discounts available for groups of 20 or more.
Membership: LCT Membership costs $50 for 12 months and provides the member with the ability to purchase one ticket for each new eligible LCT production at special member price, usually $40–$50.

From the Editors: Lincoln Center Theater is part of the massive Lincoln Center for the Performing Arts complex, virtually hidden behind the plaza and past the Met. LCT consists of two stages, the 299-seat Mitzi E. Newhouse Theater and the much larger Vivian Beaumont Theater, which has the distinction of being the only legitimate Broadway theater outside of the Times Square area.

LCT is usually regarded as the classiest (or snobbiest, depending on your point of view) of the non-profits, catering to a wealthier audience and producing a mix of handsome revivals, shows by prestigious writers like Tom Stoppard and Adam Guettel, and new plays by dramatists with whom the theater has established relationships.

Each year usually sees a full and varied season of plays and musicals, but occasionally a break-out hit like *Contact* or the *South Pacific* revival will settle into long runs at the Beaumont. A new initiative, called LCT3, is Lincoln Center Theater's effort to produce more work by emerging artists— and to do it for an affordable price (all tickets $20). Eventually LCT3 is to have its own 99-seat theater space near the Lincoln Center complex, but for now the program will use off-site venues.

MANHATTAN THEATRE CLUB
212-239-6200 • mtc-nyc.org

Venues: Samuel J. Friedman Theatre, 261 West 47th Street; Stages I and II at NY City Center, 131 West 55th Street.

Public Transportation: Excellent

Handicapped Accessibility: Good

Performances/Programs: Performance schedule is typically Tuesday–Sunday.

Ticket Prices: Single tickets are $50–$96.50, discount codes usually available through Playbill, TheaterMania, BroadwayBox, Goldstar.com and others.

Subscriptions: Seven-Play $365–$405, Five-Play $275–305, Four-Play Sampler $190–$260, Three-Play $159–$199, Flex Package (Three-Play) $199, Flex Package (Four-Play) $260, Student subscriptions available. Subscriber benefits include ticket exchanges and discounts at neighboring restaurants and bars.

From the Editors: An exclusively Off- and Off-Off-Broadway theater company for its first 30-odd years, Manhattan Theatre Club was emboldened to take up permanent residence on the Great White Way in 2003 following the hugely successful Broadway transfers of its productions of Charles Busch's *The Tale of the Allergist's Wife* and David Auburn's *Proof*. Now each MTC season includes four Off-Broadway productions on its two stages at City Center and three Broadway mountings at the Samuel J. Friedman Theatre (formerly the Biltmore).

Although it does produce some revivals (usually of rarely seen contemporary plays), the Manhattan Theatre Club displays greater commitment to new plays than the other high-profile NYC non-profits. Perhaps as a result of this laudable commitment, or because the leadership has questionable taste (or just because New York theatergoers love to complain), MTC is also often accused of producing too many mediocre plays. The company has had its share of gems, though, including Pulitzer Prize winners *Rabbit Hole* and *Doubt*. MTC also has longstanding relationships with a number of significant modern playwrights, meaning that it has been able to present several premieres by the likes of Richard Greenberg, Terrence McNally, Athol Fugard, Alan Ayckbourn, Donald Margulies, and John Patrick Shanley.

NEW WORLD STAGES
340 West 50th Street
212- 239-6200 • newworldstages.com

Public Transportation: Excellent
Handicapped Accessibility: Good
Performances/Programs: Performance schedule varies from show to show.
Ticket Prices: Single tickets vary from show to show, but generally fall between $46.50 and $80.50 (a few shows have tickets as low as $20–$25), shows sometimes available on Goldstar.com, discount codes available for most shows.

From the Editors: New World Stages, which rose from the ashes of an old Loews Cineplex in 2004, is an exciting development for the dreary commercial Off-Broadway theater scene. New World's giant underground complex contains five separate stages (ranging from 199 to 499 seats), providing a great option for producers who want to go the Off-Broadway route, but don't wish to stray from the theater district. Off-Bway smash *Altar Boyz* has made itself quite comfortable on Stage 4, while other musicals, plays, revues, solo performances, kids' shows, and various theatrical events have come and gone. Some shows, like *Naked Boys Singing* and *My First Time*, survive by doing just a couple performances a week, usually on the weekend.

The New World complex also has ample space for social gatherings and has hosted special events, ranging from a Kanye West listening party to Rosie O'Donnell's painting exhibit at the in-house art space, the Gallery. New World Stages is also home to the Time Out New York Lounge, where aspiring stars can "make their Off-Broadway debut" at open-mic Mondays (no cover, accompanist provided) or during Thursday night karaoke.

PLAYWRIGHTS HORIZONS
416 West 42nd Street
212-564-1235 • playwrightshorizons.org

Public Transportation: Good
Handicapped Accessibility: Good
Performances/Programs: Performance schedule is Tuesday–Sunday.
Ticket Prices: Single tickets are $50–$65, $15 student Rush, Live For Five Lottery $5 tickets to first preview of each show distributed via online lottery, Hot Tix limited number of $20 tickets sold one hour prior to show-

time to 30-and-unders, group discounts available, discounts occasionally available on Goldstar.com.

Subscriptions: Silver Pass $320 (one ticket to each of the six shows), Four-show ($160–$195) and Six-Show ($225–$260). FlexPass Four-Show ($200) and Six-Show ($270), Flex $40 or $60 for students; $80 or $120 for 30-and-unders. Subscriber benefits include ticket exchanges and discounts on dining and parking.

From the Editors: In the new millennium, Playwrights Horizons finds itself overshadowed a bit by the bigger non-profits that now reside on Broadway, but it has long held a well-deserved reputation for producing bold new works. Past artistic successes have included musicals *Grey Gardens*, *Floyd Collins*, *Assassins*, *Falsettos*, and *Sunday in the Park with George*, and the plays *I Am My Own Wife*, *Driving Miss Daisy*, and *The Heidi Chronicles*.

Playwrights continues to put forth a slate of entirely new work each season, and it's one of the rare theaters that accepts unsolicited scripts from playwrights—though you wouldn't necessarily know it some years, when all the shows are by established names. Playwrights is constantly developing new plays and musicals through readings and commissions and it educates performers through the Playwrights Horizons Theater School at New York University.

In 2003, Playwrights Horizons moved into its new home, a state-of-the-art facility on West 42nd St. ("Theatre Row"), which houses a mainstage and a studio theater. Also located there is Ticket Central, a box office that sells tickets for Off- and Off-Off-Broadway shows and events, as well as tickets for Playwrights Horizons own productions.

PRIMARY STAGES
59E59 Theaters, 59 East 59th Street
212-753-5959 • primarystages.com

Public Transportation: Good
Handicapped Accessibility: Good
Performances/Programs: Performance schedule is Tuesday–Sunday.
Ticket Prices: Single tickets are $60, $15 student tickets using code "STUD," PS35 $20 tickets available for 35-and-unders, usually one of the first two preview performances of a show are designated pay what you can.
Subscriptions: Four-Show Subscriptions $126–$170. Subscribers save 30%. Subscriber benefits include free ticket exchanges, discounts on courses and workshops at Primary Stages School of Theater, and special offers for other shows playing at 59E59.

From the Editors: Primary Stages has operated under the radar for many years, presenting fine productions of plays by great writers like A.R. Gurney, Horton Foote, Romulus Linney, and Lee Blessing at its little 99-seat space in Midtown West. Just a few years ago, the company moved eastward to a space twice that size at 59E59 Theaters, giving Primary Stages an opportunity to grow and present its work to a larger audience.

Primary Stages is dedicated to developing the future of playwriting in a number of ways, from development in the Dorothy Strelsin New American Writers Group to mounting full productions of plays by emerging writers. The Primary Stages School of Theater educates people in both playwriting and acting through courses and workshops. Then there's the Primetime Reading Series, a place where playwrights can have their in-process work read aloud in front of an audience of friends, fellow dramatists, and Primary Stages regulars (admission is free).

PUBLIC THEATER
425 Lafayette Street
212-539-8500 • publictheater.org

Public Transportation: Excellent
Handicapped Accessibility: Good
Performances/Programs: Performance schedule is generally Tuesday–Sunday.
Ticket Prices: Tickets usually $50, student tickets $25, Rush tickets $20, discounts for groups of 15 or more.
Subscriptions: Six-Play Package $255, Five-Play Package $227.50, Three-Play Package $142.50, Preview Pak $200 (Preview Pak holders do not receive all the benefits of regular memberships). Subscriber benefits include ticket exchanges, discounts on additional tickets, invites to special events, and discount offers for shows and local restaurants.

From the Editors: Established by Joe Papp as the Shakespeare Workshop in the mid-'50s, the re-christened Public Theater moved into the former Astor Library in the East Village in 1967 and introduced the world to *Hair* and, a few years later, *A Chorus Line*. Those shows continue to be regarded as the musical theater's most authentic responses to the '60s and '70s, respectively, and the Public struck the zeitgeist again in 1995 with the explosive tap/rap exploration of black history, *Bring in 'Da Noise, Bring in 'Da Funk*.

Though it hasn't had that kind of blockbuster success since, the Public has maintained its status as downtown's most adventurous theater by

regularly producing off-beat, multicultural, and multimedia theater pieces, fresh productions of classics, new plays by cult favorites, and plenty of
work by new and often underrepresented voices. Some of its most recent
hits include: the theatrical autobiography *Elaine Stritch: At Liberty*, Richard
Greenberg's exploration of homosexuality in *The Big Leagues*, Tony Kushner and Jeanine Tesori's Civil Rights era musical *Caroline or Change*, and the
coming-of-age rock odyssey *Passing Strange*.

The Public produces on no fewer than five different stages in its home
on Lafayette Street, which host not only its regular productions, but also
the New Work Now! play reading series and the Under the Radar Festival.

And then, of course, there's the wonderful adjoining performance
space Joe's Pub, a cross between a hip lounge and a cabaret, which has
some of the most innovative and eclectic programming of any live music
venue in New York.

ROUNDABOUT THEATRE COMPANY
212-719-1300 • roundabouttheatre.org

Venues: American Airlines Theatre, 227 West 42nd Street; Studio 54,
254 West 54th Street; Laura Pels Theatre/Roundabout Underground Black
Box Theatre, Harold and Miriam Steinberg Center for Theatre, 111 West 46th
Street.
Public Transportation: Good (all venues)
Handicapped Accessibility: Good (all venues)
Performances/Programs: Performance schedule is Tuesday–Sunday.
Ticket Prices: $66.50–$111.50 (American Airlines/Studio 54), $64–$74
(Laura Pels), $20 (Roundabout Underground); HIPTIX: $20 tickets for the-
atergoers 18–35 (must sign up for free HipTix membership in advance, one
ticket per member); $10 First Preview (100 mezzanine tickets available).
General Rush, student Rush, and half-price tickets for kids subject to avail-
ability.
Subscriptions: Four-Show $250 and Five-Show $295. Subscriber benefits include free ticket exchanges, $25 discount on additional tickets, and
restaurant and parking discounts.

From the Editors: Roundabout Theatre Company was once a Little
Non-Profit that has steadily grown to be a Great Big Non-Profit, to the point
that some even question the legitimacy of its status at this point. Ever since
its hit Sam Mendes-directed revival of *Cabaret* in 1998, Roundabout's presence on the NYC theater scene has exploded and it now has two Broadway
houses (club-turned-theater Studio 54 and the unfortunately named but

glorious American Airlines Theatre), the Laura Pels Theater Off-Broadway, and the brand new black box space, Roundabout Underground.

The Underground, which exclusively showcases new work and charges only $20 per seat, was created to make up for the sad fact that NYC's most conspicuous non-profit only produces revivals in its Broadway houses. It's unfortunate, when you consider that the money going to produce lush revivals of plays could go instead to an ambitious new drama by a contemporary writer. On the other hand, it's nice to see some wonderful—and some unjustly forgotten—old plays and musicals get top-flight productions on Broadway thanks to Roundabout.

SECOND STAGE THEATRE
212-246-4422 • 2st.com

Venues: 307 West 43rd Street (at 8th Avenue); McGinn/Cazale Theatre, 2162 Broadway (at 76th Street, 3rd Floor); Helen Hayes Theatre, 240 West 44th Street (in 2010).

Public Transportation: Excellent

Handicapped Accessibility: Good (all venues)

Performances/Programs: Performance schedule is generally Tuesday–Sunday, with an occasional Monday.

Ticket Prices: Single tickets are $50–$70, senior discounts available to some shows, Youth Advance tickets $20–$25, student Rush tickets $10–$15. See the show for free by being a volunteer usher.

Subscriptions: Three-Show $125–$149, and Four-Show $170–$205, subscription discounts available for 25-and-unders and educators. Subscriber benefits include discounted additional tickets for friends and family and free ticket exchanges.

From the Editors: Following in the footsteps of its non-profit brethren Roundabout and MTC, Second Stage Theatre is now poised to take over the littlest theater on Broadway, the 597-seat Helen Hayes, where it will begin producing shows in 2010. The Helen Hayes will make three for Second Stage, which continues to use its original home, the McGinn/Cazale on the Upper West Side, but has its main space on West 43rd St. in an old bank repurposed for Second Stage by Rem Koolhaas (the box office is in a vault!).

As its name indicates, Second Stage was originally founded in 1979 to provide a second chance to worthy contemporary plays that weren't able to find an audience during their initial runs. However, Second Stage's mission has expanded since then to include the development of new plays and musicals, leading to the world and NYC premieres of acclaimed shows like *The 25th Annual Putnam County Spelling Bee*, *The Little Dog Laughed*, *Metamorphoses*, Kenneth Lonergan's *The Waverly Gallery*, and Sarah Ruhl's *Eurydice*.

VINEYARD THEATRE
108 East 15th Street
212-353-0303 • vineyardtheatre.org

Public Transportation: Good
Handicapped Accessibility: Good
Performances/Programs: Performance schedule is Tuesday–Sunday.
Ticket Prices: Single tickets are $55–$60, $20 student Rush (two hours prior to curtain), $40 advance tickets for seniors.
Subscriptions/Memberships: Full membership is $155 and entitles you to one ticket to three mainstage shows and one lab; Show By Show membership is $55, then you pay just $25 for each member ticket per show; Under-30 membership, you pay only $30 for your membership and $15 for each member ticket per show; Theatre Artist memberships are for professional theater artists who pay only $30, then $15 for each member ticket per show, valid union ID required; Subscriber benefits include free ticket exchanges and parking discounts.

From the Editors: There's something about the Vineyard Theatre that makes it feel like the theater for cool introspective twenty- and thirtysomethings who have a good (and sometimes twisted) sense of humor. Maybe it's the fact that two of the Vineyard's biggest hits have been *Avenue Q* and *[title of show]*, both musicals about people in that age group who live in New York City and are trying to figure their lives out. The Vineyard also likes to produce work by mid-career playwrights who write about the urban experience, such as Nicky Silver and Craig Lucas.

The theater is located in the trendy Union Square area, just a bit north of NYU, but it would hardly be fair to put it into any kind of box, considering it has premiered everything from heady dramas like Edward Albee's *Three Tall Women* and Paula Vogel's *How I Learned to Drive* to moody musicals like *Eli's Comin'* and *Dream True*. The Vineyard has also mounted some downright unusual (and, yes, cool) stuff like the live-action graphic-novel *The Slug Bearers of Kayrol Island*. An eclectic slate of productions, to say the least.

YORK THEATRE COMPANY
Citigroup Center, The Theatre at Saint Peter's
619 Lexington Avenue
212-935-5820 • yorktheatre.org

Public Transportation: Good
Handicapped Accessibility: Good
Performances/Programs: Performance schedule a bit inconsistent, with various shows on every day of the week.
Ticket Prices: Single tickets for mainstage shows are $57.50, $20 student tickets, admission to readings is free.

From the Editors: The York Theatre Company's two-part mission is to develop new musicals and to preserve old ones. To realize the first part, the York facilitates dozens and dozens of free readings of new shows each year and devotes its mainstage to producing brand new musicals. As far as preserving the old tuners goes, the York Theatre's "Musicals in Mufti" series has been doing an excellent job of that for nearly 15 years, creating concert stagings of little-known gems like *Plain and Fancy*, *Celebration*, *The Grass Harp*, *Greenwillow*, and *Carmen Jones*. You can find the York Theatre Company on the lower level of St. Peter's Church, located at Lexington and E. 54th St., under the massive Citigroup Center building.

NOTABLE OFF- AND OFF-OFF BROADWAY THEATERS

CLASSIC STAGE COMPANY
136 East 13th Street
212-677-4210, ext. 10 • classicstage.org

Public Transportation: Excellent
Handicapped Accessibility: Good
Performances/Programs: Performance schedule is Tuesday–Sunday.
Ticket Prices: Single tickets are $70–$75.
Subscriptions/Membership: Four-Show membership $125–$135, MasterPass membership (five flex tickets) $250; Four-Show membership benefits include ticket exchanges and discounts at area restaurants and entertainment; MasterPass benefits include day-of-show ticket exchange, offers, and discounts at various area restaurants and entertainment venues, and private backstage tours.

From the Editors: Why wait around for the latest star-studded London production of a great Shakespeare play to transfer to Broadway when you've got the Classic Stage Company on 13th street? Under the leadership of artistic director Brian Kulick, CSC has become a magnet for renowned, adventurous New York actors, hungry to delve into great works by Shakespeare, Chekhov, Beckett, Brecht, Aeschylus, and more in the company's intimate theater. The last few years have seen Mandy Patinkin in *The Tempest*, Denis O'Hare, Peter Sarsgaard and Maggie Gyllenhaal in *Uncle Vanya*, Michael Cumpsty in *Richard III*, and Dianne Wiest and Alan Cumming in *The Seagull*.

CSC doesn't just stick to the standard repertoire—the company has also brought great literature to the stage with *The Proust Project* and staged readings of *The Iliad*, and produced new plays by writers such as David Ives *New Jerusalem* and Yasmina Reza *The Spanish Play*. Through the efforts of The Young Company, classics come alive for young audiences in performances given by Columbia University acting students, and the innovative Open Rehearsal Series allows audiences to get a glimpse into the struggles that actors and directors encounter when exploring a classic text.

CLASSICAL THEATRE OF HARLEM
The Gatehouse, Harlem Stage, 150 Convent Avenue (at 135th Street)
212-868-4444 • classicaltheatreofharlem.org

Public Transportation: Good
Handicapped Accessibility: Good
Ticket Prices: Single tickets are $22–$45, student and group discounts available.
Subscriptions: Three-Show subscription $90, subscribers save 25%.

IRISH REPERTORY THEATRE
132 West 22nd Street
212-727-2737 • irishrep.org

Public Transportation: Good
Handicapped Accessibility: Good
Performances/Programs: Performance schedule is Tuesday–Sunday.
Ticket Prices: Single tickets are $55–$60, $5 ticket discount for students and seniors, Rush tickets (for up to half-price) available one hour before each performance, discounts for groups of 20 or more, volunteer ushers get one free ticket.
Subscriptions: None offered, but you can get some benefits by joining

the Patrons' Circle for a minimum of $50 (20% discount on two tickets per production).

LA MAMA EXPERIMENTAL THEATRE CLUB
212-475-7710 • lamama.org

Venues: 1st Floor Theatre and The Club, 74A East 4th St.; Annex Theatre, 66 East 4th Street.

Public Transportation: Good

Handicapped Accessibility: Fair (the 1st Floor Theater and the Annex are accessible; the Club Theater is not).

Performances/Programs: Performance schedule generally Thursday–Sunday.

Ticket Prices: Single tickets are $15–$25, $5 discount for students and seniors, $10 tickets for children under 10, discounts for groups of 10 or more.

Note: La Mama also curates an art gallery called La Galeria, located at 6 East 1st Street. The phone number is 212-505-2476.

LABYRINTH THEATER COMPANY
212-513-1080 • labtheater.org

Venue: No fixed venue. Has been using Public Theater, 425 Lafayette Street.

Public Transportation: Good

Handicapped Accessibility: Good

Performances/Programs: Performance schedule Tuesday–Sunday.

Ticket Prices: Single tickets are $50, $25 student tickets available, $20 Rush tickets sold an hour before performances.

Membership: Lab Pass memberships available. Benefits include priority booking, ticket discounts, and exclusive invitations to private readings and benefits.

MINT THEATER COMPANY
311 W. 43rd Street, 3rd Floor
212-315-0231 • minttheater.org

Public Transportation: Excellent

Handicapped Accessibility: Good

Performances/Programs: Performance schedule is Tuesday–Sunday.

Ticket Prices: Single tickets $35–$55, "25 Under 25" $25 tickets for anyone 25 or younger.

Membership: Donate a minimum of $150 to be in the Double Mint First Priority Club and get invitations to all special events and readings, advance notice of all Mint productions, a subscription to Mint's First Priority Club newsletter, and ticket-exchange privileges. Donate $1,500 and get two tickets to each of the year's productions.

From the Editors: Many New York Off- and Off-Off Broadway theater companies do an fine job of presenting classic plays and musicals including the Classic Stage Company, Encores!, Musicals Tonight, the Pearl Theatre Company and the York Theatre Company—but no company does classic theater programming more innovatively than the Mint Theater Company on W. 43rd Street. Under the motto "lost plays found here" the Mint stages two or three productions a year of classic (as in 50–150 years old) plays you probably have never heard of (*John Ferguson*, *The Power of Darkness*, *Return of the Prodigal*, *Madras House*). In many instances you have never heard of the playwrights either (Arthur Schnitzler, Rachel Crothers, St. John Ervine) or if you have heard of them, it is due to their novels not their plays (Ernest Hemmingway, D. H. Lawrence, Leo Tolstoy). Due to the fine efforts of Artistic Director Jonathan Bank many formerly "lost plays" as well as "lost playwrights" (our favorite is Harley Granville Barker) have now become household words in the New York theater community.

MUSICALS TONIGHT!
McGinn/Cazale Theatre, 2162 Broadway
212-362-5620 • musicalstonight.org

Public Transportation: Good
Handicapped Accessibility: Good
Performances/Programs: Performance schedule is Tuesday–Sunday.
Ticket Prices: Single tickets are $20, Five-Show subscription $100. Subscriber benefits include reserved seats and ticket exchanges.

NEW GROUP
The Acorn @ Theatre Row, 410 West 42nd Street
212-244-3380 • thenewgroup.org

Public Transportation: Good
Handicapped Accessibility: Good

Performances/Programs: Performance schedule is Monday–Saturday.
Ticket Prices: Single tickets are $56.
Subscriptions: Subscriptions are $126 (renewal subs $104).

NEW YORK THEATRE WORKSHOP
79 East Fourth Street
212-460-5475 • nytw.org

Public Transportation: Good
Handicapped Accessibility: Good
Performances/Programs: Performance schedule is Tuesday–Sunday.
Ticket Prices: Single tickets are $65, CheapTix Sundays $20 ticket for Sunday evening performances, $20 tickets for full-time students, $32 senior, discounts available for groups of 10 or more; see show for free by being a volunteer usher. Shows available on Goldstar.com.
Subscriptions: Three-Play membership $142, SmartPass (four flex tickets) $190. Subscriber benefits include ticket-exchange privileges, encore admission privileges, special discounts to outside productions in the 4th Street Theatre, and discount on a Theatre for a New Audience subscription.

PEARL THEATRE COMPANY
80 Street Marks Place
212-598-9802 • pearltheatre.org

Venue: The Company is performing their 2009-2010 season at New York City Center Stage II.
Public Transportation: Excellent
Handicapped Accessibility: Good
Performances/Programs: Performance schedule is Tuesday–Sunday.
Ticket Prices: Single tickets are $45–$55, Preview tickets $25; opening-night tickets $90, Rush tickets for seniors and 24-and-unders $23–$28; remaining tickets are sold for $10 on Thursdays (15 minutes prior to curtain). Group discounts are available, TDF vouchers accepted.
Subscriptions: Six-admission Flex Pass $230, Five-Play $120–$170 (opening night Five-Play $345), Four-Play $145, Three-Play $120.

THEATRE FOR A NEW AUDIENCE
212-229-2819 • www.tfana.org

Venues: No Fixed venue. Have been using the Duke on 42nd St., 229 West 42nd St., and New York Theatre Workshop, 79 East Fourth Street.

Public Transportation: Excellent

Handicapped Accessibility: Good (both venues)

Performances/Programs: Performance schedule is Tuesday–Sunday.

Ticket Prices: Single tickets are $75 for most shows, $10 tickets available for people ages 25 and under.

Subscriptions: Four-Play $167 and Three-Play $142. Subscriber benefits include discount membership with New York Theatre Workshop and ticket exchanges.

WORKING THEATER
212-539-5675 • theworkingtheater.org

Venues: No fixed venue. Has been using Theatre for the New City, 155 First Avenue.

Public Transportation: Depends on venue (most are close to MTA transit routes).

Handicapped Accessibility: Depends on venue.

Performances/Programs: Performance schedule is Tuesday–Sunday.

Ticket Prices: Single tickets are $25, union members $23, students and seniors $21.

SHAKESPEARE IN THE PARK (summer only)
Delacorte Theatre, Central Park
(enter at 81st Street and Central Park West)
212-539-8500 • publictheater.org

Public Transportation: Good

Handicapped Accessibility: Good

Performances/Programs: Performance schedule is Tuesday–Sunday.

Ticket Prices: Tickets are free, distributed at 1 p.m. on the day of each performance at the Delacorte Theatre. Public Theater donors (usually $500 or more) qualify for reserved Shakespeare in the Park tickets. Last season, the Public introduced an online lottery for a limited number of tickets to each performance, but no certainty yet whether this will be a regular feature.

From the Editors: Every summer, the Public Theater takes its act uptown, bringing theater to all of New York with its free productions at the Delacorte Theatre in gorgeous Central Park. Shakespeare in the Park (formerly called the New York Shakespeare Festival) usually consists of two productions; one is always a play by the Bard and the other is usually either something from the classical repertoire or a modern classic.

Free tickets are handed out at 1 p.m. on the day of performance, though people start lining up at the Delacorte much earlier. When the cast is particularly starry, such as the 2001 production of *The Seagull*, featuring Meryl Streep, Kevin Kline, Philip Seymour Hoffman, Natalie Portman, John Goodman, and Christopher Walken, some people spend the whole night in the Park waiting for tickets. Fortunately, you couldn't ask for a better place to wait than lovely leafy Central Park.

The atmosphere inside the Delacorte is even better, where the drama begins just as the sun is setting.

The show will hold for rain delays, only completely calling off the performance if it gets really bad and won't let up, in which case, sadly, you'll have to return another day and wait in line for tickets all over again.

CLASSICAL MUSIC

AMERICAN COMPOSERS ORCHESTRA
212-977-8495 • americancomposers.org

Venues: Carnegie Hall, NYC; Annenberg Center for the Arts, West Philadelphia at 3680 Walnut Street.

Public Transportation: Excellent (accessible via the N, R, and Q subway at Carnegie Hall).

Handicapped Accessibility: Good

Performances/Programs: It varies, but usually six programs and eight performances per season.

Ticket Prices: Vary based on venue.

From the Editors: This group is dedicated to the performance of living American composers' music. The concerts are a great way to hear new works and gain an opportunity to learn about the composition process.

BACH VESPERS AT HOLY TRINITY
Holy Trinity Lutheran Church, 3 West 65th Street
212-877-6815 • bachvespersnyc.org

Public Transportation: Good
Handicapped Accessibility: Poor
Performances/Programs: Approximately 25 per season.
Ticket Prices: $10/$15 at door for Fourth Monday concerts and others are free.
Membership: Memberships range from $1 to $5,000+. Those whose donate $100 or more will be listed in the Vespers' program.

BARGEMUSIC
Fulton Ferry Landing near the Brooklyn Bridge
718-624-4061/718-624-2083 • bargemusic.org

Public Transportation: Good (accessible by the A, F, 2, and 3 trains).
Performances/Programs: Bargemusic presents 220 chamber-music concerts annually—four days a week, 52 weeks a year—and offers free tickets to a variety of groups every week, plus a monthly free concert open to the community.
Ticket Prices: $35, students $20, seniors $30 on Wednesday, Thursday, and Friday.

CHAMBER MUSIC SOCIETY OF LINCOLN CENTER
212-875-5788 • chambermusicsociety.org

Venues: The Chamber Music Society presents concerts in a number of venues in the Lincoln Center area, including the newly renovated Alice Tully Hall. Other venues include the Concert Hall at the New York Society for Ethical Culture, 2 West 64th Street at Central Park West; the Daniel and Joanna S. Rose Studio, Rose Building, 165 West 65th Street, 10th Floor; Merkin Concert Hall at Kaufman Center, 129 West 67th Street between Broadway and Amsterdam; the Rose Theater, Frederick P. Rose Hall, Home of Jazz at Lincoln Center, Broadway at 60th Street; the Stanley H. Kaplan Penthouse, Rose Building, 165 West 65th Street, 10th Floor.
Public Transportation: Excellent (all venues easily accessible by 1 subway).

Handicapped Accessibility: Good

Performances/Programs: Vary

Ticket Prices: Vary by performance. Discounts are sometimes available for students and seniors.

Group Discounts: Groups of 10 or more receive up to a 20% discount; student groups of 10 or more receive up to a 50% discount.

Subscriptions: Choose one of CMS's multiple Chamber Collection series or create a series of your own of 3, 4, 5, 6, or 12 events; the Chamber Music 360 for ages 21–39 is a discount package that allows subscribers to purchase three tickets for $60. Tickets can be exchanged up to two hours before the concert.

Membership: Friends level ($100–$1,499) provides invitations to open rehearsals and discounted ticket offers. Benefits increase in relation to donation amount. Patrons ($1,500+) enjoy benefits such as musical evenings in private homes, regular intermission receptions, and backstage gatherings.

Educational/Community Outreach: CMS offers an interactive program, Meet the Music. In this upbeat three-concert series, kids learn about music and hear world-class musicians who love to play for an audience of families at special afternoon concerts. CMS also offers Family Fridays, where patrons can purchase two regular Friday-evening concerts at the special subscription price of $75 and all the kids' tickets are free.

Special Group Activities: Pre-concert wine-tasting receptions take place one hour before concerts in the lobby of Alice Tully Hall several nights during the season, and are an additional $12 per person.

FRICK MUSEUM CONCERTS
Frick Museum, 1 East 70th Street
212-547-0715 • frickart.com/programs/concerts

Public Transportation: Excellent (easy access to buses and subways).

Handicapped Accessibility: Good

Performances/Programs: "Music for Exhibitions" three concerts/season, rest of season varies.

Ticket Prices: $25 each. Select concerts are offered free of charge.

From the Editors: "Music for Exhibitions" showcases a variety of music from baroque to jazz, performed in accompaniment to the museum's current exhibitions.

WORKS AND PROCESS SERIES AT THE GUGGENHEIM

The Peter B. Lewis Theater of the Sackler Center for Arts Education at the Solomon R. Guggenheim Museum, 1071 Fifth Avenue (at 89th Street)
212-758-0024
guggenheim.org/education/worksandprocess/index.html

Public Transportation: Very good (convenient to the 4, 5, 6 subways and MTA buses).

Handicapped Accessibility: Good

Performances/Programs: About 30 performances are offered a year, ranging from commissions of new compositions, opera, and ballet to poetry and lectures.

Ticket Prices: $30 (unless otherwise noted), $10 for students 25 and under. For Guggenheim members, tickets are $25; standby tickets may be available one hour before the performance for $20.

Subscriptions: Purchase tickets to four or more programs and the ticket-handling fees are waived.

Membership: Guggenheim Patrons Circle donors ($1,750+) receive complimentary tickets to Works and Process events.

From the Editors: Since 1984 and in more than 300 productions, Works and Process at the Guggenheim has been a pioneer in creating groundbreaking and carefully crafted programs that provide unprecedented access to today's leading performing artists, choreographers, composers, writers, directors, and poets. Each program blends performance, demonstration, and discussion among creative collaborators and explores the creative process. Following often sold-out performances in the intimate Frank Lloyd Wright–designed 285-seat theater, a reception for the audience and artists takes place in the museum's rotunda.

JUILLIARD SCHOOL OF MUSIC
212-799-5000 • juilliard.edu

Venues: Peter Jay Sharp Theater, Alice Tully Hall, and Avery Fisher Hall (Lincoln Center), as well as outside events performed at Carnegie Hall and around New York City.

Public Transportation: Excellent (readily accessible by 1, A, C, B, and D subways).

Handicapped Accessibility: Good

Performances/Programs: More than 30 concerts are offered each season. Juilliard has three main orchestral ensembles: Juilliard Orchestra, the New Juilliard Ensemble, and the Conductors' Orchestra. This music school has a wealth of other musical offerings, particularly in chamber music, contemporary music, and recitals.

Ticket Prices: Many events at Juilliard are free and don't require tickets. However, free tickets are required for most events in Alice Tully Hall, the Peter Jay Sharp Theater, and the Stephanie P. McClelland Drama Theater. These tickets are limited and are distributed at the box office very quickly on the day they become available.

Membership: Association members ($100–$500) enjoy advance notification for a number of classical and jazz music concerts, plays, operas, and dance productions, as well as priority ticket service by mail for many Juilliard performances.

MANHATTAN SCHOOL OF MUSIC
601 West 122nd Street
212-749-2802 • msmnyc.edu

Public Transportation: Good (easily accessible by 1 subway).

Handicapped Accessibility: Good

Performances/Programs: Manhattan School has five orchestras: Symphony, Philharmonia, Chamber Sinfonia, Conductor's, and Jazz Philharmonic. There are many other offerings in vocal, chamber music, and solo instrumental recitals, as well as selected master classes. There are multiple performances on just about any day, so it's a good idea to check the event calendar listings to see what's going on.

Ticket Prices: While most events are free, certain concerts require tickets depending on the venue. There's usually a cost for events at Carnegie Hall, but events at the Manhattan School may be free. Average ticket price for orchestra concerts ranges from $10 to $20. Student tickets are offered from $5 to $10.

Subscriptions: Purchase advance tickets to three orchestra concerts and receive a fourth free, plus priority seating for up to four people at the MSM Chamber Sinfonia concert at Carnegie Hall's Zankel Hall.

MANNES COLLEGE—THE NEW SCHOOL FOR MUSIC
212-580-0210 • www.mannes.edu

Venues: Mannes Concert Hall, 150 W. 85th Street; Alice Tully Hall, Lincoln Center; Carnegie Hall.

Public Transportation: Very good (all venues).

Handicapped Accessibility: Good

Performances/Programs: Mannes has multiple performances every day of the week. Check out the website to find information on orchestra, opera, chamber music, new music, special festivals, recitals, and master-class performances.

Ticket Prices: Many events are free and open to the public; there are some exceptions and events outside of Mannes often require a ticket for admission. When there's a charge, discounts are available to students and seniors.

METROPOLITAN MUSEUM CONCERTS
The Metropolitan Museum of Art, 1000 Fifth Avenue (at 82nd Street)
212-570-3949 • mfa.org

Public Transportation: Good (accessible from the East and West sides of Manhattan by subway and bus).

Handicapped Accessibility: Good

Performances/Programs: Approximately 15 performances given annually.

Ticket Prices: $45 for most concerts, no refunds or exchanges permitted. Concerts and lectures tickets include entrance to the museum galleries, including the Cloisters, on the day of the ticketed event. Note that the Met also offers programs that are free with museum admission, including lectures and films.

Subscriptions: Themed programs are among subscription offerings, including the Till Fellner series, Musicians from Marlboro series, From the NY Philharmonic series, Accolades series, and the Steve Ross series.

Membership: None per se. A very exclusive Friends of Concerts & Lectures membership is offered by the Met for $4,000 annually. Members of this group receive tickets to special events, followed by exclusive receptions that often provide the opportunity to meet the performers and lecturers, including museum curators.

MUSICA SACRA
212-734-7688 • musicasacrany.com

Venues: Various locations throughout NYC.

Public Transportation: Varies by venue.

Handicapped Accessibility: Most venues accessible (check with venue management for details).

Performances/Programs: Four performances are given in a season.

Ticket Prices: Prices vary by venue, but typically range from $25 to $110.

Subscriptions: Three-concert subscriptions range from $55–$280. See website or call the company information line for more details.

Membership: Memberships starting at $50 and going up to $5,000+. Depending on donation amount benefits include invites to Great Master Seminar Series, rehearsals, receptions, advance ticketing, and VIP privileges.

MUSICA VIVA OF NEW YORK
All Souls Church, 1157 Lexington Avenue (at 80th Street)
212-794-3646 • musicaviva.org

Venues: Various locations throughout NYC.

Public Transportation: Good

Handicapped Accessibility: Good

Performances/Programs: Four performances are given per season.

Ticket Prices: $25 per concert.

Subscriptions: Four concert subscription available for $90.

Membership: Memberships start at $100 and can reach up to $3,000+. Depending on donor level, benefits can include preferred seating, invites to special events and dress rehearsals, and free season subscriptions.

NEW YORK PHILHARMONIC (New York Phil)
Avery Fisher Hall, 10 Lincoln Center Plaza
212-875-5656 • nyphil.org

Public Transportation: Excellent (easily accessible by A, C, 1, D, and B subways).

Handicapped Accessibility: Good (Avery Fisher Hall is accessible to individuals with disabilities from the Josie Robertson Plaza and the North Plaza, as well as from the parking garage and the Concourse Level. Wheelchair accessible seating is also available. Please call the House Manager at 212-875-5005, on the day of the performance, to have a seat removed. Additionally, for vision-impaired guests, there are Braille and large type programs, as well as headsets available for the hearing impaired.)

Performances/Programs: Approximately 180 concerts are given per year.

Ticket Prices: Prices vary by concert. $12 student Rush tickets are available up to 10 days prior to event or day of concert at Avery Fisher box office, subject to availability. Senior Rush tickets may be available the day of the performance. For senior Rush ticket availability, please call 212-875-5656.

Group Discounts: Discounts of up to 24% are available with no service charge for ticket orders. For more information, contact 212-875-5672 or e-mail the NYP at groupsales@nyphil.org.

Subscriptions: The New York Phil offers many subscriptions, including the Regular Subscription series (six-eight concerts), Mini Series (three-four concerts), Create your own (three or more concerts of your choosing); and Inside the Music (a series of performances that gives fascinating background information about musical masterpieces). Subscriber benefits include seat upgrades, parking discounts, and free ticket exchanges.

Activities for Children and Teens: The Young People's Concerts series, programs for families with children ages 6–12, are offered, as well as the Very Young People's Concerts series, intended for families with children ages 3–5. Children ages 12–17 can attend Hear and Now, Rush Hour, and Inside the Music concerts for only $12.

Activities for Young Adults: Young New Yorkers Friends membership is designed for young donors ages 21–40. This membership includes invitations to special gatherings throughout the year. Galas and special events are listed on website. More information on this program is available on the website.

Membership: At the Supporter level ($75), donors receive special discounted ticket offers through advance email notification and two complimentary open-rehearsal tickets, as well as discounts for Lincoln Center's guided tour. Other levels include privileges such as Continental Airlines OnePass miles, free CDs, invitations to gala events, and donor recognition on website.

Other Benefits: With a donation of $1,500 or more, members receive priority ticket service, Patron Lounge access, Patron listing in Playbill, open-rehearsal tickets, and Patron Tour Gala invitations.

From the Editors: The New York Philharmonic Orchestra is the oldest orchestra in the U.S. and the third oldest in the world. The NY Phil offers a variety of music, from the standard classical repertoire to new commissions by living composers. This group is highly innovative and strives to make musical accessible to all, offering many opportunities to learn more about its programs through lectures and special concert series. For example, Hear and Now is the Phil's pre-concert lecture series that features performers and composers talking about contemporary music, specifically premieres of new works.

Keeping the concerts accessible to the general public, the NY Phil offers student and senior Rush tickets, along with multiple free concerts throughout NYC each year (Summer Concerts in the Parks and Memorial Day concert at St. John the Divine). The Very Young People's Concerts Series, for children 3–5, and the Young People's Concerts Series, for children 5–12, offer a great opportunity for young people to experience classical music.

The NY Phil website serves as a wonderful resource to online musical offerings. The website's Kidzone has fun games and information to help children learn more about music.

NEW YORK PHILHARMONIC ENSEMBLES
Merkin Concert Hall at Kaufman Center, 129 West 67th Street
212-501-3330 • nyphil.org/concertsticks/special_ensembles.cfm

Public Transportation: Excellent
Handicapped Accessibility: Good
Performances/Programs: Seven programs per season, one performance of each program.
Ticket Prices: $32, students can purchase $12 Rush tickets for select concerts up to 10 days before the concert at nyphil.org/studentrush. Concerts may also be available to purchase at the Avery Fisher Hall box office on the day of the performance only and are subject to availability. Senior tickets can only be purchased at the Avery Fisher Hall box office the day of the performance. For senior Rush ticket availability, call 212-875-5656.
Subscriptions: Six concerts for $140.

From the Editors: The New York Philharmonic Ensembles concerts are an offshoot of the New York Philharmonic and offer a great way to hear the orchestra members in a more intimate setting.

ORCHESTRA OF ST. LUKE'S
212-594-6100 • oslmusic.org

Venues: Carnegie Hall, 57th Street and Seventh Avenue; the Morgan Library & Museum, 225 Madison Avenue at 36th Street; Brooklyn Museum, 200 Eastern Parkway (Grand Army Plaza); the Beacon, 3 Beekman Street, Beacon; Caramoor International Music Festival in Katonah, New York (June, July, and August residency).
Public Transportation: Depends on venue (good in NYC).
Handicapped Accessibility: Depends on venue (NYC venues are all accessible).
Performances/Programs: About 100 performances a year.

Ticket Prices: Depends on venue, but student and senior discounts are available for most St. Luke's concerts.

Group Discounts: Up to 20% off for groups of 10 or more.

Subscriptions: Various subscriptions are offered, including the Orchestra series (tickets are available through Carnegie Hall), the Chamber Music Series, and others. Subscribers save up to 30%.

Membership: The most basic offering is the 45 Below membership, which allows people 45 years old and younger to pay their age for membership. Benefits include substantial discounts on concert tickets and area restaurants, invitations to member-exclusive events, the chance to purchase seats before they go on sale to the general public, and the Take a Friend deal.

PEOPLES' SYMPHONY CONCERTS
212-586-4680 • pscny.org

Venues: Washington Irving High School, 16th Street and Irving Place; Town Hall, 43rd Street between 6th & 7th Avenues.

Public Transportation: Very good (easy NYC subway access to both venues).

Handicapped Accessibility: Good

Performances/Programs: 12 annually

Ticket Prices: $10 and $12 for the Arens and Manns series concerts; $10, $12, and $18 for the Festival series.

Subscriptions: Offered per series at the following prices: Arens $32, Manns $32, Festival $32 (may be more, depending on seat location). With six concerts each, the Arens and Manns provide unreserved orchestra seats. The Festival subscription offers assigned seating and ticket costs reflect seat location. Subscribers save almost 50%.

From the Editors: The ticket ordering process is crude (you have to send them a check through the mail, no credit cards, no online ordering), the seats in the Washington Irving High School gym can be incredibly uncomfortable, but nowhere else on earth are you going to be able to hear world-class musicians including the Johannes String Quartet, the Parnas-Serkin Trio, Yefin Bronfman and Richard Goode for as little as $5.34 per ticket (if you buy a subscription) than at the People's Symphony Concerts. Their Festival Series at Town Hall is even more exciting, and can be enjoyed for $6.16–$9.33 per ticket (assuming you buy a subscription). One reason we stress subscriptions is that these shows almost always sell out well in advance.

VOICES OF ASCENSION
The Church of the Ascension, 12 W 11th Street
212-358-1469 • voicesofascension.org

Public Transportation: Good
Handicapped Accessibility: Good
Performances/Programs: Six performances given annually.
Ticket Prices: Varies per concert, but range $10–$55.
Membership: Memberships start at $50 and can reach up to $10,000+.
Based on donation amount, benefits can inlcude signed Voices CD, invites
to private receptions, premium seating, and free tickets.

From the Editors: Since its inception in 1990, Voices of Ascension has
been one of the world's premier professional choral groups, and has thrived
under the artistic direction of Dennis Keene for 16 seasons. The group re-
cords and performs largely at the Church of Ascension in Greenwich Village, but it has done guest appearances with the San Francisco Symphony,
the Mark Morris Dance Group, and at the Mostly Mozart Festival.

Voices of Ascension has nine recordings with Delos International, in-
cluding Beyond Chant: Mysteries of the Renaissance, The Duruflé Album,
Prince of Music: The Greatest Choral Works of Palestrina, and Hear My
Prayer, featuring soprano soloist Hei-Kyung Hong.

OPERA

METROPOLITAN OPERA
Metropolitan Opera House, Lincoln Center, 64 Broadway
212-362-6000 • metoperafamily.org

Public Transportation: Good (via 1 subway)
Handicapped Accessibility: Good
Performances/Programs: Varies, but typically more than 20 per season with multiple performances of most and special events.
Ticket Prices: Prices vary depending on date, time, performances, and
seats. Student tickets are available to full-time students under the age of 29
for $25 weekdays and $35 weekends. Student tickets are offered for select
performances, depending on availability. Students are often able to get orchestra seating (which often sell for upwards of $300), so it's an incredible

deal. Rush tickets are available to the general public for performances Monday through Thursday for $20.

Subscription: Available in a series of six–nine concerts, with prices varying considerably ($135–$3,262) based on dates, number of concerts, and seat selection. Subscriber benefits include discounts on lectures, guest pass to private intermission lounge, ticket exchange privileges, advance single ticket purchase, priority seating, and savings up to 36% off single ticket prices.

Membership: A membership is available from $65 to $25,000+. Benefits include *Opera News* subscription, merchandise discounts, invites to lectures and events, and discounted backstage tour.

From the Editors: Having recently celebrated its 125th birthday the Metropolitan Opera is one of the world's most beloved and established opera companies. The Met's productions feature the world's most prestigious vocal artists in radiant productions complete with stunning costumes, and scenery. The Met, under the leadership of esteemed musical director James Levine and general manager Peter Gelb, has taken opera into the 21st century, utilizing many new technologies to help make opera more accessible.

In addition to decades of broadcasting their productions via radio around the country, the Met now offers live HD video performances of their productions in theaters throughout the world. SIRIUS satellite radio and the Met Player allow opera fans the opportunity to listen and watch thousands of opera excerpts and complete operas online.

The Metropolitian Opera's annual outdoor concerts offer thousands of people the opportunity to attend free concerts in multiple NYC parks (usually in July). The addition of discounted student and Rush tickets make the Met's nearly 200 performances highly accessible.

NEW YORK CITY OPERA
David H. Koch Theater, 20 Lincoln Center Plaza
212-870-5570 • nycopera.com

Public Transportation: Good
Handicapped Accessibility: Fully accessible
Performances/Programs: Four–six productions per season with multiple performances and special events.
Ticket Prices: Prices vary depending on date, time, performances and seats.
Subscription: Four–five show subscription package rates vary from

$48–$688, depending on seats/dates chosen. Create-your-own subscriptions are also available. Subscriber benefits include savings of up to 20% off single ticket prices, great seats, 10% off additional single tickets, 10% gift and thrift shop discounts, free pre-performance lectures, and flexible exchange policy.

Membership: Available from $100 to $10,000+.

From the Editors: Even if it doesn't carry the prestige of its neighbor the Met, the New York City Opera has been renowned for providing NYC with adventurous and affordable opera seasons and programs. City Opera, in addition to producing traditional operas, presents concerts introducing audience members to popular works within the opera artform and educating audiences on the historical origins of opera. In conjunction with the New York City Ballet, City Opera recently undertook a $200 million renovation of their shared home the David H. Koch Theater (formerly the New York State Theater), which will be completed just in time for the start of the 2009–2010 season.

DICAPO OPERA THEATER
184 East 76th Street
212-288-9438 • dicapo.com

Public Transportation: Good

Performances/Programs: Five–six per season with multiple performances of each plus special programs such as "Jazz at Dicapo" and "Opera for Kids" performances.

Ticket Prices: $50 for opera; $20–$40 for special events; $10 (kids) to $20 (adults) for "Opera for Kids" performances.

Subscriptions: Four-Show subscription $175, seniors $165.

Membership: Donations are accepted, contact for further details.

From the Editors: Although a small company, especially by New York City standards, Dicapo Opera Theater puts on solid productions with wonderful emerging artists. Dicapo offers the rare opportunity to see classic operas, as well as some seldom-produced and contemporary works, in an intimatte setting (its space at the St. John Baptise Church on the upper east side has only 204 seats). Dicapo also showcases a number of special concerts and events, including recitals and one-hour versions of operas adapted for kids.

🎷 JAZZ/CABARET 🎷

JAZZ AT LINCOLN CENTER (JALC)
Broadway at 60th Street
212-258-9800 • jalc.org

Public Transportation: Excellent (convenient to A, B, C, D, and 1 subway and multiple bus lines).

Handicapped Accessibility: Fully accessible, with amenities for patrons with hearing or visual impairments.

Performances/Programs: Around 2000 events are presented per year, from one-night engagements to five-night stays.

Ticket Prices: $13.50–$120 and up

Group Discounts: One free ticket with every 15 purchased at full price for Rose Theater and the Allen Room.

Other Discounts: Dizzy's Club Coca Cola offers student discounts, especially for After Hours sets and the UPSTARTS! series on Monday nights. Goldstar.com occasionally promotes and discounts JaLC events.

Subscriptions: Subscriptions are purchased prior to the upcoming season or series. Seasonal subscriptions to a variety of concert series are offered (generally three-five concerts in a subscription package). Unlimited ticket exchanges are available for subscribers by phone or mail. Tickets are also transferable or can be donated through JaLC's tax-deductible donation program.

Membership: $50 for individual membership includes a membership card, 50% off JaLC tickets purchased the day of show at the box office, discounts at the gift shop and area retailers, newsletter, and a CD of the Month subscription.

From the Editors: One of the most important modern monuments to the American jazz legacy, the non-profit Jazz at Lincoln Center arrived at its Columbus Circle home in 2004 with the state-of-the-art Frederick P. Rose Hall and has been a cornerstone of the New York City jazz and arts scene ever since. JaLC has fostered the love of jazz among youth and young adults with its Jazz for Young People concerts and Swing Club subscriptions for adults (21–35). The Thursday evening Jazz Talks feature conversations with top players and historians, giving concertgoers insights into the rich context of "America's music."

Led by Artistic Director and world-renowned trumpeter Wynton Marsalis, Jazz at Lincoln Center performances range from musical legends to up-and-coming young artists from around the globe. Jazz at Lincoln Center is also home to the Nesuhi Ertegun Jazz Hall of Fame, which features a variety of interactive audio and visual presentations about past inductees to the Hall.

There are three main venues within Frederick P. Rose Hall: Rose Theater, where most of the large-scale performances are staged; the Allen Room, which has stunning views of Central Park from its 90-foot windows above the stage; and Dizzy's Club Coca Cola, the most intimate venue in the complex, offering catered dining and live jazz seven nights a week. Be sure to make a reservation for Dizzy's Club and expect to pay around $30 for the music with a $10 food/drink minimum.

THE ALGONQUIN HOTEL—OAK ROOM CABARET (The "Gonk")
59 West 44th Street
212-419-9331
algonquinhotel.com/nav_oakroom_cabaret.html

Public Transportation: Very good (near the B, D, F, and Q subways).
Handicapped Accessibility: Good
Performances/Programs: Regular weekly shows by featured performers number approximately 350 (September–July) per year.
Ticket Prices: $60–$75, plus a required prix-fixe dinner (around $70) if you go on a Friday or Saturday night. Occasional half-price tickets are available on Goldstar.com.

BIRDLAND
315 West 44th Street (between 8th & 9th Aves.)
212-581-3080 • birdlandjazz.com

Public Transportation: Very good (located a half-block from the A, C, E subways).
Handicapped Accessibility: Good
Performances/Programs: Approximately 250 performances are presented at Birdland per year.
Ticket Prices: Range from $20 to $65, depending on the performer. There is also a $10 food and drink minimum per person. Half-price tickets are occasionally available on Goldstar.com.
Group Discounts: Many party and tour-group packages are offered.

From the Editors: While today's Birdland is more than 40 years and two venue changes removed from the original club, the legacy it represents is one of the most celebrated in the jazz world. Named for bebop saxophonist Charlie "Yardbird" Parker, the original Birdland represented the epitome of jazz, with its illustrious line-up, famous clientele, and all-night jam sessions. The club also played host to a number of iconic live recording sessions by such artists such as Art Blakey and John Coltrane.

Today, Birdland's bookings generally stick to well-known jazz artists and "Songbook" revue shows. With somewhat steep ticket pricing and a required food and drink minimum, Birdland may not be the most cost effective introduction for the jazz newcomer. However, for the aficionado or the casual music-lover willing to give up stage-side seating and top-billed performers, Birdland is a perfect venue to soak up a semblance of the atmosphere that birthed the sounds of Stan Getz, Thelonious Monk, and Dizzy Gillespie. Check out the regular Sunday-night performances by Chico O'Farrill's Afro-Cuban Jazz Orchestra ($25) or the Friday-night spots by the Birdland Big Band ($25) for some smokin' jazz that won't break the bank. In the immortal words of the "Yardbird," Charlie Parker himself, "Birdland is the Jazz Corner of the World!"

BLUE NOTE/NEW YORK
131 W. 3rd Street
212-475-8592 • bluenote.net

Public Transportation: Excellent (convenient to W. 4th St./Washington Square subway stop).

Handicapped Accessibility: No

Performances/Programs: Approximately 875 performances are given annually: two sets per evening, three on Friday and Saturday, and two Sunday brunch performances.

Ticket Prices: $20 at the bar, $35 at a table. $8 tickets for the 12:30 a.m. set on Friday and Saturday. Occasional half-price tickets are available on Goldstar.com.

Membership: Membership, available on the website, features very occasional discounts and special events.

From the Editors: Blue Note has expanded from its original Greenwich Village location to become an international franchise with locations in Italy and Japan. Established in 1981, Blue Note quickly became one of the most illustrious jazz venues in New York City, dubbing itself the home of artists such as Sarah Vaughn, Lionel Hampton, Dizzy Gillespie, and Oscar Peterson.

While the die-hard jazz fan might scoff at the reputation Blue Note has garnered for itself, there's no denying the venue brings in top tier talent from around the world. Artists like Chris Botti, Chick Corea, and McCoy Tyner frequent Blue Note and the club has also incorporated a bi-weekly Late Night Groove series to showcase up and coming talent in New York.

Ticket prices are a little expensive once you tack on drinks and/or dinner. However, the 12:30 p.m. sets on Friday and Saturday feature a heaven-sent $8 cover charge and for the hungry jazz fan, $24.50 will get brunch, a show, and a drink for the Sunday brunch programs.

THE CARLYLE—BEMELMANS BAR
35 E 76th Street
212-744-1600 • thecarlyle.com/entertainment.cfm

Public Transportation: Very good (6 subway)
Handicapped Accessibility: Good
Performances/Programs: Performances are presented 2–3 times nightly.
Ticket Prices: Prices $20–$35.

THE CARLYLE—CAFÉ CARLYLE
35 E 76th Street
212-744-1600

Public Transportation: Very good (easily accessible by the 6 subway at 77th Street).
Handicapped Accessibility: Good
Performances/Programs: Approximately 448 performances are given per year: Monday–Thursday with two shows on Friday and Saturday.
Ticket Prices: Prices range from $65–$150, plus a drink minimum.

DON'T TELL MAMA CABARET AND PIANO BAR NYC
343 West 46th Street
212-757-0788 • donttellmamanyc.com

Public Transportation: Very good (convenient to all Times Square-bound subway lines).
Handicapped Accessibility: No
Performances/Programs: Two–three performances are presented every night of the week.

Ticket Prices: Generally no cover (except for benefit events), but a two-drink minimum. Occasional popular shows require a cover charge.

THE DUPLEX
61 Christopher Street
212-255-5438 • theduplex.com

Public Transportation: Excellent (very convenient to the Christopher St. subway stop on the 1, 2 and 3 lines).

Handicapped Accessibility: Poor (downstairs piano bar is accessible; upstairs bar is not).

Performances/Programs: Approximately 600 performances a year with live music seven nights a week. Two sets on Friday and Saturday.

Ticket Prices: Always a two-drink minimum and often a $10–$15 cover depending on the performers. Occasional half-price tickets offered on Goldstar.com.

FEINSTEIN'S AT LOEWS REGENCY
540 Park Avenue (at 61st Street)
212-339-4095 • feinsteinsattheregency.com

Public Transportation: Good

Handicapped Accessibility: Good

Performances/Programs: Approximately 250 performances per year. Closed during the summer.

Ticket Prices: $25–$75 and up, $25–$40 food/drink minimum. Half-price tickets on Goldstar.com. Occasional special offers through the website under "Discounts."

IRIDIUM JAZZ CLUB
1650 Broadway
212-582-2121 • iridiumjazzclub.com

Public Transportation: Good

Handicapped Accessibility: Good

Performances/Programs: Approximately 500 per year. Sets are at 8:30 and 10:30 p.m. Wednesday–Sunday, 8 and 10 p.m. on Monday.

Ticket Prices: $25–$50 cover, $10–$20 food and drink minimum, depending on the performer. Occasional half-price tickets are available on

Goldstar.com. Coupons and promotions are sometimes available on the website.

THE KITANO
66 Park Avenue
212-885-7000 • kitano.com

   Public Transportation: Good
   Handicapped Accessibility: Good
   Performances/Programs: Approximately 400 per year, Wednesday–Saturday, with sets at 8 and 10 p.m.
   Ticket Prices: $25 cover on Friday and Saturday; no cover Wednesday and Thursday.

METROPOLITAN ROOM
34 W 22nd Street
212-206-0440 • metropolitanroom.com

   Public Transportation: Good
   Handicapped Accessibility: Good
   Performances/Programs: Approximately 700 given per year, one-four sets per night.
   Ticket Prices: Most shows are $20–$30, with a $15 food and drink minimum. Occasional special offers are provided through the free membership service on the website.

SMOKE
2751 Broadway
212-864-6662 • smokejazz.com

   Public Transportation: Good
   Handicapped Accessibility: Good
   Performances/Programs: Over 1,000 performances are given per year, with three sets of live jazz every night.
   Ticket Prices: Week nights are no cover with a $20 food and drink minimum. Friday and Saturday sets are generally $25–$30 with a cover.

THE VILLAGE VANGUARD
178 7th Avenue South
212-255-4037 • villagevanguard.com

Public Transportation: Good (easily accessible via the 1, 2 and 3 subways at 14th Street).

Handicapped Accessibility: No

Performances/Programs: Two sets every evening at 9 and 11 p.m. and generally a third 12:30 a.m. set on Saturday nights. Generally, acts play five-night stays.

Ticket Prices: $30–$35 and up depending on the performers. Student discounts are offered Sunday–Thursday for the second set for $20 (which includes drink minimum). Valid student ID is required. Be sure to check with the club before to make sure the discount is valid for the evening's performance.

From the Editors: The first stop on any jazz-lover's pilgrimage to New York City must be the Village Vanguard. While other legendary venues have changed hands and locations a number of times, the Vanguard has remained in its original Greenwich location since opening in 1935.

Originally conceived as a venue for sketch comedy and poetry, the Vanguard is still run today by Lorraine Gordon, wife of the venue's original proprietor, Max Gordon. Many jazz aficionados believe Ms. Gordon is largely responsible for the Vanguard's legendary status and continued dedication to fantastic jazz.

The venue's unique acoustics have made it the gold standard in live jazz recordings, hosting seminal sessions by the likes of Bill Evans, John Coltrane, Wynton Marsalis, Sonny Rollins, Keith Jarrett, and Brad Mehldau, among many many others. Check out Monday nights with the Vanguard Jazz Orchestra, a 35-year institution in NYC and a great introduction for the jazz newcomer. In acknowledgement of the debt owed to the jazz legends who so generously passed the torch to each new player, the Vanguard offers student discounts Sunday–Tuesday for the second set.

Be forewarned: This audience isn't there for lively conversation and background music, but for the opportunity to commune with the memory of the countless players who passed through the club's doors, which lives on in the sheer unadulterated talent the Vanguard pulls in on a nightly basis. For popular acts, be sure to make reservations over the phone and get there on time, as seats are hard to come by and the club has a strict 15-minute grace period, after which your seats are given away.

 DANCE

ALVIN AILEY AMERICAN DANCE THEATER
New York City Center, 130 West 56th Street
212-514-0010 • alvinailey.org

Public Transportation: Very good
Handicapped Accessibility: Good
Performances/Programs: The programs are generally a selection from the company's extensive repertoire and the exact combination of works may vary slightly from night to night.
Ticket Prices: Tickets usually start at about $25 and can range up to around $110 for special events. Prices and special offers vary based on venue.
Membership: The basic annual membership fee is $75. This includes a subscription to the Ailey newsletter, *Revelations*, and two passes to an open rehearsal at New York City Center.

From the Editors: Alvin Ailey American Dance Theater first arrived on the New York dance scene in 1958 as a young energetic group of black dancers. Their first performance at the 92nd Street Young Men's Hebrew Association forever altered the landscape of American modern dance. Through continued expansion over the past 50 years, AAADT has not only established a lasting presence in American dance, but also proven to be one of its strongest pillars, winning two National Medals of the Arts and acting on numerous occasions as ambassadors for American culture.

Renowned for stunning athleticism, AAADT is an undeniable audience favorite. These are passionate, splashy, dramatic performers and their spiritual music is the kind that can't help but be uplifting. If you attend an Ailey concert, it's very likely that you'll see the company's signature piece, *Revelations*. Created in 1960 by Alvin Ailey himself, this piece is a tribute to the sorrow and hope of African-American heritage. It's the piece that first brought Ailey international acclaim and it's still one of the company's most extraordinary works.

AMERICAN BALLET THEATRE (ABT)
Metropolitan Opera House, Lincoln Center, 64 Broadway
212-581-1212 • abt.org

Public Transportation: Excellent (the Met and New York City Center are easily accessible by subway and bus).

Handicapped Accessibility: Good

Performances/Programs: The ABT spring season at the Met consists almost entirely of full-length classics such as *La Bayadère* and *Swan Lake*, while the fall season at City Center presents three or four shorter works (usually more contemporary) at each concert. Each individual work is performed four–eight times.

Ticket Prices: Vary from $25 to $94. At City Center, special family tickets may be available for $11. For selected performances, City Center offers $10 tickets to full-time undergraduate and graduate students under the age of 30 through the Peer-to-Peer program. Additionally, individuals can save up to 27% by purchasing tickets to three or more performances.

Group Discounts: For groups of 15 or more.

Third Party Website Discounts: Playbill Arts (playbillarts.com), High 5 (highfivetix.org/flash.html).

Other Discounts: Dance Pass (dancenyc.org/dancepass.asp).

Subscriptions: The Full subscription series consists of packages of four or six different performances, all on the same day of the week and one performance per week; Take 3 subscription is a pre-packaged trio of performances; Make 3 or More subscription is three-eight performances of your choice. ABT also offers a Family series that provides a 50% discount on tickets for children ages 4–17. Ticket exchanges are allowed within other Family series performances, pending availability and seat locations may vary for each performance. Subscribers have the flexibility to exchange any ticket in their subscription package for a ticket to any other performance within the season. Additionally, subscribers receive ABT's bi-annual news magazine, *On Pointe Magazine.*

Membership: Basic membership is $75 and includes priority notification of American Ballet Theatre's spring season at the Metropolitan Opera House (the Met), access to seats available exclusively to members for the City Center season, priority ticketing for all New York performances of the ABT Studio Company, two passes to the spring Dancers' Circle Dress Rehearsal at the Met, invitation to the Spotlight Seminar series, and subscriptions to ABT's publications *On Pointe* and *Footnotes.*

Special Young Adult Membership: Designed for young professionals ages 21–40, Junior Council members ($500) receive invitations to exclusive events with other members and ABT artists, junior-priced tickets to opening galas, a listing at abt.org, Playbill on ABT's Young Patron Evening, and access to final dress rehearsals and the Fall Season Sneak Peak.

From the Editors: Since its founding in 1939, American Ballet Theatre has distinguished itself as one of the most internationally respected ballet companies. The repertory, though grounded in the great classics of the 19th century, continues to evolve with regularly commissioned original works by acclaimed choreographers. In the past, these have included the likes of Antony Tudor, George Balanchine, Jerome Robbins, Agnes de Mille, and Twyla Tharp. Likewise, the company's dancers are among ballet's most recognizable luminaries.

The offerings for children ages 4–12 deserve special mention. The ABT Kids Performances, designed to introduce children to ballet, are priced at $25 and feature selections from company repertoire narrated by members of the ABT artistic staff.

BALLET HISPANICO
212-362-6710 • ballethispanico.org

Venues: Ballet Hispanico tours extensively and also performs an annual season in the fall at the Joyce Theater.

Public Transportation: Very good (the Joyce); other venues vary.

Handicapped Accessibility: Good (the Joyce); other venues vary.

Performances/Programs: The company performs several different programs each year consisting of selections from the six or so pieces in the current repertory. They generally perform for one-three days in each location.

Ticket Prices: Tickets are typically $25–$50. See individual venues.

Membership: Basic donor fees start at $50. Benefits include advance notice of Ballet Hispanico's New York season and other special events.

Educational/Community Outreach: Like most dance companies, Ballet Hispanico runs it share of educational and recreational programs for local youth. Unlike most dance companies, however, youth programs are actually the root of this organization and, in fact, predate the performing ensemble we know today. The company's work reaches students of all ages in the form of master classes, workshops, specialized performances, and even Latin social dance classes.

From the Editors: Ballet Hispanico Artistic Director Tina Ramirez began as a dance instructor, teaching inner-city children throughout the 1960s. In recognition of these efforts, the New York State Arts Council subsequently awarded her a grant in 1970 to found a dance company comprised of young people. Thus began the first incarnation of Ballet Hispanico. Though its performers are no longer quite so young nor the works quite so traditional, Ballet Hispanico maintains a firm grasp on its cultural roots, spotlighting Hispanic artists, dancers, and composers. Not surprisingly, extensive educational and community programs remain integral to this organization.

BILL T. JONES/ARNIE ZANE DANCE COMPANY
212-426-6655 • billtjones.org

Venues: Harlem Stage, the Joyce Theater, Brooklyn Academy of Music. For most of the year the company is on tour.

Public Transportation: Depends on venue.

Handicapped Accessibility: Depends on venue.

Performances/Programs: Currently the company tours with three different programs and will generally perform in a given location for two-three days. See the company touring calendar at billtjones.org for specific dates and venues.

Ticket Prices: Tickets for Bill T. Jones generally run between $20 and $60, depending on venue.

Third Party Website Discounts: Discounts for selected dance performances may be available through playbillarts.com. For some of Bill T. Jones' more theatrical endeavors, discounted tickets may be available through theatermania.com, ticketmayor.com, and nytix.com.

Membership: The company accepts charitable donations beginning at $50. Benefits such as invited rehearsals, salons, artistic updates and private dinners are reserved for major donors giving multi-year gifts of over $75,000.

From the Editors: Bill T. Jones and his late partner, Arnie Zane (1948–1988), challenged audiences with powerful duets dealing with issues of identity and offering social commentary. After 11 years of collaboration they founded the Bill T. Jones/Arnie Zane Dance Company and made their international debut in 1983 at BAM.

The company's work often draws from important textual sources such as Flannery O'Connor's short story, *The Artificial Nigger* and Harriet Beecher Stowe's *Uncle Tom's Cabin*.

Based in Harlem, the company is very much engaged with its surrounding community. In 2007, they launched Breaking Ground, an on-going community-dialogue series in partnership with Harlem Stage. These lively discussions are moderated by the always-articulate Bill T. Jones and focus on myriad topics, including creativity and politics. Audience participation is encouraged and everyone is invited.

The company's education program offers master classes and workshops to the greater public. Master classes are scheduled regularly around NYC and run about $15 each. In partnership with Randall's Island Sports Foundation (RISF), Bill T. Jones has also developed Kids in Motion, a pilot dance program designed to help meet the arts-education needs in Harlem's public schools.

DANCE BRAZIL
212-382-0555 • dancebrazil.org

Venues: Dance Brazil is regularly on tour throughout the United States. When at home in New York, they occasionally perform at NYU's Skirball Center for the Performing Arts at 566 La Guardia Place (at Washington Square South).

Public Transportation: Good (when in NY)

Handicapped Accessibility: Good (when in NY)

Performances/Programs: The company tours with a single show each year and performs in a single venue for up to about four days.

Ticket Prices: Venues determine prices, but in most standard theaters, tickets run between $20 and $40.

Membership: No formal membership program, but donations are accepted on the website.

LIMÓN DANCE COMPANY
212-777-3353 • limon.org

Venues: The Limón Dance Company is regularly on tour throughout the country, often appearing at university performing-arts centers and major venues. In New York City, they can sometimes be seen at the Joyce Theater.

Public Transportation: Depends on venue.

Handicapped Accessibility: Depends on venue.

Performances/Programs: The current Limón repertory contains 14 dance pieces consisting of Jose Limón's own choreography, created before he died in 1972, as well as commissioned works from other choreographers. Classics include Limón's acclaimed *The Moor's Pavane*, based on the story of Othello, and his monumental *Misa Brevis*, a tribute to human resilience in the face of destruction during World War II. The Limón Company travels to as many as four of five different locations each month and generally spends one-four days performing in each. View the upcoming performance schedule at www.limon.org/Dance/Schedule.html.

Ticket Prices: Individual venues handle all ticket sales for performances. For most, tickets are in the $20–$25 range. Depending on the venue, the best tickets can run up to about $80.

Membership: The basic donor level's donation is $5–$99. As a Friend of Limón, you receive e-communications about the company and special event invitations. Multiple membership levels exist beyond the basic Friends of Limón and include additional benefits. All contributions are matched dollar-for-dollar by Burning Media and the Francis Alexander Foundation.

MARK MORRIS DANCE GROUP
3 Lafayette Avenue, Brooklyn
718-624-8400 • markmorrisdancegroup.org

Other Venues: The company also frequently appears at Lincoln Center, Zellerbach Hall, Berkeley, CA; Krannert Center for the Performing Arts, Urbana, IL.

Public Transportation: Depends on venue.

Handicapped Accessibility: Good

Performances/Programs: Mark Morris Dance Group tours with about three or four different programs each year, made up from the dozen or so pieces in the current repertory. The company generally performs for about one week in each location.

Ticket Prices: Tickets generally range from $30–$90, depending on venue.

Third Party Website Discounts: Many third-party sites claim to offer discount tickets to MMDG concerts, but use the price estimate above as a guideline. Most of these third-party sites sell them for much more than what you'd pay through normal venue discounts.

Membership: For the basic fee of $50, anyone can become a Friend of MMDG. Benefits include advance notice of local MMDG performances and events and access to the members-only page on the website.

Special Young Adult Membership: The Junior Fan category for ages 17 and under is newly established and requests a donation of $10. Junior Fans receive a Junior Fan membership card and a MMDG pin set.

From the Editors: At one time, Mark Morris was known as the enfant terrible of modern dance. Yet since founding his company in 1980, his humor and musicality have made the Mark Morris Dance Group one of the most widely appreciated dance companies worldwide.

If ever a choreographer was committed to live music, it's Mark Morris. Noted for his gifts in translating music to movement, he has collaborated and performed with some of the most renowned orchestras, opera companies, and musicians in the world; furthermore, since 1996 live music has been a standard component of every company performance. In short, the experience of a Mark Morris Dance Group concert is a double pleasure.

In 2001, the company established the Mark Morris Dance Center in Brooklyn. The center provides rehearsal space for the dance community and offers classes in diverse styles for adults ($12 per class), as well as special programs for children (starting at $200 per semester). Since 2007, the company has also been active in helping Parkinson's disease patients through therapeutic movement classes.

MARTHA GRAHAM DANCE COMPANY
212-521-3611 • marthagraham.org/company

Venues: Although based in New York, Martha Graham Dance Company doesn't have a regular venue in the city and spends much of the year on national and international tour.

Public Transportation: Depends on venue.

Handicapped Accessibility: Depends on venue.

Performances/Programs: The company tours with various selections from their current repertory.

Ticket Prices: Depending on the venue, tickets to Martha Graham can range from about $20 to about $50.

Membership: Martha Graham Dance Company accepts tax-deductible donations in any amount, but has no formal membership/donor program.

From the Editors: Harsh, angular, spectacularly horrific—how could you not be fascinated? When Martha Graham first began to create dances in the 1920s, audiences were far from thrilled. Her work was a jolt to all who took for granted that dancers must flutter, soar, or defy gravity. The trademark pelvic contractions and rough floor work that permeated her dances created a stirring aesthetic unlike any of the glamour-clad work that came before and it indelibly changed everything that came after.

Although Graham is perhaps the most celebrated performer of her own work, her company is also exceptional in the number of former members who went on to become well-known choreographers themselves in the latter half of the 20th century. These include Merce Cunningham, Elisa Monte, Paul Taylor, Jacqulyn Buglisi, and Pascal Rioult. Certainly, this is one reason her influence on contemporary dance has been so pervasive.

MERCE CUNNINGHAM DANCE COMPANY
(Cunningham Company or MCDC)
212-255-8240 • merce.org

Venues: Lincoln Center and the Brooklyn Academy of Music. The company mostly tours and is regularly hosted by some of the world's grandest stages and esteemed university campuses, as well as other, less traditional venues.

Public Transportation: Depends on venue.

Handicapped Accessibility: Depends on venue.

Performances/Programs: The Merce Cunningham Dance Company currently maintains a repertory of a dozen or so dance pieces, spanning over six decades of Merce Cunningham's choreographic career. Evening-length concerts generally consist of a selection from the repertory and occasionally include a post-performance discussion. However, due to Cunningham's death in July 2009, the troupe will be disbanding within the next two years.

Ticket Prices: Ticket prices generally fall between $50 and $70. See individual venues for information on same-day discounts and student Rush policies.

Programs for Young People: In 1964 when Jasper Johns created the painting *Numbers, 1964* for the New York State Theater lobby, he asked his friend and collaborator Merce Cunningham to leave a footprint on it, telling him, "I think you should have your foot in the door of the State Theater." Now, Foot in the Door: Young Friends of Merce Committee, the company's aptly named membership organization, seeks to build support for the Cunningham Company from diverse groups of people.

Membership: Membership requires a donation at or above $175 and includes such benefits as invitations to showings and receptions, preferred-seating options, open rehearsals, and invitations to special workshops.

From the Editors: No question about it: Merce Cunningham was the most radically innovative figure in American dance history.

With his long-time partner and musical collaborator John Cage, he proposed the famously controversial idea that music and dance should exist independently—in the same space and time but without being connected in any intentional way. In fact, Cunningham's dancers often hear the music for the first time during the opening-night performance.

From the 1960s until his death, Cunningham was at the forefront of dance technology, which permeated almost every aspect of his work, from creating dances to final performance. He was on the development team and an active user of the choreography software program, *DanceForms* (formerly *Life Forms*); he used virtual décor and dancers in *Biped* (1999); he distributed iPod Shuffles to audience members for use during *eyeSpace* (2006); and he released open-source computer code for his choreography of *Loops* (2008).

NEW YORK CITY BALLET
212-870-4074 • nycballet.com

Venues: David H. Koch Theater at Lincoln Center, Columbus Avenue & 63rd Street, and the Saratoga Performing Arts Center in Saratoga Springs, New York, 108th Avenue of the Pines.

Public Transportation: Good (Koch Theater only; the theater in Saratoga Springs is not).

Handicapped Accessibility: Good (both)

Performances/Programs: The New York City Ballet annually presents winter and spring seasons at the State Theater. The winter season opens in November and offers about 40 performances of George Balanchine's *The Nutcracker*, plus another dozen or so programs in January and February, totaling about 150 performances altogether. Following the end of the winter season, the company has an annual engagement for a week of performances at the Kennedy Center in Washington, D.C. The spring season, from April to June, offers another 60 or so performances consisting of full-length ballets and mixed repertory programs. After the end of the spring season, the company spends three weeks in July performing at the Saratoga Performing Arts Center.

Ticket Prices: Tickets for repertory concerts range from $20 to $98. Tickets for George Balanchine's *The Nutcracker* range from $15 to $215 (you can also buy standing-room tickets for $10–$20). Student Rush tickets are available for many NYCB performances and must be purchased on the day of performance. Tickets are $12. You must be a high school or college student age 29 or under, international students welcome. Ticket availability is posted weekly on Mondays and can be checked at nycballet.com or by telephoning the student Rush ticket hotline at 212-870-7766.

Group Discounts: Discounts are available for groups of 15 or more people for repertory performances. Savings range from $3 per ticket (second seating) to $18 per ticket (orchestra seating).

Other Discounts: For a $20 membership fee, become a member of the New York City Ballet's Fourth Ring Society. As a member, you can purchase tickets located in the fourth ring of the State Theater (limited to two per performance) for $15 a ticket (approximately a 50% saving). Tickets can be ordered online, over the phone, or at the State Theater box office with the use your membership card. Additional benefits include invitations to pre-performance talks and discounts at participating nearby restaurants.

Subscriptions: Subscriptions are available for two, three or four performances. There is no immediate discount, but subscribers can get 20% off available single tickets on the day of any performance, as well as discounts at restaurants, specialty shops, and museums. Other subscriber benefits include priority seating, flexible ticket exchanges (up to 24 hours before a performance) and free copies of NYCB's bi-annual newsletter.

Educational/Community Outreach: Youngsters can attend the NYCB's Children's Workshops (aimed at children over 5), where they can meet artists, ask questions, and do fun hands-on activities.

From the Editors: New York City Ballet began with two men—one a visionary, the other a craftsman. The legacy of these two men, Lincoln Kirstein and George Balanchine, has now evolved into the largest dance organization in the United States, boasting approximately 90 world-class performers.

Unlike New York's other premier ballet company, American Ballet Theater, NYCB spends most of the year at home in New York, performing at Lincoln Center's New York State Theater, where it has been the resident ballet company since its opening in 1964.

With Balanchine as artistic director until his death in 1983, NYCB developed a strikingly sparse and elegant style. In contrast to the usual frills of Romantic-period ballets, Balanchine's dancers often wear simple practice clothing in order to emphasize the lines and angles of their limbs and his choreography de-emphasizes narrative plots in favor of complex visual patterns and musical counterpoint. For Balanchine, "Ballet may contain a story, but the visual spectacle, not the story, is the essential element."

Now under the direction of Peter Martins, NYCB continues to perform Balanchine's extensive body of work and commissions new creations from contemporary choreographers. In addition to its roster of performances, the NYCB frequently presents Studio Talks, where company dancers, choreographers, and composers discuss the various methods and processes involved in producing a ballet.

PAUL TAYLOR DANCE COMPANY
212-431-5562 • ptdc.org

Venues: New York City Center, 130 West 56th Street; this company also tours frequently both nationally and internationally.

Public Transportation: Yes

Handicapped Accessibility: Good

Performances/Programs: The Paul Taylor Company maintains a repertoire of 52 different dance pieces including Taylor's signature work, *Esplanade*. The company travels to about 30 different locations each year and spends one-three days in each, performing a selected few pieces.

Ticket Prices: Tickets are sold directly through presenting venues and generally run between $15 and $85.

Membership: The basic donor fee is $50 and includes opportunities to purchase priority seats for performances at New York City Center, a membership card offering a 10% discount on Taylor merchandise, a subscription to the newsletter, and invitations to special events throughout the year. All donations are fully tax-deductible.

Special Young Adult Membership: The Young Patrons Committee was established to introduce people in their 20s, 30s, and 40s to Paul Taylor's work. This committee helps plan events and reaches out to friends and associates. Paul Taylor hosts two exclusive Young Patrons events a year and offers specially priced Young Patrons tickets to the Annual New York Season Gala.

From the Editors: Paul Taylor is one of today's most popular choreographers. Not only is his work well-loved, but it's widely seen, having been performed in all 50 states and an impressive 62 countries. His company has also appeared on nine PBS programs, including the Emmy Award-winning "Speaking in Tongues."

Through the establishment of his second company, Taylor 2, Paul Taylor has gone to great lengths to ensure that his work can be viewed by all types of audiences, regardless of economic or technical limitations. Taylor 2's performances are flexible and can be customized to meet the needs of each community, often also including master classes, lecture demonstrations, and performances in non-traditional venues.

Before each Sunday matinée at New York City Center, everyone with tickets to that afternoon's performance is invited to attend a free 45-minute discussion. Talks center around Taylor's work, but guest speakers can be interesting, having included such people as *New York Post* dance critic Clive Barnes, former *New York Times* dance critic Anna Kisselgoff, and P.D.Q. Bach.

The Paul Taylor Company also offers occasional family matinée programs that include a performance and explanatory comments. Tickets for these educational events run about $25 for adults and $10 for children under 17.

PARSONS DANCE
212-869-9275 • parsonsdance.org

Venues: Joyce Theater, 175 8th Avenue; for the majority of the year, Parsons Dance tours nationally and internationally.

Public Transportation: Depends on venue.

Handicapped Accessibility: Depends on venue.

Performances/Programs: Parsons Dance maintains a repertoire of more than 70 different works choreographed by artistic director, David Parsons. Of these 70, they tour with about a dozen works arranged on a couple of different programs. Parsons' signature six-minute solo, *Caught*, which makes impressive use of a strobe light, is on most programs. Aside from the two weeks spent annually at the Joyce Theater, Parsons Dance generally performs for one or two days in each touring location.

Ticket Prices: Tickets for Joyce Theater season are $40–$50. Sunday-night performances may be cheaper. Tickets for most other performances are generally $30–$50. See venues for specific prices and discount offers.

Membership: Parsons Dance does not offer annual membership opportunities. Donations are welcome in any amount with a minimum of $5.

PASCAL RIOULT DANCE THEATRE
Joyce Theater, 175 8th Avenue
212-398-5901 • prdance.org

Public Transportation: Very good

Handicapped Accessibility: Good

Performances/Programs: The company repertoire fuses contemporary movement with classical scores, performing a dozen or pieces once or twice at each tour venue.

Ticket Prices: Tickets generally range between $20 and $50.

Membership: Pascal Rioult Dance Theatre does not have an annual membership fee or established gifting levels.

STEPHEN PETRONIO COMPANY
212-473-1660 • stephenpetronio.com

Venues: Joyce Theater, 175 8th Avenue; most of the year, the company is on tour.
Public Transportation: Depends on venue.
Handicapped Accessibility: Good
Performances/Programs: Stephen Petronio Company tours with programs made up of the eight or so current pieces melding kinetic choreography with cutting edge musical influences. Engagements at individual locations generally range from a day to a week. Check out the company's website for upcoming dates and locations.
Ticket Prices: Tickets generally range from $25 to $60, depending on venue.

TRISHA BROWN DANCE COMPANY
212-977-5365 • trishabrowncompany.org

Venues: Trisha Brown Dance Company does not have a regular performance venue and spends the majority of the year on tour. When in New York, check for this company at locations such as Lincoln Center, BAM, New York City Center, and the Joyce Theater.
Public Transportation: Depends on venue.
Handicapped Accessibility: Depends on venue.
Performances/Programs: The company tours with selections from their current repertoire.
Membership: Donor fees start at $50 and include Fall/Spring newsletters, company updates and program recognition.
Ticket Prices: Depending on the venue, tickets for Trisha Brown can range from about $20 to about $70.

From the Editors: Since the 1960s, Trisha Brown has been a mover and shaker in the dance world. As a member of the Judson Dance group, she began by working in alternative spaces—rooftops in SoHo became a popular stage, as did the walls of buildings.

Since the founding of her company in 1970, Brown has created intelligent and highly innovative works exploring complex movement ideas and is best known for her distinctive style, gracefully slippery and at the same time unpredictably sharp and rhythmic.

In her 50+ years of creating for the stage, she has collaborated with great artists, including Robert Rauschenberg and Laurie Anderson, most notably on her trademark piece, *Set and Reset* (1983). She has ventured into classical ballet with *O zlolony O composite* (2004) and into high-tech motion capture with *How long does the subject linger on the edge of the volume ...* (2005). She has also directed opera.

Unlike most choreographers who set work on other companies, Brown's choreography is performed exclusively by her own dancers.

JOYCE THEATERS
212-645-2904 • joyce.org

Venues: Joyce Theater, 175 8th Avenue (at the corner of 19th St.); Joyce SoHo, 155 Mercer Street (between Houston and Prince).

Public Transportation: Yes

Handicapped Accessibility: Good

Performances/Programs: The Joyce presents a different dance company every one or two weeks.

Ticket Prices: Tickets are $19, $35, and $49.

Group Discounts: Groups of 20 or more may be eligible for discounts to select performances. Call to arrange.

Subscriptions: The Joyce doesn't offer subscriptions, but with the purchase of at least one ticket to four or more different performances at the same time, tickets are discounted 25%. Additional benefits include discounts at local restaurants and businesses, priority ordering, and free ticket exchanges.

Membership: Donor fees start at $65 ($50 for students/seniors) and include advance copies of season brochures, pre-sale ticket-ordering privileges, access to open rehearsals, advance notice of Dance Talks at the Joyce Soho, and a 10% discount on Joyce merchandise.

From the Editors: A venue created by dancers specifically for dance, the Joyce Theater is a top-notch destination for seeing local, national, and international dance companies. Formerly known as the Elgin Theater, this art-deco building served as a revival movie house in the 1940s. When it later turned into a pornographic movie theater, it was closed down, stripped, gutted, and reopened in 1982 as an intimate 472-seat dance performance space. In 1996 the Joyce acquired a second property, the Joyce SoHo—a three-story firehouse now outfitted with two studio rehearsal spaces and a 74-seat flexible performance space.

At the Joyce, you can see an exciting range of dance performances unequalled anywhere in Manhattan. Additionally, the Joyce offers a range of free educational opportunities, such as the Humanities series, post-performance discussions with dance-company artists, and Dance Talks, in-depth lecture-demonstrations on current topics of interest in contemporary dance. Humanities series events are generally held following Wednesday evening performances. Dance Talks are generally held at the Joyce SoHo. See the website for scheduled events.

FILM

THE ANGELIKA FILM CENTER
212-529-6799 (Village East venue)
212-995-2000 (Houston Street venue) • angelikafilmcenter.com

Venues: Village East, 181–189 2nd Avenue; Houston Street, 18 West Houston Street (at Mercer).
Public Transportation: Good
Handicapped Accessibility: Good (ask management for details).
Performances/Programs: A blend of sophisticated mainstream and independent fare, including foreign films and some documentaries.
Ticket Prices: Approximately $10.

ANTHOLOGY FILM ARCHIVES
32 2nd Avenue
212-505-5181 • anthologyfilmarchives.org

Public Transportation: Good
Handicapped Accessibility: Fair (first-floor theater is accessible, third-floor theater is not).
Performances/Programs: A mix of American independent and avant-garde cinema, as well as classic European, Soviet, and Japanese film. Premiere screenings of original work are also a part of the Anthology's programming.
Ticket Prices: General admission $8; Essential Cinema (free for members) $7; students, seniors and children (12 & under) $6; AFA members $5.
Membership: AFA is a 503(c)(3) and there are a variety of membership opportunities.

BAM ROSE CINEMAS
Brooklyn Academy of Music, 30 Lafayette Avenue, Brooklyn
718-636-4100 • bam.org

Public Transportation: Good (easily accessible via bus and subway).
Handicapped Accessibility: Good
Performances/Programs: BAM's programming is a mix of new independent and foreign films, as well as screenings of rare classic fare.

From the Editors: The Brooklyn Academy of Music (known simply as BAM among NYC arts lovers) is Brooklyn's premier venue for both progressive live performance and independent film. In 2006, BAM began a collaboration with the Sundance Institute on a series that has brought the programming and activities of Sundance and its revered film festival to New York City through a variety of movie screenings, panels, performances, and special events.

FILM FORUM
209 West Houston Street
212-727-8112/recorded schedule: 212-727-8110 • filmforum.org

Public Transportation: Very good (easily accessible by subway).
Handicapped Accessibility: Good
Performances/Programs: Premieres of American independent and foreign art films, as well as foreign and American classics, genre works, and directors' retrospectives.
Ticket Prices: Tickets vary, but are $7 for members.

From the Editors: When it first opened as a screening room for indie films in 1970, Film Forum was just 50 folding chairs and a projector. Now, it's a three-screen movie house with 462 seats, 4,600 members, and screenings every day of the year.

One of the few autonomous non-profit cinemas in the country (and the only one in NYC), Film Forum showcases New York City premieres of American independent features and shorts, foreign films, classics, festivals, and more. Film Forum is a true home away from home for cinemaphiles.

MUSEUM OF THE MOVING IMAGE
35th Avenue at 37th Street, Astoria, Queens
718-784-4520 • movingimage.us

Public Transportation: Good (within walking distance of N, R, V, and G subways).

Handicapped Accessibility: Good

Performances/Programs: A variety of themed weekend screenings focusing on specific genres, movements, and filmmakers. Museum-sponsored screenings are frequently held at the DGA Theater in Manhattan, located at 110 West 57th Street. Filmmakers associated with the work being screened often attend these screenings to lecture beforehand.

Ticket Prices: Adults $7.50; seniors, college students with ID, and children (5–18) $5; members and children under 5 free; admission to galleries is free on Friday 4–6:30 p.m. Admission is free for educators with valid identification.

Note: As of late 2008, Museum of the Moving Image was undergoing a major expansion. During the expansion, museum galleries are open Tuesday through Thursday 10 a.m. to 4 p.m., and Friday 10 a.m. to 6:30 p.m., with admission free after 4 p.m. on Friday. During construction, visitors enter on 37th Street, near 35th Avenue.

From the Editors: There are plenty of museums out there for people who love art and sculpture, but this is the number-one museum for film buffs. It's the mission of the Museum of the Moving Image to educate people on the technology, history, technique, and art of film, as well as television and digital media. This mission is fulfilled with the museum's outstanding collection of artifacts, including costumes, photographs, publicity material, technical equipment, video games, and old movie-theater furnishings.

The Museum of the Moving Image is also great for casual movie fans and children, who enjoy learning more about the medium through interactive exhibits and special screenings. The screenings, which include a variety of motion pictures (restored prints of old films and movies currently making their way on the international festival circuit among them), are often made all the more interesting by the participation of scholars, critics, and even actors and directors.

MUSEUM OF MODERN ART—FILM
11 West 53rd Street
212-708-9400 • moma.org/calendar/film_screenings.php

Public Transportation: Very good (convenient to E, V, B, and D subways bus).
Handicapped Accessibility: Good
Performances/Programs: An array of films, running the gamut from Hollywood blockbusters to obscure and one-of-a-kind gems to classics, art-house favorites, and rare foreign films.
Ticket Prices: Free with membership. Adults $10; seniors (65 and older with ID) $8; students $6; children free, but a ticket is required.
Museum Hours: Saturday–Monday and Wednesday–Thursday 10:30 a.m.–5:30 p.m.; Friday 10:30 a.m.–8 p.m.; closed Tuesday.

From the Editors: Who would have expected the Museum of Modern Art to house such a fantastic film collection? Fortunately for movie fans, MoMA considers film to be a modern art and accordingly offers several screenings a day in its three basement theaters. The selections have an art-house slant (foreign films, silent movies, documentaries, and independents), but mainstream Hollywood flicks frequently make the cut. An admission ticket to the museum gets you into any screenings that day for free, and an annual membership gets you in all year long.

TRIBECA FILM FESTIVAL
Tribeca Cinemas, 54 Varick Street
212-941-2400 • tribecafilm.com/festival

Public Transportation: Very good
Handicapped Accessibility: Good

From the Editors: The TriBeCa Film Festival has become such an important festival so fast that it's hard to believe it's only been around since 2002. That's when Robert De Niro and Jane Rosenthal created the festival to boost morale (and business) in Manhattan's ailing downtown TriBeCa neighborhood in the wake of the September 11, 2001, attacks, while also reminding the world that New York City is an important filmmaking hub for both mainstream and independent cinema.

Every spring, the TriBeCa Film Festival screens approximately 250 movies of all varieties, from much-talked-about new indie pictures to short films and family fare. In between movies, festival attendees can sit in on special events, like panel discussions with major players in the industry and the ASCAP music lounge (which spotlights up-and-comers).

PERFORMANCE VENUES

BROOKLYN ACADEMY OF MUSIC (BAM)
718-636-4100 • bam.org

Venues: Peter Jay Sharp Building, 30 Lafayette Ave., Brooklyn; Harvey Theater, 651 Fulton St., Brooklyn.

Public Transportation: Good

Handicapped Accessibility: Good

Performances/Programs: Programming includes theater, opera, dance, films, international theater, readings, hi-def transmissions of Met Opera performances, art exhibitions and festivals. Free live music at BAM-café Live on Friday and Saturday nights. Some free community programs and events are also offered.

Ticket Prices: Vary based on program. $7–$10 Rush tickets for students (25 and under) and seniors are often available. Shows occasionally on Gold-star.com.

Group Discounts: Discounts for groups of 20 or more available for most performances.

Membership: BAM Cinema Club memberships start at $60 and include discounted admission, members-only screenings, invites to free BAMfan parties for people in their 20s and 30s, a 10% discount at BAM-café, a 20% discount at Brownstone Books, special gym rates at Crunch, and discounts to local restaurants. Friends of Bam memberships start at $75 ($60 for seniors) and include advance sales, BAMfan parties, invites to working rehearsals, access to donor lounge, waived ticket handling fee, a ticket exchange discount, a 50% discount on Artist Talks, BAMbus discount, discounts at BAMcafé and Brownstone Books, special gym rates, and area restaurant discounts.

Educational/Community Outreach: BAM's educational programs include a film literacy series, residencies and workshops and live performances for students.

CARNEGIE HALL
212-247-7800 • carnegiehall.org

Venues: Isaac Stern Auditorium/Ronald O. Perelman Stage, Joan and Sanford I. Weill Recital Hall, and Judy and Arthur Zankel Hall, all located at 881 7th Avenue.

Public Transportation: Good

Handicapped Accessibility: Good

Performances/Programs: Carnegie Hall is a premiere venue for classical and chamber music, as well as pops, jazz, world, and folk.

Ticket Prices: Vary based on program. $10 Rush tickets for students and seniors are available for some shows. $10 tickets for Weill Recital Hall events sold one hour before concert times. $10 partial view tickets sold to general public on the day of performance at noon.

Group Discounts: Discounts available for groups of 20 or more.

Subscriptions: Numerous concert packages available, starting at $89. Subscriber benefits include free ticket exchanges, discounts on restaurants and shops, a 10% discount in the gift shop, reduced-rate parking, and ticket transfers and replacement.

Membership: Membership starts at $100. Benefits include advance ticket purchase, working rehearsal passes, half-price offers, invites to member events, 50% tour discounts, and a 10% discount at the Shop at Carnegie Hall.

Educational/Community Outreach: Carnegie Hall runs numerous educational programs through its Weill Music Institute, including family concerts, professional training workshops, a fellowship program, and music classes.

KAUFMAN CENTER
212-501-3303 • kaufman-center.org

Venues: The Goodman House contains three facilities: Merkin Concert Hall, Lucy Moses School, and Special Music School.

Public Transportation: Very good

Handicapped Accessibility: Good

Performances/Programs: The Merkin Concert Hall's season runs from September to June and programming includes world music, chamber music, jazz and musical theater.

Ticket Prices: Vary based on program. Student, senior, and group discounts are available for selected Merkin shows. The Kaufman Center presentations sell half-price student tickets a half-hour before curtain.

Membership: Merkin Memberships are $80. Membership benefits include tickets to any four Musically Speaking concerts, discounts on additional Musically Speaking concerts, premium seating, free ticket exchanges, one free ticket for a guest to a Musically Speaking concert, a 10% discount on classes and group lessons at the Lucy Moses School, a 10% discount on rental of Kaufman Center studios, and practice rooms as well as restaurant discounts and an invite to the Center's annual gala.

Educational/Community Outreach: The Lucy Moses School has classes in theater, music, and dance.

LINCOLN CENTER FOR THE PERFORMING ARTS
212-721-6500 • lincolncenter.org

Venues: Alice Tully Hall, Avery Fisher Hall, the Metropolitan Opera House, the New York State Theater, the Vivian Beaumont Theater, the Mitzi Newhouse Theater, the Walter Reade Theatre, and Jazz at Lincoln Center (which includes the Allen Room, Rose Theater, and Dizzy's Club). All venues located at 70 Lincoln Center Plaza, a 16-acre complex on the Upper West Side, between Broadway and Amsterdam from 62nd to 65th Streets.

Public Transportation: Excellent

Handicapped Accessibility: Good

Performances/Programs: Lincoln Center is home to numerous resident companies, such as American Ballet Theatre, the Chamber Music Society of Lincoln Center, the Film Society of Lincoln Center, Jazz at Lincoln Center, Juilliard, Lincoln Center Presents, Lincoln Center Theater, the Metropolitan Opera, the New York City Ballet, the New York City Opera, the New York Philharmonic, the New York Public Library for the Performing Arts, and the School of American Ballet. Programming celebrates all of the arts, and includes noted series such as American Songbook, Lincoln Center Festival, Lincoln Center Out of Doors, Midsummer Night Swing, the Mostly Mozart Festival, and Live From Lincoln Center. Individual companies and series offer subscription packages.

Ticket Prices: Vary based on program. $20 student tickets available for many of Lincoln Center's shows.

Group Discounts: Group discounts are available for many performances.

Membership: Friends of Lincoln Center memberships start at $75 and include advanced ticket buying and invites to rehearsals and special events. Friends of Mostly Mozart memberships start at $75 and include early-buying privileges and priority seating. Young Patrons of Lincoln Center memberships (for people in their 20s through early 40s) start at $250 and include invites to special events, receptions, sneak previews, rehearsals, advance-buying privileges, and some discounts to Lincoln Center events.

Educational/Community Outreach: Lincoln Center houses educational institutions like Juilliard and the School of American Ballet; it's the home of the Lincoln Center Institute for the arts in education and it offers various educational programs like lectures, symposia, and the Meet the Artist series.

NEW YORK CITY CENTER
212-581-1212 • citycenter.org

Venues: Mainstage, Stage I, and Stage II, all housed at 130 West 56th Street.

Public Transportation: Very good

Handicapped Accessibility: Good

Performances/Programs: Programming includes work by resident companies, including Alvin Ailey American Dance Theater, Paul Taylor Dance Company, American Ballet Theatre, Morphoses: The Wheeldon Company, New York Gilbert & Sullivan Players, and the Manhattan Theatre Club. The popular Encores! musical concert series, Manhattan Theatre Club's Off-Broadway productions, and many additional dance performances are held at City Center.

Ticket Prices: Vary based on program. Peer-to-Peer (P2P) $10 tickets to select City Center events are available to full-time undergrad and graduate students under 30 (students can sign up for free at the City Center website and receive email notifications about offers.) Show discounts are occasionally available through Goldstar and Playbill.

Group Discounts: Discounts available for groups of 10 or more.

Membership: City Center membership starts at $65. Membership benefits include two passes per year to Encores! dress rehearsals, two passes per year to dance shows and other dress rehearsals, neighborhood discounts, and members-only presales.

Educational/Community Outreach: Educational programs include Young People's Dance Series (professional development, residencies, seminars) and Encores! In Residence.

92nd STREET Y
212-415-5500 • 92y.org

Venues: 1395 Lexington Avenue; 200 Hudson Street (92YTribeca).

Public Transportation: Very good

Handicapped Accessibility: Good

Performances/Programs: The 92nd Street Y is a Jewish institution that welcomes people of all ages, ethnicities, and religions. It's not affiliated with the YMCA. The Y functions as a performance space, lecture hall, school, health center, and community organization. Programming includes a variety of classes, lectures, concerts, readings, social events, camps, and other events.

Ticket Prices: Vary based on program. Some scholarship funds may be available to Y programs for those in financial need.

Group Discounts: 15% discount for groups of 10 or more.

Membership: No general membership, but memberships are available to certain Y programs and centers, such as the 60+ Program, the Parenting Center, the Unterberg Poetry Center, and the May Center for Health, Fitness & Sport.

ST. ANN'S WAREHOUSE
38 Water Street, Brooklyn
718-254-8779 • stannswarehouse.org

Public Transportation: Good

Handicapped Accessibility: Good

Performances/Programs: Performance schedule is Tuesday–Sunday.

Ticket Prices: Vary per production, but generally $20–$55, discounts vary per production, shows occasionally available on Goldstar.com.

Membership: You can become a member for as little as $50. Member benefits include opportunity to purchase tickets before they go on sale to the general public and free ticket exchanges.

SYMPHONY SPACE
212-864-5400 • symphonyspace.org

Venues: The 760-seat Peter Jay Sharp Theatre and the 160-seat Leonard Nimoy Thalia, both located at 2537 Broadway (at 95th Street).

Public Transportation: Very good

Handicapped Accessibility: Good

Performances/Programs: Noted Symphony Space programs include the Selected Shorts short-story readings, annual Wall-to-Wall music marathons focusing on the work of one composer/genre, and Bloomsday on Broadway, an annual James Joyce tribute. An average of 40 other organizations present roughly 125 performances at Symphony Space each year.

Ticket Prices: Vary based on program. Student discounts available for some events.

Group Discounts: Discounts available for groups of 10 or more to many events.

Subscriptions: Subscription packages are available for Symphony Space's most popular series.

Membership: Memberships begin at $75 (or $40 for students, seniors, and educators). Member benefits include 10%–40% discounts for two on all Symphony Space-produced events, a 15% discount at Symphony Space's unWINEd bar and lounge, discounts on neighborhood restaurants and shops, priority admission to Wall-to-Wall events for two, members' receptions, discounts on Selected Shorts merchandise, and other special offers.

TOWN HALL
123 West 43rd Street
212-840-2824 • the-townhall-nyc.org

Public Transportation: Very good
Handicapped Accessibility: Good
Performances/Programs: Programming includes musical theater events, concerts, film screenings and seminars, children's educational programming, comedy and other events.

Ticket Prices: Vary based on program. Sign up with Email Club for special offers. Shows also sometimes available on Goldstar.com.

Membership: Membership begins at $500. Member benefits include two tickets to selected productions and gala performance/dinner for two.

WAVE HILL
West 249th Street (at Independence Avenue), Bronx
718-549-3200 • wavehill.org

Public Transportation: Fair (accessible via combo of subway/Metro North and Wave Hill's free van service, which picks up at stations once an hour).
Handicapped Accessibility: Good
Performances/Programs: Events include concerts, art exhibits, workshops, cooking demonstrations, tours, and lectures. Wave Hill is a 28-acre public garden and features extensive gardens, woodlands, a conservatory and a greenhouse.

Ticket Prices: Wave Hill admission $2–$6. Free admission for children under 6. Tickets for events vary, but tickets are often discounted for students and seniors.

Free Days: Admission is free on Tuesday (all day on non-peak months; 9 a.m.–noon peak months May–June, Sept.–Oct.). Free admission from 9 a.m.–noon on Saturday.

Membership: Membership begins at $40 for individuals. Discounts are available to seniors ($35), senior couples ($60) and families ($75). Benefits include unlimited free admission, two guest passes, reciprocal benefits at 200+ gardens around the country, discounts on concerts/lectures/workshops, a 10% Wave Hill shop and café discount, an invite to the annual member picnic, and invites to art openings.

FESTIVALS

CENTRAL PARK SUMMERSTAGE
Rumsey Playfield, Central Park, New York
212-360-2777 • summerstage.org

Public Transportation: Very good
Handicapped Accessibility: Good
Performances/Programs: Free music, dance, spoken word and film events are performed throughout the summer. All events take place rain or shine. Performance schedule varies.

Ticket Prices: Most performances are free.

Membership: Memberships start at $150. Members get benefits such as reserved seating and free tickets.

From the Editors: Each summer, an eclectic line-up of bands and artists hit Central Park's Rumsey Playfield for the SummerStage free-concert series. Many of these are underground acts or cult faves in the jazz, soul, folk, alternative, and world-music genres. Big names do play the SummerStage as well, but they often perform in designated benefit concerts, which require a ticket purchase.

To get to Rumsey Playfield, enter the park at 69th Street on the East Side or at 72nd on the West. Bag checks at the entrance are thorough, so leave your recording devices, glass bottles, alcoholic beverages, and pets at home. Chairs aren't allowed either, but bleacher seating is available in

JUST ACROSS THE RIVER IN NEW JERSEY

While the choices in Manhattan may seem overwhelming, there are even more across the Hudson River, including the more than two dozen thriving art institutions in northeast New Jersey. Many of them are accessible by train (New Jersey Transit out of Penn Station) and make an especially delightful weekend day trip. We recommend the following:

Newark Museum (newarkmuseum.org)—New Jersey's largest museum, covering both the arts and natural sciences.

George Street Playhouse (georgestplayhouse.org)—Located in New Brunswick, the GSP hosts excellent productions of totally new work, as well as plays and musicals from the last two decades.

Paper Mill Playhouse (papermill.org)—This legendary Milburn institution is famous for its Broadway-size productions of well-known plays and musicals.

Shakespeare Theatre of New Jersey (shakespearenj.org)—Beautifully situated on the Drew University campus in Madison, the STNJ specializes in classic hits, by the Bard and beyond, and does them all very well.

Two River Theatre (trtc.org)—Another convenient source of great productions of classic plays, just a short walk from the Red Bank station.

McCarter Theatre (mccarter.org)—Located across the street from the Princeton Junction train stop and adjacent to the famous campus, the two-theater McCarter complex offers the best in all the performing arts.

While tickets to all of the above are reasonably priced, you can get even better deals at njArtstix.org.

the back if you arrive early enough (the gates open about an hour before the performance).

If you like the music, but hate the crowds, find a nice patch of grass to spread out on outside of the Playfield. Or if you're just not a fresh-air fan in general, stay at home and watch the concerts later when they're broadcast on NYC TV.

LINCOLN CENTER FESTIVAL
212-721-6500 • lincolncenter.org

Venues: Performances are given at various locations in and around the Lincoln Center complex, located at W. 65th Street, between Broadway and Amsterdam.

HOW TO GREET A CELEBRITY ...

[Editor's Note: Before joining the Arts America team, Sean spent well over a decade in the restaurant business, most notably as maitre d' for the venerable Joe Allen restaurant located in Manhattan's theater district.]

Celebrity sightings are a familiar occurrence in New York City, almost as commonplace as the unveiling of a new Duane Reade drugstore. You never know whom you might spot while taking in an art exhibit or jogging 'round the reservoir. These "special guest appearances" aren't strictly confined to hip or glamorous locations, either. I once spied an Oscar nominee in line behind me while waiting to renew my driver's license. I almost asked her if they had an express line for Oscar nominees, but refrained from doing so. That was probably a good move, since she didn't look very interested in chatting, which probably had nothing to do with her disposition and everything to do with the fact that we were at the DMV.

The point is this: In New York, famous faces can pop up anywhere. Most of us New Yorkers have learned to handle this with cool detachment, but every now and then an irresistible urge comes upon out-of-towner and local alike to approach the movie superstar, pop music idol or political giant we never thought we'd encounter in the flesh. So what's the proper etiquette for approaching a celebrity?

While working as maitre d' at one of the city's best-known theater-district restaurants, I witnessed a significant number of poorly executed celebrity encounters. After a decade of observation, I offer the following do's and don'ts of close encounters with stars.

First and foremost, be polite. Approach the person you want to meet the way you would a new friend or co-worker. Introduce yourself calmly and let the person in question know you enjoy his or her work and are pleased to be making his or her acquaintance. Pay attention to what's coming out of your mouth and be certain you're not inadvertently insulting the person you want to impress. One of the most embarrassing exchanges I ever witnessed occurred when a flustered young actor in training uttered the following sentence to a revered and still very prolific actor: "It's so great to meet you, man. You used to be amazing."

"Calmly" is the catchword here. You never want to overdo it. I strongly suggest you try not scream, yell, point, or cry. Not only will this mortify your friends and relatives, it will scare the bejezus out of the celebrity on whom you want to make a good impression. It's understandable to get excited when you see someone who you have been a fan of since you were in middle school, but for the love of God, pull yourself together! Meeting Al Roker will be a much more pleasant experience if you keep the crying and yelling to a minimum.

High-profile people expect to be recognized and more often than not, they're more than happy to make the acquaintance of fans. Things fall flat, however, when you interrupt celebrities while they're eating, talking on the cell phone, getting a bikini wax, and so on. If there's any doubt as to whether or not it's a good time to approach, it's not a good time to approach.

As for the issue of autographs, this is a matter of debate. Some famous people sign them happily while going about their daily lives, while others prefer to maintain a low profile and are none too happy about giving them. However, requesting an autograph from a performer post-performance (or at a publicity event) is completely appropriate. Other requests of celebrities are not. Don't ask a celebrity to talk to your cousin Michelle on your cell phone. Cousin Michelle is a sweetheart and yes, Courtney Cox is one of her favorites, but Courtney Cox doesn't know Cousin Michelle, so any conversation that takes place between them on your cell phone in front of the Union Square Café won't be as magical as you may have anticipated.

Being overly familiar with a celebrity can be embarrassing. So can being not familiar enough. Be certain that the celebrity you've just spotted and want to get an autograph from is, in fact, whom you think he or she is. Telling Nathan Lane how great he was on "Seinfeld" will not endear you to Nathan Lane. If you need to do a little Googling pre-approach, go ahead. It never hurts to be sure.

With the advent of the picture phone, amateur paparazzi have sprung up across the nation. However, taking unauthorized pictures and videos of celebrities (or worse yet, their children) is extremely rude no matter what the circumstances. This is the best and surest way to really infuriate your childhood idol.

By following these simple guidelines, most fans will be guaranteed a pleasant and memorable celebrity experience each and every time. For those celebrities who respond to even the most polite fan with a lousy attitude, remember this: Everyone has a bad day every now and then, even a celebrity.

Public Transportation: Excellent
Handicapped Accessibility: Good
Performances/Programs: Dance, music, theater, and opera productions from around the world presented each July. Performance schedule varies.
    Ticket Prices: Ticket prices vary considerably, $20–$270 (higher prices for multiple shows, cycles, or marathons). Some student discounts available.

    From the Editors: Lincoln Center's resident companies and artists dazzle audiences all year long, but during the Lincoln Center Festival, held every July, it is the best of the international theater community that goes on display. A collection of well-chosen productions offer the unexpected, some simple and exotic, others breathtaking in their artistry and enormity. Dramatic re-imaginings of Western classics, Mongolian songs, Iranian religious drama, and music from Bach to African pop have all been on the program. Festival audiences have seen Israel's Batsheva Dance Company move to Hebrew melodies and Springsteen tunes, Russia's Kirov Opera take on the Ring Cycle, homegrown talents Laurie Anderson and Philip Glass present intriguing new works, and Britain's finest actors do Pinter and Beckett. The Lincoln Center Festival truly is the best of all theatrical worlds.

LINCOLN CENTER OUT OF DOORS
Damrosch Park, Lincoln Center Plaza
212-875-5766 • lincolncenter.org

    Public Transportation: Excellent
    Handicapped Accessibility: Good
    Performances/Programs: Over 100 free outdoor events (music, dance, concerts, street theater, family shows, etc.) held on the plaza at Lincoln Center throughout August.
    Ticket Prices: All performances are free.

NEW YORK INTERNATIONAL FRINGE FESTIVAL (FringeNYC)
212-279-4488 • fringenyc.org

    Public Transportation: Very good
    Handicapped Accessibility: Fair (Most venues are accessible, but not all).
    Performances/Programs: Produced by the Present Company, Fringe

NYC hosts more than 200 shows in just over two weeks in various theaters throughout downtown New York City each August. Performance schedule varies with shows taking place at all times each day of the week. Tickets and show information can be found at FringeCENTRAL, the location of which is determined each year before the festival. See shows for free by volunteering with the festival.

Ticket Prices: Tickets are $15. $10 tickets available for seniors and kids under 12 (for FringeJR shows), must be purchased in person. TDF vouchers accepted.

Group Discounts: Group rates are offered for parties of 20 or more.

Subscriptions: Fiver Pass, any five shows for $70; Flex Pass, any 10 shows for $120; Lunatic Pass, all the shows you can see for $500.

Educational/Community Outreach: Educational opportunities include FringeU's free panels and events.

RIVER TO RIVER FESTIVAL
rivertorivernyc.com

Venues: Various public venues throughout downtown NYC.

Public Transportation: Very good

Handicapped Accessibility: Good

Performances/Programs: Over 500 musical and cultural events take place June through September in public venues throughout New York City. Performance schedule varies.

Ticket Prices: All events are free.

For information on Newark and Princeton, New Jersey,
visit our website at go-artsamerica.com.

CHICAGO

Chicago is the center of American culture, both geographically and intellectually. Home of Frank Lloyd Wright, Carl Sandburg, Studs Terkel, Judy Chicago, David Mamet, Tracy Letts, William Petersen, and Oprah Winfrey, the Windy City is a constant exhibit of the best that America can be, especially in the arts.

ARTS INFO

NEWSPAPERS/MAGAZINES

Chicago (chicagomag.com)—One of the best city mags in the country. Sharp writing, attractive layout, and a quick breeze to find the strongest recommendations.

Chicago Reader (chicagoreader.com)—Free weekly alternative newspaper with an excellent arts-news section and insightful reviews.

Chicago Sun Times (centerstagechicago.com)—Home to Roger Ebert.

Chicago Tribune (chicagotribune.com/entertainment)—Largest daily newspaper in the Chicago metropolitan area.

TimeOut Chicago (chicago.timeout.com)—Chi-Town's edition of the respected arts and entertainment weekly magazine. Very comprehensive.

WEBSITES

Center Stage (centerstage.net)—Chicago's original city guide and still one of the best.

League of Chicago Theatres (chicagoplays.com)—Comprehensive listings and info on Chicago theater.

DISCOUNTS

Hot Tix (hottix.org)—Half-price tickets for Chicago-area shows with two booth locations: 72 E. Randolph and 163 E. Pearson; many of the tickets can be purchased on the website.

Goldstar (goldstar.com)—National discounter offers an excellent Chicago inventory, much of it at half-price.

ART MUSEUMS

ART INSTITUTE OF CHICAGO (AIC)
111 South Michigan Avenue
312-443-3600 • artic.edu

Public Transportation: Excellent (Convenient to Brown, Green, Orange, Pink, and Purple El trains; lines all stop aboveground at Adams/Wabash, in front of the museum. The Red and Blue lines stop underground at Monroe, just a few blocks away. Also accessible by Metra.)

Handicapped Accessibility: Good

Hours: Monday–Wednesday 10:30 a.m.–5 p.m., Thursday and Friday 10:30 a.m.–9 p.m., Saturday and Sunday 10 a.m.–5 p.m.

Admission: Free general admission Thursday and Friday 5–9 p.m., all other times $18, children, students, and seniors (65+) $12, children under 14 free.

Tours: Free gallery talks are offered daily at noon, 1, and 2 p.m. and run 45–60 minutes; 30-minute Express Talks are offered Wednesday at noon and Friday at 2 p.m.

Audio Tours: $7 ($5 for members) and free to visitors with visual and hearing impairments.

Membership: Individual membership is $80 annually and provides members with unlimited access to the museum and all special exhibitions, advance notice of exhibitions and events, members-only previews for special exhibitions, member appreciation days with activities and additional discounts at the museum, the School of the Arts Institute, and the Gene Siskel Film Center. Student membership is $50 annually. Those who live more than 100 miles outside of Chicago get a 10% discount on memberships. Premium membership of $175 annually gets you reciprocal membership to 15 other museums and institutions.

From the Editors: The famous bronze-lion statues by Edward L. Kemeys that guard the Michigan Avenue entrance leading into the Art Institute of Chicago have become an unofficial mascot for the city; depending on the time of year of your visit, you could find them dressed in evergreen wreaths for the holidays or sporting a Chicago sports team's colors during playoffs.

Inside the massive Beaux-Arts-style museum, you'll find an expansive collection of Impressionist, Post-Impressionist, and American paintings, including masterworks by Cézanne, Monet (a good number of *Water Lilies*), Van Gogh, Grant Wood (*American Gothic* among the most famous in their American collection), Edward Hopper (*Nighthawks*), and, of course, *A Sunday Afternoon on the Island of La Grande Jatte* by Georges Seurat, the inspiration for Stephen Sondheim's *Sunday in the Park with George*.

Beyond this impressive collection, the museum houses medieval–Renaissance arms and armor; American decorative arts; architectural and furniture styles from America, Europe, and Asia; and ancient Egyptian, Greek, and Roman galleries displaying the mummy and mummy case of Pannkhenamun. The new glass, steel, and limestone Modern Wing, designed by Renzo Piano, opened in spring 2009, houses the Contemporary and Modern permanent collections, and provides additional education space for the museum, along with more than 20,000 square feet of green space.

All family programs are free with admission and include activities such as Drawing in the Galleries, the Artist Studio, and Gallery Walks. A free day-long event, Senior Celebrations, is held periodically for visitors 55 and older.

MUSEUM OF CONTEMPORARY ART CHICAGO (MCA)
220 East Chicago Avenue (just one block east of Michigan Avenue)
312-280-2660 • mcachicago.org

Public Transportation: Very good (convenient to the Red Line, as well as several Michigan Avenue bus routes).
Handicapped Accessibility: Good

Hours: Tuesday 10 a.m.–8 p.m., Wednesday–Sunday 10 a.m. to 5 p.m., closed Monday.

Admission: $12 (suggested donation), students with ID and seniors $7 (suggested donation), children 12 and under and members of the military free.

Free Day: Tuesday

Tours: Free. Join a docent for a tour of the museum's exhibitions and collection. Starting times vary during the week. Tours last 45 minutes.

Membership: Individual $60 annually, and includes unlimited free admission, two free guest passes, subscription to the MCA magazine and e-news, invitations to all members' previews, discounted parking, and up to 20% discounts on workshops and performances. Student and out-of-towner memberships are $30 annually. Membership for seniors (65+) is $40.

ORIENTAL INSTITUTE OF THE UNIVERSITY OF CHICAGO
1155 East 58th Street
773-702-9514 • oi.uchicago.edu

Public Transportation: Good (accessible by CTA train, bus, and Metra).

Handicapped Accessibility: Good

Hours: Wednesday 10 a.m.–8:30 p.m., Tuesday, Thursday, Friday, and Saturday 10 a.m.–6 p.m., closed Sunday and Monday.

Admission: $7 (suggested donation), children under 12 $4 (suggested donation).

Tours: Community group guided tours for 10 to 120 people are available. Fees vary based on the size of the group.

Membership: Annual individual membership is $50. This includes a free subscription to the members' newsletter; special invitations to such Institute programs as lectures, special events, and the annual dinner; discounts on classes, seminars, symposia, and workshops for adults and children; and use of the Research Archives, one of the most comprehensive libraries of ancient Near Eastern material in the United States. Multiple special discounts for membership are offered for students, educators, overseas guests, and seniors and their families. A Supporting membership ($100) earns you reciprocal admission to more than 300 other museums.

From the Editors: Part of the University of Chicago, the Oriental Institute is a research organization and museum devoted to the study of archaeology, philology, and history of early Near Eastern civilizations.

THEATER

BROADWAY IN CHICAGO
broadwayinchicago.com

Venues: Bank of America Theatre, 18 West Monroe; Cadillac Palace Theatre, 151 W. Randolph Street; Ford Center for the Performing Arts, Oriental Theatre, 24 W. Randolph; Auditorium Theatre of Roosevelt University, 50 E. Congress Parkway; Drury Lane Theatre, Water Tower Place, 175 E. Chestnut Street.

Public Transportation: Good (all)

Handicapped Accessibility: Good (all)

Performances/Programs: Performance schedules and pricing vary, since Broadway in Chicago has so many shows in so many different theaters, but it's somewhat comparable to Broadway, with Tuesday–Sunday schedules being the norm. There are some unusual prices, though, as low as $7.50 for gallery seats at *Mamma Mia!* and as high as $147 for a few of the shows. Student discounts are available, as well as discounts for seniors on weekday matinées and group discounts for parties of 20 or more. For a $25 yearly fee, you can be a member of the Broadway in Chicago Club and get special offers.

Subscriptions: Subscriptions are available for $108–$458. Subscriber benefits include ticket exchanges and the ability to request additional tickets in advance.

ABOUT FACE THEATRE
Hoover-Leppen Theatre, Center on Halsted, 3656 N. Halsted Street
773-784-8565 • aboutfacetheatre.com

Public Transportation: Good

Handicapped Accessibility: Good

Performances/Programs: Performance schedule is Wednesday–Sunday.

Ticket Prices: Single tickets are $15–$50, student and senior discounts available.

Subscriptions: For $100 you can become a member, which entitles you to one ticket to each production in the season. Subscriber benefits include members-only seating, easy ticket exchanges, and one-year subscription to *Time Out Chicago*.

AMERICAN THEATER COMPANY
1909 W Byron Street
773-409-4125 • atcweb.org

Public Transportation: Good
Handicapped Accessibility: Good
Performances/Programs: Generally Wednesday–Sunday.
Ticket Prices: $35–$40, student Rush tickets $10 (sold a half-hour before curtain); preview performances are pay-as-you-can at the door, though it's regular price if you want reserved seating.
Subscriptions: Four subscription choices: Six-Show $158–$180, Five-Show $140–$160, Flex Pass (three tickets on any combo of shows) $96, and Opening Night subscription $225. Subscribers save 20%–25% and other benefits include free ticket exchanges.

CHICAGO DRAMATISTS
1105 W. Chicago Avenue
312-633-0630 • chicagodramatists.org

Public Transportation: Excellent
Handicapped Accessibility: Good
Performances/Programs: Performances Thursday–Sunday.
Ticket Prices: Single ticket prices are $15–$28; occasional availability of $10 tickets for students and industry.
Subscriptions: Only one subscription option: Three-Ticket Flex Pass $50.

From the Editors: This theater is especially geared toward helping playwrights and developing new work, offering lots of special membership options specifically for playwrights.

CHICAGO SHAKESPEARE THEATER (CHICAGO SHAKES)
800 East Grand Avenue on Navy Pier
312-595-5600 • chicagoshakes.com

Public Transportation: Good
Handicapped Accessibility: Good
Performances/Programs: Tuesday–Sunday
Ticket Prices: Range in price, but usually between $25 and $44 per ticket.

Subscriptions: Previews $120, Wednesday matinées $138, Tuesday–Thursday $150, Friday–Sunday $198, and Sunday evenings $150; 15% discount for groups (25% discount for school groups), discounted children's tickets and occasional free summertime performances. Subscriber benefits include free coat check, free lost ticket replacement, and discounts on special events.

From the Editors: Holding the 2008 regional-theater Tony Award and a fast-growing reputation for its handsome productions of Shakespeare and modern classics, the Chicago Shakespeare Theater has become one of the city's favorite institutions.

Inside, the theater has been given a decidedly British touch with a mainstage modeled after the Royal Shakespeare Company's Swan Theatre. The Bookstall, open before the show and at intermission, is a drama-lover's dream, selling playscripts and books on the theater, as well as CST merchandise.

Chicago Shakes' diverse offerings include everything from Shakespeare-contemporary Marlowe to modern master Stephen Sondheim, along with visits from acclaimed international companies like the Globe and La Comedie Francaise.

What's most remarkable is that CST keeps finding new ways to present the Bard himself, with such imaginative productions as *Funk It Up About Nothin'* (an ad-rap-tation of *Much Ado*), *Romeo y Julieta*, and *Mac Homer: The Simpsons Do Macbeth*.

CONGO SQUARE THEATRE
Chicago Center for the Performing Arts, 777 N Green Street
773-296-1108

Public Transportation: Good
Handicapped Accessibility: Good
Ticket Prices: Single tickets are $15 to $37, student tickets $10.
Subscriptions: Season subscriptions are $60. Subscriber benefits include one free ticket exchange per show, free coat check, free or discounted parking, and free subscription to *Time Out Chicago*.

COURT THEATRE
5535 S. Ellis Avenue
773-753-4472 • courttheatre.org

Public Transportation: Excellent
Handicapped Accessibility: Good
Performances/Programs: Performances Wednesday–Sunday.
Ticket Prices: $37–$57, with various student discounts offered: University of Chicago students can get $10 tickets to any performance, while other students get a 25% discount to any performance except Saturday evenings and Sunday matinées. U of C faculty, senior, and group discounts are also available.
Subscriptions: Options include Three-Play $90–$150, Four-Play $116–$196, Five-Play $140–$240, Preview $25, Regular (not good for Saturday night and Sunday matinée) $35, and Premium $50. Flex tickets are available (minimum purchase of four). Discount student subscriptions available. Subscriber benefits include guaranteed seating, additional discounted single tickets, and free ticket exchanges.

From the Editors: The Court Theatre was founded in 1955 when a small group of like-minded theater artists at the University of Chicago got together to do a few Moliere plays. It wasn't until 20 years later that the Court was established as a professional theater, but it grew quickly and soon had its home at the Abelson Auditorium in Hyde Park.

The Court Theatre has a unique relationship with the University of Chicago: It's basically a department of the university. For many years, Moliere, Shakespeare, and Shaw served as the Court's holy trinity, but recently the company has considerably broadened its definition of classic theater, to include classics-themed works like *Radio Macbeth* and Mabou Mines's *Dollhouse*, as well as what are arguably "new classics" like *Arcadia*, *Fences*, and the musical *Caroline, or Change*.

The Court Theatre is known for rejecting any of the stuffy formality associated with classical theater, putting on lively and attractive productions in its intimate theater. It also exposes young people to classic productions by offering special matinées on weekday mornings that are performed specifically for high school students at a cost of just $10–$12 per ticket. The performances are followed by discussions between the students, cast members, and Court staff about the play.

An Artists-in-Schools program brings Court staff and artists directly into the schools, where they introduce kids to classic plays and help them to see the enduring power and relevance of these great texts.

DRURY LANE OAKBROOK TERRACE
100 Drury Lane, Oakbrook Terrace
630-530-8300 • drurylaneoakbrook.com

Public Transportation: Poor
Handicapped Accessibility: Good
Performances/Programs: Performances Wednesday–Sunday.
Ticket Prices: Single tickets are $28–$33, dinner/theater prices $42.75–$54; discounts for groups of 20 or more, senior discounts available for Wednesday and Thursday matinées.
Subscriptions: Subscriptions for a five-show season are $115–$120; benefits include ticket exchange with 48 hours notice ($2 fee applies).

GOODMAN THEATRE
170 N. Dearborn Street
312-443-3800 • goodmantheatre.org

Public Transportation: Excellent
Handicapped Accessibility: Good
Performances/Programs: Performances Tuesday–Sunday.
Ticket Prices: Albert Theatre shows $25–$82; Owen Theatre shows $10–$40; discounts on partial-view tickets, half-price tickets, and $10 tickets available day of mezzanine seating; groups can get up to 50% savings.
Subscriptions: Subscriptions for all five plays in the Albert Theatre range from $100 to $320; for all three plays in the Owen Theatre $48–$87. Subscriber benefits include the best seats, one free ticket exchange, and free *OnStage* magazine subscription. Platinum subscribers get unlimited free-ticket exchanges and a subscription to *TimeOut Chicago*.

From the Editors: The Goodman is almost as well-known to theater-going audiences outside of Chicago as it is to those in its own hometown, where it was established in 1922. One of the reasons for its notoriety is that the Goodman has been unusually successful in transferring its productions to New York. Recent productions of *Long Day's Journey Into Night* and *Death of a Salesman*, both starring Brian Dennehy and directed by Goodman artistic director Robert Falls, went on to become huge hits on Broadway.

As the recipient of the 1992 Regional Theatre Tony Award, the Goodman Theatre has also demonstrated a dedication to local artists and playwrights, such as David Mamet, Rebecca Gilman, and Mary Zimmerman, having produced several of their new works. In addition, the Goodman has a strong commitment to premiering a variety of new works by celebrated theater artists, including the play *Marvin's Room*, Kander & Ebb's *The Visit*, and Sondheim's *Bounce*.

Education and community involvement are also top priorities at the Goodman, which offers continuing-education courses in theater for Chicago public high-school teachers, and a six-week General Theater Studies program for local high-school students in which they learn about creative writing and are introduced to all the elements of theater. Events like the StoryQuilt workshop (free for kids, $5 for adults) take education to a whole new hands-on level by having families explore a theme from a current Goodman show, learn story structure and design, then go on to create quilt panels to tell their own stories.

HYPOCRITES THEATER COMPANY
The Chopin Theater, 1543 W Division Street
773-472-7352 • the-hypocrites.com

Public Transportation: Good
Handicapped Accessibility: Good
Performances/Programs: Performances Thursday–Sunday.
Ticket Prices: $20–$25; discounts available for students, seniors, and groups.
Subscriptions: Three-Play season for as low as $45.

ILLINOIS THEATRE CENTER
371 Artists' Walkway, Park Forest
708-481-3510

Public Transportation: Fair
Handicapped Accessibility: Good
Performances/Programs: Performances Wednesday–Sunday.
Ticket Prices: $19–$21, $1 discount for students and seniors.
Subscriptions: Regular Six-Play subscriptions are $100–$105, student and senior subscriptions are $95, Flex subscription is $105, tax-deductible SuperSponsor subscription is $130 and includes free or reduced admission to workshops, readings, and special events.

LIGHT OPERA WORKS
847- 869-6300 • light-opera-works.org

Venues: Mainstage, Cahn Auditorium, 600 Emerson, Evanston; Second Stage, 1420 Maple, Evanston.

Public Transportation: Good

Handicapped Accessibility: Good

Performances/Programs: Schedule varies, with most shows Friday–Sunday, but some shows on weekdays.

Ticket Prices: Mainstage shows $29–$85 for single tickets, Second Stage shows $24–$39; tickets are half-price for 21 and younger.

Subscriptions: Four-Show subscription packages are $98–$269, Three-Show and Two-Show subscriptions also available.

LOOKINGGLASS THEATRE
Water Tower Water Works, 821 N. Michigan Avenue
312-337-0665 • lookingglasstheatre.org

Public Transportation: Good

Handicapped Accessibility: Good

Performances/Programs: Performances Wednesday–Sunday (occasional Tuesday).

Ticket Prices: $25–$60, groups save 20%; for some shows, a limited number of $15 tickets for children under 12 available to subscribers (limit four per subscriber).

Subscriptions: Three-Play season ranges from $81 to $162; special Family-Series subscription includes classes and activities for children while parents enjoy the performance. Benefits include unlimited free ticket exchanges and discounts on classes.

MARRIOTT THEATRE
Ten Marriott Drive, Lincolnshire
847-634-0200 • marriotttheatre.com

Public Transportation: Poor

Handicapped Accessibility: Good

Performances/Programs: Performances Wednesday–Sunday.

Ticket Prices: $45–$55, students and seniors get a $5 discount on full-price Sunday and Wednesday matinée tickets, single tickets for Children's Theatre are $12, discounts for groups of 15 or more.

Subscriptions: Five-Show subscription packages available. Benefits include unlimited ticket exchanges ($3 fee applies), 20% savings on additional single tickets, and 20% off on guest rooms at the resort.

NEXT THEATRE COMPANY
Noyes Cultural Arts Center, 927 Noyes Street, Evanston
847-475-1875 • nexttheatre.org

Public Transportation: Excellent (Purple Line / Noyes stop)
Handicapped Accessibility: Good
Performances/Programs: Performances Wednesday–Sunday.
Ticket Prices: $23–$38, $19–$34 for seniors, $11.50–$19 for students with ID, $10 student Rush and industry discount tickets available.
Subscriptions: Gold Flex subscription $135 (anytime, any show, including Friday and Saturday nights); Sunday Flex subscriptions $105 (any Sunday matinée), followed by talk-backs with the artistic staff; Thursday Flex subscriptions $100 (any Thursday night show and dining partner deals); Preview Flex subscriptions $80 (any of four preview performances; Three-Play Gold subscriptions $110 (anytime, any date for three of the four plays per season); Three-Play Sunday subscriptions $85 (matinée performances for three of the four plays); Diamond Opening Nights $225 (includes post-show parties; $90 is tax-deductible). Subscriber benefits include free ticket exchange (with 24-hour notice).

NORTHLIGHT THEATRE
North Shore Center for the Performing Arts,
9501 Skokie Boulevard, Skokie
847-673-6300 • northlight.org

Public Transportation: Fair (somewhat accessible via CTA, Skokie Swift Yellow Line, or bus).
Handicapped Accessibility: Good
Performances/Programs: Performances Tuesday–Sunday.
Ticket Prices: $32–$56, student tickets (25 and under with valid ID) $20, group discounts available, free tickets for local hospitalized veterans, ticket exchanges are free (up to 5) for subscribers; $10 fee for non-subs.
Subscriptions: Five-Play subscription packages range from $99 to $275 (for opening nights). Benefits include one free ticket exchange per show and lost ticket replacement.

From the Editors: Each season, the multiple Joseph Jefferson award-winning Northlight Theatre produces an interesting selection of smart plays, intimate musicals, and world premieres. Some of these new works are now being developed in-house with Northlight's reading series, Interplay.

Northlight also has an overwhelming array of educational programs. Some, like the Student Theatre Arts Resource (STAR), are aimed at educating local students in the arts and giving them the opportunity to see professional productions at Chicago's best theaters at an affordable price ($3–$12). Other offerings, such as the summer-camp sessions at the Northlight Theatre Academy (NTA), are great for any child interested in the arts, but for those who are more serious about getting into the biz, the NTA has classes in acting, improvisation, and vocal technique. There's even an audition workshop for students grades 7–12 who want to learn more about getting into the Chicago entertainment industry ($675 for a one-week intensive).

PEGASUS PLAYERS
The O'Rourke Center, 1145 W. Wilson Avenue
773-878-9761 • pegasusplayers.org

Public Transportation: Good (Red Line Wilson stop or bus)
Handicapped Accessibility: Good
Performances/Programs: Performances Thursday–Sunday.
Ticket Prices: $17–$25
Subscriptions: Five-Show season subscriptions range $75–$100; no ticket exchanges for non-subscribers.

PORCHLIGHT MUSIC THEATRE
Theatre Building Chicago, 1225 W. Belmont
773-327-5252 • porchlighttheatre.com

Public Transportation: Excellent
Handicapped Accessibility: Good
Performances/Programs: Performances Friday–Sunday, with opening nights on Monday.
Ticket Prices: $34–$35, student and senior discounts available.
Subscriptions: Subscription to all three plays for $75–$85. Benefits include invites to open dress rehearsals, a season flex pass, and free ticket exchanges (with 48 hours notice).

REDMOON THEATER
Redmoon Central, 1463 W. Hubbard
312-850-8440 • redmoon.org

Public Transportation: Good
Handicapped Accessibility: Good
Performances/Programs: Performances Thursday–Sunday.
Ticket Prices: $20–$25

STEPPENWOLF THEATRE COMPANY
1650 N. Halsted Street
312-335-1650 • steppenwolf.org

Public Transportation: Excellent
Handicapped Accessibility: Good
Performances/Programs: Performances Tuesday–Sunday (occasionally Monday).
Ticket Prices: Single tickets are $20–$68, twenty $20 tickets sold at most performances starting at 11 a.m. on day of show (or 1 p.m. on Sunday), half-priced Rush tickets sold at box office one hour before performance, $15 student Rush tickets sold one hour prior to show, discounted rate for regular groups and deeper discounts for student groups.
Subscriptions: Five-Play subscriptions available for as low as $130. Benefits include free ticket exchanges (one per show).

From the Editors: This is the most famous and revered theater in Chicago and for good reason. Since its founding in a church basement in Highland Park in 1976, Steppenwolf Theatre Company has been committed to creating groundbreaking new productions through strong ensemble work and collaboration. Its name comes from the Hermann Hesse novel that one of the original organizers was reading at the time.

Steppenwolf shows, many of which went to Broadway and beyond, include *True West* with Gary Sinise and John Malkovich, *Balm in Gilead*, Frank Galati's adaptation of *The Grapes of Wrath*, and most recently Tracy Letts's Pulitzer Prize-winning *August: Osage County*.

While many companies do a token premiere now and then, Steppenwolf is always buzzing with new work. Not only does the company regularly feature new plays and adaptations of literary works (most recently *The Diary of Anne Frank* and Haruki Murakami's *after the quake*) in the Downstairs Theatre, local and international acts are always performing in the Upstairs

Theatre and the intimate Garage as a part of the Visiting Company Initiative.

The Steppenwolf for Young Adults program makes certain that kids stay involved too, with family-geared productions based on the work of writers as varied as Toni Morrison and Mark Twain.

Meanwhile, the Traffic series of one-night-only performances takes a more freewheeling approach, inviting audiences to spend *An Intimate Evening with David Sedaris* or to enjoy *A Celebration of Chicago Sketch Comedy*. Musicians like John Pizzarelli, Jon Brion, and Oleta Adams have also appeared, and Chicago Public Radio even re-broadcasts Traffic events.

But it's the mainstage productions where you really get to see the magic of the 35-strong Steppenwolf ensemble, which includes John Mahoney, Laurie Metcalf, Kevin Anderson, and of course Sinise and Malkovich. In addition to the standard (and reasonably priced) five-play mainstage subscription, Steppenwolf offers special options like the Vinci Wine Tasting Series (an expert acquaints you with Vinci's wine collection as you mingle before the show), Sign-Language-Interpreted and Audio-Described series, the Dinner & Theater Series (pre-show dinner at nearby restaurant included with each ticket), and the Student Half-Price Plan.

TEATRO VISTA
312-666-4659 • teatrovista.org

Venues: The company performs primarily at the Greenhouse Theater, 2257 N. Lincoln Ave., as well as at other venues throughout the city.

Public Transportation: Depends on venue.

Handicapped Accessibility: Depends on venue.

Performances/Programs: Usually Thursday–Sunday for the regular run, but previews and opening night sometimes fall on other days.

Ticket Prices: $25, discounts for students and seniors available at the box office with valid ID.

Subscriptions: No subscription options, but there is a Flex Pass.

THEATRE BUILDING CHICAGO (TBC)
1225 W. Belmont
773-327-5252 • theatrebuildingchicago.org

Venue: This venue has three theaters, which have been used by hundreds of artists and theater companies, in addition to TBC's own productions.

Public Transportation: Good (Belmont stop)

Handicapped Accessibility: Good

Performances/Programs: TBC produces new musicals through a variety of programs, so the performance schedule varies considerably.

Ticket Prices: Generally $10–$15; discounts available for children and groups (10 or more).

Subscriptions: No subscriptions per se, but they do have a $95 pass for the Stages new-musicals summer festival. You can also purchase a TBC Pass, which gets you any five shows (not just TBC's own productions) at any of TBC's three theaters.

TIMELINE THEATRE COMPANY
Wellington Avenue United Church of Christ
615 West Wellington Avenue
773-281-TIME (8463) • timelinetheatre.com

Public Transportation: Excellent

Handicapped Accessibility: Poor (18 steps between street level and theater).

Performances/Programs: Performances Wednesday–Sunday.

Ticket Prices: $25–$30, student tickets $15, preview tickets $15, discounts for groups of 10 or more.

Subscriptions: Two subscription options: anytime FlexPass $112 (four admissions for any time/show you choose), and weekday FlexPass $85 (four admissions to weekday performances only). Benefits include unlimited ticket exchanges and invitations to special events.

VICTORY GARDENS
Biograph, 2433 N. Lincoln Avenue
773-871-3000 • victorygardens.org

Public Transportation: Excellent

Handicapped Accessibility: Good

Performances/Programs: Schedule varies, but mostly Tuesday–Sunday, with occasional Monday performances.

Ticket Prices: $30–$45, 20% discount for seniors.

Subscriptions: Five-Play subscriptions are $80–$185, Six-Play subscriptions are $96–$222, Generation VGT subscription for people under 30 gets five plays for $80, educators can get a Five-Play package for $90, Five-Play Access subscriptions for people with disabilities are $80 for special sign-interpreted, word-captioned, or audio-described performances. Benefits include free ticket exchanges and discounts on classes at Victory Gardens Training Center.

From the Editors: Victory Gardens Theater is dedicated to the playwright and half of every VGT season consists of world premieres written by members of its Playwrights Ensemble. This group of more than a dozen writers includes Pulitzer-winner Nilo Cruz (*Anna in the Tropics*), Jeffrey Sweet (*Flyovers*), and Lonnie Carter (*The Romance of Magno Rubio*). The rest of the season is dedicated to newer works from other worthy writers, not just the same slate of recent Broadway and Off-Broadway plays that so many other regional theaters rush to produce. Although Victory Gardens is fiercely dedicated to producing original work, the company favors relatable human dramas and comedies over more overtly experimental pieces.

Through its Access Project, Victory Gardens also makes it its mission to involve people with disabilities in the theater in several ways. Workshops educate the disabled in playwriting and performing; numerous services (e.g., wheelchair seating, ASL-interpreted, captioned, and audio-described performances; Braille programs, etc.) help handicapped patrons enjoy VGT's shows; and there are programs for developing new works by disabled playwrights and/or about living with disabilities. The Sunday night series Crip Slam explores the disabled experience through movie screenings, readings, performances, and other events.

WRITERS' THEATRE
847-242-9730/847-242-9418 • writerstheatre.org

Venues: Woman's Library Club, 325 Tudor Court, Glencoe; Books on Vernon, 664 Vernon Avenue, Glencoe.

Public Transportation: Good (Metra Union Pacific North line to the Glencoe stop).

Handicapped Accessibility: Good (both venues)

Performances/Programs: Tuesday–Sunday

Ticket Prices: $60–$65, $30 tickets for people under 30, half-price student tickets available, groups of 10 or more save at least 10%, student and seniors groups of 10 or more save up to 50%.

Subscriptions: The subscription package for $200 entitles you to 25% off and lots of benefits. Becoming a member for $180 gets you up to 30% off and gives you the most flexibility (only subscribers or members may exchange tickets).

MEET THE SAINTS (OF CHICAGO THEATER)!

Do you love Chicago theater? Would you like to meet others who love Chicago theater? Would you like to be a volunteer at your favorite Chicago theater? Then consider becoming a Saint, Chicago Style.

Every year, the 1900-plus members of this unique organization help more than 80 Chicago and suburban theater, dance, and music organizations for a variety of activities, including ushering at performances. In return, Saints get to attend the activities and performances at no charge. General membership meetings are held five times a year, offering members the opportunity to learn more about the organization and its affairs, meet and socialize with other theater lovers, and participate in interesting presentations given by famous performing-arts personalities.

Annual membership is $65 and members choose the venues and performances where they want to volunteer, as often as they like. They also receive a monthly newsletter, as well as email updating them on volunteering opportunities. For complete information go to the website at saints chicago.org.

The rest of us sinners should be so lucky!

CLASSICAL MUSIC

BELLA VOCE
312-479-1096 · bellavoce.org

Venues: Numerous locations (primarily churches) throughout the Chicago area.

Public Transportation: Varies by venue.

Handicapped Accessibility: Please contact venue for details.

Performances/Programs: Three concerts (fall, spring, and holiday) with multiple performances of each.

Ticket Prices: $28–$30; premium tickets $35–$40; students and seniors $22–$25.

Group Discounts: 33% discount available for groups of 10 or more.

Subscriptions: Subscriptions are sometimes available. When available, benefits include 15% discount on single ticket prices and invites to open rehearsals.

Membership: No memberships are offered, but donations are greatly appreciated.

CHICAGO A CAPPELLA
773-435-6453 • chicagoacappella.org

Venues: Various locations throughout the Chicago area.
Public Transportation: Good
Handicapped Accessibility: All venues are accessible.
Performances/Programs: Four programs with multiple performances, plus occasional special events.
Ticket Prices: $22–$35 for most concerts; may vary depending on venue and type of performance.
Subscriptions: Flexible, create-your-own subscription, costs $100–$125, seniors (62+) $80, full-time students (23 and under) $45. Subscriber benefits include guest voucher, invites to open rehearsal, and "Meet the Singers" events, and free ticket exchanges online or by phone.
Membership: Available from $25 to $1,000+. Depending on amount of contribution, member benefits include program recognition, seating upgrade, a free CD, and invites to rehearsals.

CHICAGO CHAMBER CHOIR
312-409-6890 • chicagochamberchoir.org

Venues: Various locations throughout the Chicago area.
Public Transportation: Depends on venue.
Handicapped Accessibility: Please contact venue.
Performance/Productions: Three productions with multiple performances of each.
Ticket Prices: $18 for adults and $15 for children and students in advance, $20 for day-of tickets.
Subscriptions: Three concert series available for $50 adults, children and students $4.
Membership: Available from $1 to $5,000+. Extra special benefits for donors include a special message to a singer or the entire choir in the program ($100+), a complimentary season subscription ($250+), a singing Choirgram delivered to the recipient of your choice ($500+), dinner with the artistic director ($1,000+), and a private chamber performance for your next party or special event ($5,000+).

CHICAGO SYMPHONY ORCHESTRA (CSO)
Symphony Center, 220 South Michigan Avenue
312-294-3000 • cso.org

Public Transportation: Very good (easily reached by the Metra, CTA El Train and buses).

Handicapped Accessibility: Good

Performances/Programs: More than 150 performances are given each year.

Ticket Prices: Prices vary; student tickets $12 (bought online); student tickets day of concert $15; and senior tickets $20. These specially priced tickets may be purchased with cash at the box office only on the day of the performance (after 5 p.m., noon for matinées). Rush seating for general-admission pricing may be available immediately before the event. Some concert tickets may be obtained at a substantial discount at goldstar.com.

Group Discounts: Discounts available for groups of 20 or more.

Subscriptions: Multiple subscriptions are available, including a create your own series, where you choose up to nine concerts and save up to 20%. Multiple packages include the Chicago Symphony Orchestra Main Series, Afterwork Masterworks, Beyond the Score, and many others. Benefits include quick and easy ticket exchanges and access to discounted pre-paid parking at the Grant Park South garage.

Membership: Donor fees begin at $75 and offer discounts at Symphony Store and dining. Larger donations may be rewarded with admission to open rehearsals, invitations to galas and salon series concerts, and other perks.

Activities for Children: The Kraft Family Matinée series offers family-friendly concerts. Tickets are required.

From the Editors: Founded in 1891, the Chicago Symphony Orchestra's first music director was Theodore Thomas. Home to many of the world's finest musicians, including the largest professional chorus in America, the CSO continues its reputation as a world-renowned orchestra under the direction of Maestro Riccardo Muti.

The CSO offers over 150 performances each year, with special rates for students and seniors to help to make concerts accessible to all. For children, the Kraft Family Matinées series of family-friendly concerts is a wonderful way for kids to learn about classical music. Afterwork Masterworks concerts are a special treat for the working crowd, with an early start time of 6:30 p.m., followed by a nice wine reception.

The CSO's website offers a great resource for patrons to learn more about classical music and CSO programs. A special section titled Discover

Classical Music hosts a useful classical-music glossary, along with an Ask an Expert section dedicated to answering people's questions about classical music.

MUSIC INSTITUTE OF CHICAGO (MIC)
Nichols Concert Hall, 1490 Chicago Avenue
847-905-1500 • musicinstituteofchicago.org

Public Transportation: Good
Handicapped Accessibility: Good
Performances/Programs: MIC provides music education for people of all ages and abilities in several Chicago-area facilities. It holds frequent performances by students, faculty, guest artists, in-residence ensembles, and local arts organizations at the Nichols Concert Hall location.
Ticket Prices: Generally $20, $15 for seniors, and $7 for students. Many free events are also offered.

MUSIC OF THE BAROQUE
Harris Theater in Millennium Park, 205 East Randolph Drive
312-551-1414 • baroque.org

Other Venues: First United Methodist Church, 516 Church Street, Evanston; various church locations for holiday concerts.
Public Transportation: Good (Harris Theater)
Handicapped Accessibility: All venues are accessible.
Performances/Programs: Seven concerts, each with multiple performances.
Ticket Prices: Typically $30–$75.
Subscriptions: Three–seven concert subscriptions available for $90–$234, depending on number of shows and seats selected. Subscriber benefits include preferred seating and ticket exchange privileges.
Membership: Available from $75–$25,000+.

From the Editors: Bach, Vivaldi, and Handel are a few of the composers whose works you can expect to hear during a Music of the Baroque concert season, but the company also sometimes ventures into pre- and post-Baroque musical periods. Music of the Baroque is comprised of sixty of Chicago's finest singers and instrumentalists. The members of the chorus have careers in opera, teaching and giving recitals, while members of the orchestra perform in many other musical groups and ensembles. Since

2002, the orchestra has been under the musical direction of Jane Glover, who is in demand as a guest conductor all over the world and has become a major face in the Chicago classical music scene.

 OPERA

CHICAGO OPERA THEATER
The Harris Theater in Millennium Park, 205 E. Randolph Drive
312-704-8414 • chicagooperatheater.org

Public Transportation: Very good (easily accessible by Randolph St. METRA service).
Handicapped Accessibility: Good
Performances/Programs: Three productions per season, with multiple performances of each, plus special concerts and events.
Ticket Prices: $30–$120 for individual tickets.
Subscriptions: Available from $90 to $345, depending on seats selected. Students can get a subscription at a 50% discount.
Membership: Available from $50 to $2,500+. Mid- to high-level donors get perks like invites to dress rehearsals and cast parties.

From the Editors: The Chicago Opera Theater is one of the country's freshest and most original operas, giving emerging talent the ability to perform and produce high-quality opera in and around Chicago. Established in 1974, COT is young compared to most opera companies, and it is young in spirit as well, endeavoring to reinvent the genre's stodgy image. It does this by producing new works and giving a contemporary spin to the classics. COT proudly boasts that every one of its productions (no matter how old the opera itself may be) is brand new—new costumes, sets, lighting, musical interpretation, and staging.

LYRIC OPERA OF CHICAGO
Civic Opera House, 20 N. Wacker Drive
312-332-2244 ext. 5600 • lyricopera.org

Public Transportation: Very good
Handicapped Accessibility: Good

Performances/Programs: Eight per season with multiple performances of each plus special concerts and events such as Operathon, the Opera Ball, and Discovery Series discussions.

Ticket Prices: Prices vary depending on date, time, performances, and seats. Student tickets are available for $20 to select performances. Students must sign up as a NEXT member online to be eligible.

Group Discounts: Discounts available for groups of 15 or more.

Subscriptions: 4–8 opera subscriptions available starting at $96 for four operas, $192 for all eight, with prices based on date, time, seats, and number of performances selected. Payment plan options available. Subscriber benefits include up to 32% savings over single ticket prices, ticket exchanges, free pre-opera lectures, and invites to special events.

Membership: Available from $50–$100,000+. Depending upon amount donated, benefits include merchandise discounts, invites to special events and parties, dress rehearsal passes, and even Lyric Opera voting membership ($500+).

From the Editors: Lyric Opera of Chicago offers performances by the finest vocal artists in the world in productions of gorgeous spectacle. In addition to its repertoire of traditional favorites, Lyric has a great history of supporting and promoting contemporary opera, most recently with the premiere of William Bolcom's *A Wedding*, and a new production of Berg's *Lulu*. With over 30,000 subscribers and an attendance rate that has averaged at 100% for over 20 years, Lyric Opera of Chicago is the envy of the American opera world.

JAZZ/CABARET

ANDY'S JAZZ CLUB & RESTAURANT
11 E. Hubbard Street
312-642-6805 • andysjazzclub.com

Public Transportation: Good
Handicapped Accessibility: No
Performances/Programs: Approximately 700 performances are presented each year. Two sets nightly (5 p.m., 9 p.m. or on occasion 9:30 p.m.).
Ticket Prices: $5–$15. Discounts are available for Chicago Jazz Institute members (call ahead for information).

DAVENPORT'S PIANO BAR & CABARET
1383 N. Milwaukee Avenue
773-278-1830 • davenportspianobar.com

Public Transportation: Good
Handicapped Accessibility: Good
Performances/Programs: Approximately 700 performances are presented each year. Nightly sets Wednesday–Monday in the Lounge (See online schedule for cabaret dates and times).
Ticket Prices: No cover; $5 for the Chaise Lounge depending on the performer. Cabaret prices range $8–25 plus a two-drink minimum.

GREEN DOLPHIN STREET
2200 Ashland Avenue
773-395-0066 • jazzitup.com

Public Transportation: Good
Handicapped Accessibility: Good
Performances/Programs: Depending on the season (the club is closed for parts of the summer), live jazz is presented two to seven nights a week.
Ticket Prices: Generally, no cover is charged Tuesday, Thursday, or Sunday; a $10–$20 cover is charged Wednesday, Friday, and Saturday. If both dining and attending a performance, the cover charge is frequently waived (call ahead to make sure this discount is valid for the performer).

GREEN MILL COCKTAIL LOUNGE
4802 N. Broadway Avenue
773-878-5552 • greenmilljazz.com

Public Transportation: Good
Handicapped Accessibility: Partially (the front door is accessible, the restrooms are not).
Performances/Programs: Approximately 480 performances are presented each year. Monday–Thursday, sets are at 9 p.m.–1 a.m., Friday and Saturday two sets (8 p.m. and midnight).
Ticket Prices: Range from free to $12.

From the Editors: If you find yourself in a mobster sort of mood after gawking at the late-night Zoot Suiters, head to Green Mill Cocktail Lounge, one of the Chicago's (and the world's) oldest jazz venues, having existed in some iteration since 1907. Arrive early to soak up the atmosphere where Al Capone and his henchmen used to lord over this former speakeasy. Throughout the last century, the venue played host to a plethora of big-name musicians (Al Jolson, Eddie Cantor) and served as a favorite haunt of the likes of Charlie Chaplin and Gloria Swanson.

Rather than schedule two performers for dinner and late-night set, the club books one act for a 9 p.m.–1 a.m. stay, in the style of the all-night jazz extravaganzas of the Roaring '20s, and the sets often run far into the early morning.

Some of the best up-and-coming and established jazz performers frequently pass through Green Mill, including artists such as Kurt Elling and Randy Brecker. The club also hosts one of the world's first ongoing Slam Poetry sessions on Sunday nights. Also, for the night owl with nothing to do late on a Sunday night, stop in for the Kimberly Gordon Organ Trio with a very affordable $4 cover charge.

JAZZ SHOWCASE
Dearborn Station, 47 W. Polk Street
312-360-0234 • jazzshowcase.com

Public Transportation: Good
Handicapped Accessibility: Good
Performances/Programs: Approximately 700 performances are presented each year. Sets are scheduled at 8 and 10 p.m. Monday–Saturday; 4 p.m., 8 p.m., and 10 p.m. on Sunday.
Ticket Prices: $20–$25 cover. Senior, student, and Jazz Institute of Chicago discounts are offered for the 4 p.m. Sunday set. Children under 12 are free.

JOE'S BE-BOP CAFÉ & JAZZ EMPORIUM
600 E. Grand Avenue
312-595-5299 • joesbebop.com

Public Transportation: Good
Handicapped Accessibility: Good
Performances/Programs: Approximately 150 performances are presented each year, with sets nightly Friday–Sunday.
Ticket Prices: No cover.

KATERINA'S
1920 Irving Park Road
773-348-7592 • katerinas.com

Public Transportation: Good
Handicapped Accessibility: No
Performances/Programs: Approximately 350 performances per year. Check the calendar or call for specific times and performers as they change weekly.
Ticket Prices: Free–$15

M LOUNGE
1520 S. Wabash Avenue
312-447-0201 • mloungechicago.com

Public Transportation: Good
Handicapped Accessibility: No
Performances/Programs: Approximately 100 performances are presented annually. Sets on Tuesday and Wednesday at 7 and 10 p.m.
Ticket Prices: No cover, two-drink minimum.

NEW APARTMENT LOUNGE
504 E. 75th Street
773-483-7728

Public Transportation: Fair
Handicapped Accessibility: No
Performances/Programs: Approximately 50 performances are presented annually. Jazz by Von Freeman every Tuesday night from 10:30 p.m. to 4 a.m.
Ticket Prices: No cover, two-drink minimum.

THE VELVET LOUNGE
67 E. Cermak Road
312-791-9050 • velvetlounge.net

Public Transportation: Fair
Handicapped Accessibility: Good
Performances/Programs: Approximately 300 performances are pre-

sented annually. Monday, Wednesday and Thursday shows are at 8:30 p.m.; Friday–Sunday shows at 9:30.

Ticket Prices: $5–$20

From the Editors: While the Velvet Lounge was forced out of its original location by encroaching condominiums, the club has lost very little of the classic vibe that helped shape the face of modern free jazz. The new location is just around the corner and is still owned and operated by the indomitable Fred Anderson, a noted tenor-sax player and seminal figure in the 1960s' jazz scene. The club has played host to a variety of local legends, such as Anderson, Hamid Drake, Art Taylor, and Jim Baker. The cover charge is in the medium price range ($10–$20 usually) and can be a real bargain if you plan ahead for the bigger names.

THE WINDS CAFÉ
2657 N. Kedzie Avenue
773-489-7478 • windscafeofchicago.com

Public Transportation: Good
Handicapped Accessibility: Good
Performances/Programs: Approximately 200 performances are presented annually. Check calendar for specific days and times. Usually shows on Tuesday, Wednesday, and Saturday.
Ticket Prices: No cover.

CHICAGO JAZZ FESTIVAL
312-744-3315 • chicagojazzfest.us

Venues: Part of the festival includes a Chicago jazz-club tour at various venues around the city. Main venues are in Millennium and Grant parks (200–300 E. Jackson).
Public Transportation: Poor
Handicapped Accessibility: Good
Performances/Programs: Approximate 30 performances are given during the festival, which takes place each September.
Ticket Prices: Admission is free.

From the Editors: When Duke Ellington died in 1974, a group of musicians gathered in Grant Park to commemorate the incredible musician's life. Thousands of jazz lovers came out to celebrate and the festival was a resounding success. Several other jazz festivals at different venues in Chicago followed and the city eventually proposed a conglomerate event that combined these festivals into what has become the Chicago Jazz Festival, the largest open-admission jazz festival in the world.

Held over three days at the end of August, the festival draws hundreds of thousands of fans and the elite of the jazz world, most recently Ornette Coleman, Sonny Rollins, Herbie Hancock, and Kurt Elling. It's advisable to book hotels and amenities well in advance, as the festival attracts huge crowds from all over the world.

CITY OF CHICAGO BLUES FESTIVAL
Grant Park, 300 S. Columbus
312-744-3370 • chicagobluesfestival.us

Public Transportation: Good
Handicapped Accessibility: Good
Performances/Programs: A music festival held in early June; more than 90 performances on six stages in four days.
Ticket Prices: Admission is free. Food and beverage tickets are sold in strips of 12 for $8.

DANCE

BALLET CHICAGO
Athenaeum Theatre, 2936 N. Southport
312-251-8838 • balletchicago.org

Public Transportation: Good
Handicapped Accessibility: Good
Performances/Programs: Ballet Chicago presents two programs each year: the *Nutcracker* in December and the Spring Repertory in May. Each program is performed three–four times.
Ticket Prices: Tickets are generally $20–$30. Students get in for $12. For some performances, seniors get discounted tickets at about $16–$24.
Third-Party Website Discounts: Discounted tickets are sometimes available through ticketmaster.com.
Membership: Ballet Chicago has no annual membership. Donations are accepted in any amount via check, cash, credit card, or gift of stock.

HUBBARD STREET DANCE CHICAGO
Harris Theater for Music and Dance at Millennium Park
205 E. Randolph Drive
312-850-9744 • hubbardstreetdance.com

Public Transportation: Good
Handicapped Accessibility: Good
Performances/Programs: Four programs a year. Each program runs for one week with four or five performances.
Ticket Prices: Range from $25 to $86.
Group Discounts: Groups of 10 or more may receive discounts to select performances.
Subscriptions: Subscriptions are available for all four shows or any two shows of your choice. The approximate discount for subscribing is 25% for full-season subscriptions, 15% for the two-pack. Benefits include priority seating, flexible ticket-exchange privileges, discounts on additional single-ticket purchases, invitations to behind-the-scenes events, and a subscription to the HSDC newsletter.
Membership: Donor fees start at $50 and include 10% off two tickets to HSDC performances at the Harris Theater and one free class at the Lou Conte Dance Studio.
Educational/Community Outreach: Hubbard Street Dance has developed extensive educational and community programs, the most well-known of which is Hubbard Street 2, its young-performers company. HS2 functions both as a training ground and as a resource for HSDC's main company.

From the Editors: Hubbard Street Dance Chicago is a cocktail of ballet and contemporary styles with a twist of jazz. Founded in 1977 by Lou Conte, an ex-Broadway hoofer, this company is truly an American original. Although the overall style has developed into something more eclectically sophisticated, that show-stopping jazz-dance attitude remains delightfully prevalent.

As a formidable presence in the Chicago area, Hubbard Street Dance has a mission of identifying and supporting young talent, holding a national choreographic competition every year and awarding three emerging artists the opportunity to create original staged works for the company.

The Hubbard Street Dance Center, unveiled in 2006, now houses the main company, Hubbard Street 2 and the Lou Conte Dance Studio. The studio offers weekly classes in a variety of styles, including jazz, modern, tap, African, hip-hop, and Pilates from beginner to professional. *Chicago* magazine has called it the "Best Dance Class for Adults."

JOFFREY BALLET
Auditorium Theatre of Roosevelt University
50 E. Congress Parkway
312-739-0120 • joffrey.com

Public Transportation: Good
Handicapped Accessibility: Good
Performances/Programs: Three programs are performed each year, plus the annual *Nutcracker*. Each show runs for two weeks with seven performances. The *Nutcracker* runs for two weeks in December with one or two performances almost every day.
Ticket Prices: Range from $25 to $145.
Group Discounts: Groups of 10 or more may receive up to a 25% discount to select performances.
Subscriptions: Packages include all three programs. Subscribers select their preferred show dates. Benefits include free ticket exchanges, a pre-season lecture with Joffrey artists, priority ordering, and lost-ticket insurance.
Membership: Basic donor fees start at $50 and include priority notification of all Joffrey programs and invitations to season closing-night parties.

From the Editors: The Joffrey Ballet first emerged in 1956 as six dancers traveling across the country in a station wagon pulling a U-haul trailer. More than 50 years later, the vision of founders Robert Joffrey and Gerald Arpino has flourished into an internationally acclaimed company of over 40 performers. Although originally established in New York, Joffrey Ballet moved around the country for quite a while, maintaining resident-company status at New York's City Center and the Los Angeles Music Center before settling in Chicago in 1995. In August 2008, the city of Chicago unveiled Joffrey Tower, a commercial high-rise in Cook County that will be the company's first-ever permanent home.

This company is known for a highly original and varied repertory, including, of course, works by both Joffrey and Arpino, but also works by Ashton, Ailey, Bournonville, Forsythe, Massine, Morris, and Tharp. Slightly more unusual are the historical reconstructions of early 20th century "lost" ballets from Diaghilev's Ballets Russes. Equally unusual is the full-length ballet created to rock music by Prince.

FILM

DOC FILMS
212 E 59th Street
773-702-8574 • docfilms.uchicago.edu

Public Transportation: Good (accessible by CTA and METRA)

Handicapped Accessibility: Good (call theater to arrange accommodation).

Performances/Programs: The screenings are usually themed and feature rare gems, essential classics, and special retrospectives, often with guest lectures by celebrated filmmakers.

Ticket Prices: General admission is $5. Quarterly and summer memberships are available for $26 and $18, respectively.

From the Editors: For 75 years, Doc Films has served students of the medium. The University of Chicago-based Doc is in fact one of the oldest student-film societies in the country, and its programming is even informed by proposals made by the university's student body.

As its name indicates, the organization began as a showcase for "the realist study of our time via nonfiction film," but documentaries were not enough to keep Doc Films going, so the group soon expanded its interests to include fictional films, particularly of the educational and experimental ilk.

Doc, which screens films nightly at the Max Palevsky Cinema in Ida Noyes Hall on the U of C campus, has done series on topics such as human rights and feminism, and frequently shows prints from leading film archives around the nation.

GENE SISKEL FILM CENTER
164 North State Street
312-846-2600 • siskelfilmcenter.org

Public Transportation: Very good (accessible from all CTA L lines)

Handicapped Accessibility: Good

Performances/Programs: Independent, international and classic cinema.

Ticket Prices: General admission is $9; students $7; students, faculty, and staff of the School of the Art Institute $4. All screenings are $5 for Film Center members.

From the Editors: The Film Center of the School of the Art Institute of Chicago, renamed the Gene Siskel Film Center in 2000 in honor of the renowned Chicago movie critic, has been a haven for film lovers for more than 30 years. With its sophisticated new facilities at 164 North State Street, the center serves more than 65,000 film fans a year with approximately 1,500 screenings in a comfortable intimate setting. First runs of new foreign and indie pictures are shown here and the programming includes screenings of movies by Chicago directors and regular appearances by guest artists.

The Gene Siskel Film Center is also a first-rate revival house, hosting major retrospectives and screening classics and long out-of-print films by major international directors. Even the concessions surpass the usual junk-food fare, offering coffee, tea, wine, chocolate, and beer.

MUSIC BOX THEATRE
3733 N. Southport Avenue
773-871-6607 • musicboxtheatre.com

Public Transportation: Good (accessible by CTA bus and train)
Handicapped Accessibility: Good
Performances/Programs: Independent and foreign films
Ticket Prices: General admission is $9.25; first-show-of-the-day discount (Monday–Thursday only) $8.25; Saturday and Sunday matinée films at 11:30 a.m. are $7.25.

From the Editors: Independently owned, the Music Box Theatre is the largest dedicated theater space in Chicago. It's one of the city's prime art-house movie theaters, screening foreign and independent films.

One of the Music Box's greatest assets is its old-fashioned ambience. The design is a mix of Spanish and Italian by way of Hollywood. The dark-blue-clouded ceiling has a twinkling-stars effect and the walls are decorated in a style that evokes an Italian courtyard, making the audience feel as though they're viewing the film out on the palazzo. Adding to the Hollywood magic is the Music Box Theatre's homegrown ghost story: Legend has it that the theater's former manager, Whitey, continues to watch over the theater even today.

PERFORMANCE VENUES

AUDITORIUM THEATRE OF ROOSEVELT UNIVERSITY
50 East Congress Parkway
312-922-2110 • auditoriumtheatre.org

Public Transportation: Good
Handicapped Accessibility: Good
Performances/Programs: Programming includes ballet, dance companies, concerts, musicals, and other cultural offerings.
Ticket Prices: Vary based on program. Discounted tickets sometimes available via HotTix. Student Rush is sometimes available, depending on policies set by individual shows. Shows also occasionally available on Goldstar.com.
Group Discounts: Discounts may be available for groups of 10 or more.
Subscriptions/Membership: Several different subscription series available. Benefits include 10%-20% discounts on tickets, Fireside Chat discussions and receptions, ticket exchanges, priority ticketing, and discounted pre-paid parking.

CHICAGO CULTURAL CENTER
78 E. Washington
312-744-2947 • egov.cityofchicago.org

Public Transportation: Good
Handicapped Accessibility: Good
Performances/Programs: Hundreds of free arts programs and exhibitions (music, dance, theater, lectures, films, exhibitions, tours, and more) are presented here year round, almost every day. The Center includes galleries, concert and exhibit halls, a studio, a rotunda, a café, Studio Theater, and the Claudia Cassidy Theater.
Membership: Mosaic membership starts at $55 for individual, $25 for student, and $75 for household. Benefits include invitations to openings, reserved seating, and discounts at shop, café, and on DCA theater productions.

THE DOWNBEAT CAFÉ
1202 N. Alvarado Street, Echo Park
213-483-3955 • thedownbeatcafe.com

Public Transportation: Poor
Handicapped Accessibility: Good
Performances/Programs: Approximately 50 performances given each year. Live jazz performed by the house band every Wednesday at 7:30 p.m.
Ticket Prices: No cover.

FESTIVALS

GRANT PARK MUSIC FESTIVAL
205 East Randolph Drive
312-742-7638 • grantparkmusicfestival.com

Public Transportation: Good
Handicapped Accessibility: Good
Performances/Programs: 10 weeks of free (mostly classical) music performances from mid-June to mid-August each year. The Festival takes place in venues at Millennium Park, with most concerts being in the Jay Pritzker Pavilion. Schedule varies, with performances generally given Wednesday through Sunday.
Ticket Prices: Free admission. Priority seating for members.
Ticketing for Groups: For groups of 20 or more, call 312-744-4159 to reserve seats.
Membership: Memberships start at $80. Membership benefits include reserved seating and special discounts.

From the Editors: Chicago's favorite free summer-concert series, the Grant Park Music Festival is conveniently located in Millennium Park, right by the Loop. Over 10 weeks, evening concerts featuring the Grant Park Orchestra and Chorus are held in the Frank Gehry-designed Jay Pritzker Pavilion, where Chicagoans picnic and enjoy the state-of-the-art sound out on the lawn (festival donors can get priority seating closer to the stage).

On selected Saturdays, the concerts are preceded by a CoffeeTalk discussion about the evening's program in the Choral Hall (on the east side of the Pavilion) and on some Wednesdays a TalkBack with artists and festival

WHAT MAKES CHICAGO CHICAGO?

by Howard Simpson

[Editor's Note: Howard Simpson, a fourth-generation Chicagoan, has traveled the world extensively and seen many wonderful places, but proudly calls Chicago home.]

A bustling urban center located in the corner of a mostly rural state, Chicago still maintains a bit of the frontier: wide open, boisterous, a can-do philosophy. In fact, it's still thought of by its citizens as a young vital Midwest community. Although many of the big meat-packing plants, steel companies, and great merchants that formed the city's character have diminished their respective roles, much of the pulse of the city harkens back to those beginnings.

Here, people are more likely to be judged by their accomplishments than by their individual or family backgrounds as I've seen in other cities. The major improvements and leaps forward have, for the most part, been led by civic groups, not government. The rebuilding of the city after the Chicago fire allowed alleys to become the spine of the physical city; the reversal of the Chicago River, the development of the Burnham Plan that created the new shoreline of Lake Michigan with a vast interconnected park and road system, two world fairs, the bid for the 2016 Olympics, and the Millennium Park have all come from groups of citizens identifying the need, developing the funding scheme, and implementing the plan.

This, citizen participation at the highest levels, is the strength of Chicago, renders it unique, and will continue to make it culturally significant in the future. From our cherished jazz, R&B, and blues clubs to our quirky elevated subway system; from our legendary steakhouses to our magnificent buildings that make up the Chicago School of Architecture; from our quiet little inner-city neighborhoods to our sprawling open parks and beachfronts; from our three major hubs: air, rail and truck; from the Field Museum to Steppenwolf, Chicago is dynamic, alive, full of promise and a great place to live, work, and especially visit!

organizers follows the concert right in front of the Pavilion stage. Free daytime "open-rehearsals" are also available for groups, with docents on hand to talk about the music and field questions.

LOLLAPALOOZA
Grant Park, 331 E. Randolph Street
888-512-SHOW • lollapalooza.com

Public Transportation: Good
Handicapped Accessibility: Good
Performances/Programs: Lollapalooza has evolved over the years, but in its current form is a three-day summer festival in Chicago running Friday–Sunday.
Ticket Prices: Tickets are $80 (single day) to $205 (three-day pass). VIP LollaLounge and private cabana packages also available.

PITCHFORK MUSIC FESTIVAL
Union Park, 1501 W. Randolph Street
pitchforkmusicfestival.com

Public Transportation: Good (easily accessible by bus or train).
Handicapped Accessibility: Good
Performances/Programs: This three-day July music festival features more than 40 indie bands and musicians on three stages. Performances are held on Friday evening and throughout the day on Saturday and Sunday.
Ticket Prices: Single-day passes are $30. Saturday and Sunday two-day passes are $50. Three-day passes are $65. Free admission for children under 10 when accompanied by an adult. No re-issues for lost or stolen tickets.

RAVINIA
Ravinia Park, 200 Ravinia Park Road, Highland Park
847-266-5100 • ravinia.org

Public Transportation: Good (Easily accessible via Metra; also free Park 'n' Ride bus available).
Handicapped Accessibility: Good
Performances/Programs: Annual summer festival taking place from late May to mid-September; also offers indoor Rising Stars concerts from October to May. Performances almost every day.
Ticket Prices: Lawn seats are $3–$25. Reserved seats $20–$100. Premium-priced seats $75–$250. $5 lawn tickets are available for children 10 and younger. Some concerts and master classes offered free of charge. Free lawn passes are available for college students for Chicago Symphony Orchestra concerts and Martin Theatre concerts on the evening of per-

formance. Students may also purchase available reserved-seat tickets for these same concerts for only $10 with valid ID (one ticket per ID). Reserved seat tickets may be exchanged up to 24 hours before the date of the concert. Dated lawn tickets may not be exchanged.

Group Discounts: Discounts for groups of 20 or more available for Rising Stars concerts.

Educational/Community Outreach: Educational initiatives include the Steans Institute for Young Artists professional studies program, and Ravinia U—which has online courses that tell you about the kinds of classical music that is performed at the actual festival.

From the Editors: With its long history, beautiful atmosphere, and a yearly roster full of great performing artists in all genres (Willie Nelson, Tony Bennett, B.B. King, Chicago Symphony Orchestra, etc), Ravinia has become a beloved tradition for many Chicago-area residents. To some, who set their picnic tables with candelabras and feasts fit for the gods, it's nearly sacred. But other festival goers are less than impressed, complaining that despite the fact that lawn seats can cost up to $25, you can't actually see the stage, and the big-name concerts are so crowded that it's even a challenge to simply relax in the grass and enjoy the music. Furthermore, traveling to Ravinia, located out in suburban Highland Park, can be a pain in the neck because of limited parking and an overwhelmed Metra full of thousands of festival attendees. Ravinia's most satisfied customers are invariably those that stick to going to the less popular (but just as excellent) classical music programs, or those who pony up the extra cash to pay for reserved Pavilion seats.

For information on Ft. Wayne and Indianapolis, Indiana;
Louisville, Kentucky; and Milwaukee, Wisconsin,
visit go-artsamerica.com.

LOS ANGELES

The City of Angels can be an angelic arts destination. There are several world-class museums, orchestras, and choruses, and theater with world-renowned stars in intimate productions at excellent prices. They also make good movies here!

But the L.A. downside is that you really need a car here (we also recommend a GPS). Not only are these cultural arts institutions spread over 500 square miles, but the various public-transportation systems are meager, poorly coordinated, and not at all user-friendly.

However, if you don't mind driving and parking, the benefits can be well worth the investment. At least, that's what we tell ourselves when we're mired in traffic.

ARTS INFO

NEWSPAPERS/MAGAZINES

L.A. Weekly (laweekly.com)—Free newspaper with the best Los Angeles arts listings. We also recommend its sister publication, the *OC Weekly* (as in Orange County).

Los Angeles Times (theguide.latimes.com)—Since its acquisition by the *Chicago Tribune*, arts coverage has seriously declined, but the big daily is still worth picking up and checking out the Calendar Section.

WEBSITES

Both of the above publications run excellent websites, better than the publications, in our opinion.

DISCOUNTS

GoldStar (goldstar.com)—Headquartered in Altadena, this national discount-entertainment service has a tremendous Los Angeles inventory of every type of entertainment, from ballet to Lakers tickets.

LATix (lastagealliance.com)—Operated by the Los Angeles Stage Alliance, this site offers online discount tickets to almost every play in L.A. The website is very informative regarding the L.A. theater scene, though it does seem to have technical issues from time to time.

On the House un-Ltd (onthehousetickets.com)—L.A.'s only papering service. Members pay (a rather high) $225 per year, or $135 for six months, but there's no per-performance charge. (Note: As we go to press, there are plans for New York's Theater Extras to open an L.A. site.)

Plays411 (plays411.net)—Another online source for theater tickets, many (but not all) at a discount.

ART MUSEUMS

GETTY CENTER
1200 Getty Center Drive
310-440-7300 • getty.edu

Public Transportation: Excellent (Metro Rapid Line 761 stops at the museum's main gate).

Handicapped Accessibility: Good

Hours: Tuesday–Friday 10 a.m.–5:30 p.m., Saturday 10 a.m.–9 p.m., Sunday 10 a.m.–5:30 p.m., closed Monday.

Admission: Free, but an advance time-specific ticket is required (you can book online). Parking is $15 per car, free after 5 p.m.

Tours: Getty Center Architecture Tours are 30- to 45-minute tours of the site and its architecture. Tuesday–Sunday 10:15 a.m., 11 a.m., 1, 2, and 3 p.m., and on Friday and Saturday there is also a 4 p.m. tour. Collection Highlights Tours are one-hour overviews of major works in the museum,

Tuesday–Sunday at 11 a.m. Exhibition Tours are one-hour guided tours of a current exhibition, Tuesday–Sunday at 1:30 p.m. Focus Tours are one-hour thematic gallery tours whose topic changes daily, Tuesday–Sunday at 3 p.m.; Getty Center Garden Tours are 45-minute tours of the grounds and Central Garden, Tuesday–Sunday at 11:30 a.m. and 12:30, 2:30, and 3:30 p.m.; Masterpiece of the Week Talks are 15-minute explorations of a specific object that changes weekly, Tuesday–Sunday at 4 p.m.

Audio Tours: $5

Membership: Not available, as the entire museum is funded by the Getty Foundation.

From the Editors: The Getty Center is situated on a 110-acre site overlooking the Los Angeles skyline. The jaw-dropping location is a match (to some it's more than a match) for what's housed inside the J. Paul Getty Museum: five museum galleries showcasing pre-20th-century European paintings, drawings, and decorative arts; a collection of 19th- and 20th-century American and European photography; contemporary and modern sculpture; and a selection of Greek and Roman antiquities.

The collection boasts (albeit minor) works by Gauguin, Puryear, Van Gogh, and decorative arts dating back to the 1700s. The paintings are viewed in natural light, thanks to the computer-controlled skylight windows on the second-floor galleries.

The museum offers a packed schedule of events and public programs, including Friday Night at the Getty, a free-of-charge contemporary performance series featuring music, dance, theater, and spoken-word events.

During museum hours, families can visit the Family Room, a place for children of all ages to learn about art together by participating in hands-on projects. The award-winning "GettyGuide" is the portable audio tour on sale for $5 and comes in various versions catering to age group and interest.

The real gem of the Getty Center grounds is its Central Garden, a 134,000-square-foot garden chiefly the work of artist Robert Irwin. More than 500 plant varieties are used to create a masterpiece of greenery that includes a tree-lined walkway descending to a central plaza, stone waterfall, and pool.

GETTY VILLA MALIBU
17985 Pacific Coast Highway
310-440-7300 • getty.edu

Public Transportation: Very good (Metro Bus 534 stops directly across from the Getty Villa entrance). Note: Passengers exiting at PCH (Pacific

Coast Highway) and Coastline Drive to visit the Getty Villa must have their admission ticket hole-punched by the driver before exiting the bus in order to enter.

Handicapped Accessibility: Good

Hours: Thursday–Monday 10 a.m.–5 p.m., closed Tuesday and Wednesday.

Admission: Free. An advance timed ticket is required. Each Villa ticket allows you to bring up to three children ages 15 and under with you in one car. This doesn't apply to tickets for events, such as lectures and performances. Parking is $15 per car, free after 5 p.m.

Tours: Free. Orientation Tours are 45-minute overviews of the Villa and its history, renovation, and mission, Thursday–Monday at 10:30 a.m. and 12:30 and 2:30 p.m. Getty Villa Architecture and Gardens Tours are 45-minute tours of the site and its architecture and gardens, Thursday–Monday at 11:30 a.m. and 1:30 and 3:30 p.m. Spotlight Talks are 20-minute discussions of a single object, Monday, Thursday, and Friday at 11 a.m. and Saturday and Sunday at 1:30 p.m. Collection Highlights tours are one-hour overviews of major works in the museum, Monday, Thursday, and Friday at 2 p.m. and Saturday and Sunday at 11 a.m. Focus Tours are one-hour thematic tours of the collection and exhibitions, Thursday–Monday at 3 p.m.

Audio Tours: Free

Membership: Not available, as the entire museum is funded by the Getty Foundation.

From the Editors: In 1968, J. Paul Getty replaced his hacienda house-museum with a 2,000-year old villa that had been buried in the Mount Vesuvius eruption in 79 A.D. Since the opening of the Getty Center, this breathtaking property now appropriately houses his extensive ancient Greek and Roman art collection.

HUNTINGTON LIBRARY, ART COLLECTIONS, AND BOTANICAL GARDENS
1151 Oxford Road, San Marino
626-405-2100 • huntington.org

Public Transportation: Poor (Metro Rail Gold Line Allen Avenue station is about 1-1/2 miles north of the Huntington. Nearest buses stop approximately one mile away).

Handicapped Accessibility: Fair (all areas are accessible, although some of the garden is steep and should be avoided; the Visitor's Guide contains recommended routes for wheelchairs).

Hours: Monday, Wednesday–Friday noon–4:30 p.m., Saturday and

Sunday 10:30 a.m.–4:30 p.m., closed Tuesday.

Admission: $15 weekdays, $20 weekends and Monday holidays, seniors (65+) $12/$15, students (12–18) $10, youth (5–11) $6, children (under 5) free; discounts for groups of 15 or more.

Free Day: Admission to the Huntington is free to all visitors on the first Thursday of every month with advance tickets. Hours on Free Day are 10:30 a.m.–4:30 p.m.

Tours: Free daily tours of the garden are offered with the price of admission.

Membership: Sustaining membership is $120 annually and includes full membership privileges for two adults at the same household, unlimited free admission during public hours, unlimited free admission during public hours for your children or grandchildren under 18 accompanied by a cardholder, a complimentary one-day Guest Pass, express entry so members can bypass admission lines, discounts on selected lectures, classes, and museum bookstore purchases, and invitations to special members-only events. Senior discounts are $90 (65+) and include all Sustaining membership benefits.

From the Editors: The Huntington Library, Art Collection, and Botanical Garden resides on an estate in San Marino that you may recognize from the movies. The gardens cover 120 acres and contain rare plants from around the world, separated by theme (Palm Garden, Rose Garden, Japanese Garden, Desert Garden, etc.). After taking in the sunshine and exotic greenery, inside you'll find an art collection that consists of works of 18th- and 19th-century British and French artists, and 18th–20th-century American artists.

In addition to astonishing holdings in the library (a Gutenberg Bible, for one) is the recently acquired William Morris collection, made up of books, textiles, ceramics, drawings, embroidery, wallpaper, and stained-glass relating to the pre-Raphaelite artist and designer. Programming for adults includes lectures, symposia, and films.

LOS ANGELES COUNTY MUSEUM OF ART (LACMA)
5905 Wilshire Boulevard
323-857-6000 • lacma.org

Public Transportation: Good
Handicapped Accessibility: Good
Hours: Monday, Tuesday, and Thursday noon–8 p.m., Friday noon–9 p.m., Saturday and Sunday 11 a.m.–8 p.m., closed Wednesday.

Admission: $12, seniors (62+) and students $8, children (17 and under) free. After 5 p.m. admission is pay what you wish. Discounts are available for groups of 10 or more.

Free Day: On the second Tuesday of each month, general admission to the permanent galleries and non-ticketed exhibitions is free to all. Target also sponsors free holiday Mondays throughout the year.

Tours: Free docent-led In Focus Tours are offered most days at 1 p.m.

Membership: For $90, members are entitled to unlimited free general admission to LACMA's permanent collection and non-ticketed special exhibitions for two adults and children under 18; two free tickets to specially ticketed exhibitions; a members-only line, preview and priority admission for major special exhibitions; a members-only window at the museum's box offices; and various discounts at the museum and surrounding businesses and on all museum lectures and educational programs.

Other Benefits: Patron membership ($200/annually) gets you reciprocal memberships to other area museums, as well as invites to opening parties and special museum events.

From the Editors: The Los Angeles County Museum of Art (LACMA) is a seven-building complex located in the heart of Los Angeles. Currently undergoing a 10-year expansion, the museum is growing substantially in order to display its collection of works from around the world that span, as the museum claims, "the entire history of art." This is the largest museum west of Chicago, whose impressive holdings include the collection of Asian art housed in Bruce Goff's Pavilion for Japanese Art, a wide range of Latin American art, including works by Kahlo and Rivera, and a new 60,000-square-foot space devoted to contemporary art featuring the works of Baldessari, Basquiat, Rauschenberg, Serra, and more.

Children of all ages (under 18) can join Arts for NexGen LACMA, a free membership program that offers events just for kids. After Dark is a program just for teens, which presents exhibition openings exclusively for this age group.

MUSEUM OF CONTEMPORARY ART LOS ANGELES (MOCA)
213-626-6222 • moca.org

Venues: MOCA Grand Avenue, 250 South Grand Avenue; Geffen Contemporary Art at MOCA, 152 North Central Avenue; MOCA Pacific Design Center, 8687 Melrose Avenue.

Public Transportation: Good (MOCA Grand and Geffen are located off the Metrolink Redline; the Pacific Design Center is not easily accessible by public transport).

Handicapped Accessibility: Good

Hours: MOCA Grand Avenue and Geffen Contemporary Art at MOCA Monday and Friday 11 a.m.–5 p.m., Thursday 11 a.m.–8 p.m., Saturday and Sunday 11 a.m.–6 p.m., closed Tuesday and Wednesday. MOCA Pacific Design Center Tuesday–Friday 11 a.m.–5 p.m., Saturday and Sunday 11 a.m.–6 p.m., closed Monday.

Admission: MOCA Grand Avenue and Geffen Contemporary Art at MOCA regular admission $10, seniors (65+) and students $5; free admission at MOCA Grand Avenue and the Geffen Contemporary at MOCA every Thursday 5–8 p.m. MOCA Pacific Design Center free.

Tours: Free. MOCA Grand Avenue and the Geffen Contemporary Art at MOCA offer tours throughout the day as a part of museum programming.

Membership: Basic membership is $75 annually and includes unlimited free admission for two, discounted weekend parking for MOCA Grand Avenue, invitations to all members' openings and behind-the-scenes tours.

From the Editors: The Museum of Contemporary Art Los Angeles has three functioning locations in L.A.: the MOCA Grand Avenue downtown, the Geffen Contemporary in Little Tokyo, and the Pacific Design Center in West Hollywood.

The main location, MOCA Grand Avenue, houses upwards of 5,000 contemporary artworks (from 1940 forward). Here you'll find works by de Kooning, Hockney, Lichtenstein, Rothko, and more, as well as high-profile traveling exhibitions (recently Louise Bourgeois, which originated at the Tate Modern in London and traveled to the Guggenheim Museum in New York).

The Geffen Contemporary building was originally used as a temporary space for the collection in 1983. An old 1940s hardware store renovated by Frank Gehry, the space proved to be an excellent exhibition space and continues to be utilized as the museum's space for large-scale sculptural works and installations, and as a gallery for works by lesser-known artists.

The Design Center, opened in 2000, presents new work, exhibition programming (in its 384-seat theater), and showrooms of traditional and contemporary furnishings.

Educational programming takes place at all three locations and includes excellent free programs, like First Sundays are For Families workshops, which are drop-in programs featuring hands-on activities for all ages. The second Sunday of each month is reserved for teens invited to join TOCA (Teens of Contemporary Art) in free exhibition explorations and art workshops.

NORTON SIMON MUSEUM
411 W. Colorado Boulevard, Pasadena
626-449-6840 • nortonsimon.org

Public Transportation: Excellent (bus lines 180 and 181 and the Pasadena ARTS Bus shuttle stop directly in front of the museum; rail service is also convenient).

Handicapped Accessibility: Good

Hours: Monday, Wednesday, Thursday, Saturday, and Sunday noon–6 p.m., Friday noon–9 p.m., closed Tuesday.

Admission: $8, seniors (62 and above) $4, students and patrons under 18 free; admission is free for all visitors the first Friday of every month from 6 to 9 p.m. Free admission for staff of other museums and one guest upon presentation of identification.

Tours: Free. The museum offers public tours on the first Friday of every month and free Spotlight Talks, also on Fridays. Both programs are led by museum educators. Tours start at 7 p.m. in the entrance gallery and last approximately 45 minutes. Spotlight Talks start at 2 p.m. and last approximately 15 minutes.

Audio Tours: $3

Membership: The Active membership is $65 annually and includes unlimited free admission for two adults, invitations to exhibition previews and special events, and a 20% discount in the museum store.

From the Editors: The Norton Simon Museum is named for the private collector who saved the museum when it was in the midst of financial crisis in the early 1970s. At the time, industrialist and art enthusiast Norton Simon had acquired a collection of more than 4,000 objects and was looking for a place to house the works; thus, the ailing Pasadena Art Museum became the Norton Simon Museum.

Built in 1969 from the design by Thornton Ladd and John Kelsey (the exterior is covered with 115,000 tiles made by Edith Heath), the museum underwent a major renovation and redesign in 1995.

The museum offers an impressive collection of European art from the Renaissance to the 20th century, south and southeast Asian art spanning 2,000 years, and modern and contemporary art from Europe and the U.S. Although it contains more than 12,000 objects, only about 1,000 are on view at any given time in the galleries and gardens. The museum makes use of three temporary exhibition galleries for rotating installations of artworks from the permanent collection, so it's a good place to frequent for fans of the 19th-century masters and Impressionists.

Illuminating short films about the collection, including *The Art of Nor-*

ton Simon and *Sister Wendy at the Norton Simon Museum*, are shown daily in the Norton Simon Theater, free with admission.

ORANGE COUNTY MUSEUM OF ART
850 San Clemente Drive, Newport Beach
949-759-1122 • ocma.net

> **Public Transportation:** Good (55, 57, 75, and 79 buses service the area).
> **Handicapped Accessibility:** Good
> **Hours:** Wednesday–Sunday 11 a.m.–5 p.m., Thursday 11 a.m.–8 p.m., closed Monday and Tuesday.
> **Admission:** $12, seniors (65+) and students $10, children under 12 free, 2-for-1 admission for KCRW members with valid membership.
> **Free Day:** Second Sunday of the month.
> **Tours:** Free public tours of the permanent collection are offered Thursday, Saturday, and Sunday at 1 p.m.; free tours of special exhibitions are also offered, though times vary with each exhibition.
> **Membership:** $60 annual membership entitles two people to unlimited museum visits, invitations to members' openings for major exhibitions and events, and a free subscription to the members' newsletter. Student membership is offered for $25.
> **Other Benefits:** Friend membership ($250/annually) will get you reciprocal admission to other museums.

From the Editors: Originally incorporated in the Laguna Beach Art Association, the museum took the name Orange County Museum of Art in 1996. The primary focus of the collection is modern and contemporary art focusing on California artists and art movements; there's also a strong international collection.

THEATER

A NOISE WITHIN
Masonic Temple Building, 234 S. Brand Boulevard, Glendale
818-240-0910 • anoisewithin.org

> **Public Transportation:** Good
> **Handicapped Accessibility:** Good

Performances/Programs: Performance schedule is Wednesday–Sunday.

Ticket Prices: Single tickets are $40–$44, preview tickets are $28, student Rush tickets are $20 (one hour before curtain); discounts are available for groups of 10 or more. Select performances are designated pay what you can.

Subscriptions: Six-Play premiere package $156–$240, Four-Play Patron's Choice $104–$168, Six-Play for seniors $156–$228. As You Like It Flex Pass: six vouchers $240, eight vouchers $320; 25 and Under Package: Four-Play $100, Six-Play $150.

From the Editors: If you love classic theater, (Shakespeare, Moliere, Ibsen, Shaw, Arthur Miller), then A Noise Within could easily become your favorite Los Angeles theater company. Not only do they produce exceptional productions of the great plays, they are the only company in Southern California operating in repertory (rotating productions). Over one weekend, you can easily enjoy three superb theatrical experiences.

ACTORS CO-OP THEATRE COMPANY
1760 North Gower Street, Hollywood
323-462-8460 • actorsco-op.org

Public Transportation: Good
Handicapped Accessibility: Good
Performances/Programs: Performance schedule is Friday–Sunday.

Ticket Prices: Single tickets are $30–$34; discounts available for groups of six or more; tickets can be exchanged with 24-hour notice.

Subscriptions: Subscriptions are $75–$100. Subscribers save 24%–40%. Benefits include free tickets to other co-op productions and free parking.

ANTAEUS COMPANY
Antaeus Company at Deaf West Theater
5112 Lankershim Boulevard, North Hollywood
866-811-4111 • antaeus.org

Public Transportation: Good (easily accessible by Metro Rail/North Hollywood Red Line stop).
Handicapped Accessibility: Good
Performances/Programs: Performance schedule is Friday–Sunday.

Ticket Prices: Single tickets are $20–$30; student discounts sometimes available.

THE BLANK THEATRE COMPANY
The Blank's 2nd Stage Theatre, 6500 Santa Monica Boulevard, Hollywood
323-661-9827 • theblank.com

Public Transportation: Good
Handicapped Accessibility: Good
Performances/Programs: Performance schedule is Thursday–Sunday.
Ticket Prices: Single tickets are $22–$38; shows available on Goldstar.com.
Memberships: Two membership options: $50 Gold Level (six tickets per year) and $100 Platinum Level (12 tickets). Purchase a year-long membership to get "subscriber benefits," including easy ticket exchanges and additional ticket discounts.

BROADWAY IN L.A.
Pantages Theatre, 6233 Hollywood Boulevard, Hollywood
323-468-1770 • broadwayla.org

Public Transportation: Good
Handicapped Accessibility: Good
Performances/Programs: Performance schedule is Tuesday–Sunday.
Ticket Prices: Single tickets are $32–$95. Discounts for groups of 15 or more and additional discounts vary per show.
Subscriptions: Seven-Show package $235–$644, Four-Show package $136–$365. Benefits include ticket forwarding (email tickets to family and friends if you can't use them), ticket exchanges, and lost-ticket insurance.

CABRILLO MUSIC THEATRE
Thousand Oaks Civic Arts Plaza, 2100 E. Thousand Oaks Boulevard
Thousand Oaks
805-449-2787 • cabrillomusictheatre.com

Public Transportation: Good
Handicapped Accessibility: Good
Performances/Programs: Performance schedule is Thursday–Sunday.
Ticket Prices: Single tickets are $42–$78, group discounts available.

Subscriptions: Seasonal subscriptions are $104–$236. See website for more details.

CALIFORNIA REPERTORY (CAL REP)
The Armory, 854 E. 7th Street, Long Beach
562-985-5526 • calrep.org

Public Transportation: Good
Handicapped Accessibility: Good
Performances/Programs: Performance schedule is Tuesday–Saturday.
Ticket Prices: Single tickets are $20, student $17, senior and military $15, preview performances $12.
Subscriptions: Four-Pack $64, Eight-Pack $128, Opening-Night Club $250. Benefits include invites to special events, subscriber newsletter, and free family/friend pass.

CENTER THEATRE GROUP
213-628-2772 • centertheatregroup.org

Venues: The Mark Taper Forum & Ahmanson Theatre at the Music Center, 135 N. Grand Ave; the Kirk Douglas Theatre, 9820 Washington Blvd., Culver City.
Public Transportation: Good (both venues)
Handicapped Accessibility: Good
Performances/Programs: Performance schedule is Tuesday–Sunday.
Ticket Prices: Single tickets are $30–$100; discounts available for groups of 10–20 or more (varies per show).
Subscriptions: Four-Show Ahmanson subscription $99–$420, Five-Show Kirk Douglas subscription $112–$260; discounted student subscriptions available. Benefits include money-back guarantee, free ticket exchange/replacement, and free parking.

From the Editors: The Center Theatre Group runs two of L.A.'s most distinguished theaters, the Ahmanson Theatre (often home to shows both going to and coming from Broadway) and the Mark Taper Forum (*Angels in America* and *Children of a Lesser God* started here), as well as a third that's gaining in reputation, the Kirk Douglas Theatre. The former are both located at the Music Center right in Los Angeles, and the 317-seat Kirk Douglas, which opened in 2002, is in Culver City.

CTG programs strong seasons for all three of its theaters, with the larger shows going into the mammoth Ahmanson, the midsize going into the more modest Mark Taper, and the off-beat and intimate settling into the Kirk Douglas. Each theater sells its own season subscription, but CTG also allows you to mix and match by creating your own custom subscription. Another option for people looking for flexibility is the $100 annual Passport membership, which entitles you to most of the regular subscriber benefits. Passport members can get up to two tickets at a 50% discount for each show at the three theaters.

THE CHANCE THEATER
5552 E. La Palma Avenue, Anaheim Hills
714-777-3033 • chancetheater.com

Public Transportation: Good
Handicapped Accessibility: Good
Performances/Programs: Performance schedule is Thursday–Sunday.
Ticket Prices: Single tickets are $15–$45, $3 discount for students, seniors, and military for most shows; $15–$20 student Rush tickets for students under 25 (30 minutes before curtain, cash only). Discount rates available for groups of 15 or more. No refunds or exchanges.
Subscriptions: First Three Weeks series $110 and Chance Flex Pass $120. Subscribers save 30%. Benefits include opportunity to vote on and attend the Chance's very own awards show ("the Chancies"), invites and discounts to special events, and easy ticket exchanges.

THE COLONY THEATRE
The Burbank Center Stage, 555 N. 3rd Street, Burbank
818-558-7000 • colonytheatre.org

Public Transportation: Good
Handicapped Accessibility: Good
Performances/Programs: Performance schedule is Wednesday–Sunday.
Ticket Prices: Single tickets are $37–$50, Preview tickets are $20–$25, special pay-what-you-can performances, discounts available for students, seniors, and groups.
Subscriptions: $90–$195, student (full-time) and seniors $75–$170, children (under 18, purchased with an adult subscription) $45–$75. Benefits include free ticket exchanges and free ticket replacement.

CORNERSTONE THEATER COMPANY
213-613-1700 • cornerstonetheater.org

Main Venue: 708 Traction Avenue; many performances held at alternate sites.
Public Transportation: Depends on venue.
Handicapped Accessibility: Depends on venue.
Performances/Programs: Performance schedules are generally Thursday–Sunday.
Ticket Prices: Tickets are usually a $20 suggested donation or pay what you can.

EAST WEST PLAYERS
The David Henry Hwang Theater at the Union Center for the Arts
120 North Judge John Aiso Street
213-625-7000 • eastwestplayers.org

Public Transportation: Very good (via DASH)
Handicapped Accessibility: Good
Performances/Programs: Performance schedule is Wednesday–Sunday.
Ticket Prices: Single tickets are $30–$50, Preview tickets $20–$25, opening night $60–$70, $10 tickets to previews for students or anyone under 18, plus $5 off regular performances; seniors get $5 off regular performance price. $20 tickets for deaf and hard-of-hearing people who attend special ASL-interpreted performances. Discounts for groups of 15 or more. No exchanges for single tickets.
Subscriptions: Subscriptions are $125, $200 for opening night; $85 for preview; $85 for ASL; $110 for student and senior. Subscribers save 20%. Benefits include free ticket exchanges and replacements.

THE FOUNTAIN THEATRE
5060 Fountain Avenue
323-663-1525 • fountaintheatre.com

Public Transportation: Good
Handicapped Accessibility: Good
Performances/Programs: Performances are Thursday–Sunday.
Ticket Prices: Single tickets are $25–$30, previews $15, $18 student tickets (Thursday and Friday), $23 senior tickets (Thursday and Friday).

Membership: Opening-Night memberships $100, Regular Show memberships $84, Preview memberships $52. Benefits include preferred seating, free parking and discounts to other theaters.

FULLERTON CIVIC LIGHT OPERA
Plummer Auditorium, 201 E. Chapman Avenue, Fullerton
714-879-1732 • fclo.com

Public Transportation: Good (accessible via Amtrak and local bus lines)
Handicapped Accessibility: Good
Performances/Programs: Performance schedule is Thursday–Sunday.
Ticket Prices: Single tickets are $25–$52; 50% discount for active military personnel. Discounts available for groups of 20 or more.
Subscriptions: Four-Show subscriptions $75–$156, Flex Pass $128 (same benefits as above, except for exchange privileges). Benefits include ticket replacement and one free exchange per production ($5 fee for additional exchanges).

GEFFEN PLAYHOUSE
Geffen Playhouse and Audrey Skirball Kenis Theater
10886 Le Conte Avenue
310-208-5454 • geffenplayhouse.com

Public Transportation: Good
Handicapped Accessibility: Good
Performances/Programs: Performance schedule is Tuesday–Sunday.
Ticket Prices: Single tickets are $40–$115. Occasional discounts for students, seniors, and educators.
Subscriptions: Subscriptions are $170–$425. Subscribers save an average of $80. Benefits include free ticket exchange (with 24-hours notice). Non-subscribers are not eligible for ticket transfers.

From the Editors: Originally called the Westwood Playhouse, the Geffen was later renamed for its benefactor, movie bigwig David Geffen. Appropriately, Geffen Playhouse productions often star Hollywood actors, which may account for its ticket prices being higher than most local theaters. The discount options aren't overwhelming, but the Geffen does have an Industry Insider program that notifies people by email when discounted tickets (as low as $10) become available. Sign up for free at: geffenplayhouse.com/industry.

The Geffen Playhouse's Signature Series helps make the theater experience a more social affair. Jazz and complimentary wine tastings are on the menu on Wine Down Sundays, while vodka, beer, and appetizers are on hand during the post-show party at selected Girls Night Out shows. On Talk Back Tuesdays, coffee and tea are offered before the show and a stimulating Q&A is held afterwards. Lounge Fridays bring a laid-back club experience right to the Geffen, providing theatergoers with music, eats, and cocktails before the performance. The Geffen also has a family series called Saturday Scene that presents music programs and children's shows at 11 a.m. on Saturday mornings.

INTERNATIONAL CITY THEATRE
Center Theater, Long Beach Performing Arts Center
300 E. Ocean Boulevard, Long Beach
562-436-4610 • ictlongbeach.org

Public Transportation: Good
Handicapped Accessibility: Good
Performances/Programs: Performance schedule is Thursday–Sunday.
Ticket Prices: Single tickets are $19–$42, $5 discount for full-time students under 24, seniors, and Chamber of Commerce members (limit two). KCRW Fringe Benefits cardholders and DLBA Passport holders get 2-for-1 admission for Thursday and Friday performances (limit two). Discounts for groups of 15 or more.
Subscriptions: Subscriptions are $109–$250; Flex subscription $175; student subscription $74; educator subscription $109. Benefits include free ticket exchanges, free ticket insurance, 50% off parking, and discounts on ICT's Summer Youth Conservatory tuition.

L.A. THEATRE WORKS
681 Venice Boulevard, Venice
310-827-0808 • latw.org

Public Transportation: Good
Handicapped Accessibility: Good
Performances/Programs: Performance schedule varies, but generally Wednesday–Sunday.
Ticket Prices: Single tickets are $39.50–$47, student tickets are $20, subscribers save up to 20%.

Subscriptions: VIP subscription $365–$375; Five-Play subscription $200; Three-Play subscription $127. Benefits include lost-ticket insurance (for VIP subscribers only) and free parking.

LAGUNA PLAYHOUSE
Moulton Theater, 606 Laguna Canyon Road, Laguna Beach
949-497-ARTS (2787) • lagunaplayhouse.com

Public Transportation: Good
Handicapped Accessibility: Good
Performances/Programs: Performance schedule is Tuesday–Sunday.
Ticket Prices: Single tickets are $25–$65. Students, educators, and active military personnel are eligible for discounts. Full-time students eligible for 50% discount on tickets at some performances, $25 Rush tickets available for some performances. Discounts available for groups of 10 or more. Non-subscribers can exchange tickets for a $10 fee ($20 if less than 24 hours notice).
Subscriptions: $175–$413, subscribers save up to 20%. Benefits include one free ticket exchange per show and discounts on additional single tickets.

MUSICAL THEATRE WEST
Carpenter Performing Arts Center
(Cal State University/Long Beach Campus)
6200 Atherton Street, Long Beach
866-710-4MTW (4689) • musical.org

Public Transportation: Good (accessible by bus)
Handicapped Accessibility: Good
Performances/Programs: Performance schedule is Thursday–Sunday.
Ticket Prices: Single tickets are $25–$53. Some discounts available for children, students, and seniors.
Subscriptions: Four-Show subscriptions are $100–$200. Subscription discounts available for children (16 and under) $75–$100, and teachers $100–$180.

NORTH COAST REPERTORY THEATRE
987 Lomas Santa Fe Dr., Suite D, Solana Beach
858-481-1055 • northcoastrep.org

Public Transportation: Fair
Handicapped Accessibility: Good
Performances/Programs: Performance schedule is Wednesday–Sunday.
Ticket Prices: Single tickets are $28–$48. Discounts are available to active duty military, students, educators and seniors for most performances. Ticket exchanges are $2 for non-subscribers.
Subscriptions: 7-Show season subscriptions $162–$255; students, seniors, and military, $155–$241. Subscriber benefits include free unlimited ticket exchanges and ticket insurance.

ODYSSEY THEATRE ENSEMBLE
2055 S. Sepulveda Boulevard
310-477-2055 • odysseytheatre.com

Public Transportation: Good
Handicapped Accessibility: Good
Performances/Programs: Performance schedule is Wednesday–Sunday.
Ticket Prices: Single ticket prices are $25–$30. Discounts are available for students and members of Actor's Equity/SAG/AFTRA. Discounts for groups of 10 or more.
Subscriptions: Six-Play subscriptions are $90–$135; Nine-Play subscriptions $120–$190. Flex option: six vouchers for $140.

PASADENA PLAYHOUSE
39 South El Molino Avenue, Pasadena
626-356-7529 • pasadenaplayhouse.org

Public Transportation: Fair (accessible via combo of Metro Gold Line and Metro bus).
Handicapped Accessibility: Good
Performances/Programs: Performance schedule is Tuesday–Sunday.
Ticket Prices: Single ticket prices are $25–$72, $15–$25 tickets for full-time students under 30. Discounts are available for groups of 15 or more.

Subscriptions: Multiple subscription packages, including those that include tickets for an entire season's worth of shows as well as a flex-pass option, are available. Discount subscription rates offered for full-time students under 25. Benefits include free ticket exchanges and free tickets to Hothouse New Play Development Series.

From the Editors: Founded in 1917 and declared the State Theatre of California in 1937, the beautiful Pasadena Playhouse enjoyed a reputation as "Hollywood's talent factory" for many years as it churned out great actors like William Holden, Eve Arden, Robert Preston, Gene Hackman, and Dustin Hoffman. Superman's (George Reeve's) 1959 memorial service was held here. Financial woes forced the Playhouse to close in 1969, but it reopened several years later and is going strong, once more.

Diversity is the name of the game these days, and Pasadena Playhouse's seasons are invariably full of new musicals, classics, contemporary dramas, and light-hearted fare. The Playhouse's Theatrical Diversity Project and the Hothouse reading series help ensure that it has a steady stream of interesting new projects, while the Directors Lab West program nurtures new directors and other artists.

The 99-seat Carrie Hamilton Theatre (which is undergoing a Frank Gehry-designed renovation) provides a venue for the Playhouse's developmental work; it's also home to edgy artist-in-residence, the Furious Theatre Company.

REPRISE THEATRE COMPANY
The Freud Playhouse (on the UCLA campus), MacGowan Hall
405 Hilgard Avenue
310-825-2101 • reprise.org

Public Transportation: Good
Handicapped Accessibility: Good
Performances/Programs: Performance schedule is Tuesday–Sunday.
Ticket Prices: Single tickets are $60–$75. Ticketmaster discounts are often available. No ticket exchanges for non-subscribers.
Subscriptions: Four-Show packages $220–$260. Benefits include ticket exchanges, lost-ticket insurance, and new tickets issued for missed shows.

RUBICON THEATRE COMPANY
1006 E Main Street, Ventura
805-667-2900 • rubicontheatre.org

Public Transportation: Good
Handicapped Accessibility: Poor (house is accessible, but no handicapped restrooms or parking).
Performances/Programs: Performance schedule is Wednesday–Sunday.
Ticket Prices: Single tickets are $29–$57, seniors get $5 discount (except for previews), $20 tickets for students and members of Actors Equity. Discounts are available for groups of 12 or more.
Subscriptions: Six-Play $161–$278, Seven-Play $185–$322, and Eight-Play packages $198–$345. Student and teacher subscriptions are $120 (Six-Play), $140 (Seven-Play), and $160 (Eight-Play). Flex passes available $227–$366. Benefits include ticket exchanges and lost-ticket insurance.

SOUTH COAST REPERTORY
655 Town Center Drive, Costa Mesa
714-708-5555 • scr.org

Public Transportation: Good
Handicapped Accessibility: Good
Performances/Programs: Performance schedule is Tuesday–Sunday.
Ticket Prices: Single ticket prices are $20–$62. Discounts are available for full-time students, patrons 25 and under, educators, and seniors. Pay-What-You-Will shows offered occasionally ($7 minimum). Discounts available for groups of 15 or more.
Subscriptions: Five-Play Segerstrom Stage $155–$275, Four-Play Argyros Stage $124–$220, entire Nine-Play season $279–$495, and Three-Play Theatre for Young Audiences Season $45–$72. Subscription discounts available for seniors, full-time students 25 and under, and first-time subscribers under 35. Benefits include free ticket exchanges, lost-ticket insurance, and $40 off South Coast Rep acting classes.

From the Editors: New plays, premieres, multicultural works, classics, and the occasional musical can be found at South Coast Repertory, which each year produces six shows on its main stage, five on its smaller second stage and three family shows (Theatre for Young Audiences).

SCR's holiday traditions include not only the perennial favorite *A Christmas Carol*, but also *La Posada Magica* (*The Magical Journey*), Octavio Solis and Marcos Loya's imaginative tale about a little girl's Christmas Eve adventures in her community. *La Posada Magica* is in English, but it's infused with Latin music and spirit. SCR encourages other such works with its Hispanic Playwright Project, a program that began in 1986 and since then has workshopped more than 50 pieces by such playwrights as Eduardo Machado, Jose Rivera, Edwin Sanchez, Nilo Cruz, and Caridad Svich (over half of the plays have gone on to receive full productions at the Rep). Other development programs include Collaboration Laboratory, the staged reading series NewSCRipts, and the annual Pacific Playwrights Festival.

Each year, SCR also offers its subscribers theatrical excursions to New York City and London, which include airfare, hotel, sightseeing tours, and tickets to three productions. It's all for a price, of course, but it's a great way to enjoy Broadway and the West End with your fellow theater fanatics.

THEATRE WEST
3333 Cahuenga Boulevard West
323-851-7977 • theatrewest.org

Public Transportation: Good
Handicapped Accessibility: Fair (house is accessible, bathrooms are not).
Performances/Programs: Performance schedule is Friday–Sunday.
Ticket Prices: Single tickets are $10–$40. Discount available for groups of 12 or more.

WILL GEER THEATRICUM BOTANICUM
1419 N. Topanga Canyon Boulevard, Topanga
310-455-3723 • theatricum.com

Public Transportation: Poor
Handicapped Accessibility: Good
Performances/Programs: Performance schedule Thursday–Sunday.
Ticket Prices: Single tickets are $15. Discounts available for children (under 12) and veterans.
Subscriptions: Five-Play $126 and Four-Play $100. Significant subscription discounts for students, seniors, families, Actors Equity members, and Iraq War veterans.

CLASSICAL MUSIC

LOS ANGELES CHAMBER ORCHESTRA (LACO)
213-622-7001 • laco.org

Venues: Alex Theatre, 216 North Brand Boulevard, Glendale; Royce Dr & W. Sunset Blvd, Westwood; Zipper Concert Hall, 200 South Grand Avenue, Los Angeles

Public Transportation: Depends on venue.

Handicapped Accessibility: Depends on venue.

Performances/Programs: Between 16 and 21 concerts are performed annually.

Ticket Prices: Prices range from $18 to $95, depending on seat. Student Rush tickets are available for $10 one hour before show time; students and seniors may purchase tickets for Section D for Orchestral Series concerts at the Alex Theatre and Royce Hall for $42 (regularly $50).

Group Discounts: Groups of 12 or more may receive discounts up to 15% off.

Subscriptions: Various options are offered, including the Orchestral series, which includes tickets to all seven orchestral concerts given in a season, and the Flex series, offering four concerts of your choosing. Conversations is a four-concert series with each performance ending with a question-and-answer forum. Baroque and Family subscriptions are also available. Benefits include free ticket exchange and lost-ticket replacement.

Activities for Children: The Family Concert series offers a musical experience appropriate for families with children five years and older. From 1 to 2 p.m., these concerts feature an instrument "petting zoo" where children get to try out instruments, followed by a 2 p.m. family concert.

LOS ANGELES CHAMBER SINGERS & CAPPELLA
310-575-9790 • lacs.org

Venues: Various locations.

Public Transportation: Varies based on venue.

Handicapped Accessibility: Please contact venue for accessibility info

Ticket Prices: General admission $25, advance purchase $20, students and seniors $15.

Group Discounts: Discounts available for groups of 10 or more.

Subscriptions: Available, inquire for prices through website.

LOS ANGELES MASTER CHORALE
Walt Disney Concert Hall, 111 South Grand Avenue
213-972-7282 • lamc.org

Public Transportation: Good
Handicapped Accessibility: Good
Performances/Programs: Nine performances per season and various special events such as L.A. Philharmonic appearances.
Ticket Prices: $32–$110 for single tickets.
Group Discounts: Discounts available for groups of 8 or more.
Subscriptions: Full seven-concert series available for $231–$749, or four-concert series for $132–$428, depending on seat selection. Create your own series option also available. Subscriber benefits include free ticket exchanges and lost ticket replacement.
Membership: Available from $100–$5,000+. Based on donation amount, membership benefits include program recognition, rehearsal invite, and self-park vouchers.

   From the Editors: The Los Angeles Master Chorale is the resident chorus of the Walt Disney Concert Hall, notable for both its eye-popping Frank Gehry design and its outstanding acoustics. Since 2001, the Chorale has been under the musical direction of Grant Gershon, who has assisted the chorus in building a large audience base and a more extensive musical repertoire. Some of the L.A. Master Chorale's exciting projects have included the multi-year "Homage to Haydn" and outreach programs that bring the Chorale's masterful musicianship to wider audiences. The Chorale has even been heard in movie theaters around the world on the soundtracks to films like *My Best Friend's Wedding*, *Bram Stoker's Dracula*, and *Lady in the Water*.

LOS ANGELES PHILHARMONIC (L.A. PHIL)
Walt Disney Concert Hall, 111 South Grand Avenue
323-850-2000 • laphil.com

Public Transportation: Good (accessible by Red Line Metro)
Handicapped Accessibility: Good
Performances/Programs: Over 200 performances annually.
Ticket Prices: Prices range from $24 to $195. Students and seniors with valid ID can purchase $10 tickets, based upon availability, beginning two hours prior to select concerts.
Group Discounts: Offered for groups of 10+.

Subscriptions: There are many options available for classical, jazz, contemporary, and world-music subscriptions, as well as a Choose Your Own option. There are also special discounts for students and seniors. Subscription tickets can be exchanged, subject to availability. Emergency ticket exchanges can only be made at the box office, up to 5 p.m. on the day of the performance you wish to exchange. Exchanges cannot be made on the day of a matinée concert. The emergency exchange fee is $10 per ticket.

Subscriber Benefits: Subscribers (except Choose Your Own patrons) receive a 20% discount on additional tickets for regular Los Angeles Philharmonic concerts, as well as other discounts for performances at Hollywood Bowl, subject to availability. Additional discounts are offered by local merchants and restaurants with an L.A. Phil subscriber ID Card.

Membership: Prelude Membership begins at $75 (tax-deductible). Benefits include a Friends membership card offering a 10% discount at the L.A. Phil and Hollywood Bowl stores and exclusive access to Friends helpline for inquiries about Friends membership and benefits.

Special Memberships for Families, Children and Young Adults: Junior Patron membership is an annual option at a cost of $75 for the first two children and $25 for each additional child. In addition to all the benefits your child receives, $58 of your contribution is tax-deductible. Benefits include a Junior Patron membership card with 10% discount at the L.A. Phil store in Walt Disney Concert Hall and at the Hollywood Bowl store; your child's name listed in the Toyota Symphonies for Youth programs; a Junior Patron T-shirt; an invitation to a Meet the Artist event following the final Toyota Symphonies for Youth concert; an invitation to a Hollywood Bowl rehearsal (including refreshments); and year-round listing on the L.A. Phil/Hollywood Bowl website.

From the Editors: In 1919, a multi-millionaire and amateur musician established Los Angeles' first permanent symphony orchestra, the Los Angeles Philharmonic. Under the direction of Walter Henry Rothwell, 94 musicians brought from the St. Paul Symphony in Minnesota came together to perform at the Trinity Auditorium in L.A. The next year, the Orchestra built the Philharmonic Auditorium, which it called home for the next 44 years.

Today, under the direction of Esa-Pekka Salonen, the L.A. Philharmonic enjoys world recognition. In addition to its regular series concerts, the Phil offers free community concerts, which they post on their website, along with special concerts designed especially for young people. Toyota Symphonies for Youth, a Saturday-morning concert series, is geared toward children 5–11 years old. Before the concert there are many special activities for the kids. SummerSounds, a program that began in 1968, is a performing arts festival for youth at the Hollywood Bowl that takes place each summer. The festival, a six-week series from July to August, offers two concerts each weekday morning designed especially for kids 3–10 years old.

PACIFIC CHORALE
Orange County Performing Arts Center
615 Town Center Drive, Cost Mesa
714-662-2345 • pacificchorale.org

Public Transportation: Accessible via OCTA.

Handicapped Accessibility: Good

Performances/Programs: Five performances per season, plus special concert events.

Ticket Prices: $20–$140, discounts for students and seniors are available by phone.

Subscriptions: Three-concert subscriptions $45–$400, and five-concert subscriptions $90–$500, with prices varying based on seat selection. Students and seniors eligible for subscription discount. Subscriber benefits include 20% savings, seating priority, ticket exchanges, and 10% discount on additional single ticket purchases.

Membership: Yearly dues to join the Pacific Chorale Guild are $50 per individual/family. Guild benefits include newsletter subscription, priority invites to benefits and special events, and discounts on Guild-sponsored events.

From the Editors: Founded in 1968, the Pacific Chorale is made up of 140 professional-level singers and has long been under the musical direction of John Alexander. The group has toured internationally several times and collaborated with many international symphonies. The Pacific Chorale also has a 24-member ensemble, known as the John Alexander Singers, that specializes in chamber music. Given that the group's eclectic concerts feature everything from beloved holiday songs and hymns to great choral masterpieces and little-known classical works, it's no wonder that the Pacific Chorale received the 2005 ASCAP Chorus America Alice Parker Award for adventurous programming. For an excellent primer on choral music, visit the "Discover Choral Music" section of the Pacific Chorale website.

WORLD FESTIVAL OF SACRED MUSIC
310-825-0507 • festivalofsacredmusic.org

Venue: Venues throughout Los Angeles
Public Transportation: Depends on venue.
Handicapped Accessibility: Depends on venue.
Performances/Programs: Festival occurs every three years (next in 2011), 41 events are offered.
Ticket Prices: Prices vary. Some are suggested donation. Student and senior tickets may be available at a discounted rate for select performances and events.
Membership: Mandala Level membership begins at $250 and benefits include two tickets for the Opening Gala concert, two tickets to VIP Donor reception with international artists at Opening Concert, plus name recognition in the Opening Concert program book.

From the Editors: Over the past ten years, WFSM-LA has brought together tens of thousands of people of diverse ethnic, religious, and cultural backgrounds, including artists of all types, community and religious leaders, educators, and students. With a combined total of 185 multidisciplinary events presenting the work of 6,000 artists in 180 diverse venues across Los Angeles and an attendance of 200,000 people at the 1999, 2002, and 2005 Festivals, WFSM-LA is the largest citywide festival currently active in Los Angeles.

OPERA

LOS ANGELES OPERA
Dorothy Chandler Pavilion, 135 N. Grand Avenue
213-972-7219/213-972-8001 • laopera.com

Public Transportation: Good
Handicapped Accessibility: Good
Performances/Programs: Eight–nine full productions and recitals with notable opera singers per season.
Ticket Prices: $15–$260 for opera productions, depending on date, time, performances, and seats selected. $25–$100 for recitals.
Subscriptions: Four to nine show subscriptions available, prices vary

depending on date, time, and performances selected; contact for details. A flexible design your own series is also available.

Membership: Available from $75–$3,500. Benefits include restaurant discounts, 10% off merchandise at the Opera Shop and Dutton's bookstores, and an invite to the Opera Insights event; higher level donors get dress rehearsal passes and access to the Members Lounge.

From the Editors: In just over 20 years of existence, the Los Angeles Opera has become the fourth largest opera company in the United States and gained international recognition. The company has a celebrity for its general director, famed tenor Plácido Domingo, who actually starred in LA Opera's premiere production of Verdi's Otello in 1986. Domingo has also sung in over 100 performances with the Opera and conducted many other performances. LA Opera sponsors several notable Education and Community Programs that have served over 1 million people to date, especially low-income groups and people who don't normally get much exposure to opera in all its grandeur.

JAZZ/CABARET

THE BAKED POTATO
3787 Cahuenga Boulevard West, Studio City
818-980-1615 • thebakedpotato.com

Public Transportation: Poor
Handicapped Accessibility: Good
Performances/Programs: Approximately 350 performances per year. Sets begin at 9:30 and 11:30 p.m. nightly.
Ticket Prices: $15–$20 cover and a two-drink minimum.

CATALINA JAZZ CLUB
6725 W. Sundayset Boulevard, Ste. 100
323-466-2210 • catalinajazzclub.com

Public Transportation: Good
Handicapped Accessibility: Good
Performances/Programs: Approximately 180 performances per year.

Shows Monday–Saturday at 8 and 10 p.m.; Sunday at 7:30 and 9:30 p.m.

Ticket Prices: $20–$30, plus dinner or two-drink minimum. Half-price tickets are sometimes available on Goldstar.com.

HIP KITTY JAZZ & FONDUE
502 W 1ˢᵗ Street, Claremont
909-447-6700 • hipkittyjazz.com

Public Transportation: Poor
Handicapped Accessibility: Good
Performances/Programs: Approximately 300 performances are presented annually. Live jazz is played Tuesday–Sunday 8 p.m.–midnight.
Ticket Prices: A $5 cover is charged Thursday–Saturday.

JAZZ BAKERY
3233 Helms Boulevard, Culver City
310-271-9039 • jazzbakery.com

Public Transportation: Poor
Handicapped Accessibility: Good
Performances/Programs: Approximately 300 performances are given each year.
Ticket Prices: $25–$40. A student Rush discount with ID is offered. Not valid for reservations. Occasional half-price tickets on Goldstar. Admission is free for small children (sit-on-lap, no-charge policy).
Group Discounts: 10% discount for groups of 10 or more.
Subscriptions: Two tiers of donation levels are offered for $500 and $1,000. These Upper Crust cardholders and their guests receive tickets for a maximum of 15 or 30 performances, respectively, depending on the donation level.

From the Editors: The Jazz Bakery, one of Los Angeles' premier musical venues, is any jazz-lover's dream. Rather than a supper club or bar with a jazz afterthought, the Bakery is a theater-style venue with the music as the one and only focus. It's also one of the only non-profit jazz venues on the West Coast and as a result draws some of the world's greatest.

Begun 11 years ago, the Jazz Bakery was conceived by Ruth Price as a no-frills all-about-the-music space that features live performances almost every night, usually two sets at 8 and 9:30 p.m. There's also a 4 p.m. Sunday matinée. The ticket prices can be a bit steep, but remember that this venue runs solely on the ticket sales and donations. There are no $10 cocktails to pad the profit margin. Tickets are generally $25–$35.

LA VE LEE
12514 Ventura Boulevard, Studio City
818-980-8158 • laveleejazzclub.com

Public Transportation: Poor
Handicapped Accessibility: Good
Performances/Programs: 240 performances per year. Live jazz is performed Tuesday–Saturday, with sets at 8:30 and 10:30 p.m.
Ticket Prices: Usually a $10 cover, plus two-drink minimum per person. Occasional half-price tickets are available on Goldstar.com.

PASADENA JAZZ INSTITUTE
260 East Colorado Boulevard, Ste. 206, Pasadena
626-398-3344 • pasjazz.org

Public Transportation: Poor
Handicapped Accessibility: Good
Performances/Programs: About 300 performances per year. Live jazz is played most nights of the week at 8 p.m.
Ticket Prices: From $10–$20. Occasionally half-price tickets are available through Goldstar.

SPAZIO
14755 Ventura Boulevard Ste. D, Sherman Oaks
818-728-8400 • spazio.la

Public Transportation: Poor
Handicapped Accessibility: Good
Performances/Programs: Approximately 300 performances annually. Live Jazz nightly at 8 p.m. Jazz brunch on Sunday from 10:30 a.m. to 2 p.m.
Ticket Prices: No cover charge.

VIBRATO GRILL & JAZZ
2930 N Beverly Glen Circle
310-474-9400 • vibratogrilljazz.com

Public Transportation: Poor
Handicapped Accessibility: No
Performances/Programs: Approximately 260 performances per year. Hours are Tuesday–Sunday from 6:30 p.m. till close.
Ticket Prices: No cover.

ANGEL CITY JAZZ FESTIVAL
Barnsdall Art Park, 4800 Hollywood Boulevard
angelcityjazzfestival.com

Public Transportation: Poor
Handicapped Accessibility: Good
Performances/Programs: All performances take place one day per year (generally Labor Day). Approximately 15 performances are given during the festival on two different stages.
Ticket Prices: $25 presale, $35 at the door. A $50 VIP pass is also available. Tickets are $15 for students with ID. Children under 13 are free.

From the Editors: The Angel City Jazz Festival has a wide range of different styles and genres, from straight-ahead jazz to hard bop, acoustic piano to avant-garde. This Labor Day festival even features performance art from time to time. Tickets are best purchased online, as there's a $10 discount for presale purchases. The festival is based at the Barnsdall Art Park overlooking Los Angeles.

 DANCE

DIAVOLO
714-979-4700 • diavolo.org

Venue: Recent performance locations have included the Hollywood Bowl and UCLA's Freud Playhouse.
Public Transportation: Poor
Handicapped Accessibility: Good

Performances/Programs: Diavolo tours with selections of about a dozen pieces and generally performs in each location for one or two days. The company also regularly holds open informal showings of their work at their own studio located at 616 N. Moulton Avenue. Contact the company business manager for exact dates.

Ticket Prices: Tickets generally run $15–$40.

LOS ANGELES BALLET (LAB)
310-998-7782 • losangelesballet.org

Venues: Alex Theatre Glendale, 216 North Brand Avenue, Glendale; Broad Stage Santa Monica, 1310 11th Street, Santa Monica; Freud Playhouse, UCLA, MacGowan Hall; Redondo Beach Performing Arts Center, 1935 Manhattan Beach Blvd., Redondo Beach; Royce Hall, UCLA, 340 Royce Drive, Los Angeles; Irvine Barclay Theatre, 4242 Campus Drive, Irvine.

Public Transportation: Depends on venue.

Handicapped Accessibility: Good (all venues)

Performances/Programs: Three programs per year, five performances each.

Ticket Prices: Range from $30 to $95. Seniors (65+) and children (12 and under) receive 20% off all standard ticket prices. For the *Nutcracker* Family Package series, children 12 and under receive 50% off standard ticket prices and students ages 13 to 17 receive 20% off.

Group Discounts: Groups of 15 or more may purchase tickets at a discounted rate. Actual discounts vary.

Subscriptions: Subscriptions are available for each presenting venue and within each venue selection there are two or three packages available. Packages generally include multiple themed performances. All ticket sales are final. Benefits include priority seating and ticket exchanges.

Membership: Membership is $125 and includes a subscription to LAB online newsletter, a LAB T-shirt, and 10% off merchandise at the LAB Gift Boutique.

Special Young People's Membership: Friends of LAB (for children 14 and under) membership is $35 and sponsors small items for dancers such as make-up and shoes. Friends of LAB receive a LAB T-shirt and 15% off merchandise at the LAB Gift Boutique.

LULA WASHINGTON DANCE THEATRE
Harriet & Charles Luckman Fine Arts Complex, CSU Los Angeles
5151 State University Drive
323-292-5852 • lulawashington.com

Public Transportation: Good
Handicapped Accessibility: Good
Performances/Programs: Two programs each year, one performance each.
Ticket Prices: $30. Students and children 18 and under may purchase specially priced tickets. Actual prices vary by performance. Seniors may purchase tickets at a 20% discount. Members of DRC, K-JAZZ, KCET, KMZT, KCRW, and KUSC receive 20% off regular prices. Additionally, Cal State L.A. faculty, staff and alumni-association members receive 20% off regular prices. Members of the military also receive 20% off regular prices.
Group Discounts: Groups of 15 or more receive a 20% discount on all tickets booked in advance.

CADANCE/LAGUNA DANCE FESTIVAL
Artists' Theatre, 625 Park Avenue, Laguna Beach
949-715-5578 • dancelaguna.com

Public Transportation: Poor
Handicapped Accessibility: Good
Performances/Programs: CaDance is a non-profit organization that presents the Laguna Dance Festival each September. Events and performances stretch over about two weeks.
Ticket Prices: Many of the events happening on the Main Beach are free. Concert tickets run about $50. Seniors can purchase tickets for $45 and student tickets are $35.

FILM

ACADEMY OF MOTION PICTURE ARTS AND SCIENCES
310-247-3000
oscars.org/events-exhibitions/venues-ticketing/index.html

Venues: The Academy Foundation and the Samuel Goldwyn Theater,

8949 Wilshire Boulevard, Beverly Hills; the Linwood Dunn Theater, 1313 Vine Street, Hollywood.

Public Transportation: Good (venues are all accessible by public buses).

Handicapped Accessibility: Good (all venues)

Performances/Programs: The Academy screens a variety of fare, including Oscar award-winning films, acclaimed documentaries, Hollywood blockbusters, foreign classics, and more.

Ticket Prices: Ticket prices vary, but can be purchased by mail, online, or in person at the box office.

From the Editors: Hollywood legends Louis B. Mayer and Douglas Fairbanks helped found the Academy of Motion Picture Arts and Sciences in 1927. The organization was created for the purpose of appreciating, developing, and preserving the American film institution, a mission that it continues to fulfill to this day by maintaining an enormous film library and by offering its members screenings in its state-of-the-art theaters.

AMPAS is best known to the general public for its creation and annual presentation of the Academy Awards (the Oscars), which honor the achievements of great films and the people who make them.

AMERICAN FILM INSTITUTE
2021 N. Western Avenue
323-856-7600 • afi.com

Venues: Screenings are held at multiple venues including the Silver Theater and the Arclight Cinemas in Hollywood and Sherman Oaks. See AFI website for more details.

Public Transportation: Depends on venue.

Handicapped Accessibility: Good (all venues)

Performances/Programs: Vary, but include everything from *Duck Soup* to *Dirty Dancing*.

Ticket Prices: Vary, but members receive discounts and special invitations to advance screenings.

From the Editors: Founded in 1967 with a mission to preserve the heritage of American film, the American Film Institute has the largest library of feature films in the world. As a result, AFI screenings include the widest possible variety of titles, from silent classics to modern hits. With generous funding from organizations like the MPAA and the NEA, the American Film Institute was able to create a training program that has educated such distinguished directors as Paul Schrader, Terrence Malick, and David Lynch. AFI is also known for compiling lists of the best films in different categories, based on polling done among notables in the film industry.

NEW BEVERLY CINEMA
7165 West Beverly Boulevard
323-938-4038 • newbevcinema.com

Public Transportation: Very good (easily accessible by MTA 14, 714 and 712 buses).
Handicapped Accessibility: Fair (theater is accessible, restrooms are not).
Performances/Programs: Hollywood classics, independent film, European and Asian favorites.
Ticket Prices: All shows are double features, cash only. General admission is $7; students with ID $6; seniors and kids $4.

NUART THEATRE
11272 Santa Monica Boulevard
310-281-8223
landmarktheatres.com/market/LosAngeles/NuartTheatre.htm

Public Transportation: Poor
Handicapped Accessibility: Good
Performances/Programs: Independent and foreign films, documentaries, animation festivals, and restored prints of classics.
Ticket Prices: Vary based on program.

From the Editors: Located on Santa Monica Boulevard, the Nuart Theatre is the best art-house movie theater in Los Angeles. Foreign films, independent features, documentaries, and old classics all figure into Nuart's regular programming, and world premieres and festivals can regularly be seen here as well. Other special events include question-and-answer sessions with filmmakers, actor appearances, and a weekly midnight screening of the interactive cult favorite, *The Rocky Horror Picture Show*.

PERFORMANCE VENUES

THE BARCLAY
Irvine Barclay Theatre, 4242 Campus Drive, Irvine
949-854-4646 • thebarclay.org

> **Public Transportation:** Very good (easily accessible by bus).
> **Handicapped Accessibility:** Good
> **Performances/Programs:** The Barclay is 750-seat theater located near the University of California at Irvine campus. Programming includes ballet, modern dance, jazz, classical and choral music, world-music artists, vocalists, chamber music, musical theater, film, family shows, opera, and more. Shows available on Goldstar.com.
> **Ticket Prices:** Vary by program. See website for schedule and details.
> **Subscriptions/Membership:** NEXT@thebarclay is a group aimed at young professionals ($60 for individuals, $100 for couples). NEXT membership includes discount tickets to select performances and invites to special events.

CERRITOS CENTER FOR THE PERFORMING ARTS
Cerritos Towne Center, 12700 Center Court Drive, Cerritos
800-300-4345 • cerritoscenter.com

> **Public Transportation:** Very good
> **Handicapped Accessibility:** Good
> **Performances/Programs:** Season runs from August to May an annual schedule includes over 150 performances. Programming includes concerts, dance, cabaret, comedy, musicals, family shows, orchestras, opera, magic, jazz, circus, and other events.
> **Ticket Prices:** Vary based on program.
> **Group Discounts:** Discounts available for groups of 20 or more.
> **Subscriptions/Membership:** Subscription discounts available for some series, such as the What Makes It Great series.

FORD AMPHITHEATRE
John Anson Ford Theatres, 2580 Cahuenga Boulevard East
323-461-3673 • fordamphitheater.org

Public Transportation: Very good
Handicapped Accessibility: Good
Performances/Programs: The Ford's summer season runs May to October. Summer-season programming includes the Los Angeles Film Festival, the Big!World!Fun! family series ($5 tickets for adults, free for children), world music and dance, and all kinds of American music, classical music, theater, and other performance events. The Ford opens its terraced entryway two hours prior to each performance for picnics (you can bring your own meal or order a box dinner in advance from Ford's caterers, or purchase from on-site concessions). In addition to its summer slate, the Ford offers Inside: the Ford New Play Series, which runs from November to May each season.
Ticket Prices: Vary based on program. Students pay $12 for single tickets (regular single ticket price is $20). Additionally, students and children (ages 12 and under) pay only $5 for tickets to dance events. J.A.M. Sessions offered for free.
Group Discounts: Discounts available for groups of eight or more.
Subscriptions/Membership: The Summer Season subscription offers a 20% savings when buying tickets for three or more events. Inside subscriptions ($45–$60) offer a 25% savings. Shows available on Goldstar.com.

GALLIMAUFRY PERFORMING ARTS
949-499-5060 • gallimaufry.info

Venues: Multi-faceted innovative arts organization uses multiple venues in and around Laguna Beach.
Public Transportation: Varies by venue.
Handicapped Accessibility: Varies by venue.
Performances/Programs: Programming includes Gallimaufry Arts Festival (two weeks of theater, dance, music, and film), Family Festival, plays and musicals, performances by the teen theater company The Generation Gap, Lagunatunes community chorus, Gallimaufry & Greene contemporary dance company, Promiscuous Assemblage repertory company, and the Ridiculous Medley vocal performance group.
Ticket Prices: Vary by program. Free events include master classes and performances on Dance Day, as well as various free concerts.

Group Discounts: Group discounts are available for some performances. See website for details.

Subscriptions/Membership: Membership begins at $35; at the $500 Patron level, you get VIP priority seating; at the $1,000 donation level, you get two free tickets to any production.

Educational/Community Outreach: Gallimaufry Arts Project provides free educational programs for both kids and adults throughout its season.

LOS ANGELES MUSIC CENTER
(Performing Arts Center of Los Angeles County)
135 North Grand Avenue
213-972-7211 • musiccenter.org

Venues: Music Center is home to the Dorothy Chandler Pavilion, the Ahmanson Theater, the Mark Taper Forum and Walt Disney Concert Hall.

Public Transportation: Very good

Handicapped Accessibility: Good

Performances/Programs: Companies in residence at Music Center include the Los Angeles Philharmonic, the Center Theater Group, the Los Angeles Opera, and the Los Angeles Master Chorale.

Ticket Prices: Varies by company.

Subscriptions/Membership: Individual companies have their own subscription plans and discount ticket options. The Music Center has many membership groups, including Center Dance Arts, the Fraternity of Friends, the Blue Ribbon, and Club 100.

Other Items of Interest: World City (performances by international artists) and Pillow Theatre (shows for families with kids) are admission-free programs.

THE PASADENA CIVIC
The Pasadena Conference Center, 300 East Green Street, Pasadena
626-449-7360 • thepasadenacivic.com

Public Transportation: Very good (easily accessible by Metro).

Handicapped Accessibility: Good

Performances/Programs: Opened in 1932, the Pasadena Civic Auditorium is one of the nation's most renowned performance venues; it has hosted the Emmy Awards more than 20 times, TV specials, and the People's Choice Awards. The venue regularly hosts musicals, symphony orchestras, lectures, family shows, awards shows, and other special events.

Ticket Prices: Varies by program. Shows occasionally available on Goldstar.com.

Group Discounts: Group discounts available for some events.

Subscriptions/Membership: Subscriptions available for the Pasadena Symphony, the Distinguished Speaker Series, and the Broadway Musical Series.

ORANGE COUNTY PERFORMING ARTS CENTER
600 Town Center Drive, Costa Mesa
714-556-ARTS • ocpac.org

Venues: The Renee and Henry Segerstrom Concert Hall, the Samueli Theater, Segerstrom Hall, and Founders Hall.

Public Transportation: Very good (easily accessible via OCTA).

Parking: The Center Town parking structure is recommended for visitors to Segerstrom Hall and Founders Hall; the Plaza Tower parking struc-

IN CASE OF "SHIRLEY MACLAINE," DON'T PANIC!

In 1955, Carol Haney, star of Broadway's *The Pajama Game*, broke her ankle. Her understudy (a totally unknown actress named Shirley MacLaine) replaced her for six weeks. One of the people to catch the show was Hal Wallis, head of Paramount Studios, and the rest is one of the best stories in theater history.

Forty years later Jeffrey and William Compton found out that, due to illness, Glenn Close wouldn't be appearing in that night's performance of *Sunset Blvd.* (in L.A.'s now-defunct Shubert Theater). Having no alternative (all other shows with Close were sold out), they watched understudy Karen Mason win over a very unfriendly audience. In the end, she got a standing ovation.

Whenever you see a note in the lobby that "for this performance, the role of Carrie will be played by Ida Newface," don't panic. If the replacement involves a major soloist, conductor, or star whose name is above the title of the show (or the theater has to send on an unprepared actor with script in hand), ticket refunds or replacements should be willingly offered. Most of the time we wouldn't consider taking them up on it. Based on our experience, Ms. Newface will probably be the best thing on that stage. After all, it's her night to shine!

ture is recommended for those attending performances at Segerstrom Concert Hall and the Samueli Theater.

Handicapped Accessibility: Good

Performances/Programs: Companies in residence at the Center include the Pacific Symphony, the Philharmonic Society of Orange County, Opera Pacific, and Pacific Chorale.

Ticket Prices: Vary by program. Rush tickets are available to some performances for students and seniors. Discounts are also occasionally available for AAA members.

Group Discounts: Discounts available for groups of 15 or more.

Subscriptions: Broadway, Dance, Jazz Club, Cabaret, Concert, and Family series subscriptions are offered.

Membership: Center Access membership allows students, teachers, retired people, members of the armed forces, and clergy to get discounted tickets for select events (there is an annual $10 processing fee).

Educational/Community Outreach: Educational initiatives at the Center include the Family series aimed at kids 4–8, free Masters at the Center classes, Summer at the Center workshop for at-risk high school students, the ArtsConnect residency program, and the comprehensive Arts Teach program (including family nights, residencies, professional development workshops, student workshops, school assemblies, and more). Free public tours are also available.

SKIRBALL CULTURAL CENTER
2701 N. Sepulveda Boulevard
877-SCC-4TIX • skirball.org

Public Transportation: Very good (easily accessible by bus).

Handicapped Accessibility: Good

Performances/Programs: Jewish cultural institution that features a museum and exhibitions, theater, music, comedy, family, and literary programs.

Ticket Prices: Vary by program. Discounts are often available for students, members, and seniors. All exhibitions are free on Thursday. Film screenings are also usually free; additionally, family and dance programs are usually free with museum admission. Shows available on Goldstar.com.

Membership: Membership starts at $55. Benefits include unlimited free general admission to museum, two complimentary passes, free admission to the Hanukkah Family Festival, discounts on Skirball public programs and Learning for Life courses, and invites to members-only events.

FESTIVALS

HOLLYWOOD BOWL
2301 North Highland Avenue, Hollywood
323-850-2000 • hollywoodbowl.com

Public Transportation: Good (Park 'n' Ride shuttles are available from over a dozen locations for $5 roundtrip).

Handicapped Accessibility: Good

Performances/Programs: 14 weeks of concerts from June to September. Performance schedule varies; generally Tuesday through Sunday, with some Mondays.

Ticket Prices: Ticket prices range from $5 to $125. Join the Email Club on the website to find out about special offers.

Group Discounts: Group discounts available for parties of 10 or more for most performances.

Subscriptions: Numerous subscriptions available from $100 to $1,140. Subscriber benefits include priority upgrades, 20% discounts on additional tickets, dining, purchases at the Bowl Store, lost-ticket replacement, and ticket exchanges (with $4 fee).

Educational/Community Outreach: Educational programs include professional development training for musicians and teachers, initiatives for young musicians, and free pre-concert talks with artists and musicologists.

For information on Santa Barbara, California, and
Honolulu, Hawaii, visit go-artsamerica.com.

SAN FRANCISCO BAY AREA

Rich in Latin and Asian influences, as well as a major epicenter for gay and lesbian culture and art, San Francisco is one of the most visited cities in the United States. In addition to its reputation as a premier dining destination, the City by the Bay's variety of professional theaters, music venues, art galleries, and dance companies enjoys international acclaim.

Recognized as one of the most beautiful cities in the world, its superior public-transit choices put all of the Bay's cultural attractions (including those in San Jose) within easy reach.

ARTS INFO

NEWSPAPERS

San Francisco Chronicle (sfgate.com)—Best daily newspaper for Bay Area arts news and reviews.

San Francisco Bay Guardian (sfbg.com) and *SF Weekly* (sfweekly. com)—Free weeklies with comprehensive arts coverage.

WEBSITES

funcheapSF (sf.funcheap.com)—Fun cheap things to do in the San Francisco Bay area. Sign up for email updates.

Only in San Francisco (onlyinsanfrancisco.com)—The official website of San Francisco. Very helpful.

SF Arts (sfarts.org)—Comprehensive guide to San Francisco arts.

DISCOUNTS

GoldStar (goldstar.com)—National entertainment-discount service offers discounts to all types of Bay Area entertainment with an inventory of every type of entertainment.

Tix Bay Area (tixbayarea.com)—A program of Theatre Bay Area, a nonprofit organization that promotes theater and dance in the Bay Area. Strong inventory of discount seats.

ART MUSEUMS

ASIAN ART MUSEUM OF SAN FRANCISCO
200 Larkin Street
415-581-3500 • asianart.org

Public Transportation: Very good (Muni rail, bus, streetcar, and cable car; BART Civic Center station is close).

Handicapped Accessibility: Good

Hours: Tuesday–Sunday 10 a.m.–5 p.m. (The museum is open until 9 p.m. from February–September.)

Admission: $12; seniors 65 and older with ID $8; college students with ID and youths 13–17 $7; members, children 12 and under, and SFUSD students with ID free; Thursday evenings after 5 p.m. $5.

Free Days: The first Sunday of every month is free.

Basic Tour: There are two types of tours available daily, an introductory tour of the museum's collection and tours that highlights specific areas of the collection or special exhibitions.

Audio Tours: Free

Membership: Membership begins at the Active level ($75) and your contribution is fully tax-deductible. Membership benefits include two personalized cards, unlimited free admission for two adults, priority entry, exhibition previews, a 10% discount at the museum store, a subscription to *Treasures* (the Asian's beautifully illustrated magazine), and reduced admission to lectures, films, and special events. A Senior Active membership is also available for $55. Additional packages are offered for Family & Friends ($100), as well as a Contributor membership ($150) that includes additional benefits, such a s reciprocal membership at over 350 museums nationwide and invitations to exclusive Contributor receptions.

From the Editors: As one of the world's largest collections of Asian art, the Asian Art Museum of San Francisco was founded through the generosity of Avery Brundage in an effort to promote Asian and American cultural understanding. The museum holds a massive collection of more than 17,000 pieces, which cover 6,000 years of history. A prime example is its gilt bronze Buddha, dating all the way to 338 A.D.—the oldest known dated Chinese Buddha in the world. In addition, the range of its rotating exhibitions is a great asset.

Past, present, and future exhibitions include a painting-based show of Lords of the Samurai, a sculpture collection of Emerald Cities: Arts of Siam and Burma, and jewelry and stone-based exhibition Later Chinese Jades: Ming Dynasty to Early Twentieth Century.

A lesser-known feature of this museum is its extensive and diverse Family Program line-up, which is free and includes yoga, storytelling, and writing workshops.

BERKELEY ART MUSEUM AND PACIFIC FILM ARCHIVE (BAM/PFA)
510-642-0808 • bampfa.berkeley.edu

Venues: BAM, 2626 Bancroft Way; PFA, 2575 Bancroft Way (both between College and Telegraph).

Public Transportation: Very good (AC Transit buses; about a mile from downtown Berkeley BART station).

Handicapped Accessibility: Good

Hours: BAM, Wednesday–Sunday 11 a.m.–5 p.m.; PFA, Monday–Thursday, 1–5 p.m.

Admission: Adults (18–64) $8; non-UC Berkeley students, seniors (65+), disabled persons, young adults (13–17) $5; UC Berkeley students, faculty and staff, and children (12 & under) free.

Free Day: First Thursday of the month.

Tours: Public guided tours of current BAM exhibitions are usually held on Thursdays at 12:15 p.m. and Sundays at 2 p.m.

Membership: Individual membership is $50 annually and includes free admission to the BAM galleries for two, discounted PFA Theater tickets for two, invitations to exhibition previews and special events, free lectures, seminars, and discussions with artists, free access to the PFA Library and Film Study Center, and reciprocal membership privileges at over 30 university art museums. A student/senior/disabled membership is $35 annually. UCB Individual membership is $45 annually.

From the Editors: Besides a large Hans Hofmann collection and an extensive 20th-century American/European painting collection, the UCBAM houses the largest collection of Japanese movies outside of Japan.

CALIFORNIA PALACE OF THE LEGION OF HONOR (THE LEGION)
34th Avenue at Clement Street
415-750-3600 • famsf.org/legion

Public Transportation: Very good (Muni buses)
Handicapped Accessibility: Good
Hours: Tuesday–Sunday 9:30 a.m.–5:15 p.m.
Admission: $10, seniors (65+) $7, youth (13–17) $6, children (12 and under) free.
Free Day: First Tuesday of each month is free. Special exhibition surcharges still apply. Admission tickets to the Legion may be used on the same day for free entrance to the de Young. Muni riders with Fast Pass or transfer receive a $2 discount.
Tours: Regularly scheduled drop-in tours available Tuesday–Sunday.
Audio Tours: Audio tours are available for $6.
Membership: Individual membership, $80 annually, includes unlimited free admission for one member and a guest to the permanent collections and most special exhibitions at the de Young and the Legion of Honor, invitations to special members-only events and viewing hours, priority ticketing for special exhibitions, as well as exclusive offers and discounts on museum special events, films, lectures, and concerts. Special discounts are offered on memberships for the following: student $45/annually; senior $50/annually; teacher $55/annually; out-of-state $60/annually.

From the Editors: The Palace of the Legion of Honor is a three-quarter-scale replica of the 18th-century building of the same name (the Palais de la Légion d'Honneur) in Paris. This version was built in 1924 to commemorate California soldiers who died in WW I. Its site is known as Land's End, located in Lincoln Park and overlooking the Pacific Ocean, Golden Gate Bridge, and the entire cityscape. The Court of Honor, an outdoor portion of the breathtaking grounds, is where you'll find *Rodin's Thinker*, one of the more than 70 Rodin sculptures in the collection.

The museum itself contains a great collection of European art; fans of the Impressionists and post-Impressionists will delight in the many works of Degas, Monet, and Renoir that the galleries have to offer. If you visit on a weekend at 4 p.m. you'll be lucky enough to catch a recital on the museum's symphonic organ, commissioned in 1924 and housed above the main galleries. The single instrument is capable of producing sounds similar to that of a full orchestra with its various sonics, including bass drum, castanets, crash cymbal, echo, and more. The informal twice-weekly recitals are a transporting experience, and not to be missed if your visit happens to coincide. Membership benefits at the Legion also apply at the M.H. de Young Memorial Museum.

IRIS & B. GERALD CANTOR CENTER FOR VISUAL ARTS
Stanford University Campus
328 Lomita Drive (at Museum Way), Stanford
650-723-4177 • museum.stanford.edu

Public Transportation: Good (the local transit hub for bus and train services at Stanford is the Palo Alto Caltrain Station).

Handicapped Accessibility: Good

Hours: Wednesday–Sunday 11 a.m.–5 p.m., Thursday 11 a.m.–8 p.m., closed Monday and Tuesday.

Admission: Free

Tours: Multiple public tours are offered throughout the week. All meet in the main lobby unless otherwise specified. These include an introduction to the Cantor Arts Center, the Outdoor Sculpture Walk, the B. Gerald Cantor Rodin Sculpture Garden and Rodin Gallery tour, and tours of changing exhibitions. The museum also offers tours of other attractions on the complex, such as the Stanford Memorial Church and the Papua New Guinea Sculpture Garden.

Membership: Individual memberships are $50 annually and include invitations to opening receptions for major exhibitions, the center's newsletter and monthly calendar, art-related travel opportunities, and access to art study groups.

From the Editors: Formerly the Leland Stanford Jr. Art Museum, the Cantor Center was re-opened in 1999 after being extensively damaged in two earthquakes. Check out the Rodin sculpture garden, which contains 20 bronzes, and the center's excellent collection of ancient Mediterranean, Asian, African, and Native American art. The modern and contemporary American art collection is also recommended.

M.H. DE YOUNG MEMORIAL MUSEUM
Golden Gate Park, 50 Hagiwara Tea Garden Drive
415-750-3600 • famsf.org/deyoung

Public Transportation: Very good (serviced by Muni bus and streetcar).
Handicapped Accessibility: Good
Hours: Tuesday–Sunday 9:30 a.m. to 5:15 p.m., Fridays 9:30 a.m. to
8:45 p.m., mid-January through November, otherwise 5:15 p.m.
Admission: $10, seniors 65 and over $7, college students and youths
13–17 $6, children 12 and under free; Muni riders with Fast Pass, transfer,
or CultureBus ticket receive a $2 discount. Admission tickets can be used
(same-day) for the Legion of Honor.
Tours: Free. Regularly scheduled docent tours are available Tuesdays
through Sundays. No reservations required; visitors are welcome to join the
tours in progress.
Audio Tours: $6
Membership: Individual membership is $80 annually and includes un-
limited free admission for one member and a guest to the permanent collections and most special exhibitions at the de Young and the Legion of
Honor, invitations to special members-only events and viewing hours, as
well as priority ticketing for special exhibitions. Several special discounted
memberships are also available: senior $50/annually; teacher $55/annually;
student $45/annually; out-of-state $60/annually.
Other Benefits: A Contributing-level membership ($175/annually) gets
you reciprocal admission to other museums.

From the Editors: The de Young Museum has been a part of Golden
Gate Park—and San Francisco's cultural make-up—since 1895. Inside you'll
find collections of American art from the 17th through the 20th centuries,
along with art of the native Americas, Africa, and the Pacific. Largely due
to the acquisition of the Rockefeller Collection of American Art, the de
Young's collection of paintings is one of the finest in the U.S., comprising
more than 1000 artworks that represent the spectrum of the nation's history, with works by George Caleb Bingham and Frederic Edwin Church, as
well as 20th-century artists such as Edward Hopper, Georgia O'Keefe, and
Grant Wood. Also unique to the collection—and always worth perusing despite which touring exhibition is currently at the museum—the African-art
collection features nearly 1,500 works from sub-Saharan Africa.

The museum's educational program offers free after-school classes for
children under 12 based on the Get Smart with Art curriculum. For the general public, the Docent Council keeps a busy schedule of public lectures
by scholars, faculty, and curators. Membership benefits at the de Young

also apply to the Legion of Honor. For visitors to the city, the location—in historic Golden Gate Park—can't be beat and the museum is a must-stop on your tour.

OAKLAND MUSEUM OF CALIFORNIA
1000 Oak Street, Oakland
510-238-2200 • museumca.org

Public Transportation: Very good (AC Transit buses; two blocks from the BART Lake Merritt Station).
Handicapped Accessibility: Good
Hours: Wednesday–Saturday 10 a.m.–5 p.m., Sunday noon–5 p.m., closed Monday and Tuesday. (First Friday of each month open until 9 p.m.)
Admission: $8, students and seniors are $5, children under six are free; group discounts are offered for all nonprofit groups and are 50% off general admission prices (special exhibition rates still apply).
Free Day: Second Sunday of the month.
Membership: Individual membership is $40 annually and includes unlimited year-long admission, home delivery of @CALIFORNIA, the museum's quarterly events calendar, invitations to member previews, and one-time use guest passes for general admission. Students, educators, and seniors can become members for $35 annually.

From the Editors: Fascinating collection devoted to California's history and art.

SAN FRANCISCO MUSEUM OF MODERN ART (SFMOMA)
151 Third Street (between Mission and Howard Streets)
415-357-4000 • sfmoma.org

Public Transportation: Excellent (Montgomery Street BART station, Muni bus and Metro lines, Golden Gate Transit, SamTrans, and Caltrain).
Handicapped Accessibility: Good
Hours: Monday and Tuesday 11 a.m.–5:45 p.m., Thursday 11 a.m.–8:45 p.m., Friday–Sunday 11 a.m.–5:45 p.m., closed Wednesday. Museum opens at 10 a.m. June–August.
Admission: $15, students and seniors (62+) $9, group discounts available. Thursday evenings 6–9 p.m. admission is half-price.
Free Day: First Tuesday of each month.
Tours: Tours are led daily by SFMOMA docents.

Audio Tours: $3

Membership: Individual membership is $80 annually and includes one personalized membership card, unlimited free admission for you and a friend, express entry, invitations to exhibition previews and receptions, as well as discounts on tickets to screenings, lectures, and special events. SF-MOMA offers special discounted memberships for seniors, working artists, teachers, students, and out-of-town residents. Working artist, teacher, and student memberships require current proof of status and can be purchased at the museum or by mail. A $250 supporting membership gets you reciprocal membership to other area and national museums.

From the Editors: The San Francisco Museum of Modern Art (referred to as SFMOMA by locals) was the first museum on the West Coast to be devoted entirely to 20th-century art. Opened in 1935, it wasn't until 40 years later that the museum added "Modern" to its title, which described the collection more accurately and established it internationally as an important collection of contemporary art.

The collection includes works by Ansel Adams, Duchamp, Klee, Mondrian, Pollack, Rauschenberg, and others. The museum moved to its current location in 1995, and is in the heart of San Francisco's SOMA (South of Market) neighborhood, which has a long tradition as a haven for artists and industrial live-work loft spaces. Adjacent to the museum are the lovely Yerba Buena Gardens and atop the museum is the Rooftop Garden, opened in spring 2009, which acts as a gallery without a ceiling.

The museum houses an education center on the second floor; the Koret Visitor Education Center is open to all visitors for drop-in activities and interactive learning, and offers a wide range of scheduled public programs. Open during museum hours, the center is a great place to drop in to view daily screenings of videos focused on artists in the permanent collection, a full library of SFMOMA's catalogues (as well as art books for all ages), multimedia kiosks with interactive educational programs, and it's a comfortable and welcoming place to drop in if you need a break from the 50,000 square feet of gallery space.

THEATER

ACTORS THEATRE OF SAN FRANCISCO
855 Bush Street
415-345-1287 • actorstheatresf.org

Public Transportation: Very good (accessible by Muni bus).
Performances/Programs: Performance schedule is Thursday–Saturday.
Ticket Prices: Single tickets are $30–$35, student and senior tickets are $20, Thursday nights are on a sliding scale of $10 to $30; group discounts available for most shows; shows available on Goldstar.com.

AMERICAN CONSERVATORY THEATER
415-749-2ACT (2228) • act-sf.org

Venues: Zeum Theater, 221 Fourth Street; Yerba Buena Center for the Arts, 415 Geary Street.
Public Transportation: Very good
Handicapped Accessibility: Good
Performances/Programs: Performance schedule is Tuesday–Sunday.
Ticket Prices: Single tickets are $14–$82, one Pay What You Wish/Bring What You Can performance for each show (bring a food item for a community-service organization, then pay what you like); discounts available for groups of 15 or more; shows available on Goldstar.com.
Subscriptions: Seven-Play $101–$570, Five-Play $85–$410, Four-Play $70–$250, and Three-Play $55–$190 packages available, 50% discount on subscriptions available for full-time students and educators; subscription discounts available for seniors. Benefits include ticket exchanges, ticket insurance, restaurant benefits, and one free seat upgrade at the performance of your choice.

From the Editors: San Franciscans love their theater, and along with notoriously vociferous New Yorkers, they're probably the most passionate and opinionated theater-goers in the country. American Conservatory Theater, one of the nation's most distinguished theaters, draws strong reactions from locals. Many adore A.C.T. for its exceptional production values, excellent talent pool (with A.C.T.'s own resident acting company at the center), and beautiful historic theater, even if it is lacking in legroom and bathroom stalls. They're impressed by A.C.T.'s renowned MFA train-ing program, which has produced such fine actors as Denzel Washington, Danny Glover, Annette Bening, and Anika Noni Rose. And they appreciate free events, such as the Visiting Artist Series panel discussions (featuring artists as varied as Tom Stoppard and Tracy Chapman) and Theater on the Couch, an analytical talk on the play led by members of the SF Center for Psychoanalysis.

However, American Conservatory Theater's detractors feel that al-though the theater's productions always look good, A.C.T. lacks vision and soul: It's a regional theater with Broadway pretensions and very little artis-tic daring.

Perhaps the best way to determine which camp you're in is to visit A.C.T. for yourself on a designated pay-what-you wish/bring-what-you-can night, when audiences can pay whatever they want if they bring a food item to donate. Even if you don't like what you see, you may find you want to get involved with the theater in other ways, like through the A.C.T. Stu-dio, which offers performing-arts classes for people of all backgrounds and experience levels.

AURORA THEATRE COMPANY
2081 Addison Street, Berkeley
510-843-4822 • auroratheatre.org

Public Transportation: Very good (one block from downtown Berkeley BART station; also AC Transit buses).

Handicapped Accessibility: Good

Performances/Programs: Performance schedule is Wednesday–Sun-day.

Ticket Prices: Single tickets are $28–$50, $20 Rush tickets sold to any-body a half-hour before curtain, half-price tickets for full-time students, $10 tickets for under-18-year-olds when accompanied by full-price-paying adult, $5 discount for anyone with a California Alumni Association mem-bership, free preview performances for low-income students and seniors, discounts for groups of 20 or more.

Subscriptions: Season subscriptions $130–$210, discounts for full-time students, educators, and parents bringing underage children. Benefits include free ticket exchanges, guest ticket discounts, and dining discounts.

BERKELEY REPERTORY THEATRE (BRT)
2025 Addison Street, Berkeley
888-4BR-TIX (27–8849) • berkeleyrep.org

Public Transportation: Very good (one block from downtown Berkeley BART station; also AC Transit buses).

Handicapped Accessibility: Good

Performances/Programs: Performance schedule is Tuesday–Sunday.

Ticket Prices: Single tickets are $27–$71, Rush tickets for students and seniors $10, half-price tickets for anyone under 30 for most shows. Join the CYBERrush email list to receive half-price discount offers. Other discounts for are available for: members ($5 off); Cal Rep Sports and California Alumni Association members; and groups of 10 or more. No exchanges for non-subscribers.

Subscriptions: $25–$65 per play, subscription discounts available for educators, seniors, and students.

From the Editors: The Berkeley Repertory Theatre is San Francisco's premier spot for dynamic, innovative, and unusual theater by multidisciplinary artists, theater newcomers, and veteran risk-takers (we would name them, but you probably haven't heard of most of them, which is sort of the point). That's not to say that Berkeley Rep doesn't produce work by more well-known writers. There have been productions of new plays by Tony Kushner, Terrence McNally, and Mary Zimmerman, revivals of classic dramas, imaginative stage adaptations of both classic and modern literature, and world premieres by Danny Hoch and Sarah Ruhl. Sarah Jones's tour-de-force *Bridge & Tunnel* and Stew and Heidi Rodewald's rock musical *Passing Strange*, both of which went on to Broadway, began here.

Berkeley Rep has a "green policy," meaning that the company is striving for energy efficiency and waste reduction in every facet of its operation. Patrons will find that trash cans for recyclable materials are provided in the restrooms and they're strongly encouraged to come to the theater via public transportation (there's a very convenient BART stop nearby). If you must drive, though, there's inexpensive parking across the street.

The theater also offers such free events as Teen Nights, a treat for teenagers who not only get discounted tickets to the show that night, but also enjoy dinner and a discussion with Berkeley Rep artists. The 30-Below program is a favorite of cash-strapped theater lovers under 30, who qualify for half-price tickets to most performances. What's more, under-30s who attend designated performances also get free admission to the 30-Below post-show party with live music and free food and drinks.

CUTTING BALL THEATER
415-419-3584 • cuttingball.com

Venues: EXIT Theatre, EXIT Stage Left, and EXIT Café, 156 Eddy St.; EXIT on Taylor, 277 Taylor St.; Magic Theatre, Fort Mason, Building D.

Public Transportation: Good

Handicapped Accessibility: Good

Performances/Programs: Cutting Ball does a lot of readings, workshops, and festivals, with only a few full productions. Performance times and dates vary.

Ticket Prices: Tickets range from free to $30, discounts available for students, seniors, and groups, $15 tickets on Under 30 Thursday, shows sometimes available on Goldstar.com.

42nd STREET MOON
215 Jackson Street (between Battery and Front Streets)
415-255-8207 • 42ndstmoon.org

Public Transportation: Very good (Muni streetcar, buses; six blocks from Embarcadero BART station)

Handicapped Accessibility: Good

Performances/Programs: Performance schedule is Wednesday–Sunday.

Ticket Prices: Single tickets are $22–$38, students and seniors are $22–$33, $5 family-matinée tickets for anyone under 18, discounts for groups of 10 or more.

Subscriptions: Season subscriptions are $94–$162; subscription discounts available for students and seniors.

GOLDEN THREAD
415-626-4061 • goldenthread.org

Venue: Frequently uses Thick House, 1695 18th Street.

Public Transportation: Good (Muni buses)

Handicapped Accessibility: Good

Performances/Programs: Performance schedule is Thursday–Sunday.

Ticket Prices: Single tickets are $20–$25, discount tickets for students and seniors available, previews are pay what you can, group discounts available.

Subscriptions: Season passes available.

MAGIC THEATRE
Fort Mason Center, Building D, 3rd Floor
415-441-8822 • magictheatre.org

Public Transportation: Good (Muni buses)
Handicapped Accessibility: Good
Performances/Programs: Performance schedule is Wednesday–Sunday.
Ticket Prices: Tickets are $20–$45, students, seniors, educators, and people with disabilities get $5 off regular-priced tickets, $10 Rush tickets available for students, seniors, educators, and anyone under 30, $5–$25 tickets available on Sliding-Scale Wednesdays, discounts available for groups of six or more.
Subscriptions: Six-Play $120–$450, Flex Six-Ticket pass $144–$240, and Under-30 subscription $30. Benefits include free ticket exchanges and unlimited free repeat viewings of shows you have already seen.

MARIN THEATRE COMPANY (MTC)
397 Miller Avenue, Mill Valley
415-388-5200 • marintheatre.org

Public Transportation: Good (Golden Gate Transit)
Handicapped Accessibility: Good
Performances/Programs: Performance schedule is Tuesday–Sunday.
Ticket Prices: Single tickets $31–$51, student tickets are $20, certain nights designated pay what you can, group discounts for parties of 15 or more, shows available on Goldstar.com.
Subscriptions: Five-Play Season subscription $130–$230, student subscriptions $100, senior subscriptions (matinées) $95–$130, first-time subscribers (previews only) $105. Benefits include free ticket exchanges, dining discounts, and lost-ticket replacement.

From the Editors: Marin Theatre Company is a professional theater with the intimacy of a community playhouse. Founded in the early '60s as a multi-arts organization called the Mill Valley Center for the Performing Arts, MVCPA changed its name to the Marin Theatre Company in the '80s to reflect its change of focus and relocated to its current home on Miller Avenue.

Though it doesn't have the cachet of local giants like A.T.C. and Berkeley Rep, MTC provides its loyal base with just as many interesting new plays and premieres, as well as highly polished productions of classics. MTC's inspired Words + Music series, presented on selected Monday nights, explores elements of the current mainstage show through a live presentation that offers a mix of live performance, film, and discussion with guest speakers. Each Marin Theatre season also includes four new plays in the Nu Werkz staged reading series, also held on Monday nights.

NEW CONSERVATORY THEATRE CENTER
25 Van Ness Avenue, Lower Lobby
415-861-8972 • nctcsf.org

Public Transportation: Very good (Muni Metro and buses; five blocks to Civic Center BART station).

Handicapped Accessibility: Good

Performances/Programs: Performance schedule is Wednesday–Sunday.

Ticket Prices: Single tickets are $18–$40, half-price student Rush tickets sold half-hour before show, group discounts available for parties of 15 or more, shows available on Goldstar.com, no ticket exchanges for non-subscribers.

Subscriptions: Season subscriptions $120–$260, subscriptions for 30-and-under are $99, Three-Show Sampler Pass $50–$100.

NORTHSIDE THEATRE COMPANY
The Black Box Theatre, 848 East William Street, San Jose
408-288-7820 • northsidetheatre.com

Public Transportation: Fair (Santa Clara Valley Transportation Authority).

Handicapped Accessibility: Good

Performances/Programs: Performance schedule is Thursday–Sunday.

Ticket Prices: Single tickets are $20, $15 tickets for seniors and children under 18, group discounts available for parties of 10 or more.

Subscriptions: Season subscriptions are $80, under 18 and senior packages are $60, Six-Pack Flex pass $90. Benefits include free ticket insurance.

SAN JOSE REPERTORY THEATRE
101 Paseo de San Antonio, San Jose
408-367-7255 • www.sjrep.com

Public Transportation: Excellent (Santa Clara Valley Transportation Authority bus, light rail, and Caltrain).

Handicapped Accessibility: Good

Performances/Programs: Performance schedule is Tuesday–Sunday.

Ticket Prices: Single tickets are $27–$55, $6 discount for seniors and teachers, half-price tickets for students, Rush tickets available (for balcony price), groups discounts for parties of 10 or more; non-subscribers can exchange tickets for a fee and with 48-hour notice.

Subscriptions: Five-Play $115–$260 and Six-Play $138–$312 offerings, also a Design Your Own option (discounts for students). Benefits include ticket exchanges, lost-ticket insurance, and free parking.

From the Editors: Founded in 1980, the San Jose Repertory Theatre was the city's first resident professional theater and has since gained a reputation for being one of the country's pre-eminent regional houses. Part of the Rep's mission is to produce works that speak to San Jose's diverse community—and "diverse" perfectly describes this theater that recently offered a classic French play, a Reduced Shakespeare Company show, a political thriller, adaptations of both *Jekyll & Hyde* and *It's a Wonderful Life*, and a quirky musical all in one season.

Young professionals around 25–39 who want to get the Rep experience, but would also like to make a full night of it, should join the Scene, a group of young theater lovers who get together for a great meal before the show, then meet at a hip joint afterwards for drinks and discussion (all planned by the Rep and offered for a reasonable fixed price).

San Jose Rep also has many educational initiatives, the most notable being its Red Ladder Theatre Company, an outreach program that uses performance techniques and creative expression to show at-risk youth and other disadvantaged or troubled individuals how they can better their lives through the arts.

SAN FRANCISCO MIME TROUPE (SFMT)
415-285-1717 • sfmt.org

Venues: Various

Public Transportation: Varies by venue.

Handicapped Accessibility: Varies by venue.

Performances/Programs: These aren't mimes in the commonly under-stood sense; instead, SFMT mostly does broad social and political satire. SFMT does not have a fixed performance space; the company performs mostly in parks from July 4 to Labor Day. These performances are free, though they pass around a hat to collect donations afterwards (usually suggesting that people pay the same price as a movie ticket). The company also tours schools and other venues.

Ticket Prices: Some of the company's indoor touring shows have an admission price set by the host organization, usually $15–$20.

SF PLAYHOUSE
533 Sutter Street
415-677-9596

Public Transportation: Very good (Muni buses and cable car, five blocks to Powell Street BART station).

Handicapped Accessibility: Good

Performances/Programs: Performance schedule is Tuesday–Saturday.

Ticket Prices: Single tickets are $20 previews, $38 regular performances, $65 for grand opening, discounts available for students, seniors, and groups, shows available on Goldstar.com.

Subscriptions: Six-Show $90–$350, Six-Show flex pass $190. Benefits include free ticket exchanges and discounted tickets for friends.

SHAKESPEARE SANTA CRUZ
831-459-2121 • shakespearesantacruz.org

Venues: Theater is located on the campus of University of California–Santa Cruz: UCSC Theatre Arts Mainstage, 1156 High St., Santa Cruz.

Public Transportation: Good

Handicapped Accessibility: Good

Performances/Programs: Performance schedule is Tuesday–Sunday.

Ticket Prices: Single tickets are $22–$44, student Rush available for some performances $14, students, seniors, UCSC staff and alumni (weekdays and Sunday evening) $29, youth $12 (available with full-price adult ticket purchase), discounts for groups of 15 or more.

Subscriptions: Season subscriptions $75–$144.

SHOTGUN PLAYERS
Ashby Stage, 1901 Ashby Avenue, Berkeley
510-841-6500 • shotgunplayers.org

Public Transportation: Very good (easily accessible by BART and bus).
Handicapped Accessibility: Good
Performances/Programs: Performance schedule is Thursday–Sunday.
Ticket Prices: Single tickets are $7–$25, first weekend of performances is pay what you can, shows available on Goldstar.com.
Subscriptions: Five-Show "Select Membership" subscription $80–$125, 38 Special (anyone 38 and younger) $60, Opening Week subscriptions are $60. Benefits include ticket exchanges.

THEATRE OF YUGEN AT NOHSPACE
2840 Mariposa Street
949-394-8776 • theatreofyugen.org

Public Transportation: Yes (easily accessible via Muni and BART).
Handicapped Accessibility: Good
Performances/Programs: Performance schedules vary considerably.
Ticket Prices: The offerings vary and so do the ticket prices, but shows most often average at $10–$20, student and senior discounts offered for some shows, some performances offered for free, some shows have pay-what-you-can performances.

THEATRE RHINOCEROS
1360 Mission Street
415-861-5079 • therhino.org

Public Transportation: Good
Handicapped Accessibility: Good
Performances/Programs: Performance schedule is Wednesday–Sunday.
Ticket Prices: Single tickets are $15–$25, $5 discounts for students and seniors for most performances.
Subscriptions: Season subscriptions $110–$235, $335 for opening-night subscription.

THEATREWORKS
650-463-1960 • theatreworks.org

Venues: Mountain View Center for the Performing Arts (MVCPA), 500 Castro St., Mountain View; Lucie Stern Theatre, 1305 Middlefield Rd., Palo Alto.

Public Transportation: Fair/Poor (MVCPA is accessible via Caltrain; Lucie Stern only somewhat accessible).

Handicapped Accessibility: Good (both venues)

Performances/Programs: Performance schedule is Tuesday–Sunday.

Ticket Prices: Single tickets are $36–$64, discounts available for seniors, educators, and students. Quick Tix: Register online and get special last-minute ticket offers.

Membership: Package prices are $165–$410, discounts available for seniors, students, and educators. Pay $40 for Theatreworks membership, then get discounted tickets for the shows of your choice at $27 for plays and $32 for musicals.

From the Editors: The majority of the shows produced on TheatreWorks's two stages, the Mountain View Center for the Performing Arts and the Lucie Stern Theatre, are appearing in Northern California—if not on the entire West Coast—for the first time. Most seasons also feature the world premier of a show that has been developed through the New Works Initiative, a program that gives new musicals (and plays with music) readings and workshops, culminating in the exciting annual New Works Festival.

Not even 10 years old yet, the New Works Initiative has already nurtured new musicals by Stephen Schwartz, Andrew Lippa, Joe Dipietro, Bill Russell, Henry Krieger, Hunter Foster, Marsha Norman, and many rising theater writers.

Meanwhile, the Workshop, the umbrella term for TheatreWorks's community and education programs, is training the playwrights and stage stars of the future through residencies, classes, and day camps for kids and teens.

The Children's Healing Project takes it a step further by bringing drama teachers right into the Lucile Packard Children's Hospital, where they brighten the patients' spirits by engaging them in improvisational activities and creative exercises.

TRAVELING JEWISH THEATRE
470 Florida Street
415-522-0786 • atjt.com

Public Transportation: Fair/ Good (accessible by BART, but requires a 12-minute walk to the theater).
Handicapped Accessibility: Good
Performances/Programs: Performance schedule is Thursday–Sunday.
Ticket Prices: Single tickets are $15–$34, discounts available for groups, seniors, students and teachers, designated pay-what-you-can nights, shows available on Goldstar.com.

TEATRO VISION
Mexican Heritage Plaza, 1700 Alum Rock Avenue, Suite 265, San José
408-928-5587 • teatrovision.org

Public Transportation: Good
Handicapped Accessibility: Good
Ticket Prices: Single tickets $14–$24, discounts available for students, seniors, and groups.
Subscriptions: Season subscriptions $30–$114. Benefits include free ticket exchanges and discounts on extra tickets.

WILLOWS THEATRE COMPANY
925-798-1300 • willowstheatre.com

Venue: Willows Theatre (Main Stage), 1975 Diamond Blvd., Concord; Campbell Theatre/Willows Cabaret, 636 Ward Street, Martinez; John Muir Amphitheater on the Martinez Waterfront, Martinez; Alhambra Performing Arts Center, Alhambra Avenue at E Street, Martinez.
Public Transportation: Fair (venues reachable by a combo of BART and bus lines).
Handicapped Accessibility: Most venues
Performances/Programs: Performance schedule is Wednesday–Sunday.
Ticket Prices: Single tickets are $17–$40, discounts available for students and seniors, $10 student Rush tickets available for full-time students and teachers, group discounts available.
Subscriptions: Subscriptions are $13–$215, youth (6–18) or college student $72–$96.

WOODMINSTER SUMMER MUSICALS
Woodminster Amphitheater, Joaquin Miller Park
3300 Joaquin Miller Road, Oakland
510-531-9597 • woodminster.com

Public Transportation: Poor
Handicapped Accessibility: Good
Performances/Programs: Performance schedule is Friday–Sunday, with some Thursdays.
Ticket Prices: Single tickets are $23–$38, $2 discount for seniors and children (16 and under), kids 16 and under get in for free when accompanying a paying adult, groups of 25 or more can get half-price tickets.
Subscriptions: Three-Show subscription $59–$97, Flex pass $84.

SAN FRANCISCO SHAKESPEARE FESTIVAL
800-978-PLAY (7529) • sfshakes.org

Venues: Multiple venues throughout the San Francisco area, including San Mateo's Central Park, 5th Avenue and El Camino Real; the Presidio's Main Post Parade Ground Lawn; Cupertino's Memorial Park Ampitheater; and many others.
Public Transportation: Varies by venue.
Handicapped Accessibility: Varies by venue.
Performances/Programs: SF Shakespeare Festival offers free Shakespeare productions in numerous parks and tours productions to schools. Free park performances generally take place between Friday and Monday from June to September.

SAN FRANCISCO THEATER FESTIVAL (SFTF)
Yerba Buena Gardens, 3rd and Mission Streets
sftheaterfestival.org

Performances/Programs: The San Francisco Theater Festival (SFTF) produces an annual event held at Yerba Buena Gardens in both indoor and outdoor venues. The festival promotes the region's many live-stage theaters to a broad and diverse audience. Intended to reach small children, adults, those with low incomes, and others, the festival strives to increase appreciation for, and build attendance of, the Bay Area's culturally and artistically varied theatrical institutions.
Ticket Prices: Free admission.

CLASSICAL MUSIC

AMERICAN BACH SOLOISTS
415-621-7900 • americanbach.org

Venues: Grace Cathedral, 1100 California Street; Robert & Margrit Mondavi Center for the Performing Arts, 9399 Old Davis Rd., Davis; St. Stephen's Church, 3 Bayview Avenue, Belvedere; First Congregational Church, 2345 Channing Way, Berkeley; St. Mark's Lutheran Church, 1111 O'Farrell Street, San Francisco; Davis Community Church, 412 C Street, Davis.

Public Transportation: Depends on venue.

Handicapped Accessibility: Depends on venue.

Performances/Programs: Programs and performances vary annually.

Ticket Prices: $18–$60/ticket, discounts available for students and seniors at a reduced rate beginning as low as $10.

Subscriptions: Subscribers save almost 20%. Subscriptions are based on venue and area and include either five concerts including the *Messiah* or four concerts not including the *Messiah*. Only subscribers can exchange tickets. Along with your regular subscription(s), you can purchase additional tickets for family and friends at the same discounted rate offered to you as a subscriber.

From the Editors: Named "the best American specialists in early music" by the *Washington Post*, the American Bach Soloists (ABS) was founded in 1989 with the mission of introducing contemporary audiences to the cantatas of Johann Sebastian Bach through historically informed performances, recordings, and educational programs. Since then, the ensemble's repertoire has expanded to include masterpieces from the Baroque, as well as the Classical and Romantic eras, and beyond.

CHANTICLEER
415-252-8589 • chanticleer.org

Venues: Various locations throughout the Bay area.

Public Transportation: Varies by venue.

Handicapped Accessibility: Most venues should be accessible; call venue management for details.

Performances/Programs: In addition to its worldwide touring schedule, Chanticleer does a Bay Area Season each year made up of four programs with multiple performances of each.

Ticket Prices: $25–$40

Subscriptions: Two–four concert series available from $84–$160, or $76–$147 for students and seniors.

Membership: Available from $50 to $25,000+. Depending on donation amount, donor benefits include limited edition Chanticleer memorabilia, invites to special events, and complimentary tickets.

From the Editors: The name refers to the "clear-singing" rooster in Chaucer's *Canterbury Tales*, and if you've ever heard the strikingly crisp vocals of the 12-member Chanticleer, you'll appreciate the choice. A world-renowned all-male chorus with over two dozen CD releases under its belt, Chanticleer has a demanding concert schedule that keeps these fellows on the road regularly. However, the group is San Francisco-based and programs a four-concert season each year that has it performing in several Bay Area venues. Since its founding in 1979 by the late Louis Botto there is no period or style of music that Chanticleer hasn't sung, and the dulcet-toned ensemble is also dedicated to supporting new music by commissioning original works from composers such as Mark Adamo and Jake Heggie.

VOLTI
415-771-3352 • voltisf.org

Venues: St. Gregory of Nyssa 500 De Haro Street (San Fransisco), St. Mark's Episcopal Church, 2300 Bancroft Way (Berkeley); All Saints' Episcopal Church, 555 Waverley Street at Hamilton (Palo Alto).

Public Transportation: Call venue management for details.

Handicapped Accessibility: All venues should be accessible; call venue management for more details.

Performances/Programs: A few concerts each season in the Bay area, some with multiple performances.

Ticket Prices: Generally $25 in advance, $30 at the door, $18–$22 for seniors, and $10 student Rush at the door; prices may vary for special events or performances at other venues.

Subscriptions: Available for $99 (general admission) or $83 (seniors)

Membership: No set membership packages are offered, but donations are accepted and greatly appreciated.

SAN FRANCISCO CHAMBER ORCHESTRA (SFCO)
415-248-1640 • sfchamberorchestra.org

Venues: The Contemporary Jewish Museum of San Francisco; Herbst Theater, 401 Van Ness Avenue; San Francisco Conservatory of Music, 50 Oak Street; Julia Morgan Theater, 2640 College Avenue, Berkeley.
Public Transportation: Depends on venue.
Handicapped Accessibility: Depends on venue.
Performances/Programs: Approximately nine programs and 24 performances.
Ticket Prices: Free (except for special events).
Membership: Individual $50, Family $95. Benefits include reserved seating for all concerts, advance reservations, a "Best of Season" CD, recognition in programs and online, a monthly e-newsletter, invitations to house concerts and special events, members-only events and post-concert receptions and 2-for-1 tickets to "Classical at the Freight."

From the Editors: Founded by conductor Adrian Sunshine, the first concert of the SFCO took place in April 1953 in Berkeley's Hillel Foundation. The musicians in the early years were all members of the San Francisco Symphony, which was then a very part-time engagement. The name San Francisco Chamber Orchestra wasn't used until 1957, when the orchestra made its "debut" at the University of San Francisco under Maestro Sunshine's direction.

SAN FRANCISCO CONSERVATORY OF MUSIC
50 Oak Street
415-503-6275 • sfcm.edu

Public Transportation: Yes (multiple MUNI stops are convenient to the Conservatory).
Handicapped Accessibility: Good
Performances/Programs: Varies per year.
Ticket Prices: Some events are free; prices for others range $15–$20.

From the Editors: In 1917, local pianists Ada Clement and Lillian Hodghead opened the doors of the Ada Clement Piano School. Located in the remodeled home of Lillian's parents, the school began with three pianos, four studios, two blackboards, and 40 students. Enrollment grew quickly and, recognizing the need for a music conservatory on the West Coast, the school became the San Francisco Conservatory of Music in 1923.

From the beginning, chamber music has been an important part of the Conservatory. The first faculty chamber group, the California String Quartet, was formed in 1926. In 1948, the internationally renowned Griller Quartet established a summer school at the Conservatory, attracting students from across the United States. The ensemble returned for three more summers and served on the faculty for many years.

The renowned Alma Trio began a summer residence program in 1952, and the ensemble's pianist, Adolph Baller, subsequently joined the Conservatory's faculty.

Today, the Conservatory hosts approximately 407 students enrolled from 35 states and 31 countries to study with distinguished faculty members who include more than two dozen members of the San Francisco Symphony, Opera, and Ballet orchestras.

SAN FRANCISCO SYMPHONY (SFS)
415-864-6000 • sfsymphony.org

Venues: Davies Symphony Hall, 201 Van Ness Ave; Flint Center, 21250 Stevens Creek Boulevard, Cupertino.

Public Transportation: Good (take MUNI or BART to the Civic Center station)

Handicapped Accessibility: Good

Performances/Programs: 230 per season.

Ticket Prices: From $30 to $135. On the day of select concerts, Rush tickets are $20 each, limit two per person.

Group Discounts: Groups of 10 or more save 10%–20%.

Subscriptions: With the Davies Symphony Hall Classical series, you can choose from more than 20 different classical concerts performed throughout the season at Davies Symphony Hall. Tickets are available by day of the week and time of performance. Other subscriptions include the Great Performers, Flint Center Classical, Katharine Hanrahan Open Rehearsal, Davies Symphony Hall Chamber Music, and Youth Orchestra series. Benefits include discounts on additional ticket purchases and ticket exchanges.

Membership: Dolce Society membership begins at $75. Benefits include a membership card providing a 10% discount at the symphony store, an annual calendar with advance notice of events, and free admission for two to a Friends private rehearsal.

From the Editors: Founded in 1911 to help revitalize the city of San Francisco after the famous earthquake, the San Francisco Symphony has grown to international acclaim. Today under the direction of Michael Tilson

Thomas, SFS continues to develop new programs to make classical music more accessible.

Keeping Score, launched in 2006, is anchored by a PBS television series, an interactive website, a national radio series, DVDs, and an educational program for grades K–12. Concerts for Kids and Music for Families concerts are specially geared toward children.

SFSkids.com is SFS's website that provides children with the opportunity to learn about music online. The site's music lab helps children learn music basics, including tempo, rhythm, harmony, pitch, and music symbols; Instruments of the Orchestra allows users to learn about the instruments of the orchestra by sound and sight.

Throughout its history, the SFS has presented more than 200 world premieres, commissioned more than 100 new works, and received 12 awards from ASCAP for adventurous programming and a commitment to American music.

Thousands of free tickets to SFS events are provided to a variety of groups each season. Ticket Reach distributes more than 2,000 complimentary tickets each year through charities such as Big Brothers/Big Sisters and the Chinatown Youth Center.

Davies After Hours is a fun and free post-concert experience held on three special dates during the season. Part performance and part reception, Davies After Hours features different performers, including SFS musicians showcasing their non-classical pursuits (including SFS violist, Christina King, on electric violin!) and DJ/composer Mason Bates with the SFS's own Benjamin Schwartz.

BERKELEY FESTIVAL AND EXHIBITION
University of California, Berkeley Campus, Berkeley
bfx.berkeley.edu

Public Transportation: Very good (easily accessible by Richmond and Concord transit lines, as well as AC Transit bus).

Performances/Programs: Approximately 13 performances are given per year.

Ticket Prices: Prices range from $16 to $56. Student tickets may be available for certain events as noted in the performance calendar.

Subscriptions: Subscription is activated if you purchase tickets to three or more events, which entitles you to a 10% discount. Only subscribers may exchange their tickets free of charge for another Berkeley Festival and Exhibition concert of their choice.

Membership: Individual membership begins at $75 and entitles you

advance ticket-purchasing options. Higher levels of donation provide you with access to open rehearsals, invitations to Friends Appreciation Nights, reserved-parking passes, an invitation to the annual Home Concert, an invitation to the annual Director's Dinner, and more.

From the Editors: The Berkeley Festival and Exhibition is an early music festival that occurs each summer. It's produced by Cal Performances in association with the Department of Music, University of California, Berkeley, the San Francisco Early Music Society, and Early Music America.

CABRILLO FESTIVAL OF CONTEMPORARY MUSIC
cabrillomusic.org

Venues: Santa Cruz Civic Auditorium, 307 Church Street, Santa Cruz; Mission San Juan Bautista, corner of 2nd Street and Mariposa Street.
Public Transportation: Poor
Handicapped Accessibility: Good
Performances/Programs: Approximately eight performances annually. Summer Festival takes place first two weeks in August.
Ticket Prices: $20–$41 depending on concert; Family concert is free (tickets required).
Membership: No membership packages are offered, but tax- deductible donations are accepted.

 OPERA

POCKET OPERA
415-972-8934 • pocketopera.org

Venues: Florence Gould Theater at the Palace of the Legion of Honor, 100 34th Avenue at Clement Street (San Francisco); Napa Valley Opera House, 1030 Main Street (Napa); Julia Morgan Theater, 2640 College Avenue (Berkeley).
Public Transportation: Depends on venue.
Handicapped Accessibility: Good (all venues)
Performances/Programs: Six productions per season with multiple performances of each.
Ticket Prices: $35; youth tickets $20, seniors $31.

Group Discounts: Discounts available for groups of 10 or more.

Subscriptions: Full Six-show subscription is $174. Mini subscriptions (four or five operas) also available for $30 per show. Subscriber benefits include great seats, flexible ticket exchanges, lost ticket insurance, and un-limited single ticket add-on for $30 each.

Membership: Available from $250–$10,000 and up. Members receive all subscriber benefits, plus extra benefits when donating $500 or more.

From the Editors: Pocket Opera provides a straightforward ap-proach to opera, with the hope that the audience will leave with a bet-ter understanding and appreciation for the production and the art form itself. English translations often replace original librettos, and introductions and narratives are added to offer a deeper explanation of the story. The productions are intimate and modest, with a chamber orchestra of 15 or fewer musicians. The multi-talented Donald Pippin founded Pocket Opera, serves as its artistic director, narrates and plays piano for the productions, and has translated dozens of major and lesser-known operas to English for the company.

SAN FRANCISCO OPERA
San Francisco War Memorial Opera House, 301 Van Ness Street
415-864-3330 • sfopera.com

Public Transportation: Good

Handicapped Accessibility: Good

Performances/Programs: Six productions per season with multiple performances of each plus special free events like Opera in the Park.

Ticket Prices: $15–$245, based on date, time, and performances select-ed. Student Rush $25, and $30 senior and military Rush sometimes avail-able. $10 standing room tickets available for each performance.

Group Discounts: Discounts available for groups of 10 or more.

Subscriptions: Available from $60–$2,700, depending on date, time, and performances selected. Full (nine-performance), Half (four- or five-per-formance), Mini (three- and four-performance), Out of Town (three perfor-mances in three days), and Design-Your-Own (three or more). Subscriber benefits include 30% savings, priority ordering, easy ticket exchanges, in-vites to subscriber events, and discounts to the gift shop and area busi-nesses.

Membership: Available from $75–$25,000+. Students can join at the lowest level for just $40.

From the Editors: The San Francisco Opera was founded in 1923 and has since grown to be the second largest opera company in North America. The beautiful and renowned War Memorial Opera House has been the exclusive performing center for the San Francisco Opera since 1932. The Opera has offered several high definition simulcasts in recent years, in order to reach audiences outside of the Opera House. The San Francisco Opera has recently signed a deal for the distribution of six productions per year to movie theaters using the feature film quality digital format, this being a first for the opera community. For people who want to see the San Francisco Opera in person but still pay movie prices, the Opera offers an impressive 200 Standing Room tickets per performance for a mere $10.

 JAZZ/CABARET

ANNA'S JAZZ ISLAND
2120 Allston Way, Berkeley
510-841-JAZZ (5299) • annasjazzisland.com

Public Transportation: Good
Handicapped Accessibility: Good
Performances/Programs: Approximately 280 performances each year. Showtimes vary, but the club is open Tuesday–Sunday from 5 p.m. until the music ends.
Ticket Prices: $5–$10.

LES JOULINS JAZZ BISTRO
44 Ellis Street
415-397-5397 • jazzbistrosf.com

Public Transportation: Good
Handicapped Accessibility: Good
Performances/Programs: Approximately 300 performances per year. Performance schedule is seven nights a week from 7:30 p.m. till close.
Ticket Prices: No cover charge.

RASSELAS JAZZ CLUB
1534 Fillmore Street
415-346-8696 • rasselasjazzclub.com

Public Transportation: Good
Handicapped Accessibility: Good
Performances/Programs: Approximately 280 performances per year. Performances run Thursday–Tuesday; times vary depending on the night and the performer. See online calendar for details.
Ticket Prices: Occasional cover of $5–$10.

RRAZZ ROOM AT HOTEL NIKKO
222 Mason Street
415-394-1189 • therrazzroom.com

Public Transportation: Good
Handicapped Accessibility: Good
Performances/Programs: Approximately 300 performances per year. Performance nights vary; see schedule for details.
Ticket Prices: $25–$60. Half-price tickets sometimes available on Goldstar.com.

SAVANNA JAZZ
2937 Mission Street
415-285-3369 • savannajazz.com

Public Transportation: Good
Handicapped Accessibility: Good
Performances/Programs: 280 performances per year. Performances are given on Sunday, Tuesday and Wednesday at 8 p.m.; Thursday, Friday and Saturday at 8:30 p.m.
Ticket Prices: $5–$10. Some shows offer a $5 discount before 9:30 p.m.

YOSHI'S SAN FRANCISCO
1330 Fillmore Street
415-655-5600 • yoshis.com

Public Transportation: Good
Handicapped Accessibility: Good

Performances/Programs: 14 shows per week. Schedule of performances are Monday–Saturday at 8 and 10 p.m., Sunday at 7 and 9 p.m.

Ticket Prices: From $10 to $35 with a one-drink minimum.

YOSHI'S OAKLAND
510 Embarcadero West, Oakland
510-238-9200 • yoshis.com

Public Transportation: Good

Handicapped Accessibility: Good

Performances/Programs: 15 performances are given each week. Monday–Saturday at 8 and 10 p.m.; Sunday at 7 and 9 p.m.; Sunday kids' matinée at 2 p.m.

Ticket Prices: Ranging from $10 to $40, with a one-drink minimum. Admission is $5 for children 15 and under for the Sunday matinée.

From the Editors: Yoshi's Oakland and Yoshi's San Francisco are two of the premier jazz clubs on the West Coast, boasting some of the most sophisticated acoustics to be found and a stellar lineup of contemporary jazz and pop.

The Oakland location began in 1973 in North Berkeley as a sushi bar that soon expanded into a world-class restaurant and jazz club that has hosted the likes of McCoy Tyner, Harry Connick, Jr., Oscar Peterson, Diana Krall, Dizzy Gillespie, and many more. The club moved to Jack London Square in 1997 as part of an effort to revitalize the arts in Oakland.

The San Francisco location opened its doors in 2007 with 28,000 square feet in San Francisco's historic Fillmore District.

Ticket prices are generally reasonable and many of the later shows are discounted to keep the club's many fans coming back for more. Be sure to get there early, even with tickets, to snag that table near the stage. If you're dining in the restaurant beforehand, your table in the club can be reserved to avoid the last-minute scramble to find seats.

Yoshi's Oakland hosts a Sunday Kids' Matinée with $5 admission for young jazz lovers 15 and under.

SAN JOSE JAZZ FESTIVAL
408-288-7557 • sanjosejazz.org

Venues: 10 stages centered around Plaza de César Chávez, Park & Market Streets, San Jose.

Public Transportation: Good
Handicapped Accessibility: Good
Performances/Programs: Approximately 100 performances over three days in August.
Ticket Prices: $10 per day, $25 for all three days. $350 for VIP admission.
Group Discounts: Tickets are $20 per person for groups of 20 or more.

From the Editors: San Jose Jazz continues to be one of the best jazz advocates on the West Coast and its annual festival is also one of the best. Tickets can be purchased on site the day of the festival (though VIP passes must be purchased beforehand). With more than 10 different venues and plenty of activities aside from the music, the festival will keep even the most intrepid jazz lover busy all weekend long.

DANCE

ALONZO KING'S LINES BALLET (ALONZO KING)
Novellus Theater at Yerba Buena Center for the Arts
700 Howard Street at 3rd Street
415-978-2787 • linesballet.org

Public Transportation: Good
Handicapped Accessibility: Good
Performances/Programs: Two seasonal programs (one in the fall and one in the spring), each with about eight performances over two weeks.
Ticket Prices: Range from $15 to $65. Student tickets for select performances are $15 and are located in the upper terrace section.
Group Discounts: Groups of 10 or more receive a 20% discount.
Subscriptions: Subscriptions are available for either the fall or spring seasons and include priority seating and flexible ticket-exchange privileges. Subscribers save 20%.
Membership: Starting with contributions of $100, donors receive a subscription to the donor newsletter, recognition in home season programs, and a 10% discount on all LINES Ballet merchandise.

BALLET SAN JOSE
San Jose Center for the Performing Arts, 255 Almaden Boulevard
408-288-2800 • balletsanjose.org

Public Transportation: Good

Handicapped Accessibility: Good

Performances/Programs: Four different programs each year, plus the annual *Nutcracker*. There are three or four performances of each program. The *Nutcracker* runs about three weeks.

Ticket Prices: Range between $25 and $85. Students and seniors receive small discounts in selected seating areas.

Group Discounts: Packages are customized for groups of 10 or more. Discounts start at $5 per ticket.

Subscriptions: Subscriptions include performances of all four programs. Subscribers choose a Thursday, Friday, Saturday, or Sunday series and seating preferences. Small discounts are available for children and senior subscriptions. All ticket sales are final. Benefits include priority seating, ticket insurance, free or low-cost parking, invitations to subscribers-only events, and free ticket exchange privileges.

ODC/DANCE (ODC)
Yerba Buena Center for the Arts, 701 Mission Street
415-863-6606 • odcdance.org

Public Transportation: Good

Handicapped Accessibility: Good

Performances/Programs: Two annual home seasons of about two weeks each.

Ticket Prices: From $15 to $45. Discounts are available for students, seniors, and educators; actual amounts vary by performance. Free admission to the ODC Gallery is included with the purchase of a ticket.

Group Discounts: Groups of 10 or more receive a 15% discount.

Membership: Annual membership to ODC Verge is $35 and includes invitations to special events, 20% off prime seats at ODC performances, and 2-for-1 tickets at select shows at the ODC Theater.

Special Membership for Young Adults: Although ODC Verge doesn't have an official age limit, this organization is aimed at young and avid dance fans in the Bay Area. In addition to the offerings mentioned above, the organization offers networking parties and opportunities to participate in the Verge Leadership Council, which strives to cultivate new support for contemporary arts in the Bay Area.

SAN FRANCISCO BALLET
War Memorial Opera House, 301 Van Ness Avenue (at Grove Street)
415-861-5600 • sfballet.org

Public Transportation: Good

Handicapped Accessibility: Good

Performances/Programs: Eight programs a year, plus the annual *Nutcracker*. Each program runs for two weeks with seven performances. The *Nutcracker* runs for two-and-a-half weeks in December with performances almost every day.

Ticket Prices: Range from $25 to $250. Discounts for individual shows are available to seniors (68+), students, and military personnel on the day of the performance up until the hour before the performance.

Group Discounts: Groups of 20 or more can receive discounts to select performances. Flex and standard plans are available.

Subscriptions: Subscription packages are available for three, five, or eight shows. Only subscribers may exchange tickets free of charge up until 24 hours before a performance. Other benefits include a 15% discount at the Ballet Shop, discounts on additional single-ticket purchases, waived handling fees, a subscription to *Backstage* magazine, savings at local restaurants, and lost-ticket insurance.

Membership: Donor fees start at $75 and include a complimentary season program guide and a subscription to *Backstage* magazine.

Special Membership for Young Adults: ENCORE! is a membership program for young men and women. Annual membership is $75 and includes invitations to special events, preferred seating at select San Francisco Ballet performances, subscriptions to *Backstage* magazine and *On Pointe* newsletter, and special notice of Junior League previews during the repertory season.

From the Editors: San Francisco Ballet is proud to be America's oldest professional ballet company, dating back to 1933. What started as a regional ballet company is now one of the three largest ballet companies in the country and undoubtedly one of the most diverse. Under the direction of current artistic director, Helgi Tomassaon, this company has become an international success story.

The Ballet features leading interpreters, not only of George Balanchine's classical ballets, but also of contemporary works by Nacho Duato, William Forsythe, and Mark Morris. In 2005, San Francisco Ballet won a Laurence Olivier Award for its fall season at London's Sadler's Wells Theatre. In 2006, it was the first non-European company to be voted "Company of the Year" by *Dance Europe* magazine.

The year 2008 marked San Francisco Ballet's 75th anniversary. Celebratory events included hosting a New Works Festival with 10 new works by 10 choreographers and producing a televised *Nutcracker* project with KQED Public Television. The company is currently the spotlight of a curated exhibit at San Francisco International Airport and has released a commemorative book: *San Francisco Ballet at 75*.

SMUIN BALLET
415-495-2234 • smuinballet.org

Venues: Yerba Buena Center for the Arts, 701 Mission Street; Lesher Center for the Arts, 1601 Civic Drive, Walnut Creek; Mountain View Center for the Performing Arts, 500 Castro Street, Mountain View; Sunset Center, San Carlos Street at Ninth Avenue, Carmel-by-the-Sea.

Public Transportation: Yes (Lesher Center and Yerba Buena).

Handicapped Accessibility: Good

Performances/Programs: Three programs each year with about 20 performances each.

Ticket Prices: $40 to $55. Student and senior discounts vary by venue.

Group Discounts: Groups of 10 or more receive discounts of up to 25%.

Subscriptions: Season subscriptions are available at each of Smuin's four regular venues. Subscriptions include performances of all three shows and vary in price according to seating preferences. Subscribers save up to 15% with subscriptions and receive free ticket exchanges. All sales are final.

Membership: Donors contributing $50 or more receive e-newsletters and other special notices.

FILM

THE CASTRO THEATRE
429 Castro Street
415-621-5288 • thecastrotheatre.com

Public Transportation: Good (accessible via MUNI Metro, F Market streetcar, and multiple bus lines).

Handicapped Accessibility: Good

Performances/Programs: Revival screenings of classic American and foreign films.

Ticket Prices: Varies, based on program.

From the Editors: The Castro Theatre is one of the great icons of San Francisco. This landmark theater, built in 1922, is located in the city's well-known Castro, a largely gay neighborhood. Decorated in a Spanish Renaissance style, the beautiful old movie palace features Art Deco touches throughout and has a luxurious interior that even includes a chandelier.

Outside, the theater's enormous neon "Castro" sign, which can be seen from many spots in San Fran, beckons movie lovers to its doors.

Visitors will be pleased to find that the Castro Theatre hosts an eclectic array of movies, with a special focus on films that appeal to the gay community. Numerous festivals, such as the Silent Film Festival, the SF International Film Festival, the SF Jewish Film Festival, and the Asian-American Film Festival, are held at the Castro, and most movie screenings here are preceded by a recital on the theater's Wurlitzer pipe organ.

SAN FRANCISCO FILM SOCIETY
39 Mesa Street, Ste. 110, The Presidio
415-561-5000 • sffs.org

Venues: Varies, based on program; see website for details.
Public Transportation: Depends on venue.
Handicapped Accessibility: Depends on venue.
Ticket Prices: Varies, based on program.

From the Editors: The non-profit San Francisco Film Society presents movie screenings and film festivals in the city throughout the year. The society hosts a number of unique events that will intrigue movie buffs, including the San Francisco International Animation Showcase (a collection of the best animated movies from around the globe), Film in the Fog (an annual end-of-summer series of outdoor screenings for the whole family held at the Presidio), New Italian Cinema, and the San Francisco International Film Festival.

SAN FRANCISCO CINEMATHEQUE, EXPERIMENTAL FILM AND VIDEO
145 Ninth Street, Suite 240
415-552-1990 • sfcinematheque.org

Venues: Yerba Buena Center for the Arts; San Francisco Art Institute
Public Transportation: Good

Handicapped Accessibility: Good
Performances/Programs: Mostly experimental and classic works.
Ticket Prices: Vary based on program.

From the Editors: The San Francisco Cinematheque, founded in 1961, is like a library, museum, lab, and screening room all rolled into one— in short, a cinema fan's paradise. The Cinematheque shows experimental films, digital media, and performative cinema, and it works to further the public's appreciation of these through showcases, publications, exhibitions, and other activities.

Numerous programs offered throughout the year often include in-person presentations from distinguished scholars and film practitioners, historical works from American and international cinema, experiments in film, and the development of video and film presentations for showcases in America and abroad. Students and scholars of film will find a treasure trove of information on the art available at the San Francisco Cinemateque through its archival services, publications library, lectures, panels, and retrospectives.

SUNDANCE CINEMAS: THEATRE KABUKI
1881 Post Street at Fillmore
415-346-3243 • sundancecinemas.com/kabuki.html

Public Transportation: Good
Handicapped Accessibility: Good
Performances/Programs: A blend of independent and mainstream American and foreign films.
Ticket Prices: Vary based on seat location and program.

From the Editors: Sundance Kabuki is a multiplex that elevates the movie-going experience by adding a little extra class. That means no commercials before the feature and the food and drink options offered outside the auditorium include cheese plates, crème brulee, and keoke coffee.

Built at the tip of the Japan Center complex, the Kabuki plays independent features, art films, foreign films, documentaries, *and* major Hollywood releases, and it has served as a key venue for the San Francisco International Film Festival.

TELLURIDE FILM FESTIVAL
510-665-9589 • telluridefilmfestival.org

Venues: Screenings held in venues in and around the Berkeley area.

From the Editors: Founded in 1974 by Tom Luddy, James Card, and Bill and Stella Pence, the Telluride Film Festival is headquartered in Berkeley, California and held amidst the breathtaking beauty of the Colorado mountains in the town of Telluride. The annual four-day festival, which takes place over Labor Day weekend, features a schedule (which isn't revealed until opening day) that includes exciting premieres, gems from the past, and three "tributes" that honor the work of a trio of guest artists who have made fundamental contributions to film.

PERFORMANCE VENUES

CAL PERFORMANCES
510-642-9988 • calperfs.berkeley.edu

Venues: The Zellerbach Auditorium, Zellerbach Playhouse, Hearst Greek Theatre, and Wheeler Auditorium, all located on the University of California-Berkeley campus, 101 Zellerbach Hall #4800, Berkeley.
Public Transportation: Very good (easily accessible by BART)
Handicapped Accessibility: Good
Performances/Programs: Programming includes theater, dance, opera, classical music, jazz, recitals, world music, family shows, and a discussion/lecture series.
Ticket Prices: Vary based on program. Children under 16 get tickets for 50% off for selected matinées. A $5 discount for students, seniors, and UC Berkeley faculty and staff is offered. UC Berkeley students receive a 50% discount on tickets; $20 Rush tickets are available one hour before show for select performances ($10 for UCB students, $15 for seniors and UCB faculty/staff). Ticket exchanges are $5 for single-ticket buyers.
Group Discounts: Discounts available for groups of 10 or more.
Subscriptions: Numerous subscription series choices, including a choose your own option, are offered. Benefits include free ticket exchanges.

GRACE CATHEDRAL
1100 California Street
415-749-6300 • gracecathedral.org

Public Transportation: Very good
Handicapped Accessibility: Good
Performances/Programs: Music programming includes sacred music, holiday music, classical, jazz, recitals, and sometimes performers from the world of popular music. Other events include film screenings, literary events, sing-alongs and "The Forum at Grace Cathedral" live talk show.
Ticket Prices: Vary based on program. Many events are free. Shows occasionally available on Goldstar.com.

JEWISH COMMUNITY CENTER OF SAN FRANCISCO (JCCSF)
3200 California Street
415-292-1200 • jccsf.org

Public Transportation: Very good (easily accessible by MUNI bus or BART).
Handicapped Accessibility: Good
Performances/Programs: The JCCSF offers everything from fitness programs to adult-education classes. Arts & Ideas programming includes literary events, film screenings, concerts, discussions with notable people, dance, and other performance events.
Ticket Prices: Vary based on program. Ticket discounts are available for members, as are frequent student discounts. Discounts also available on Goldstar.com.
Subscriptions: Several different subscription series choices available, including a create-your-own series option. Subscriber benefits include preferred seating and free ticket exchanges.
Membership: Community membership is $180 per year for a household ($125 for individuals, $100 for seniors). Benefits include discounts on classes and programs, discounts on special events, priority registration, members-only special offers, $1 off general admission price at Balboa Theatre, 50% off a subscription to J (the Jewish News Weekly of Northern California), and numerous discounts at local shops and restaurants. Center membership includes the same benefits, plus access to the fitness and aquatics facilities, a parking discount at the JCCSF garage, priority registration for classes and sports leagues, and priority use of drop-in childcare.

MASONIC CENTER
Nob Hill Masonic Center, 1111 California Street
415-292-9191 • masonicauditorium.com

Public Transportation: Very good
Handicapped Accessibility: Good
Performances/Programs: The Masonic Center hosts concerts, comedy shows, lectures, and various private events.
Ticket Prices: Varies, based on program. Some shows available on Goldstar.com.

OLD FIRST CONCERTS
Old First Church, 1751 Sacramento Street
415-474-1608 • oldfirstconcerts.org

Public Transportation: Very good
Handicapped Accessibility: Good
Performances/Programs: Old First Concerts feature classical, chamber, jazz, avant-garde, blues, folk, and world music. The venue has hosted notable musicians like Ali Akbar Khan and the Kronos Quartet, but it's dedicated to providing a platform for emerging and niche artists and frequently premieres brand new work.
Ticket Prices: Ticket prices tend to be around $15. Old First Concerts also offers a discount-ticket program. Patrons receive a 10% discount when buying a book of five tickets or a 20% discount when purchasing a book of 10 tickets. Further discounts are available for students and seniors (for both discount books and for single tickets).
Subscriptions/Membership: None, as such, but people who donate $100 or more to Old First Concerts receive invitations to rehearsals.

POST STREET THEATRE & MARINES MEMORIAL THEATRE
415-771-6900 • unionsquaretheatres.com

Venues: Post Street Theatre, 450 Post Street; Marines Memorial Theatre, 609 Sutter Street.
Public Transportation: Very good
Handicapped Accessibility: Good
Performances/Programs: Shows produced at these theaters include plays, musicals, dance shows, solo pieces, concerts, and comedy performances.

Ticket Prices: Vary based on presentation. The following discount ticket packages are available: buy tickets for two shows in one transaction and get $10 off each ticket; get $15 off when you buy tickets for three shows at once.

Group Discounts: Group discounts are available for some shows.

SAN FRANCISCO WAR MEMORIAL & PERFORMING ARTS CENTER (SFWMPAC)
401 Van Ness Avenue, Room 110
415-621-6600 • sfwmpac.org

Public Transportation: Very good
Handicapped Accessibility: Good
Performances/Programs: The SFWMPAC contains the War Memorial Opera House, the War Memorial Veterans Building (including the Herbst Theatre and Green Room), Louise M. Davies Symphony Hall, Harold L. Zellerbach Rehearsal Hall, and the Memorial Court. Events held in these facilities include opera, classical music, dance, recitals, plays, lectures, meetings, receptions, special screenings, gala events, and various other types of theatrical performance.

Ticket Prices: Vary based on program. Discounts for students, seniors and children are sometimes available. Shows available on Goldstar.com.

YERBA BUENA CENTER FOR THE ARTS
415-978-2787 • ybca.org

Venues: Novellus Theater at YBCA, 700 Howard Street at 3rd; YBCA Galleries & Forum Building, 701 Mission Street.
Public Transportation: Very good
Handicapped Accessibility: Good
Performances/Programs: YBCA produces 12–15 events per year; other companies also produce at the Novellus and Forum. Programming includes multimedia performance, dance, world theater, comedy, solo shows, performance art, and more.

Ticket Prices: Vary based on presentation. $5 discounts are offered for seniors, students and teachers for all YBCA performances. Shows available on Goldstar.com. Film or performance ticket includes free same-day admission to the gallery.

Group Discounts: Discounts available for groups of 10 or more to YBCA shows, and some group discounts available to other shows.

Subscriptions: A Pick 4 subscription package gets you $5 off regular ticket prices ($10 off if you're a YBCA member). Pick 4 benefits include free ticket exchanges and an invite to the season-announcement party. Ticket exchanges are available for non-subscribers with a $2 fee.

Membership: Membership starts at $65 ($25 off for working artists, seniors, full-time students, and full-time teachers). Benefits include $5 off all tickets to YBCA shows, a 10% discount at local eateries, an invitation to the annual season-announcement preview party, free gallery and opening-night-party admission, discounts on film and performance tickets, and waived ticket-handling fees. At the $165 member level, benefits also include reciprocal member privileges at more than 100 arts venues throughout the country.

For information on Reno, Nevada, and
Sacramento, California, visit go-artsamerica.com.

WASHINGTON, D.C.

The United States is one of the few countries where the political capital is not the cultural capital, but America's capital city still has an excellent arts scene, in particular several world-class museums that are totally free of charge, plus a theater with an interesting historical past.

ARTS INFO

NEWSPAPERS

Washington City Paper (washingtoncitypaper.com)—Free weekly newspaper with excellent reviews and art listings.

Washingtonian (washingtonian.com)—Glossy monthly with good arts articles and listings.

Washington Post (washingtonpost.com)—Though more famous for its political coverage, this daily newspaper does a fine job of covering the high points of the D.C. arts scene.

WEBSITES

Cultural Alliance of Greater Washington (cultural-alliance.org)—Dedicated to sustaining and increasing regional leadership, appreciation, support, and resources for arts and culture.

D.C. Theater Scene (dctheatrescene.com)—"Washington's Liveliest Theater Website."

DISCOUNTS

Goldstar (goldstar.com)—National site offers good selection of discounts in and around Washington.

TicketPlace (ticketplace.org)—Non-profit site offering half-price tickets to a variety of D.C.-area performances. Booth at 407 7th Street NW.

ART MUSEUMS

CORCORAN GALLERY OF ART, COLLEGE OF ART AND DESIGN
500 17th Street NW
202-639-1700 • corcoran.org

Public Transportation: Excellent (easily accessible from the Metro Orange, Blue, and Red lines, as well as Metro bus).

Handicapped Accessibility: Good (wheelchair access provided at E Street entrance, located near the intersection of 17th and E Street NW).

Hours: Wednesday, Friday–Sunday 10 a.m.–5 p.m., Thursday 10 a.m.–9 p.m.

Admission: Regular admission is $10, special exhibitions are $14, seniors and military $12; students $10, children 6 and under free; groups are accommodated with occasional discounts. The Corcoran's permanent collection is on view free of charge for all reciprocal members (reciprocal membership privileges do not apply for admission to ticketed exhibitions).

Tours: Free tours are given daily at noon, except on Tuesdays. Lasting approximately 45 minutes, they provide an overview of the Corcoran's collections and include an introduction to the building.

Membership: Individual membership is $60 annually and includes free year-round admission, invitations to preview days for special exhibitions, free or reduced admission to public programs, and advance opportunity to register for continuing-education courses at the Corcoran College of Art and Design. Discount packages are available: student membership (with valid ID) $30/annually; national membership $45/annually (for those living 250 or more miles from Washington, D.C.); senior membership (62+) $50/annually.

Other Benefits: Supporting membership ($160/annually) gets you reciprocal admission to select museums nationwide.

From the Editors: The Corcoran Gallery, including its renowned art school, is housed in an ornate 1897 Beaux-Arts building. The museum is famous for its Dutch 17th-century and French 19th-century works, along with one of the best American painting collections found anywhere in the world. Also check out the Salon Doré, a sumptuous French period room.

DUMBARTON OAKS
32nd Street between S and R Streets
(one block east of Wisconsin Avenue in Georgetown)
202-339-6401 • doaks.org

Public Transportation: Excellent (Metrobus routes 30, 32, 34, 36, D2, D4, and M12 come within two blocks of the garden and museum entrances).
Handicapped Accessibility: Good (Note: The hillside gardens may present challenges for some visitors).
Hours: Tuesday–Sunday 2–6 p.m. (summer), 2–5 p.m. (winter), closed Monday.
Admission: Museum is always free. Summer Season garden admission $8, students, seniors, and children under 12 $5.
Tours: A brief introductory tour of the gardens takes place daily at 2:15 p.m. (except Mondays). In-depth guided tours of the gardens are available for a fee of $8 per person, and must be arranged in advance. Docent-led tours are offered to eligible groups of 10 to 45 people on Tuesday, Wednesday, Thursday, and Saturday by advance reservation and for a fee of $8 per person.

From the Editors: The former Georgian mansion of Robert Woods Bliss and his wife Mildred, Dambarton Oaks has a fine collection of Byzantine and pre-Columbian art, plus a lovely 16-acre garden.

HILLWOOD ESTATE, MUSEUM AND GARDENS
4155 Linnean Avenue NW
202-686-5807 • hillwoodmuseum.org

Public Transportation: Fair (accessible by Metrobus L1 or L2. Also accessible by Metrorail, but requires a 20-minute walk from the Van Ness/UDC Metro station on the Red Line).

Handicapped Accessibility: Good

Hours: Tuesday–Saturday 10 a.m.–5 p.m., Sundays by reservation only. (Note: On the days of your visit, go to the Visitor Center to make arrangements, or if you prefer call 202-686-5807 to make advance reservations, or reserve online. On spring weekends, daily availability may be limited, so advance reservations are preferred. Reservations are required for most Sunday visits.)

Admission: $12, seniors (65+) $10, full-time college students $7, children (6–18) $5.

Tours: Tours of the Mansion are offered Tuesday–Saturday at 11:30 a.m. and 1:30 p.m., and on select Sundays at 1:30 p.m. Garden tours are offered in the spring and fall at 10:30 a.m. and 12:30 p.m. All tours require advance reservations.

Audio Tours: Free

Membership: Individual Friends membership is $50 annually. Membership provides guaranteed access to tour the estate, guaranteed access for Friends' guests in groups of eight or fewer, two guest passes per year, as well as invitations to annual exhibition previews and Friends-only events.

From the Editors: The former 25-acre estate of cereal heiress Marjorie Merriweather Post has the largest collection of Imperial Russian decorative art outside of Russia.

THE KREEGER MUSEUM
2401 Foxhall Road NW
202-337-3050 • kreegermuseum.org

Public Transportation: Good (easily accessible by D6 bus; nearest Metro stop is Tenleytown on the Red line, which requires a taxi to reach the museum).

Handicapped Accessibility: Fair (the main floor of the museum, the sculpture terrace, and restrooms are wheelchair accessible; the museum's lower galleries are not).

Hours: Saturday 10 a.m.–4 p.m.; Tuesday–Friday, reservations are required for all museum visits. Museum is closed in August.

Admission: $10, students and seniors $7, group discounts are available for groups of 10 to 45 individuals; a non-refundable check for $8 per person ($5 for seniors 65+ and students) must be submitted two weeks in advance of a scheduled tour.

Tours: Weekday visitors may choose to make reservations for the

10:30 a.m. or 1:30 p.m. tour. On Saturday, optional guided tours are given at 10:30 a.m., noon, and 2 p.m.

Membership: Friend membership is $100 annually and entitles members to complimentary museum admission with one guest, an invitation to the Friends of the Kreeger Museum reception, and discounted tickets to select public programs.

From the Editors: Located in the former residence of David and Carmen Kreeger, this museum showcases a collection of 19th- and 20th-century paintings and sculptures, including works by Monet, van Gogh, Picasso, Renoir, Cézanne, Chagall, Rodin, Miro, Moore, and Kandinsky.

NATIONAL GALLERY OF ART
4th and Constitution Avenue NW
(on the National Mall between 3rd and 7th Streets)
202-737-4215 • nga.gov

Public Transportation: Excellent (convenient to multiple Metro stops and buses).
Handicapped Accessibility: Good
Hours: Monday–Saturday 10 a.m.–5 p.m., Sunday 11 a.m.–6 p.m.
Admission: Free
Tours: The museum offers ongoing Gallery Talks of the touring exhibitions and permanent collection.
Audio Tours: $5

From the Editors: Like many of the museums you'll find on the Mall in the nation's capital, the National Gallery of Art has a free-of-charge admission policy for all visitors. Enjoy the expansive collection of Western sculpture and painting, housed in two buildings connected underground by a spacious passageway. The original West Building was designed by John Russell Pope, the designer of the Jefferson Memorial. The East building, designed by I.M. Pei, was opened in 1978. The grounds are completed by the National Gallery of Art Sculpture Garden, which provides an outdoor setting for exhibiting select sculptures from the collection—and is the site of the popular ice-skating rink in the winter months (mid-November to mid-March, $7 adults/two-hour session).

Inside the neo-classical West Building and the more modern East building, you'll find a grand collection of European and American paintings, sculpture, photographs, and decorative arts. Originally created as a collection for the people of the United States by a joint resolution of Congress accepting the gifts of collector Andrew Mellon in 1937, it has grown considerably to include an impressive Italian Renaissance collection and Western sculpture, featuring Botticelli, Bellini, Degas, Leonardo, Raphael, Rodin, Titian, and Vermeer.

NATIONAL MUSEUM OF WOMEN IN THE ARTS
1250 New York Avenue NW
202-783-5000 • www.nmwa.org

Public Transportation: Very good (accessible by Red, Blue or Orange Metro lines, as well as local buses).

Handicapped Accessibility: Good

Hours: Monday–Saturday 10 a.m.–5 p.m., Sunday noon–5 p.m.

Admission: $10, students and seniors (65+) $8, youth (18 and under) free.

Free Day: First Sunday of every month.

Tours: Walk-in tours are offered throughout the week when guides are available. Walk-in tours give a brief overview of the museum and last about 20 minutes. For those who prefer to visit on their own, the wall texts in the permanent-collection galleries provide an overview and guide.

Membership: Individual membership is $40 annually. It includes free unlimited admission to the museum's collections and exhibitions, a personalized membership card, and special member trip and event invitations, as well as a subscription to NMWA's award-winning quarterly magazine, *Women in the Arts*.

Other Benefits: The Young Professional's Forum ($75/annually) offers individual membership benefits for patrons between the ages of 18 and 30, as well as invitations to cultural, social, and networking events. The $100 annual Friend membership gets you reciprocal admission to other museums. The Sustainer membership ($250/annually) gets you reciprocity, plus additional special visiting privileges and invites to opening parties.

From the Editors: The permanent collection and temporary exhibitions highlight achievements by women in the arts.

THE PHILLIPS COLLECTION
1600 21st Street NW
202-387-2151 • phillipscollection.org

Public Transportation: Very good (easily reachable by the Metro Red Line).

Handicapped Accessibility: Good

Hours: Tuesday–Saturday 10 a.m.–5 p.m., Thursday (extended hours) 10 a.m.–8:30 p.m., Sunday 11 a.m.-6 p.m., closed Monday.

Admission: Free (donations accepted). Special exhibitions $12, students and seniors (62+) $10.

Tours: The Phillips Collection offers one-hour guided tours of special exhibitions. Tours are given by professionally trained staff and are presented in the spirit of the museum's tradition, described by Duncan Phillips as a "joy-giving, life-enhancing influence, assisting people to see beautifully as true artists see." Tours are available on the following schedule: Tuesday–Friday 10 and 11:30 a.m., 1:30 and 3 p.m., and Thursday evenings at 6:30 p.m. The prices for tours are adults $15, students and seniors (62+) $13.

Membership: Individual membership is $60 annually and includes unlimited free admission to the permanent collection and all special exhibitions, two Member-for-a-Day guest passes, plus members-only preview days. Also included is free admission to the acclaimed Sunday Concerts and Thursday Phillips After 5 parties.

Other Benefits: Associate membership ($175/annually) gets you reciprocal admission to other museums, plus special visiting privileges and invites to special opening parties.

From the Editors: For a great museum that's off the beaten path of Washington, D.C.'s mall, look no further than the Phillips Collection, the oldest museum of modern art in the U.S. (opened in 1921).

Housed in founder Duncan Phillips's 1897 home in the Dupont Circle neighborhood, the setting is intimate; the venue is outstanding for viewing the American and European impressionist and modern art on display. On the walls you'll find Klee, Renoir, Rothko, and Whistler, among many esteemed others. With more than 2,500 artifacts in the collection, the museum expanded in 2006 to accommodate its impressive holdings and offer more on-view to the visitor. The expansion includes a new gallery designated for post-1950s works, a large auditorium for public programs, and an outdoor courtyard.

Programming is rich and popular with locals and visitors. Ongoing programs include the Sunday concerts, held weekly from October through May and featuring intimate performances from solo pianists to chamber ensembles. Phillips was known for collecting extensive compilations from artists he especially favored. These compilations are known by the museum as "collection units" and offer the visitor a unique experience unlike at any other modern art museum; you can peruse the Rothko room, which houses Rothko's work exclusively, and is designed in accordance with both the artist's and Phillips' original aesthetic preference and intention for the work.

SMITHSONIAN MEMBERSHIP

Researching which Smithsonian membership program will work best for you can be frustrating. Each of the nineteen principal museums has a separate (and very different) membership structure. There are also several national plans (National Associate Level, Resident Associate Membership, Contributing Membership, James Smithson Society) which unfortunately are not clearly explained on their website (si.edu/membership).

If you live in the Washington DC area and are a frequent Smithsonian visitor (to any of their museums, including the National Zoo), you should consider getting a Resident Associate Membership ($35 Individual, $50 family) which includes free and discounted admission to a more than 1,000 educational and cultural programs.

SMITHSONIAN AMERICAN ART MUSEUM (SAAM)
8th and F Streets NW
202-357-2700 • americanart.si.edu

Public Transportation: Excellent (conveniently located on the Red, Yellow and Green lines off the Gallery Place-Chinatown Metro station).
Handicapped Accessibility: Good
Hours: Open daily 11:30 a.m.–7 p.m.
Admission: Free
Membership: Associate membership is $50 annually and includes store discounts.
Other Benefits: Sponsor membership ($150/annually) gets you reciprocal benefits at other museums. Sustainer membership ($250/annually) entitles members to special visiting privileges and invitations to opening parties.

From the Editors: Celebrate 300 years of arts America at this collection of 38,000-plus works in all media and from all American periods, including Colonial and Federal, Hispanic, PWA works from the New Deal, and a large compilation of works by Native American and African American artists. The National Portrait Gallery has the only complete collection of portraits of American presidents.

SMITHSONIAN FREER & SACKLER GALLERIES
202-633-1000 • asia.si.edu

Venues: Sackler, 1050 Independence Avenue SW; Freer Gallery of Art, Jefferson Drive at 12th Street SW (Note: The two museums are connected by an underground exhibition space.)

Public Transportation: Very good (convenient to Metrorail and D.C. Circulator bus).

Handicapped Accessibility: Good (accessible entrance to the Freer Gallery is located on Independence Avenue at 12th Street, SW.)

Hours: Open from 10 a.m.–5:30 p.m. daily.

Admission: Free

Tours: Free. A variety of complimentary walk-in tours are offered in both galleries on most days. In addition, Highlights tours of the Freer Gallery of Art are offered at 12:15 p.m. on weekdays (except Wednesdays and federal holidays) and at 1:15 p.m. on weekends, unless other programs are taking place. Free guided group tours are available with four weeks' advance registration, subject to availability, from 10:15 a.m. to 2:15 p.m. daily, except Wednesdays and federal holidays.

Audio Tours: $5

Membership: Unlike many museums, the lowest level for membership at the Freer & Sackler Galleries is quite high: Patrons' Circle $1,200–$2,999. This entitles members to three exhibition opening receptions, in-depth tours of special exhibitions led by curators, and other discounts and amenities.

From the Editors: The Freer and Sackler Galleries feature an extensive and exquisite collection of bronzes, jades, sculptures, ceramics, and glass from Japan, China, India, Iran, Syria, and other places in Asia and Asia Minor. Early Christian art and the largest collection of James Whistler paintings also make up an important part of the collection.

SMITHSONIAN-HIRSHHORN AND SCULPTURE GARDEN (HIRSHHORN)
Independence Avenue (at 7th Street SW)
202-633-4674 • hirshhorn.si.edu

Public Transportation: Excellent
Handicapped Accessibility: Good
Hours: Open daily 10 a.m.–5:30 p.m. (except for December 25). Plaza hours are 7:30 a.m.–5:30 p.m. daily. The Sculpture Garden is open daily 7:30 a.m.–dusk.
Admission: Free
Basic Tour: From 10:30 a.m. to noon, group tours scheduled in advance meet at the Information Desk. Schedule your tour by calling 202-633-2796 or 202-633-8043 (TTY). From noon until 4 p.m., docents help you plan your visit and lead you on impromptu 30-minute tours. Interpretive guides also roam the galleries to answer your questions and discuss the special exhibitions on the second level.
Audio Tours: Free
Membership: Beginning at the Associates Circle level ($100–$249), members receive free admission to After Hours (for one), special curator-led Last Look exhibition tours, a 10% discount in the Hirshhorn and Smithsonian museum shops, a subscription to the Hirshhorn magazine, and a donor listing in the spring issue.

From the Editors: Here you'll see modern American and European sculpture by Moore, Rodin, and Picasso, plus gyrating mobiles by Alexander Calder and paintings by 20th-century American artists, all in a doughnut-shaped building. Outside is a sculpture garden which includes works by Auguste Rodin and Alexander Calder.

SMITHSONIAN NATIONAL MUSEUM OF AFRICAN ART (NMAFA)
950 Independence Avenue SW
202-633-4600 • africa.si.edu

Public Transportation: Excellent (accessible by Blue and Orange Metro lines).
Handicapped Accessibility: Good
Hours: Open daily 10 a.m.–5:30 p.m.
Admission: Free
Tours: Tours are based on objects and themes reflected in the museum's collections and exhibitions. Visitors and groups of no more than 15

may request an unscheduled tour at the information desk in the museum's pavilion, subject to docent availability.

Membership: Donor membership is $50 annually and provides the member with recognition as a member of the National Museum of African Art (NMAfA) on the museum's electronic member and donor scrolls.

Other Benefits: An Associate membership ($250/annually) gets you special visiting privileges and invites to opening parties

From the Editors: This collection of African art concentrates on south of the Sahara, with the earliest dating before 1700 B.C.E. Much of the exhibition space is underground.

THEATER

AFRICAN CONTINUUM THEATRE
Atlas Performing Arts Center, 1333 H Street NE
202-399-7993 • africancontinuumtheatre.com

Public Transportation: Very good
Handicapped Accessibility: Good
Performances/Programs: Performance schedule is generally Thursday–Sunday.
Ticket Prices: Single tickets are $25, discounts for groups of 10 or more, shows available on Goldstar.com.

ARENA STAGE
202-488-3300 • arenastage.org

Venues: Lincoln Theatre, 1215 U Street NW; Arena Stage in Crystal City, 1800 South Bell Street, Arlington.
Public Transportation: Very good (both venues)
Handicapped Accessibility: Good (both venues)
Performances/Programs: Performance schedule is Tuesday–Sunday.
Ticket Prices: Single tickets are $47–$66, full-time students get 35% off, $20 tickets for Southwest D.C. residents on specially designated Friday-evening performances, $10 tickets for 30-and-under. HotTix: Limited number of half-price tickets go on sale 90 minutes before curtain. Target Fam-

ily Fun Pack: four seats, four non-alcoholic drinks, and four snacks for only $100. Discounts for groups of 15 or more.

Subscriptions: Eight-Show $336–$448, Seven-Show $302–$414, Six-Show $266–$350, Four-Show $188–$244, and Three-Show $146–$188. Benefits include Bring a Friend discount coupons, unlimited exchanges, and $100 off a four-week session at Camp Arena Stage.

From the Editors: There is rich variety in every Arena Stage season, which has just been expanded to include an incredibly ambitious 10 productions. Golden Age and contemporary musicals, new plays and classics, solo shows and intimate musical revues—everything has a place here.

Arena's shows reflect the theater's dedication to producing American work (a fitting mission for the premier theater of the nation's capital). Audience-enrichment activities include lively pre-show discussions with Arena artists at the Salon (free for subscribers, $3 for non-subs) and free post-show chats with the cast on selected Tuesdays and Thursdays.

Arena also has a dizzying array of educational initiatives, including the Student Playwrights Project, Camp Arena Stage, the after-school drama program Voices of Now, a teaching artists-in-residence program for university students, and Moving Stories, a classroom-based program that has Arena Stage artists using creative techniques to bring literature to life.

The Arena Stage is in a transition period right now, as its home is undergoing a massive renovation. When the newly dubbed Mead Center for American Theater opens in 2010, the Fichandler Stage and Kreeger Theater will have had state-of-the-art makeovers, and a new black box space, The Cradle, will have been added. In the meantime, Arena shows are being produced at Arena Stage at Crystal City and the Lincoln Theatre.

FOLGER THEATRE
201 East Capitol Street SE
202-544-7077 • folger.edu

Public Transportation: Very good
Handicapped Accessibility: Good
Performances/Programs: Performance schedule is generally Wednesday–Sunday, with some Tuesdays.
Ticket Prices: Single tickets are $25–$55, group discounts available, some shows available on Goldstar.com.
Subscriptions: Three-show season subscription $95–$156. Benefits include free ticket exchanges and discounts to Capitol Hill restaurants.

FORD'S THEATRE
511 10th Street NW
202-347-4833 • fordstheatre.org

Public Transportation: Very good
Handicapped Accessibility: Good
Performances/Programs: Ford's Theatre produces plays and musicals year round.
Ticket Prices: Vary based on presentation. Discounted show tickets are sometimes available on Goldstar.com.
Group Discounts: Discounts available for groups of 20 or more.
Membership: Friends of Ford's Theatre membership begins at $50. Benefits include a 20% discount on two tickets during the first two week of most productions, preferred seating, members-only ticket priority, ticket exchanges, invites to members-only events, a 10% discount in Ford's Theatre bookstore, and access to members-only VIP Hotline.

From the Editors: Ford's Theater is the site of Abraham Lincoln's assassination, and the theater celebrates the president's legacy with a museum and educational programming.

GALA THEATRE
GALA Theatre-Tivoli, 3333 14th Street NW
800-494-TIXS (8497) • galatheatre.org

Public Transportation: Good
Handicapped Accessibility: Good
Performances/Programs: Performance schedule varies, but generally Thursday–Sunday.
Ticket Prices: Single tickets are $32–$36, discounts available for students, seniors, and military, discounts for groups of 10 or more, shows available on Goldstar.com.
Subscriptions: Season subscription $125, Flex (four-pack) $130. Benefits include unlimited exchanges and discounts for friends.

ROUND HOUSE THEATRE
Round House Theatre, 4545 East-West Highway, Bethesda, Maryland
240-644-1100 • roundhousetheatre.org

Other Venues: Round House Theatre Silver Spring, 8641 Colesville

Road, Silver Spring, Maryland.

Public Transportation: Good (both venues)

Handicapped Accessibility: Good

Performances/Programs: Performance schedule is Wednesday–Sunday.

Ticket Prices: Single tickets are $25–$50, $25 tickets for people 25-and-under, 20% discounts for seniors, two pay-what-you-can performances offered for each production, discounts for groups of 10 or more, shows available on Goldstar.com.

Subscriptions: Five-Show $185–$255, Four-Show $151–$207, and Three-Show $117–$159. FlexPass: five-admission $240, four-admission $195, and three-admission $150. Benefits include ticket exchanges.

From the Editors: The Round House Theatre produces plenty of new plays, but the company's true love is the literary adaptation, as evidenced by its Helen Hayes Award-nominated Literary Works Project. Through this project, Round House has produced numerous stage versions of classics as varied as *Camille* and *Crime and Punishment*, adaptations of contemporary novels like *A Prayer for Owen Meany*, and both dramatic and musical renderings of children's favorites.

To fulfill its mission of making theater a community-building pursuit, Round House has found a number of wonderful ways to get people of all ages and backgrounds into the act. *The Sarah Play* is an annual show entirely put together by area high schoolers, who do all onstage, backstage, and creative duties (Round House simply provides the resources). On the other end of the spectrum is the Heyday Players, a senior-citizen performance troupe that puts together theatricals that they perform for other seniors at community centers, libraries, and schools throughout the D.C. area.

Young, old, and everyone in between is invited to take free 60-minute theater classes during Free-for-All Fridays at the Round House Theatre Education Center. And for artists in need of support, Round House has created a theater lab known as the Kitchen, where "the Cooks" (i.e., writers, designers, actors, and other artists) can get rehearsal and performance space, classes at the Education Center, and opportunities for development—all at no cost.

THE SHAKESPEARE THEATRE COMPANY
202-547-1122 • shakespearetheatre.org

Venues: Lansburgh Theatre, 450 7th Street NW; Sidney Harman Hall, 610 F Street NW

Public Transportation: Good (both venues)
Handicapped Accessibility: Good (both venues)
Performances/Programs: Performance schedule is Tuesday–Sunday.
Ticket Prices: Single tickets are $23–$79, discounts available for students, seniors, and military, limited number of $10 tickets for 35-and-unders, $10 tickets for full-time students during previews, $10 Standing Room Only tickets available when show is sold out, discounts for groups of 10 or more, shows available on Goldstar.com.
Subscriptions: Prices vary; $287–$476, $140 subscriptions for full-time students and 35-and-unders. Benefits include free ticket exchanges and discounted parking.

From the Editors: Founded in 1985 and formerly housed in the Folger Library, the Shakespeare Theatre Company is one of the country's foremost champions of classic theater. The Shakespeare lives up to its name, producing three plays by the Bard every year and filling out the rest of the season with work by other great dramatists, from Aeschylus to Tennessee Williams.

The company tackles five more plays each season with its Monday-night ReDiscovery series, a reading series that spotlights seldom-produced works by the famed (e.g., Oscar Wilde), the overshadowed (Ben Jonson), and the obscure (Alfred de Musset). The Shakespeare Theatre's most beloved offering is the annual Free For All, a set of 10 free performances of one of the theater's Shakespeare productions, performed each summer at the Carter Barron Amphitheatre in Rock Creek Park.

SIGNATURE THEATRE
4200 Campbell Avenue, Arlington
703-820-9771 • sig-online.org

Public Transportation: Good (Accessible by bus, somewhat accessible by Metro train).
Handicapped Accessibility: Good
Performances/Programs: Performance schedule is Tuesday–Sunday.
Ticket Prices: Single tickets are $44–$86, Cabaret tickets are $30, $30 Rush tickets go on sale one hour before performances, discounts available for groups of 10 or more, shows available on Goldstar.com.
Subscriptions: Five-Show subscription $229–$338. Benefits include free ticket exchanges.

From the Editors: Few theaters have shown as much dedication to modern musical theater as Washington, D.C.'s Signature Theatre. The Signature first became known for its frequent and innovative productions of Stephen Sondheim musicals, going on to produce works by the celebrated "new guard" of musical theater writers that includes such notables as Adam Guettel and Michael John LaChiusa. Most Signature seasons boast a world premiere of a new musical, and productions of cult favorites like *Side Show* and *Hedwig & the Angry Inch* are also common.

Aspiring songwriters are supported through programs like the two-week Musical Theatre Institute training program and recently The American Musical Voices Project: The Next Generation gave three promising composers a good chunk of money to develop new full-length musicals that will later be developed at the Signature through readings and performances.

But the Signature doesn't allow its love of new musicals to completely overshadow other worthy ventures—exciting new plays (often premieres) are regularly produced here, and even an old tuner like *My Fair Lady* occasionally makes the cut.

THE STUDIO THEATRE
1501 14th Street NW
202-332-3300 • studiotheatre.org

Public Transportation: Good
Performances/Programs: Performance schedule is Tuesday–Sunday.
Ticket Prices: Single tickets are $25–$67, $5 discount for students, seniors, and military, half-price student Rush tickets for full-time students, discounts for groups of 10 or more, $10 tickets for residents of the Studio District on designated nights, shows available on Goldstar.com.
Subscriptions: Five-Show subscription $140–$309. Benefits include ticket exchanges.

THEATER J
Aaron & Cecile Goldman Theater; Jewish Community Center
1529 16th Street NW
800-494-TIXS (8497) • washingtondcjcc.org/center-for-arts/theater-j

Public Transportation: Very good
Handicapped Accessibility: Good
Performances/Programs: Performance schedule generally Tuesday–Sunday.
Ticket Prices: Vary based on program, half-price tickets for under-25s, discounts for seniors and Washington DCJCC members, limited number of

Rush tickets sold half-hour before each performance, discounts for groups of 10 or more, shows available on Goldstar.com.

Subscriptions: Four-Show $155–$185 and Five-Show $90–$270; Flex packages: eight-ticket $310–$370, and 10-ticket $370–$440 available, subscription discounts for seniors and Washington DCJCC members. Benefits include unlimited ticket exchanges.

WASHINGTON SAVOYARDS
Atlas Performing Arts Center, 1333 H Street NE
202-399-7993 • savoyards.org

Public Transportation: Good
Handicapped Accessibility: Good
Performances/Programs: Performance schedule generally Friday–Sunday.
Ticket Prices: Single tickets are $45, senior tickets $40, for 17-and-unders $20, student Rush tickets available for $10, shows sometimes available on Goldstar.com.

WOOLLY MAMMOTH THEATRE COMPANY
641 D Street, NW (7th & D)
202-393-3939 • woollymammoth.net

Public Transportation: Very good
Handicapped Accessibility: Good
Performances/Programs: Performance schedule is Wednesday–Sunday, some Mondays and Tuesdays.
Ticket Prices: Single tickets are $24–$57, $15 tickets for 25-and-unders; Stampede Seats: 10 or more side-balcony seats for all performances are $15 each (sold two hours before showtime); pay-what-you-can tickets for the first two performances of every production, discounts available for groups of six or more, shows available on Goldstar.com.
Subscriptions: Three-Show $72–$168 and Five-Show $90–$310 subscriptions available. Benefits include no ticket-handling or facility fees and unlimited ticket exchanges.

CLASSICAL MUSIC

THE CATHEDRAL CHORAL SOCIETY
Washington National Cathedral, 3001 Wisconsin Avenue NW
202-537-5527 • cathedralchoralsociety.org

Public Transportation: Good
Handicapped Accessibility: Good
Performances/Programs: Several concerts of choral, sacred, and holiday music each season, as well as sing-alongs and special events.
Ticket Prices: $20–$80. Student Rush tickets are sold at the door at half-price when available.
Subscriptions: Four-event subscription is $76–$304, based on seat selection. Subscribers can purchase additional single tickets at a reduced price.
Membership: Available from $100–$20,000+. Depending on donation amount, donor benefits include program recognition, free concert tickets, and invites to receptions and dress rehearsals.

THE CHORAL ARTS SOCIETY OF WASHINGTON
John F. Kennedy Center for the Performing Arts, 2700 F Street NW
703-244-3669 • choralarts.org

Other Venue: Saint Matthew's Cathedral, 1725 Rhode Island Avenue, NW.
Public Transportation: Good
Handicapped Accessibility: Good (both venues)
Performances/Programs: Several concerts per season with special events.
Ticket Prices: $15–$65
Group Discounts: Discounts available for groups of 10 or more.
Subscriptions: Full four-concert series $52–$192 (based on seat selection), or custom three-concert subscription $13–$55 (per concert). Subscriber benefits include up to 20% savings, great seats, no-hassle ticket exchanges, discount rate for extra tickets, and invites to special concerts, receptions, and lectures.
Membership: Available from $50–$25,000+.

FOLGER CONSORT
201 East Capitol Street, SE
202-544-4600 • folger.edu/consort

Performances/Programs: A full schedule of concerts performed at the Folger Shakespeare Library. Check website for full details.

Musicians: Artistic Directors and Founding Members Robert Eisenstein and Christopher Kendall form the core of the ensemble, with other musicians joining them per performance.

Repertory Selection: The Folger Consort specializes in performances of early music and other classical selections.

NATIONAL SYMPHONY ORCHESTRA (NSO)
The Kennedy Center, 2700 F Street NW
202-467-4600 • kennedy-center.org/nso

Public Transportation: Good (Orange and Blue lines get you close to the Kennedy Center and a free shuttle is available if you choose to skip the walk. The Kennedy Center is also accessible by 80 bus).

Handicapped Accessibility: Good

Performances/Programs: About 175 per season.

Ticket Prices: From $20 to $85, depending on the performance.

Group Discounts: Discounts are available at most performances for groups of 20 or more.

Subscriptions: Available in Mini Packs (Choral, Friday Matinée, Meet the Maestro, Family, and Pops). You may also create your own series of three or more performances. Benefits include a subscription to *Kennedy Center News* and limited ticket exchanges.

Kids Chats: Following each of the 3 p.m. NSO Family concerts, young audience members can ask questions of the concert artists and hear their stories in an up-close and personal forum.

Membership: National Symphony Orchestra membership begins at $60. Benefits include members-only ticket priority, an exclusive subscription to the *On the Aisle* newsletter, a subscription to the Kennedy Center news magazine, and discounts to Performance Plus events.

From the Editors: Founded in 1931, the National Symphony Orchestra regularly performs for official state occasions, presidential inaugurations, and other events of national and international importance. With a strong commitment to music education, the NSO offers many educational concerts and activities for both children and adults. Sunday afternoon family concerts are designed for parents and children (ages 7+); Kinder Konzerts are small ensemble performances geared toward introducing young children (4+) to the orchestra and its instruments. Instrument "petting zoos" offer a chance for children and their parents to see the instruments played by the orchestra up-close. NSO Ensembles for children 9 and up utilize multimedia to demonstrate the connection between music and other disciplines.

A special series, NSO Composer Portraits, is a wonderful way for adults to learn more about a particular composer. The first half of the performance offers background information about the composer with excerpts of his works in chronological order, demonstrating the development of his style, while the second half features the performance of an entire single work by that composer.

Following NSO Classical Subscription concerts, Composer Portraits performances, and Kennedy Center Chamber Players concerts throughout the season, ticket holders are invited to AfterWords for a discussion about the evening's performance.

THE WASHINGTON CHORUS
202-342-6221 • thewashingtonchorus.org

Venues: John F. Kennedy Center Concert Hall, Music Center at Strathmore, National Presbyterian Church, Atlas Center for the Performing Arts, and other venues.

Public Transportation: Good to most venues.

Handicapped Accessibility: Most venues accessible.

Performances/Programs: Several classical/choral music concerts and special events each season.

Ticket Prices: $15–$60

Subscriptions: Four-concert subscriptions ranging from $60–$187, based on seating. Subscriber benefits include 15% off additional single tickets, great seats, and ticket exchanges.

Membership: Available from $1,000–$25,000, though smaller donations are greatly encouraged.

OPERA

WASHINGTON NATIONAL OPERA
John F. Kennedy Center for the Performing Arts Opera House
2700 F Street NW
202-295-2420 • dc-opera.org

Public Transportation: Excellent
Handicapped Accessibility: Good
Performances/Programs: Several full opera productions per season with multiple performances, plus special events.
Ticket Prices: $50–$300
Subscriptions: Full season subscriptions start at $300, Mini subscriptions begin at $150. Subscriber benefits include flexible ticket exchanges, access to lectures and Q&As, free newsletter, free season preview CD, special offers, and payment plan options. Full season subscriber benefits include all that plus 10% discount on additional tickets to mainstage operas, two free ticket exchange vouchers, and waived handling fees.
Membership: Available from $75–$25,000+.

From the Editors: Under the direction of opera legend Placido Domingo (who is doing double duty, serving as general director for the LA Opera as well), the Washington National Opera has recently been designated "The National Opera" by the U.S. Congress. The company offers a mixture of standard operas alongside contemporary and lesser-known works, with consistently high standards of production. The Generation O program for young professionals supplies members with a variety of special events and opportunities to support their appreciation and understanding of opera. Out @ the Opera, for the GLBT community, features special receptions, artist meetings, and other events. O-Zone lectures and Opera Insights, for all ticketed patrons, offer additional insights into the opera productions. Also, check out Artist Q&A, after the Sunday matinées.

JAZZ/CABARET

BLUES ALLEY
1073 Wisconsin Avenue, NW
202-337-4141 • bluesalley.com

Public Transportation: Good
Handicapped Accessibility: No
Performances/Programs: Approximately 240 per year. Live jazz most nights. Two sets, at 8 and 10 p.m.
Ticket Prices: Prices range from $15 to $60. Occasional half-price offers for mailing list members.
Group Discounts: Some group discounts for parties of 12 or more. Call ahead for full details.

From the Editors: As the quintessential D.C. jazz supper club, Blues Alley has played host to any number of legendary jazz players since its opening in 1965. (The club claims to be the longest continuously running jazz supper club in the country.) Dizzy Gillespie, Sarah Vaughn, Nancy Wilson, and Maynard Ferguson have all graced the stage in this very intimate setting.

Located in the heart of historic Georgetown, the club features live jazz every night of the week and augments the music with classic Creole cuisine. Even if you make a reservation, get there early. Seating is first-come-first-served and you can count on a number of diehards getting in the line a good hour ahead of time. Remember to purchase tickets early as well, as shows sell out early for big names. Also note that these jazz enthusiasts have no problem shushing chatty audience members. This club is all about the music.

BOHEMIAN CAVERNS
2001 11th Street NW
202-299-0800 • bohemiancaverns.com

Public Transportation: Good
Handicapped Accessibility: No
Performances/Programs: Approximately 270 performances per year. Shows performed at 8 p.m. Monday–Thursdays, 9 and 11 p.m. on Friday and Saturday.
Ticket Prices: $15–$20.

HR-57
1610 14th Street NW
202-667-3700 • hr57.org

Public Transportation: Poor
Handicapped Accessibility: No
Performances/Programs: Approximately 160 performances per year. Jam sessions takes place Wednesday, Thursday, and Sunday; a variety of performers take the stage on Friday and Saturday at 9 p.m.
   Ticket Prices: $5–$15.

THE KENNEDY CENTER (KC JAZZ)
2700 F Street NW
202-467-4600 • kennedy-center.org/programs/jazz

Public Transportation: Good
Handicapped Accessibility: Good
Performances/Programs: Approximately 30 performances per year.
   Ticket Prices: Prices range from $15 to $50. Students, seniors, military, and people with permanent disabilities are eligible for 50% off. These tickets must be purchased in person and availability is limited for each performance.
   Group Discounts: Discounts are offered for groups of 20 or more.
   Subscriptions: For the jazz series, subscribers pick three or more performances. Desired shows can be changed at any time. Benefits include guaranteed seats before public sale and subscription to *Kennedy Center News*.

   From the Editors: The Kennedy Center is one of the nation's most important arts venues and as such, its jazz series draws some of the most important and celebrated musicians in the U.S. to Washington, D.C. KC Jazz recognizes the diversity within the jazz world and frequently expands beyond traditional jazz to incorporate blues, world music, and even hip-hop into its series, which runs from September to May. The Kennedy Center utilizes several different venues in the series aside from its world-renowned concert halls. Purchase tickets well in advance for big names and be sure to check the Center's website for updates and special offers.

TRYST
2459 18th Street NW
202-232-5500 • trystdc.com

Public Transportation: Poor
Handicapped Accessibility: Good
Performances/Programs: Approximately 140 performances a year. Live jazz every Monday, Tuesday, and Wednesday 8–11 p.m.
Ticket Prices: No cover.

TWINS JAZZ
1344 U Street NW
202-234-0072 • twinsjazz.com

Public Transportation: Very good
Handicapped Accessibility: No
Performances/Programs: Approximately 270 performances per year. Live jazz is played Tuesday–Thursday and Sunday at 8 p.m.; Friday and Saturday at 9 and 11 p.m.
Ticket Prices: $10–$30, plus a two-drink minimum. Students occasionally get half-price tickets for select Friday night sets.

UTOPIA BAR & GRILL
1418 U Street NW
202-483-7669 • utopiaindc.com

Public Transportation: Good
Handicapped Accessibility: Good
Performances/Programs: Approximately 280 performances given each year. Jazz nightly Tuesday–Thursday, and Sunday at 9 or 9:30 p.m.; Friday and Saturday at 11 p.m.
Ticket Prices: No cover. $15 food-and-drink minimum.

DANCE

CITY DANCE ENSEMBLE
Music Center at Strathmore
5301 Tuckerman Lane, North Bethesda, Maryland
202-347-3909 • citydance.net

Other Venues: Harman Center for the Arts, Lansburgh Theatre, 450 7th Street NW; Kennedy Center, Terrace Theater, 2700 F Street NW
Public Transportation: Good
Handicapped Accessibility: Good
Performances/Programs: Five different programs, two or three performances each.
Ticket Prices: Range between $15 and $55.
Membership: Annual contribution fees start at $250 and include discounts at Strathmore's Music Center and the Shops at Strathmore, access to a members-only concessions line at the Lansburgh Theatre, invitations for two to open rehearsals, name listing on recognition panels, and invitations to special events.

SUZANNE FARRELL BALLET
The Kennedy Center, 2700 F Street NW
800-444-1324 • kennedy-center.org/programs/ballet/farrell

Public Transportation: Very good
Handicapped Accessibility: Good
Performances/Programs: The company performs annually at the Kennedy Center for one week.
Ticket Prices: Range from about $30 to $85. Discounts of 50% off are available to students, seniors (65+), military, disabled, and people on fixed incomes. Standing-room tickets are available if a show sells out. All ticket sales are final.
Group Discounts: Customized packages are available to groups of 20 or more.

WASHINGTON BALLET
Eisenhower Theater, Kennedy Center
2700 F Street NW
202-362-3606 • washingtonballet.org

Other Venues: Warner Theatre, 13th and E Streets NW; Harman Center, Sidney Harman Hall, 610 F Street NW.

Public Transportation: Yes (all venues)

Handicapped Accessibility: Good (all venues)

Performances/Programs: Four programs each year, plus the annual *Nutcracker*. Each program runs for one week with about six performances. The *Nutcracker* runs for two and a half weeks in December.

Ticket Prices: Range from $20 to $120. Student and senior discounts are available at some venues.

Group Discounts: Groups of 10 or more receive discounts of up to 20%.

Subscriptions: A Four-Series subscription and Family series packages are available. All sales are final. Benefits include 10% off *Nutcracker* ticket purchases, as well as invitations to in-studio performances and special events.

Membership: Begins at $75 and includes advance notice of purchasing options and special prices on TWB special events.

Special Membership for Young Adults: The Jeté Society is a group for young professionals 21 to 45. Membership starts at $50 and includes invitations to social events and discounts on single ticket prices.

Educational/Community Outreach: The Washington Ballet offers extensive and innovative community arts programs including Dance D.C., a program integrating movement with the language-arts curriculum in local public schools.

From the Editors: The Washington Ballet School was founded in 1944 by Mary Day, a Washington native who sought to establish her hometown as an elite training ground for talented young dancers. Further inspired by later travels to the Soviet Union, Miss Day expanded her organization in the 1960s to offer training in both dance and academics, modeling it after the famed Russian Academy of Ballet. Out of this unique training center emerged the company now known as the Washington Ballet.

Although the academic department of the Washington Ballet School closed only a year after the company began in 1976, the dance-training program continues today and, not surprisingly, education and training still remain a vital part of this organization's mission. In addition to the Dance D.C. program, each November the company also performs an abridged version of the *Nutcracker* at Arts Day at THEARC, a free community arts festival held at the Town Hall Education, Arts, and Recreation Campus in Anacostia.

DANCE PLACE
3225 8th Street NE
202-269-1600 • danceplace.org

Public Transportation: Good (conveniently located two blocks from the D. C. Brookland/CUA Red Line stop).

Handicapped Accessibility: Good

Performances/Programs: Dance Place regularly presents local and visiting dance companies throughout the year. Generally a different company performs every week for two-three days (fewer companies in the summer months).

Ticket Prices: Prices vary across events, but tickets generally range between $20 and $30. For select performances, Dance Place members, seniors, and students receive $5 discounts. Children (under 17) can purchase tickets at around $8. At other performances, pre-K-12 teachers receive $5 discounts.

Group Discounts: Groups of 10 or more receive a 20% discount.

Membership: Basic membership starts at $50. Friends of Dance Place receive discounts on tickets and classes, as well as invitations to master classes, receptions, and after-performance parties.

FILM

AMERICAN FILM INSTITUTE (AFI) SILVER THEATRE AND
CULTURAL CENTER
8633 Colesville Road, Silver Spring, Maryland
301-495-6700 • afi.com/silver/new

Public Transportation: Good (easily accessible by Metro Red line)

Handicapped Accessibility: Good

Performances/Programs: Mainstream and art-house films, as well as screenings of classic fare.

Ticket Prices: $10, students and seniors $9, members $8.50, children $6.

From the Editors: Located a little north of Washington, D.C. in Silver Spring, Maryland, the AFI Silver movie theater complex has three screens that showcase both mainstream flicks and the usual art-house fare. Originally designed by architect John Eberson and opened in 1938, the theater was recently restored and reopened in 2003. Since the AFI Silver is run by the American Film Institute, it should be no surprise that the theater is committed to excellence in film in terms of both artistic and technical quality. In fact, it's currently the most technically advanced outlet for motion picture exhibition in all of North America, capable of showing 16, 35, and 70mm vertical, Betacam, Betacam SP/SX, DigiBetacam, HDCAM, DVCAM, MiniDV, D5, DVCPRO, DVD, and VHS, and all in state-of-the-art projectors. The AFI Silver is also the host of the annual Silverdocs documentary festival.

WASHINGTON'S DOWNTOWN ARTS COMPLEX
1017-1021 7th Street NW
202-783-3933 • warehousetheater.com

Public Transportation: Good (easily accessible via Metro Green, Yellow, and Red lines).
Performances/Programs: Mostly locally made or low-budget independent films.
Ticket Prices: Vary based on program.

From the Editors: Washington's Downtown Arts Complex is home to the Warehouse Screening Room, a 50-seat venue that holds small-scale film festivals, showcases the work of local filmmakers, and does private screenings.

PERFORMANCE VENUES

ARTS CLUB OF WASHINGTON
Monroe House, 2017 I Street NW
202-331-7282 • artsclubofwashington.org

Public Transportation: Very good
Handicapped Accessibility: Poor (not wheelchair accessible and no handicapped parking nearby).
Performances/Programs: Programming at the club includes cabaret, jazz, classical-music concerts, seminars, literary events, art exhibits, theatrical presentations, classes, and other arts events. Events take place at the club regularly throughout the year from September to July.

Ticket Prices: Vary based on program. Some events, such as the Friday Noon Concert series, are free and open to the public.

Membership: Membership starts at $750 per year, $400 for Junior (35 and under), $450 for Daytime, $150 for nonresident. Prospective members must formally apply and there's a $150 application fee. Arts Club of Washington has a reciprocal relationship with the following clubs and organizations: Arts Club of Chicago, the Scarab Club (Detroit), Kansas City Club, Franklin Inn Club (Philadelphia), Racquet Club of Philadelphia, the Providence Art Club, the United Arts Club (Dublin), Glasgow Art Club, the Arts Club (London), the Chelsea Arts Club (London), the National Liberal Club (London), the Penzance Arts Club, the Coffee House (NYC), the Midtown Executive & Chemist's Club (NYC), National Arts Club (NYC), Salmagundi Club (NYC), and the Montauk Club.

ATLAS PERFORMING ARTS CENTER
1333 H Street NE
202-399-7993 • atlasarts.org

Public Transportation: Good (accessible by Metrobus and free shuttle service provided from the Union Station MetroRail stop on Friday and Saturday evenings).

Handicapped Accessibility: Good

Performances/Programs: The Atlas complex comprises four theaters, three dance studios, a café, and production and rehearsal space. The Atlas has partnerships with the following groups: African Continuum Theatre Company, Capital City Symphony, Catalyst Theater Company, Congressional Chorus, the In Series, Joy of Motion Dance Center, Levine School of Music, MusicLink, Step Afrika!, Washington Musica Viva, Washington Performing Arts Society, Washington Savoyards (light opera company), and Zoon Vader Productions.

Ticket Prices: Vary based on presentation. Shows available on Goldstar.com. $5 fee for ticket exchanges.

Subscriptions: The various companies that perform at Atlas offer their own subscription packages and discounts.

Membership: Atlas membership starts at $25. Member benefits include 10% off single ticket orders, a 10% discount off Joy of Motion classes, and invites to events like tours, post-show Q&As, and cast meet-and-greets.

THE LINCOLN THEATRE
1215 U Street NW
202-328-6000 • thelincolntheatre.org

Public Transportation: Very good
Handicapped Accessibility: Good
Performances/Programs: The Lincoln Theatre hosts comedy shows, TV specials, concerts, awards shows, movie screenings, theatrical and dance performances, benefits, and other special events.
Ticket Prices: Vary based on presentation. Shows sometimes available on Goldstar.com.
Membership: Membership begin at $50.

THE KENNEDY CENTER
2700 F Street NW
800-444-1324 • kennedy-center.org

Venues: The Kennedy Center encompasses several performance venues, including the Opera House, Concert Hall, Eisenhower Theater, Family Theater, Terrace Theater, Theater Lab, Millennium Stage, and Jazz Club.
Public Transportation: Very good (easily accessible via bus or Metro, with free shuttle service between Metro stop and the Kennedy Center).
Handicapped Accessibility: Good
Performances/Programs: The Kennedy Center presents more than 2,000 performances each year, consisting of plays, musicals, dance, classical, chamber, jazz, pop, folk music, family and children's shows, multimedia performances, and more. Resident companies at the Center include the National Symphony Orchestra, Washington National Opera, Washington Ballet, and the American College Theater Festival. Additionally, hundreds of free performances are offered every year. The Millennium Stage has free performances every evening at 6 p.m.
Ticket Prices: Vary based on program. Specially Priced Tickets or SPTs (tickets priced at a 50% discount) are offered for students (elementary through grad school), seniors, military, people on fixed incomes (less than $9,800 a year), and people with permanent disabilities. Standing-room tickets are available for shows at the Opera House, Eisenhower Theater, and Terrace Theater when the performance is sold out. Shows are also available on Goldstar.com.
Group Discounts: Discounts are available for groups of 15–20 or more.
Subscriptions: Several subscription packages available. See website for more details.
Membership: Kennedy Center membership begins at $60, with ben-

efits including a 10% gift-shop discount and discounts to Performance Plus events.

Educational/Community Outreach: The Kennedy Center has numerous educational initiatives, among them professional development opportunities for teachers, performances for students, and partnerships with D.C. schools.

NATIONAL THEATRE
1321 Pennsylvania Avenue NW
202-628-6161 • nationaltheatre.org

Public Transportation: Very good

Handicapped Accessibility: Good

Performances/Programs: The National is the oldest operating major touring house in the U.S. It first opened in 1835 and today primarily hosts Broadway touring shows. The National also offers many free programs, such as Saturday-morning children's theater, Monday-night showcases of local talent, and free films in the summer.

Ticket Prices: Vary based on program. A limited number of half-price tickets are offered to people with disabilities, students, seniors, military, and people with low fixed incomes.

Group Discounts: Discounts for groups of 20 or more people sometimes available.

OLNEY THEATRE CENTER
2001 Olney-Sandy Spring Road, Olney, Maryland
301-924-3400 • olneytheatre.org

Public Transportation: Fair (accessible by a combo of Metro and bus, plus a 10-minute walk; bus stops running at 11 p.m.).

Handicapped Accessibility: Good

Performances/Programs: Olney Center programming includes plays, musicals, children's shows, and musical performances; it's also the home of the National Players.

Ticket Prices: Vary. A $5 discount is always available for students and $10 student Rush tickets are frequently available on the day of performance. Some pay-what-you-can performances are also offered. Free summer Shakespeare performances are presented, as well. Shows also frequently available on Goldstar.com.

Group Discounts: Discounts available for groups of 15 or more.

Subscriptions: Subscriptions start at $186 for a six-show subscription.

Benefits include a $5 discount on additional tickets, discounted tickets to family events, unlimited free ticket exchanges, lost-ticket replacement, and priority seating.

ROUND HOUSE THEATRE
4545 East-West Highway, Bethesda, Maryland
240-644-1100 • roundhousetheatre.org

Public Transportation: Very good
Handicapped Accessibility: Good
Performances/Programs: Round House produces and presents plays, musicals, solo shows, family shows, and other performance events. Nearly 200 performances are presented every season.
Ticket Prices: 25 and under $25. A 20% discount is standard for seniors. Two pay-what-you-can performances are offered for each production. Shows are also occasionally available on Goldstar.com.
Group Discounts: Discounts are given for groups of 10 or more.
Subscriptions: Subscriptions start at $117. Flex passes start at $150. Benefits include ticket exchanges.

STRATHMORE
Music Center at Strathmore, 5301 Tuckerman Lane
North Bethesda, Maryland
301-581-5100 • strathmore.org

Other Venue: The Mansion at Strathmore, 10701 Rockville Pike, North Bethesda, Maryland.
Public Transportation: Very good
Handicapped Accessibility: Good
Performances/Programs: Programming includes concerts (pop, rock, jazz, musical theater, classical, choral), art exhibitions, lectures, theatrical performances, and other events, as well as festivals, camps, and art classes. Resident partners at the Strathmore include the Baltimore Symphony Orchestra, National Philharmonic, Washington Performing Arts Society, Levine School of Music, CityDance Ensemble, Maryland Classic Youth Orchestras, and interPLAY.
Ticket Prices: Vary based on program. Discounted last- call tickets are sometimes available. Sign up for Strathmore's mail list for special offers.
Group Discounts: Discounts are given for groups of 15 or more.
Subscriptions: Create-your-own subscription by choosing four or more

events. Ticket exchanges free for subscribers; $5 fee for non-subscribers.

Membership: Membership to Strathmore (for two) starts at $75. Benefits include invites to special receptions, a complimentary summer parking pass for free outdoor concerts, a 10% discount on Tea Room reservations, and a 10% discount on gift-shop merchandise.

WASHINGTON PERFORMING ARTS SOCIETY (WPAS)
2000 L Street NW, Suite 510
202-785-9727 • wpas.org

Performances/Programs: WPAS presents more than 60 performances each year on the following subscription series: Great Orchestras, Stars, Hayes Piano, Kreeger String, Celebrity, Jazz, Dance All Over, On the Edge, World Music and Movement, and American Roots. These performances are held at numerous D.C. area venues, including the Kennedy Center, Strathmore, and Warner Theatre.

Ticket Prices: Vary based on program. Join the Email Club for special offers.

Group Discounts: Discounts for groups of 15 or more.

Subscriptions: The create your own series (five or more) or create a mini-series (three or four) are among the most popular subscriptions at WPAS. Benefits include free ticket exchanges and priority seating.

Membership: WPAS membership starts at $50. Member benefits include members-only pre-sales, three members-only concert previews, no handling charges on ticket orders placed through WPAS ticket services, a 15% discount on select performances, and discounts at the Strathmore Café, Olsson's Books and Records, Music Box Center, M Street Bar and Grill, Hela Spa, Mar de Plata, and Artmosphere Digital Café.

WARNER THEATRE
513 13th Street NW
202-783-4000 • warnertheatre.com

Public Transportation: Very good

Handicapped Accessibility: Good

Performances/Programs: Programming includes Broadway plays and musicals, concerts, comedy shows, holiday shows, classical music, dance, and other performances and special events.

Ticket Prices: Vary based on program. Shows available on Goldstar.com.

Group Discounts: Group discounts are available for select events.

WOLF TRAP FOUNDATION FOR THE PERFORMING ARTS
Filene Center at Wolf Trap National Park, 1551 Trap Road
Vienna, Virginia
703-255-1868 • wolf-trap.org

Other Venues: The Barns at Wolf Trap, 1635 Trap Road; Center for Education at Wolf Trap, 1645 Trap Road, all located in Vienna, Virginia.

Public Transportation: Very good (easily accessible via Metrorail and Wolf Trap shuttle).

Handicapped Accessibility: Good

Performances/Programs: Over 100 performances of modern and classical dance, pop, rock, jazz, classical, and world music, musical theater and opera, children's shows, and even films and multimedia events throughout the summer. Also around 100 performances October through May at Wolf Trap's indoor venue. Performances given most days throughout the summer.

Ticket Prices: Tickets are $8–$80. 50% discounts are offered for seniors. Ticket exchanges available for $5.

Group Discounts: Group discounts are available.

Membership: Memberships start at $50 and include invites to special events and gift-shop discounts.

Educational/Community Outreach: Educational programs include artsplay classes for infants/toddlers, private music classes, master classes, group music classes for adults, internships, residences, and field trips for students.

From the Editors: A wild variety of performers come out every year to play at Wolf Trap, located on the woodsy rolling terrain of a national park. Wolf Trap devotees brave the muggy Virginia weather and risk the chance of getting wet (concerts go on rain or shine) to see artists like Bonnie Raitt, Linda Ronstadt, Elvis Costello, Jewel, Rufus Wainwright, Morrissey, the Beach Boys, and even the National Symphony Orchestra, while picnicking out on the expansive lawn of the Filene Center. Tuesday through Saturday mornings, all summer, Children's Theatre-in-the-Woods has something for the whole family (kids under 3 get in for free), and during the rest of the year there are indoor concerts at Wolf Trap's 400-seat the Barns venue.

For information on Richmond, Virginia, and
Raleigh, North Carolina, visit go-artsamerica.com.

MORE
ARTS AMERICA DESTINATIONS

ATLANTA, GEORGIA

The "Gateway to the South," Atlanta offers a tremendous array of cultural offerings to thrill any arts lover. Known especially for its booming popular music and club scene, the city is also home to a number of first-class art and theater venues.

ARTS INFO & DISCOUNTS

Creative Loafing (creativeloafing.com)—Atlanta newspaper with great arts coverage and listings.

artscard.com—For a $15 membership ArtsCard holders receive discounts to a variety of museums and theaters in Atlanta, and Dallas, Texas.

artsinatlanta.org—Links to art organizations and institutions in Atlanta.

accessatlanta.com—Search for Atlanta events listings on the site operated by the *Atlanta Constitution*.

atlantaperforms.com—Provides show listings as well as substantial ticket discounts through AtlanTix.

THE ARTS

HIGH MUSEUM OF ART ATLANTA
1280 Peachtree Street, NE
404-733-4444 • high.org

Public Transportation: Excellent (the museum and Woodruff Arts Center are located directly across the street from MARTA Arts Center N5 station).

Handicapped Accessibility: Good

Hours: Tuesday–Wednesday and Friday–Saturday 10 a.m.–5 p.m., Thursday 10 a.m.–8 p.m. (Note: Friday Jazz is held on the 3rd Friday of every month from 5 to 10 p.m. The museum is closed on major holidays.)

Admission: $18, students and seniors (65+) $15, children (6–17) $11, children (5 and under), members, Fulton County residents, and military are free.

Tour: Free with cost of admission. Tours are available on a regular basis. The 45-minute Daily Highlights tour of the permanent collection is available Tuesday–Sunday at 1 p.m., and leaves from the Wieland Pavilion. The museum also offers complimentary Weekend Family Tours on Saturdays and Sundays at 2 p.m. (These tours leave from the Greene Family Learning Gallery.)

Audio Tour: Free audio tours are available for selected exhibitions.

Membership: Individual membership is $65; Dual/Family membership is $90. All members receive free, unlimited admission to the museum collections, special exhibitions, Friday Jazz, discounted parking in the Woodruff Art Center parking garage, invitations to members-only previews, and events and select tickets to the Alliance Theatre and Atlanta Symphony Orchestra. Discounted memberships are available to students, educators and seniors.

Other Benefits: Reciprocal membership to other museums is available at the Patron Level ($1,000+).

From the Editors: With more than 11,000 pieces in its permanent holdings, the High has a marvelous array of work (including a wide range of lesser-known pieces by international heavy-hitters) and a variety of worthwhile special exhibitions. Some of its areas of strength are its 19th- and 20th-century American art collection, European art, African American art, and modern/contemporary art holdings. Some specific artists with particularly strong pull include Chuck Close, Claude Money, Rodin, Dorothea Lange, and Mary Cassat.

The museum also places a special emphasis on supporting and collecting pieces by Southern artists; if Howard Finster is your cup of tea, the High's collection will be sure to please.

Another interesting and well-stocked area of the museum's holdings is its curatorial department specifically devoted to the genre of self-taught art.

Another pocket of particular strength is the tie to international world-class museums, such as the Louvre and Opificio delle Pietre Dure in Florence. The result of these partnerships is particularly strong special exhibitions (i.e., the Van Gogh to Mondarian Exhibit, which showcased works from the Kroller-Muller Museum in the Netherlands). The High Museum of Art has a little bit of everything without losing its level of superior quality— certainly a museum worth its price of admission.

7 STAGES
1105 Euclid Avenue
404-523-7647 • 7stages.org

Venues: Performances are held at the Mainstage (202 seats) and Back Stage Theaters (a black box space seating 65–90). 7 Stages shares this facility with several other theater companies, including the Synchronicity Performance group, Out of Hand Theatre, Essential Theatre, and Teatre du Reve.

Public Transportation: Good (accessible by public transportation, including the MARTA East-West line).

Handicapped Accessibility: Good

Performances/Programs: Schedule varies.

Ticket Prices: Tickets are usually $25, $15 for students, seniors and educators. Discounted offerings, including specially priced morning performances for school groups, are also offered.

Group Discounts: Group rates are available (10–49 at $12.50 each; $10 each for 50 or more).

Subscriptions: The Seven-Play Season, Seven-Play Flex package, and Seven-Play Opening-Night Party subscription (including pre- and post-show receptions) are offered. Benefits include free parking, priority seating, local dining discounts, easy ticket exchanges, and discounts to other Atlanta theater companies. Subscribers save approximately 25% off the single ticket price.

ACADEMY THEATRE
119 Center Street, Avondale Estates
404-474-8332 • academytheatre.org

Venue: This space is shared with the Laughing Matters Improvisational Comedy Troupe, Gateway Performance Productions, Peachtree Theatre Company, and Working Title Playwrights.

Performances/Programs: Performances are presented Thursdays–Sundays.

Ticket Prices: Single tickets are $20; $15 for students and seniors.

Group Discounts: Tickets are $12 each for groups of 10 or more.

Educational/Community Outreach: In addition to its production slate, the Academy Theater is a school for the performing arts.

ACTOR'S EXPRESS THEATRE
King Plow Arts Center
887 West Marietta Street NW, Suite J-107
404-607-SHOW (7469) • actors-express.com

Public Transportation: Good (accessible by MARTA and 14 and 52 buses).

Handicapped Accessibility: Good

Performances/Programs: General schedule of performances are Wednesday–Sunday.

Ticket Prices: Individual tickets $22–$27. For students, seniors and groups (nine or more), tickets are $16 ($22 on Saturdays). Preview tickets are just $11.

Subscriptions: The Open Run subscription is $115 and offers a range of performance choices, free readings, and five half-price ticket passes for friends and family. Subscribers can see a show a second time for free if they're accompanied by full-price paying person. (Note: No late seating is permitted for any shows due to the intimacy of the space.)

ALLIANCE THEATRE
Woodruff Arts Center, 1280 Peachtree Street NE
404-733-5000 • alliancetheatre.org

Venues: The Alliance utilizes two performance spaces: the Alliance (770-seat) and Hertz (200-seat) stages. The Alliance shares the Woodruff

Center with the 14th Street Playhouse, Atlanta Symphony Orchestra, Young Audiences Arts for Learning, and the High Museum of Art.

Public Transportation: Good (easily accessible by MARTA).

Handicapped Accessibility: Good

Performances/Programs: Performances throughout the week, though often dark on Mondays.

Ticket Prices: Vary, but signing up for both the Alliance's Email Club and monthly *The Insider* e-newsletter allows you to get extra discounts and promotions.

Subscriptions: Several subscription packages are offered including Build-Your-Own Season, Alliance Stage series (four mainstage productions), Turner Series on the Hertz (three new intimate shows at the Hertz), Family series (two family-friendly plays) and Flex Pass. Subscribers save up to 40% and enjoy great seats, insurance for missed performances, a 15% discount on additional single tickets, and discount parking.

Educational/Community Outreach: The Company's renowned Theatre for Youth produces two shows (one intended for elementary-school audiences and the other for middle-school students) each season. The Theatre for Youth's latest endeavor, the Collision Project, gets high-school students directly involved in the creative process by immersing them in a classical text, used as a jumping-off point for the students to devise their own original play with the help of a playwright. On the collegiate level, there is the Kendeda Graduate Playwriting Competition, which accepts submissions from students in playwriting programs across the country. At the conclusion of the competition, a winning play is produced at the Alliance.

From the Editors: One of the largest and most prominent theaters in the Southeast, the Alliance Theatre is the recipient of the 2007 Regional Theatre Tony Award for its commitment to excellence.

The Alliance has been the launching pad for three very different shows that went on to Broadway: Alfred Uhry's semi-autobiographical play *The Last Night of Ballyhoo*, Disney's *Aida* (scored by Elton John and Tim Rice), and the musical version of *The Color Purple*. This diversity is reflective of the Alliance's varied programming, which features plays and musicals of every stripe, while staying true to the hometown crowd by including many Southern-themed works.

A host of events, from free acting workshops to post-show expert panels and special family nights, make visiting the Alliance Theatre an experience that goes beyond just seeing a show. It's a top-notch professional theater that creates a genuine community experience.

ART STATION
Art Station Theatre, 5384 Manor Drive
Stone Mountain Village
770-469-1105 • artstation.org

Public Transportation: Good (easily accessible by MARTA)
Handicapped Accessibility: Good
Performances/Programs: The theater company performs Thursday, Friday, and Saturday at 8 p.m. and Sunday at 3 p.m. (there are also occasional Wednesday performances at 8 p.m.). In addition to its performances, Art Station also maintains five art galleries, an arts-education program, rehearsal space, and dance and music studios.

Ticket Prices: $26; students and seniors $20. Preview tickets are $16. Additional discounts are available on the company website or by signing up for the Art Station newsletter.

Subscriptions: No subscription packages available, but you can get ticket discounts and other perks by becoming a member of Art Station. See website for more details.

THE ATLANTA LYRIC THEATRE
Ferst Center for the Arts, Georgia Tech
349 Ferst Drive NW
404-894-9600 • atlantalyrictheatre.com

Other Venue: The Byers Studio Theatre at the Lyric, 1705 Commerce Drive.

Public Transportation: Good (both locations accessible via MARTA bus and rail service).

Handicapped Accessibility: Good

Performances/Programs: Performance schedule is Friday-Sunday for Ferst Center shows and Thursday-Sunday for Byers Studio shows.

Ticket Prices: $38–$49; seniors $33–$44; students $22–$33 (higher price is for better seating). Tickets for Byers shows are $27, students and seniors $22.

Group Discounts: Discounts are offered for groups of 10 or more.

Subscriptions: Series A offers two shows at the Ferst; Series B offers two Ferst shows, plus all four Byers shows; and Series C offers two Ferst shows and a choice of Byers shows. Seating at Byers is general admission, but there is designated premium seating for subscribers. Subscribers can also exchange their tickets for another performance for free, while non-subscribers must pay $2 to do an exchange. The Ferst Center also offers free parking.

CENTER FOR PUPPETRY ARTS
1404 Spring Street NW at 18th
404-873-3391 • puppet.org

Public Transportation: Good (easily accessible by MARTA).

Handicapped Accessibility: Good

Performances/Programs: The Center for Puppetry Arts is the largest non-profit theater company dedicated to puppetry in the U.S. Performance schedule varies.

Ticket Prices: Ticket prices vary, but generally Family tickets are $16 (this includes admission to Create-A-Puppet workshop and museum); tickets to adult and teen performances are $20–$24 (includes museum admission). Special promotions and discount offers are available by signing up for the Center's e-newsletter.

Membership: A variety of membership levels (as low as $45/year) include free and substantially discounted shows, events, workshops, etc. Members save up to 45%.

DAD'S GARAGE THEATRE
280 Elizabeth Street, Suite C-101
404-523-3141 • dadsgarage.com

Venues: Dad's Garage has two stages, the Mainstage (140 seats) and the Top Shelf (50 seats). The following companies frequently perform in the Top Shelf: Jack in the Black Box, Out of Hand Theatre, Process Theatre Company, TwinHead Productions, and VisionQuest.

Public Transportation: Good (easily accessible by MARTA).

Handicapped Accessibility: Good

Performances/Programs: Performance schedule is Thursday–Saturday at 8 and 10:30 p.m.

Ticket Prices: Ticket prices range from $10 to $28. Thursday shows are quite a bit cheaper than Saturday shows and tickets are cheaper if you get them in advance rather than at the door. Tickets also cost less at the beginning of a show's run than closing weekend. Student tickets are available for Thursday shows at $10 each for 8 p.m. shows; $7.50 for 10:30 p.m. shows.

Group Discounts: Discounts are available for groups of 10 or more if you pay in advance via phone.

Subscriptions: Subscription options include the Beer Me Pass ($40, any five improv shows and a beer at each show) and the Gimme Everything package ($125, admission to any 10 plays and/or improv shows).

GEORGIA SHAKESPEARE

Conant Performing Arts Center, Ogelthorpe University
4484 Peachtree Road NE
404-264-0020 • gashakespeare.org

Public Transportation: Fair (accessible by a combination of MARTA rail and bus service).

Handicapped Accessibility: Good

Performances/Programs: Performances throughout the week; Mondays are usually dark.

Ticket Prices: Ticket prices average $15–$40. Discounts are available for educators, students, children, and seniors. Special offers, such as 2-for-1 tickets, are sometimes available. The best way to find out about these offers is to subscribe to the email list.

Group Discounts: Group discounts are available at a 15% savings.

Subscriptions: Numerous subscription package options are available. Benefits include free ticket exchanges, lost-ticket replacement, excellent seats, admission to special events, and free parking.

Educational/Community Outreach: Georgia Shakespeare dedicates a tremendous amount of time and effort to educating young people about drama through touring productions, workshops, and the Camp Shakespeare summer program. Even in the off season, the company offers winter classes and special 50-minute versions of Shakespeare favorites for students.

From the Editors: Georgia Shakespeare kicks off its season each May with Shake at the Lake, a week of free fully staged performances on the dock of Lake Clara Meer in Piedmont Park. Free tickets for the upcoming evening performance are distributed at 10 a.m. each morning at the Piedmont Park Visitors Center and at the Georgia Shakespeare box office (they're popular, so arrive early!). The season then resumes at Georgia Shakespeare's regular home, the Conant Performing Arts Center at Ogelthorpe University. This college campus location helps create a wonderful Shakespeare in the Park vibe by giving attendees a picturesque place to picnic before the show. (Too lazy to make your own sandwich? Order a prepared picnic in advance from Panera Bread.) Other pre-show fun includes musical entertainment and Terrace Talks, in which a company member offers a synopsis and orients everybody to the world of the play that they're about to see. Audiences then proceed indoors to enjoy the play in a comfortable state-of-the-art theater.

The main GA Shakes season is three plays in repertory performed throughout the summer, but the company has expanded its season to include a special Family Classics series and a fall production. Georgia Shakespeare isn't just limited to the Bard either; classic works by Chekhov, Moliere, and Arthur Miller are also frequently on the bill.

HORIZON THEATRE COMPANY
1083 Austin Avenue
404-584-7450 • Horizontheatre.com

Public Transportation: Good (easily accessible by MARTA).
Handicapped Accessibility: Good
Performances/Programs: Performance schedule is generally Wednesday–Sunday.
Ticket Prices: Single tickets are $20–$35. Discounted prices are available for students and seniors. The theater also offers occasional pay-what-you-can nights. Single tickets can be exchanged for another performance for a $5 fee with a 24- hour notice.
Group Discounts: Discounts are available for groups of 10 or more.
Subscriptions: Subscriptions are available for as little as $50. Benefits include ability to exchange tickets for free, reserved seating, discounts to the company's holiday show, and free admission to New South Festival events.

THE NEW AMERICAN SHAKESPEARE TAVERN/
ATLANTA SHAKESPEARE COMPANY
499 Peachtree Street NE
404-874-5299 • shakespearetavern.com

Public Transportation: Good (easily accessible by MARTA).
Handicapped Accessibility: Good
Performances/Programs: Performances are given Thursdays, Fridays, and Saturdays at 7:30 p.m. and Sundays at 6:30 p.m. with 10 a.m. student matinées most Tuesdays and Wednesdays during the school year.
Ticket Prices: Single tickets range from $12–$32, depending on days and seating (cheapest tickets are in the balcony, as well as on Thursdays and Sundays). Special morning matinées for students are priced at $12 for students, teachers, and chaperones. Preview performances are $12.
Other Discounts: Discounts on regularly scheduled performances are available for students and educators ($5 off adult price), as well as for seniors and military ($3 off).
Group Discounts: Discounts are offered for parties of 10 or more.
Subscriptions: A subscription is available in the form of a membership

to the Shakespeare Club, which gets you a deeply discounted ticket voucher for each show, as well as $5 off any additional tickets purchased.

SYNCHRONICITY PERFORMANCE GROUP
7 Stages Theatre, 1105 Euclid Avenue
404-484-8636 • synchrotheatre.com

Public Transportation: Good (easily accessible by MARTA).
Handicapped Accessibility: Good
Performances/Programs: Performance schedule is Thursday–Sunday.
Ticket Prices: Single tickets are $15–$20 (the cheaper price is for the Thursday shows). Tickets are discounted to $12–$15 for students, seniors, and artists. For Family Series shows, tickets are $12 and $15 for children 12 and under. No refunds or exchanges for single tickets.
Group Discounts: Discounts are available for groups of 10 or more.
Subscriptions: Five different season-pass options are offered, ranging from the $35 Budget pass (one ticket to all three mainstage plays) to the $225 Supper Club Special (where an elegant dinner is provided before each show). Season-pass holders save 20% over single-ticket prices.

THEATRE IN THE SQUARE
11 Whitlock Avenue, Marietta
770-422-8369 • theatreinthesquare.com

Venues: The theater has two stages: the Main Stage (225 seats) and Alley Stage (120 seats).
Public Transportation: Poor
Handicapped Accessibility: Good
Performances/Programs: Performance schedule is Tuesday–Sunday.
Ticket Prices: Single tickets for Mainstage shows range from $18 to $35; Alley Stage tickets are $15–$20; kids shows are $10, $7 for children 12 and under. No refunds or exchanges on single tickets.
Group Discounts: A $2 per ticket discount is given for groups of 12 or more.
Subscriptions: Season subscriptions are available. Benefits include free ticket exchanges.

THEATRICAL OUTFIT

The Balzer Theater at Herren's, 84 Luckie Street NW
678-528-1500 • theatricaloutfit.org

Public Transportation: Good (easily accessible by MARTA).
Handicapped Accessibility: Good
Performances/Programs: Performance schedule Wednesday–Sunday.
Ticket Prices: $25. Single-ticket holders can exchange tickets if they do so 24 hours in advance, but there's a fee. Special offers are available by subscribing to the company's email newsletter.
Group Discounts: Discounts available for groups of 10 or more (even deeper discounts for 25 or more).
Subscriptions: Several subscription packages are available, ranging from $70 to $130. Students can get a season subscription for just $40. Subscribers can exchange tickets in advance free of charge.

THE ATLANTA SYMPHONY ORCHESTRA (ASO)

Symphony Hall, Woodruff Arts Center
1280 Peachtree Street NE
404-733-4900 • atlantasymphony.org

Other Venues: Verizon Wireless Amphitheatre at Encore Park, 2200 Encore Parkway, Alpharetta; Delta Classic Chastain, 4469 Stella Drive NW.
Public Transportation: Very good (Woodruff Arts Center easily accessible by MARTA and shuttle bus).
Handicapped Accessibility: Good
Performances/Programs: More than 200 per year.
Ticket Prices: Each performance is priced individually. Discounts are frequently available for students and seniors. For selected performances, tickets are available for $10 at the Woodruff Arts Center box office. Tickets can only be purchased the day of a performance for that day or evening's performance. Payment is cash only. Discounts are available for most concerts for groups of 10 or more. If you cannot attend a performance, simply exchange tickets at least one hour before the show.
Subscriptions: Multiple options are available; Classical, Pops, Family, Youth Orchestra, Special Presentations, Holiday Music, and a Compose-Your-Own series of six concerts. Subscribers may exchange tickets at no charge.
Membership: Basic annual membership/donor fee begins at $50 and up. Members receive an ASO membership card, 10% discount at the Atlanta Symphony store, invitation for two to members-only open rehearsals, and invitations for two to Starbucks Lectures of Note series.

Other Benefits: Donors at higher levels receive tickets to appreciation concerts, invitations to opening-night receptions invitations to travel with the ASO, and exclusive use of the elegant Robert Shaw Room for a personal reception or event.

From the Editors: The Atlanta Symphony, led by musical director Maestro Robert Spano (Musical America's 2008 Conductor of the Year), offers a strong classical tradition mixed with new ideas and repertoire. Many offerings are suitable to all ages and tastes. In addition to its main series and family concerts, the ASO also offers a pops series and free community concerts in the parks.

The Atlanta Symphony is dedicated to expanding its audience throughout the community, particularly youth, through the Coca-Cola Family Concerts series, school outreach programs, and free memberships to ASO's Kid's Club with games, contests, and giveaways. The younger affiliate, the Atlanta Symphony Youth Orchestra, features 120 high-school-age members from throughout Atlanta and northern Georgia. The ASYO has three performances of its own each year.

The ASO frequently commissions new works, believing in the importance of contemporary repertoire. Recent projects have included commissions for video and animated installations in the concert hall and video interviews with living composers.

ATLANTA OPERA
Cobb Energy Performing Arts Centre
2800 Cobb Galleria Parkway
404-881-8885 • atlantaopera.org

Public Transportation: Fair
Handicapped Accessibility: Good
Performances/Programs: Four productions and 16 performances per season.
Ticket Prices: $27.50–$133.50
Subscriptions: Four-opera subscriptions cost $99–$538. Subscribers receive exclusive deals around town, subscriber prices on additional tickets, and flexible ticket exchange policy.
Membership: Memberships begin at $50.

From the Editors: Now over 30 years old, the Atlanta Opera has entertained more than 800,000 patrons during more than 250 performances of 75 exciting productions. Led by General Director Dennis Hanthron, the company attracts the finest international, national, and regional singers, conductors, stage directors and designers. The Atlanta Opera runs an impressive array of educational initiatives that include Student Shorts (special one-hour versions of Atlanta Opera productions), touring productions, opera workshops, and helpful online resources like an Opera Glossary and a "First Time Expectations" guide that dispels many myths about opera-going.

CAFÉ 290
290 Hilderbrand Drive
404-256-3942 • cafe290atlanta.com

> **Public Transportation:** Poor
> **Handicapped Accessibility:** No
> **Performances/Programs:** Live music nightly, ranging from open-mic night on Monday to jazz jam sessions on Sunday. Shows generally begin at 8:30–9 p.m.
> **Ticket Prices:** $5–$15

CHURCHILL GROUNDS
660 Peachtree Street
404-876-3030 • churchillgrounds.com

> **Public Transportation:** Poor
> **Handicapped Accessibility:** No
> **Performances/Programs:** Approximately 240 performances are given per year. Performance schedule is Tuesday–Saturday at 9 and 11:30 p.m.
> **Ticket Prices:** $5–$10, plus $10 food/drink minimum.

DANTE'S DOWN THE HATCH
3380 Peachtree Road NE
404-266-1600 • dantesdownthehatch.com

> **Public Transportation:** Poor
> **Handicapped Accessibility:** No
> **Performances/Programs:** Live jazz performed nightly, Monday, Friday, and Saturday at 6 p.m., Tuesday–Thursday and Sunday at 7 p.m.
> **Ticket Prices:** No cover

LONDZELL'S JAZZ & BLUES CAFÉ

2300 Holcomb Bridge Road, Ste. 309, Roswell
678-795-9100 • londzellsjazzandblues.com

Public Transportation: Poor
Handicapped Accessibility: No
Performances/Programs: Live music performed Tuesday–Sunday at
8 p.m., Friday–Saturday at 8:30 p.m.
Ticket Prices: $5–$10

SAMBUCA

3102 Piedmont Road NE
404-237-5299 • sambucarestaurant.com

Public Transportation: Poor
Handicapped Accessibility: Good
Performances/Programs: Approximately 350 performances are given
per year. Many genres represented, with jazz concerts at least one night a
week.
Ticket Prices: $1 added to dinner bill to cover music costs.

ATLANTA JAZZ FESTIVAL

Woodruff Park, Auburn Avenue NE & Peachtree Street NE
404-817-6818 • atlantafestivals.com

Public Transportation: Good
Handicapped Accessibility: Good
Performances/Programs: Three days of performances every Memorial
Day weekend. Approximately 20 performances are presented during the
festival.
Ticket Prices: Free

From the Editors: The Atlanta Jazz Festival is a three-day event,
founded in 1977, that takes place over Memorial Day weekend. Most recently, the festival expanded to a 31-day event commemorating its 31st
anniversary and brought some of America's top talent to the stage in the
Big Peach. The festival is traditionally held in Woodruff Park in the heart
of downtown Atlanta. Past performers have included Tito Puente, Lena
Horne, McCoy Tyner, and, of course, Ray Charles.

ATLANTA BALLET
Cobb Energy Performing Arts Centre
2800 Cobb Galleria Parkway
404-892-3303 • atlantaballet.com

Other Venues: Fox Theatre, 660 Peachtree Street NE
Public Transportation: Good
Handicapped Accessibility: Good
Performances/Programs: Five programs per year, plus the annual *Nut-cracker*. Each program runs for two weeks with four to six performances. The *Nutcracker* runs regularly throughout the month of December.

Ticket Prices: Range from $15 to $115; college students receive discounts on season packages. Students (and their parents) of the Atlanta Ballet Centre for Dance Education receive a 20% discount on tickets to select performances.

Group Discounts: Groups of 10 or more receive discounts of up to 30%.

Subscriptions: Subscribers can build their own package by choosing any 3 ballets. A Flex-pass package is also available. All sales are final. Benefits include lost-ticket insurance and discounts on additional single-ticket purchases.

Membership: The basic donor fee is any amount up to $99 and includes a subscription to Atlanta Ballet e-news, a 10% discount at the Atlanta Ballet Boutique, and a listing in the annual report.

From the Editors: Atlanta Ballet is the oldest professional dance company still functioning today in the United States. Founded in 1929 under the name the Dorothy Alexander Dance Concert Group, the company has grown to become Georgia's largest self-supported arts organization. The ballet has a strong presence in Atlanta's cultural community, having distinguished itself as international performers and as innovative collaborators with other artists, such as the Indigo Girls and OutKast's Big Boi.

As with most arts organization, funds are consistently uncertain and in the summer of 2006 the company scrapped its orchestra and switched to digital music as a cost-saving strategy. The issue was (and still is) controversial and it's far from solved, yet through a generous gift, Atlanta Ballet has been fortunate enough to secure the benefits of a live orchestra—at least for the time being—once again.

FOX THEATRE—THEATER OF THE STARS
660 Peachtree Street NE
404-252-8960 • www.theaterofthestars.com

Public Transportation: Very good (easily accessible via MARTA).
Handicapped Accessibility: Good
Performances/Programs: Performance schedule is Tuesday–Sunday.
Ticket Prices: Single tickets are $20–$68.
Subscriptions: Season subscriptions cost between $135 and $410. Benefits include guaranteed seats for all sell-out shows, lost-ticket replacement, easy ticket exchanges, and special deals on dining and other Atlanta events.

For information on Birmingham, Alabama; Savannah, Georgia; Charleston, South Carolina; and Columbia, South Carolina; visit go-artsamerica.com.

BALTIMORE, MARYLAND

Somewhat overshadowed by its proximity to Washington, D.C., "Charm City" has a vibrant arts scene in its own right. This mid-sized blue-collar urban center boasts an excellent selection of arts options, including theater, music, and an especially plentiful number of impressive museums.

ARTS INFO AND DISCOUNTS

Baltimore City Paper (citypaper.com)—Alternative weekly arts paper with comprehensive arts listings and coverage.

Baltimore Sun (baltimoresun.com)—Arts news/reviews for both Baltimore and Washington, D.C.

baltimore.metromix.com—Events listings and coverage.

bop.org—Baltimore Office of Promotion and the Arts.

baltimore.org/deals-and-discounts—Half-price arts discounts in Baltimore.

THE ARTS

AMERICAN VISIONARY ART MUSEUM (AVAM)
800 Key Highway (at the base of Federal Hill)
401-244-1900 • avam.com

Public Transportation: Fair (the nearest bus stop is Light St. and Key Highway, approximately a 10-minute walk; Camden Yard Light Rail is about a 20-minute walk from the AVAM).

Handicapped Accessibility: Good

Hours: Tuesday-Sunday 10 a.m.–6 p.m., closed Monday (except some holidays).

Admission: $14, students and seniors (60+) $10, children $8; group discounts available.

Tours: Group and school tours are offered at $5 per person, adults/chaperones $7 (chaperones are free for groups of 70 or more, and a group of 10 or more is required for a group discount).

Membership: Family Fans membership covers four immediate family members for $100 and includes unlimited free admission for one year to AVAM, and all special exhibitions, two Big Fan guest passes, and advance mailings for programs and special events. Student membership is $25. Senior and out-of-town visitor membership is $35. Individuals can join at a cost of $50 a year.

From the Editors: A unique museum, AVAM solely houses works of art produced by self-taught individuals, the great majority of whom have never received any form of formal training. All pieces are examples of "visionary art." In other words, every piece emerges from an inner vision of the artist, unconstrained by outer teachings or restrictions.

The museum houses a permanent collection of 5,000 pieces and rotates special exhibitions—often one-of-a-kind and interdisciplinary. The special exhibit that ran between October 2008 and September 2009, *The Marriage of Art, Science and Philosophy*, is a prime example. Encompassing 50 visionary artists, the event focuses on new and artistic takes to the concepts of sound, color, scale, and number, providing a twist to the traditional. Certainly an off-beat take on the expected, AVAM provides a distinct experience—this is indeed the Dave Eggers of museums. Where else can you find a Sculpture Barn converted from an old Whiskey Production Center, Giant Whirligig, and Wildflower Garden?

BALTIMORE MUSEUM OF ART (THE BMA)
10 Art Museum Drive
443-573-1700 • artbma.org

Public Transportation: Good (easily accessible by the MTA 3 and 11 buses).

Handicapped Accessibility: Excellent (including Sculpture Touch tours for the blind and visually impaired, sign-language interpretation, and selected foreign-language interpretation for non-English speakers).

Hours: Wednesday–Friday 11 a.m.–5 p.m., Saturday and Sunday 11 a.m.–6 p.m., closed Monday and Tuesday.

Admission: Free (fees for some special exhibitions).

Tours: Multiple free tours are offered: Treasures at the BMA (45 minutes) Saturdays 11:30 a.m. and 2 p.m., Sunday Shorts (focusing on a single piece of art or gallery; 30 minutes) Sundays 2:30 p.m., Exhibition Tours Wednesdays 2 p.m., Third Thursday curatorial tours.

Audio Tours: Cell phone and Podcast tours available.

Membership: $50–$60 membership includes free admission to special exhibitions, invitations to members First Nights, member preview days, and special member events, shop and restaurant discounts, and quarterly magazine.

From the Editors: With traditional heavy-hitters like Cezanne, Picasso, and Van Gogh, as well as works by the more modern majors Andy Warhol, Georgia O'Keeffe, and Kara Walker, the BMA offers an all-around powerhouse for free. Another area of strength lies within the great variety of special exhibitions provided, from a traditional Taking in the View: English Watercolors and Prints to Front Room: Jim Dine in the Experimental Project space. The program schedule is just as strong; three regulars include Artblast! Big and Small (an event of various options including art-making and gallery activities); Free-Fall Baltimore; and Mapping Baltimore's Monuments, which takes you through a tour of 14 area monuments, led by authors, curators, local artists, and historians.

THE WALTERS ART MUSEUM
600 N. Charles Street
410-547-9000 • thewalters.org

Public Transportation: Excellent (adjacent to Light Rail service as well as multiple MTA bus lines).

Handicapped Accessibility: Excellent (docent-led touch and multi-sensory tours are available for the physically and sense impaired).

Hours: Wednesday–Sunday 10 a.m.–5 p.m., closed Monday and Tuesday.

Admission: Free

Tours: Individual, family and self-guided tours are free. Guided group tours are $7 adult, $4 student.

Audio Tours: Free

Membership: Individual membership is $50. Slightly discounted membership available to students, seniors, and educators.

Other Benefits: Supporter membership ($125) provides members with reciprocal membership to 30 museums nationwide.

From the Editors: The Walters Art Museum's well-rounded collection is internationally recognized for its breadth, incorporating pieces from pre-dynastic Egypt, Greek sculpture, Art Deco jewelry, as well as 19th- and 20th-century European masterpieces. Former exhibitions have included Gee's Bend: The Architecture of the Quilt, Salviati and the Antique, and The Special Dead: A Medieval Reliquary Revealed.

Perhaps a lesser-known, but equally enriching, aspect of the museum is its library. Rich in resources for art-history students and enthusiasts, it's open to the public by appointment. To book, call 410-547-9000 ext. 297.

CENTERSTAGE
700 North Calvert Street
410-332-0033 • centerstage.org

Public Transportation: Good

Handicapped Accessibility: Good

Ticket Prices: $10–$65, half-price Rush tickets available for seniors and full-time students on the day of the show, $10 off Rush tickets can be bought in advance for Friday shows by calling, at the box office, or via theater website. Multiple other discount programs include: Day of Show discounts, pay-what-you-can for low-income audience members, and special rates for teachers and students. Group rates for 15 or more.

Subscriptions: Traditional subscriptions range from $60 to $300. Flex memberships provide all the benefits of traditional subscriptions, but with the flexibility and convenience of choosing your own date and time. Preview Flex memberships start at just $25 a ticket. High school or college students can get a modified Flex membership with proof of full-time enrollment. Other extensive student discounts are available. Parents may add a Preferred Seat membership for any child under 18 at 50% off the adult prices.

From the Editors: In a city that's sadly lacking in professional theaters, Centerstage really stands out. The 45-year-old organization, which always offers a slate of classics, new plays, and innovative musicals, has earned a reputation as Baltimore's premier theater company. Centerstage courts all kinds of audiences with special programs that aim to make show-going an integral part of its patrons' social lives.

Pre-show festivities include a party with discounted beer and wine, free eats, and raffle prizes for students and their guests, known as College Night, a cocktail hour for members of the GLBT community (only $5, and free for subscribers), and a family-style dining night for kids and their parents. The First Look series presents readings and workshops of new and in-development works for five bucks. The company's Young Playwrights Festival invites Maryland K-12 students to submit their plays, and the Student Critics program gives young people attending student matinées a crash course in how to be a critic, with winning reviewers getting free theater tickets and having their reviews posted on the Centerstage website.

Centerstage is also ready to help out parents when they need it. Child's Play is in-house daycare that provides kids ages 4–10 with theater-related activities while Mom and Dad watch a Saturday matinée. The cost is $15 per child.

EVERYMAN THEATER
1727 N. Charles Street
410-752-2208 • everymantheatre.org

Public Transportation: Excellent

Handicapped Accessibility: Very good (also providing listening devices, large print programs, and audio description devices for patrons with hearing and vision problems).

Performances/Programs: Performances scheduled Wednesday–Sunday.

Ticket Prices: Single tickets $18–$35; discounts on certain performances for students and seniors, savings of up to 20% for groups of 10 or more. (Seating is general admission.)

Subscriptions: Subscribers get all five plays of the season for prices ranging from $75 to $150. Benefits include 10% off Everyman theater classes, ticket insurance, free ticket exchanges (free exchanges on any extra tickets you purchase as well); although exchanges are free, up charges may apply if you want to exchange tickets for a more expensive performances.

REPSTAGE

Howard Community College
10901 Little Patuxent Parkway, Columbia
410-772-4900 • repstage.org

Public Transportation: Poor
Handicapped Accessibility: Very good (also special sign-language-interpreted performances and audio description for selected shows).
Performances/Programs: Performance schedule Wednesday–Sunday.
Ticket Prices: $15–$25, no refunds; student tickets are $12, $2 off for seniors, military and their families, and Howard Community College staff/faculty. Discounts for groups of seven or more. Some Wednesday performances are pay-what-you-can; non-subscribers must pay $3 fee to do a ticket exchange.
Subscriptions: Two basic subscription packages (full season of six plays or choose four) ranging from $48 to $132. Subscriber benefits include preferred seating, special discounts for extra tickets, and free ticket exchanges.

THEATRE PROJECT

45 West Preston Street
410-752-8558 • theatreproject.org

Public Transportation: Good
Handicapped Accessibility: Good
Performances/Programs: In addition to its own productions, Theatre Project invites numerous other artists and international acts to present work in its space. Performance dates and times vary.
Ticket Prices: $20, $15 for seniors and artists, $10 for students.
Subscriptions: Subscription gets you six shows for $80; the Kids Subscription series (four family-friendly shows) is $25 for kids, $35 for adults.

BALTIMORE SHAKESPEARE FESTIVAL

BSF at St. Mary's Outreach Center (indoor)
3900 Roland Avenue
410-366-8596 • baltimoreshakespeare.org

Other Venue: BSF at the Evergreen Museum and Library (outdoor), 4545 N. Charles Street.

Public Transportation: Poor

Handicapped Accessibility: Fair (both venues are wheelchair accessible, but the restrooms at St. Mary's are not).

Performances/Programs: Performances run Wednesday–Sunday.

Ticket Prices: $25; $20 for students and seniors, $5 fee to have tickets mailed to you (rather than picking up at will call), credit cards only accepted on phone orders; must pay cash at the door.

Subscriptions: Subscribers get both summer productions for a discounted $40. Unlimited free ticket exchanges and the ability to reserve seats for indoor performances reserved for subscribers only.

BALTIMORE SYMPHONY ORCHESTRA (BSO)

Joseph Meyerhoff Symphony Hall, 1212 Cathedral Street
410-783-8000 • bsomusic.org

Other Venue: Music Center at Strathmore, 5301 Tuckerman Lane, North Bethesda.

Public Transportation: Very good (the Meyerhoff is easily accessible by light rail and bus and is a short cab ride from Penn Station; the Strathmore is accessible by DC Metro and bus lines).

Performances/Programs: Varies; check BSO website for schedule.

Ticket Prices: Prices vary per program. Special admission prices are offered for students and seniors; student Rush tickets can be purchased at either the Meyerhoff or the Strathmore ticket office for just $10. For select concerts, $10 student Rush tickets may be purchased online or in person. Group discounts are offered for parties of 15 or more. $20 unreserved seating is also offered; for just $20, you get the best available seat on the day of the concert. $25 tickets at Strathmore are regularly updated on the BSO website; check frequently to find these discounted tickets available for upcoming events.

Subscriptions: Multiple subscription options are offered at the Meyerhoff, including a Choose Your Own series, Off the Cuff series, Symphony with a Twist series, as well as an offer of student subscriptions of five concerts for $40. Free ticket exchanges are given with subscription via the Internet. There's a $3 fee for phone exchanges and online ticket exchanges are only available to subscribers. Convenient pre-paid parking is also an option at certain subscriber rates.

Activities for Young Adults and Children: Forte is an opportunity for young professionals, ages 21–40, to enjoy a world-class orchestra and meet fellow music-lovers. Members take advantage of exclusive benefits, including $40 tickets in orchestra-level seats, post-concert networking events, and unique opportunities to meet BSO musicians and guest artists. Family-Musical Adventures (for children ages 3–6) and Family-Classically Kids (for children ages 7–12 and their families) are family-friendly programs offered by the BSO for young music aficionados.

Membership: Membership begins at $75. Benefits include two complimentary tickets to the annual donor-appreciation concert and the opportunity to purchase tickets prior to public sale, as well as access to exclusive events, parties, trips, and tours.

From the Editors: Founded in 1916, the Baltimore Symphony Orchestra was originally established as a branch of the municipal government. In 1942 it was reorganized into a private institution. Even still, it maintains a close relationship with the Baltimore community and government.

The BSO is led by Maestra Marin Alsop, who became the Orchestra's 12th music director in 2007 and is the first woman to become head of a major American orchestra.

In addition to its regular series concerts, the BSO offers many great opportunities for children: Family-Musical Adventures and Family-Classically Kids concerts for children ages 3–6 and 7–12 respectively, along with a BSO Kids section of their website, which offers a free educational outlet for children to learn about classical music. College Nights and $10 student tickets provide additional incentive for students to come to the BSO and enjoy an after party with free food, prizes, and drink specials. The young-professionals membership group, Forte, gives patron ages 21–40 exclusive benefits, including reduced-priced seating, post-concert networking events, and opportunities to meet guest artists and the musicians of the BSO.

BALTIMORE CHORAL ARTS SOCIETY
410-523-7070 • baltimorechoralarts.org

Venues: Various locations, including Meyerhoff Symphony Hall, Kraushaar Auditorium at Goucher College, and The Basilica of the Assumption.

Public Transportation: Depends on venue.

Handicapped Accessibility: Most venues accessible; contact venue management for details.

Performance/Productions: Several concerts per season, with multiple performances of each, plus special events such as sing-alongs and performances with the Baltimore Symphony Orchestra.

Ticket Prices: Not listed, contact for details.

Subscriptions: Three-concert series $89–$113.

Membership: Donations accepted, contact for details.

From the Editors: Now in its 44th year, the Baltimore Choral Arts Society is a major player in the cultural life of Maryland, the mid-Atlantic region, and beyond. In fact, in 2007, BCAS Artistic Director Tom Hall took the chorus on a successful three-city tour in France. The chorus, which regularly performs with the Baltimore Symphony Orchestra, has also been featured on TV specials, radio broadcasts, and recordings.

AN DIE MUSIK LIVE
409 N Charles Street, 2nd Floor
410-385-2638 • andiemusiklive.com

Public Transportation: Poor

Handicapped Accessibility: No

Performances/Programs: Approximately 50 performances are presented per year. Every Monday night is Peabody student jazz at 7:30 p.m.

Ticket Prices: $8

COCO'S BUTTER CAFÉ
7361 Assateague Drive, Unit 1040, Columbia
443-755-9595 • cocosbuttercafe.com

Public Transportation: Poor

Handicapped Accessibility: Good

Performances/Programs: Approximately 60 performances are given per year. Fridays and Saturdays have regular live jazz and open-mic/jam sessions 6–10 p.m.

Ticket Prices: Saturday night cover is $15.

THE CHARLES
1711 N. Charles Street
410-727-3456 • thecharles.com

Public Transportation: Good
Handicapped Accessibility: Good
Performances/Programs: A mix of mainstream and offbeat new films, as well as classics, including documentaries and obscure fare.
Ticket Prices: Matinées $6; evenings $8.

From the Editors: The Charles is Baltimore's oldest theater and fittingly, it has the ambience of a bygone era. Screenings of Hollywood classics like *King Kong* raise the nostalgia factor, but the Charles shows plenty of new movies, independents, documentaries, and foreign films as well.

THE PATTERSON
3134 Eastern Avenue
410-267-1651 • creativealliance.org

Public Transportation: Good (accessible by Baltimore's MTA bus lines).
Handicapped Accessibility: Good
Performances/Programs: Focuses mainly on films of local or regional interest.
Ticket Prices: Usually around $8. Some programs are free.

From the Editors: The Patterson is a favorite haunt for Baltimore filmmakers and people interested in local art. The Creative Alliance MovieMakers Salon, a free forum held the first Monday of every month, gives regional movie makers an opportunity to show their work and get feedback from the audience. In addition to the Salon screenings, the Patterson's 180-seat theater is also used for concerts, film-series screenings, and documentaries. Baltimore-area artists display their works in the galleries outside the theater.

THE FRANCE-MERRICK PERFORMING ARTS CENTER
(formerly the The Hippodrome)
12 North Eutaw Street
410-547-7328 • france-merrickpac.com

Public Transportation: Good (accessible via Metro, light rail, and MTA bus service)

Handicapped Accessibility: Good

Performances/ Programs: The Hippodrome serves as the Baltimore-area's primary venue for touring Broadway shows and special musical and theatrical events.

Subscriptions: Available for Broadway Across America subscriptions. See Hippodrome website or broadwayacrossamerica.com for details.

From the Editors: Originally constructed in 1914 by acclaimed theater architect Thomas Lamb as a luxurious movie and vaudeville showcase, Baltimore's Hippodrome Theatre fell into disrepair in the late 1970s, eventually closing in 1990. In 2006, the venue was rechristened the France-Merrick Performing Arts Center and reopened after an extensive renovation that restored the theater to its former grandeur. The Hippodrome is now Baltimore's premier touring house, presenting major plays, musicals, and special engagements year round.

BOSTON, MASSACHUSETTS

One of America's oldest cities, Boston is the cultural (and economic) hub of New England. With some of the finest universities in the nation, Boston also boasts tremendous arts options. Besides being rich in history, the city is also well-known for its stellar theatrical and visual-arts exhibits (several of which are affiliated with Harvard University).

ARTS INFO AND DISCOUNTS

The Boston Phoenix (thephoenix.com)—Newsweekly with comprehensive arts and entertainment listings.

boston.com/ae—News and listings for arts and entertainment events from the *Boston Globe*.

cityofboston.gov/ARTS—Boston arts and events information.

BosTix—Boston's answer to the TKTS booth, with two booths, at Faneuil Hall and Copley Square.

bostix.org—Purchase half-price tickets in advance for some Boston shows.

goldstar.com—Another good choice for discounts.

showofthemonth.com—Discounts on good seats for theater and arts events in Boston.

THE ARTS

ADDISON GALLERY OF AMERICAN ART
*The Addison Gallery is currently closed until spring
2010 for renovations and expansions.*
Phillips Academy, 180 Main Street, Andover
978-749-4015 • addisongallery.org

Public Transportation: Fair (the museum is accessible through the Andover Stop on the Haverhill commuter rail line; it's about a one-mile walk from the station to the museum).
Handicapped Accessibility: Good
Admission: Free
Tours: Free. Tours are available to school, community and adult groups. Age-appropriate guided tours of all exhibitions are available. If you're coming with a group of eight or more, call ahead at 978-749-4037, even if not requesting a tour.
Membership: Friends of Addison (for a donation of $50+) receive advance notice of all events and exhibitions, as well as acknowledgement in the Addison's annual report.
Other Benefits: Director's Circle members (for a donation of $1,000+) are entitled to all the benefits of Friends of Addison, in addition to complimentary exhibition catalogues, invitations to special programs, and dinner with the Director and visiting artists.

From the Editors: As a department of Phillips Academy, the main focus of Addison is academic. Its collection is devoted to acquiring, preserving, interpreting, and exhibiting works of art for the education and general enjoyment of the public, with a specific bent toward the students, faculty, and staff of Phillips Academy and other students, teachers, and scholars.

With a permanent collection of more than 16,000 pieces, Addison offers a powerhouse for American art. Its original founding collection included works by Winslow Homer, John Singer Sargent, and James McNeill Whistler. It now also holds works by Georgia O'Keefe, Jackson Pollock, Hans Hoffmann, and Edward Hopper. Over its 77-year span, the museum has amassed 7,000 photographs covering the entire span of the history of American photography.

BOSTON MUSEUM OF FINE ARTS (THE MFA)
465 Huntington Avenue
617-267-9300 • mfa.org

Public Transportation: Good (convenient to MBTA subway Orange Line and local buses).

Handicapped Accessibility: Good

Hours: Monday–Tuesday 10 a.m.–4:45 p.m., Wednesday–Friday 10 a.m. –9:45 p.m., Saturday-Sunday 10 a.m.–4:45 p.m.

Admission: $17, students and seniors 18+ $15, youths (7–17) $6.50 (admitted free on weekdays after 3 p.m., weekends, and public-school holidays), Boston-area college students free ($8 special-exhibition tickets). General admission includes one free repeat visit to the MFA's collections within 10 days.

Free Day: Wednesdays, 4–9:45 p.m.

Tours: Free guided tours and gallery talks.

Audio Tour: Members $5, nonmembers $6, youths (7–17) $4.

Membership: Individual membership is $55–$100 and includes members-only previews to major exhibitions, 15% discounts at all museum dining venues, discounts on parking, lectures, concerts, and museum-store purchases, *Preview* (the MFA members' magazine), access to the members' room to relax, read, or meet friends, monthly member news email with museum updates.

Other Benefits: Supporting members ($750) receive reciprocal membership at 21 major art museums, including the Art Institute of Chicago, Los Angeles County Museum of Art, and the Metropolitan Museum of Art.

From the Editors: With installations of art ranging from ancient to modern, the MFA holds pieces geographically spanning Asia, Africa, Oceania, the Americas, and Europe; there's indeed something for everyone. Not only is the permanent collection strong, but its rotating exhibits in the past have offered, and continue to provide, an enormous range of artists and movements: from Ansel Adams to David Hockney, from a special 2007 Summer of Love collection to a richly represented Facets of Cubism in 2005.

The MFA's permanent collection and its rotating exhibition strengths are likewise matched in its various programs, particularly the film niche. With its annual culturally telling exhibit the Best British Commercials and a likewise yearly Boston Palestine Film Festival, the museum provides an ongoing look into the connections between art, its ever-changing place within society, and its lasting impacts.

FOGG ART MUSEUM, BUSCH-REISINGER MUSEUM AND ARTHUR M. SACKLER MUSEUM
485 Broadway, Cambridge
617-495-9400 • artmuseums.harvard.edu

Public Transportation: Very good (easily accessible from the Red subway line).

Handicapped Accessibility: Good

Hours: Monday-Saturday 10 a.m.–5 p.m., Sunday 1–5 p.m., closed major holidays.

Admission: $9, seniors (65+) $7, college students $6; Harvard students, Cambridge Library Card Holders and children under 18 free. Group rates are available.

Tours: Free

Membership: Individual membership is $55 annually and includes unlimited free admission to all three art museums and Agnes B. Mongan Center, invitations to special events and members-only receptions, including fall and spring exhibition celebrations, and reciprocal admission to Harvard's Museum of Natural History and Peabody Museum. Student and senior memberships are available for $45. Dual memberships are $75.

Note: Fogg Art Museum and Busch-Reisinger Museum are closed for renovation; select work is on display at Arther M. Sackler Museum, which is open to the public.

ISABELLA STEWART GARDNER MUSEUM (THE GARDNER)
280 The Fenway
617-566-1401 • gardnermuseum.org

Public Transportation: Good (accessible via 39 bus or the Green line E train).

Handicapped Accessibility: Good (most of the museum's galleries, the museum shop, Gardner Café, and restrooms are wheelchair accessible; information is also available in Braille and in large print at the Visitor Information Desk).

Hours: Tuesday–Sunday 11 a.m.–5 p.m.; closed Monday (open some Monday holidays; closed Independence Day, Thanksgiving, and Christmas).

Admission: $12, seniors $10, college students $5; everyone named Isabella admitted free; $2 off adult/senior admission when visiting both the MFA and Gardner Museum within a two-day period.

Free Day: Columbus Day (Monday October 13) free admission 10 a.m. –5 p.m.

Tours: Guided tours may be arranged three weeks in advance; modest fees are charged. Discounted rates are available to adult, senior, and student groups with more than 15 people.

Audio Tours: $4

Membership: Individual membership ($60, fully tax deductible) includes unlimited free admission for one adult for one year, invitations to members-only exhibition previews and special events, and special member prices and advance notice for concerts and lectures. Special membership fees available to students ($25, fully tax deductible) and non-residents ($50, fully tax deductible). Dual/family memberships are also offered ($85, fully tax deductible).

Other Benefits: Supporters ($250, $235 is tax deductible) receive reciprocal membership to more than 25 participating museums, as well as complimentary museum passes admitting four guests. Contributor ($500, $465 is tax deductible) and Courtyard Circle members ($1,000, $955 is tax deductible) receive additional perks and benefits.

From the Editors: The Isabella Stuart Gardner Museum is the work of one person. Isabella Stuart Gardner and her husband were not only avid art collectors whose collection contains more than 2,500 pieces, including European tapestries, furniture, mosaics, manuscripts, and paintings by Sargent, Degas, Raphael, and Matisse, Gardner also designed the building and even hung the objects. Very little has changed since her death in 1924. Resembling a Venetian Palace, the museum is centered on a Palazzo courtyard, home of the museum's long-running concert series (see below).

AMERICAN REPERTORY THEATRE (ART, AMREP)
Loeb Drama Center (Mainstage), Harvard University
64 Brattle Street, Cambridge
617-547-8300 • amrep.org

Other Venue: Zero Arrow Theatre (300 seats), 2 Arrow Street, Harvard Square, Cambridge.

Public Transportation: Good (Red Line/Harvard Square stop).

Handicapped Accessibility: Good

Performances/Programs: Performances scheduled Tuesday–Sunday.

Ticket Prices: Single tickets at Zero Arrow Theatre are $39 ($52 for Friday and Saturday nights) for table seating; $25 for stool seating; $18 student and seniors tickets available for many shows, student Rush tickets for $15 on day of performance, by phone or in person. 50@$15 is a Rush-ticket program available to anybody, starting at noon on the day of the performance; up to 50 tickets are available to buy in person. Group tickets are available for groups of 10 or more ($10 to $20 off each ticket, depending on the size of the party), A.R.T. student pass is good for up to 80% savings on tickets for full-time college students, $60 for five shows.

Subscriptions: Multiple subscription options include the Assigned series: Choose day of week, time, and seating section, receive the best seats, guaranteed, for all productions and an option to renew with same seats for subsequent seasons; Choose Your Own Series: Choose peak (Friday or Saturday evenings) or off-peak days (weekdays, matinées) and seating section, choose specific dates for each play, receive priority seating before single tickets go on sale. (Seats may change from show to show.). For the Flex series, choose peak (Friday and Saturday evenings) or off-peak days (weekdays, matinées) and seating section. Benefits include a subscription to *ARTicles*, A.R.T.'s behind-the-scenes magazine, Zipcar membership, tickets to A.R.T. Institute productions, drink coupons for use at the A.R.T. bar and easy ticket exchanges.

From the Editors: Located in Cambridge, the American Repertory Theatre was founded in 1980 by drama historian and critic Robert Brustein, longtime theater reviewer for *The New Republic*. A.R.T.'s main theater is on the Harvard campus, and adding to the company's academic feel is the fact that it has its own school, the Institute for Advanced Theatre Training (a two-year program that teaches acting, dramaturgy, and special studies, and includes a three-month residency at the Moscow Art Theatre School). Institute students do their own shows apart from A.R.T.'s season, and they're cheaply priced at $5–$10.

A.R.T., which regularly works with some of the finest and most daring artists in the theater world, is well-known for producing premieres of new work and modern interpretations of classics. The company has even taken to doing stage versions of noted independent films, like *Donnie Darko* and *Wings of Desire*.

A.R.T productions are always of high quality and the theater's fans appreciate the company's willingness to take risks.

Pre-show activities for the LGBT community and under-35s are frequently held, and on-site childcare is available for select Saturday matinées at $10 per child. Regulars say that the theater has good views all around, but that finding a good parking spot near the theater is another matter entirely.

HUNTINGTON THEATRE COMPANY
Boston University Theatre, 264 Huntington Avenue
617-266-0800 • huntingtontheatre.org

Other Venue: Calderwood Pavilion, 527 Tremont Street
Public Transportation: Good
Handicapped Accessibility: Good
Performances/Programs: Performance schedule is Tuesday–Sunday.
Ticket Prices: $30–$75; $25 tickets for people aged 21–35 who sign up with the 35 Below/Pay Your Age program, $12 student tickets, limited number of free first-come first-served tickets, groups of 10 or more get 20% off.
Subscriptions: Subscription packages allow you to choose four-seven shows that you want to see. Subscribers save up to 50%. The theater also offers a special FlexPass subscription that allows you to pay a flat rate of $50 per ticket. Student subscription (25 and under with ID) is $15 per play. B.U. faculty/staff/alumni get to deduct $10 from each play in their subscription; seniors and military personnel deduct $5 per ticket. Benefits include free ticket exchanges.

From the Editors: The Huntington Theatre, founded in 1982 (just two years after the American Rep), is the other big kid on the block in Boston. It has a well-deserved reputation for not just taking on edgy work, but for having an older audience base.

In addition to offering generous ticket price discounts to college aged patrons, the theater also hosts College Nights for the matriculated crowd. Students who want to spread the word can join the Huntington Student Ambassador Program.

For people who have some relevant experience, the Huntington Literary Office takes on a few volunteer readers each season who help read and evaluate the many play submissions that the company receives. If you're lacking the right credentials for that job, but would still like to be on the ground floor (literally), the Huntington also takes on volunteer ushers, who get to see the show for free.

Although the word on the street about the quality of Huntington's productions is mostly very positive and audiences also seem to love the ambience of the old theater that the company performs most of its shows in, some people may still be hesitant to shell out the money for a subscription. Unlike many other theaters of similar note, the Huntington offers a money-back guarantee to its audience members: If you attend your first show and aren't satisfied, you can turn in your remaining tickets for a full refund.

THE LYRIC STAGE COMPANY OF BOSTON

140 Clarendon Street
617-585-5678 • lyricstage.com

Public Transportation: Good (Green Line to Copley Square, Orange Line to Back Bay).

Handicapped Accessibility: Good

Performances/Programs: Performance schedule is Wednesday–Sunday.

Ticket Prices: Single tickets $25–$54, 10% discounts available for groups of 10 or more (15% for 25 or more), special student matinées at 10 a.m. $14 each, and one free teacher ticket for every 10 paid student tix; student groups of 10 or more can also attend regular performances for $20 per ticket.

Subscriptions: Three main subscription packages: Seven-Show (greatest savings, best seats) $125–$260; Four-Show Flex $146–$182; Six-Tix packages (the most flexibility) $270 for preferred seating, $60 for students. Benefits include great seats and free ticket exchanges with 24-hour notice (no exchanges for non-subscribers). Subscribers save up to 32%.

MERRIMACK REPERTORY THEATRE

Liberty Hall, 50 E Merrimack Street Lowell
978-654-4MRT (4678) • merrimackrep.org

Public Transportation: Fair

Handicapped Accessibility: Good

Performances/Programs: Performance schedule is Wednesday–Sunday (with occasional Tuesdays).

Ticket Prices: $26–$61, seniors are eligible for a small discount on tickets, students can get $15 tickets in the balcony, groups of 6 or more get 25% off (30% off for 26 or more).

Subscriptions: Three subscription packages available: Full Season (all six plays, biggest savings, $132–$282); Custom Season (three, four, or five plays); FlexPass (choice of four or six tickets to use in any combination you choose). Seniors pay $20 less for any subscription package; student subscriptions range from $45–$84. Benefits include free parking and easy ticket exchange if you give 24-hour notice.

NEW REPERTORY THEATRE

Arsenal Center for the Arts, 321 Arsenal Street, Watertown
617-923-8487 • newrep.org

Public Transportation: Good
Handicapped Accessibility: Good
Performances/Programs: Performance schedule generally Wednesday through Sunday.
Ticket Prices: $10–$59; discounts for seniors, students (under 25), and WGBH members, 20% off for groups of 10 or more (25% for 20 or more, 30% for 50 or more), groups of students numbering 10 or more can save up to 65%, $10–$15 exchange fee for non-subscribers.
Subscriptions: Seven-, Five-, and Three-Play mainstage subscriptions are available, as well as the Downstage@New Rep subscription, which offers savings on all of the programming in New Repertory Theatre's Black Box performance space. Additionally, the theater provides the option of the A La Carte subscription, a customizable selection of up to four mainstage and downstage shows.

SPEAKEASY STAGE COMPANY

Calderwood Pavilion at Boston Center for the Arts
527 Tremont Street
617-933-8600 • speakeasystage.com

Public Transportation: Fair (accessible via bus or MBTA, but must walk a few blocks).
Handicapped Accessibility: Good
Performances/Programs: Generally Wednesday through Sunday (with occasional Tuesdays).
Ticket Prices: $25–$54; $14 student Rush tickets sold an hour before curtain (subject to availability).
Subscriptions: Four-Show $160–$180, Five-Show $190–$215, Four-Show Flex $192, Five-Show Flex $230. Benefits include priority seating, easy ticket exchange, and a 2-for-1 discount card to use at over 30 other Boston theaters.

WHEELOCK FAMILY THEATRE
Wheelock College, 200 The Riverway
617-879-2300 • wheelock.edu/wft

Public Transportation: Good (five-minute walk from Fenway T stop required).

Handicapped Accessibility: Good

Performances/Programs: Performance schedule is Friday through Sunday, with some special events and performances on other days.

Ticket Prices: $15–$23, discounts available for groups of 15 or more (discount is $3 off each ticket).

Subscriptions: Subscriptions are $60 per person, including one Section A seat to each of the three productions, also available is the Family Flex Pass, $125 for six Section A seats to be used for any productions of your choice. Benefits include preference on all seating requests, discounts on guest tickets, and free ticket exchanges. An annual $25 member's fee in addition to the purchase of a subscription gets you additional benefits, such as 10% off theater classes, invitations to special theater events, and discounts for many area attractions and businesses.

BOSTON BAROQUE
New England Conservatory's Jordan Hall
30 Gainsborough Street
617-484-9200 • bostonbaroque.org

Other Venue: Sanders Theatre, 45 Quincy Street, Cambridge.

Public Transportation: Good (both venues are close to T stops).

Handicapped Accessibility: Good

Performances/Programs: Five programs, 10 performances.

Ticket Prices: $25–$73

Subscriptions: Three-, Four-, or Five-concert packages are offered from $79–$336. Ticket exchanges are only available for subscribers. Additional benefits include free ticket replacement, discounted parking, easy ticket exchanges, and 15% discount on additional tickets and CDs.

Membership: Contributions from $25–$10,000+ for the Annual Fund are welcome. Based on donation amount, benefits include program listing, complimentary Boston Baroque CDs, invites to meet-the-artist receptions, private recitals, and dress rehearsals.

From the Editors: Founded by harpsichordist and conductor Martin Pearlman, Boston Baroque is North America's oldest orchestra and chorus dedicated to performing Baroque music. The group uses period instruments and is one of the leaders in the authentic performance movement, serving as the resident professional ensemble for the Historical Performance Program at Boston University.

BOSTON SYMPHONY ORCHESTRA (BSO)
also Boston Pops and Tanglewood Music Festival
Symphony Hall, 301 Massachusetts Avenue
888-266-1492 • bso.org

Public Transportation: Very good (easily accessible by Green and Orange Lines and bus).

Handicapped Accessibility: Good

Performances/Programs: 250+ performances given annually.

Ticket Prices: $29–$115, depending on seat location and day of week. Discounts for students. Groups of 25 or more receive discounts to most concerts; 5% on Saturday evenings, 10% all other concerts, 20% on Chamber Players, 10% on Open Rehearsals. A limited number of $9 Rush tickets for BSO concerts on Tuesday and Thursday evenings and Friday afternoons are set aside to be sold on the day of the performance. Tickets to Open Rehearsals are offered at a discounted price and are priced for general admittance. Seating is on a first-come first-served basis. Tickets are $19.

Subscriptions: Subscription packages are offered based on day-of-week performance selection, type of music desired, variety of programs, and so on. Ticket insurance and reserved parking (for a fee) are also included as part of the BSO's Patron Privilege program.

Membership: Donors who give $75 or more become members of the Friends of the BSO. Those who give $3,000 or more become members of the Higginson Society. Benefits begin with discounts at the Symphony Shop, a monthly newsletter, and admission to BSO or Pops working rehearsal and reception.

Other Benefits: Invitations to special receptions, lunches, dinners, July 3 boat cruise, reserved seating for July 3 Esplanade Concert, opportunity to travel with the BSO.

Other Activities for Groups (children/students/singles): Numerous programs and discounts are offered for elementary-school-aged children, primary-school-aged children and their families, as well as college students.

From the Editors: The first BSO performance took place in the Old Boston Music Hall, under the baton of Georg Henschel, more than 100 years ago. In 1900 the orchestra moved to Symphony Hall, where it still performs today and is the largest (based on budget) professional orchestra in the United States. Since 2001, Maestro James Levine has led the BSO as its music director. His programs include a wide range of classical, opera, and contemporary repertoire. Under his direction, the BSO has commissioned works from many of the best-known American composers of today, such as Milton Babbitt, Elliott Carter, John Harbison, Peter Lieberson, and Charles Wuorinen.

In addition to its commitment to performance excellence, the BSO is highly committed to musical outreach and to keeping classical music accessible to the general public and, in particular, youth. In 1888 the BSO launched its first concerts for young people, which were revived in 1959 by Harry Ellis Dickson and are still an important part of the BSO today. In fact, the BSO offers many opportunities for young people to enjoy its concerts. The Concerti Club membership offers family concerts and events. The BSO Kids' Club includes access to special members only activities on family concert days, along with Backstage Pass mailings with special Kids' Club news, games, and fun facts. The Young Musician's Card allows high-school students to enjoy up to 19 concerts for only $15; the College Card program, a $25 membership, grants 100+ tickets to members for 25 pre-determined concerts on a first-come first-serve basis; and Repartee, a musical enthusiasts group for 21–40 year olds, allows members $40 concert tickets along with invitations to pre-concert receptions and lectures. There's even Bolero, a group for singles over 40 that also offers pre-concert receptions and lectures.

BOSTON POPS AT THE BSO (BSO)
Symphony Hall, 301 Massachusetts Avenue
617-266-1492 • bso.org

Public Transportation: Very good (easily accessible by Green and Orange Lines and bus).

Handicapped Accessibility: Good

Performances/Programs: About 30 Holiday Pops concerts, plus a limited number of spring, touring, and free concerts, are offered.

Ticket Prices: $27–$122 for Holiday Pops; the annual Esplanade concert is free. Groups of 25 or more receive discounts to most concerts. A limited number of Rush tickets for Boston Symphony Orchestra concerts on Tuesday and Thursday evenings and Friday afternoons are set aside to be sold on the day of the performance. Rush tickets cost $9, are limited to one per customer, and must be paid for with cash only. Open Rehearsals are open to the public and are offered at a discounted price from the actual performance ticket prices. Tickets to Open Rehearsals are priced for general admittance and seating is on a first-come first-served basis. Tickets are $19.

From the Editors: The Boston Pops is a holiday staple, known not only in Boston but all over the world for its programming of classical favorites. It's particularly well-known for holiday concerts, performing numerous shows during the Christmas season and a large concert on the Esplanade for the 4th of July celebration.

CANTATA SINGERS
161 First Street, Cambridge
617-868-5885 · cantatasingers.org

Venues: Primarily New England Conservatory's Jordan Hall (30 Gainsborough Street) and various locations throughout the Boston area.
Public Transportation: Good (Jordan Hall)
Handicapped Accessibility: Good (Jordan Hall)
Performance/Productions: Usually four–six performances per season.
Ticket Prices: $17–$52
Group Discounts: Discounts available for groups of 10 or more.
Subscriptions: Available from $68–$168 depending on the type of seats and date of performances selected. Season ticket holders get 10% off recordings, priority seating, ticket insurance, sell-out protection, and a Greater Boston Choral Consortium VIP Discount Card that gets you discounts on concerts by dozens of nearby choral groups.
Membership: Contributions from $25–$2,500+ are most welcome.

From the Editors: With longtime music director David Hoose at the helm, the Cantata Singers & Ensemble have premiered several new choral and orchestral works that the group commissioned by American composers and it has spotlighted seldom sung works of old, all the while staying true to its commitment to the music of the cantata master himself, J.S. Bach.

HANDEL AND HAYDN SOCIETY
617-266-3605 • handelandhaydn.org

Venues: Symphony Hall, 301 Massachusetts Ave; New England Conservatory's Jordan Hall, 30 Gainsborough Street; Old South Church, 645 Boylston Street.
Public Transportation: Good

Handicapped Accessibility: Good

Performance/Productions: Nine Baroque and Classical concerts per season, with multiple performances of each.

Ticket Prices: Vary by concert and venue, contact for exact pricing details. Sign up with e-mail newsletter to keep informed on student discounts available.

Group Discounts: Discounts available for groups of 10 or more.

Subscriptions: Available from $189–$540, depending on the type of package preferred and performances selected. Create-your-own subscriptions (choose four concerts or more and save 10%). Subscriber benefits include free ticket exchanges, 10% off additional tickets, and free, reserved, or discounted parking. Student Flex Pass available.

Membership: Available from up to $75–$50,000+. Annual Fund contributor benefits include 10% discount at the Society's Boutique, program recognition, and special ticket offers.

ISABELLA STEWART GARDNER MUSEUM CONCERTS

Isabella Stewart Gardner Museum, 280 The Fenway
617-566-1401 • gardnermuseum.org

Public Transportation: Yes (easily accessible by MBTA Green Line E train).

Handicapped Accessibility: Good

Performances/Programs: 40 are given per year.

Ticket Prices: $23, seniors $18, members $15, college students $10; children ages 5–17 $5 (children under 5 not admitted).

Membership: Museum members ($60 per year) get tickets for a reduced fee of $15.

From the Editors: The longest-running museum music program in the nation, the Gardner Museum's concert series is held in the museum's intimate and atmospheric Tapestry Room gallery, including performances by the museum's own Gardner Chamber Orchestra, world-renowned chamber music groups and soloists, and several of the most talented young musicians performing today, many of whom have won prestigious international competitions.

BOSTON LYRIC OPERA
Shubert Theater, Citi Performing Arts Center
617-542-6772 • blo.org

Public Transportation: Good
Handicapped Accessibility: Venue is accessible.
Performances/Programs: Four-five per season with multiple performances of each.
Ticket Prices: $34–$195, with prices varying by date and seat selection. Students get a 50% discount on single tickets.
Group Discounts: Discounts available for groups of 10 or more.
Subscriptions: Three-show subscription $96–$555, depending on date and seats selected. Subscriber benefits include 5% discount on single tickets, priority seating, ticket exchange privileges, ticket replacement for lost tickets, invites to special events, and potential seating upgrades.
Membership: Donations from $75–$150,000+ are welcome. Annual Fund donor benefits include program recognition, restaurant discounts, dress rehearsal passes, and more, depending on donation amount.

From the Editors: Boston Lyric Opera, the largest opera company in New England, is highly dedicated to presenting quality mainstage productions, as well as many outreach events. BRAVO!, a program for young professionals, offers a variety of educational, social, and networking opportunities throughout the year. Family Day at the Opera includes fun pre-performance activities along with lunch and a matinée performance of a kid-friendly production. In addition, family performances, a part of the Opera for Young Audiences program, are performed in a variety of venues throughout the greater Boston area.

THE BEEHIVE
541 Tremont Street
617-423-0069 • beehiveboston.com

Public Transportation: Good
Handicapped Accessibility: No
Performances/Programs: 300 performances per year. Shows are generally 9 p.m. during the week and 10 p.m. on weekends.
Ticket Prices: No cover.

REGATTABAR
1 Bennett Street
617-395-7757 • regattabarjazz.com

Public Transportation: Good
Handicapped Accessibility: Good
Performances/Programs: Approximately 300 performances are presented annually. Live jazz is usually performed Thursday–Saturday at 7:30 and 10 p.m.
Ticket Prices: $10–$30. Occasional discounts are offered if tickets are purchased before day of show.

RYLES
212 Hampshire Street, Cambridge
617-876-9330 • ryles.com

Public Transportation: Poor
Handicapped Accessibility: Good
Performances/Programs: Approximately 750 performances are presented each year, with live jazz or Latin selections almost every night. A Sunday jazz brunch occurs from 10 a.m. to 3 p.m.
Ticket Prices: $5–$20.

SCULLER'S JAZZ CLUB
Doubletree Guest Suites, 400 Soldiers Field Road
617-562-4111 • scullersjazz.com

Public Transportation: Poor
Handicapped Accessibility: Good
Performances/Programs: Approximately 800 performances are presented per year. Show schedule is Tuesday–Saturday. Sets are usually at 8 and 10 p.m.
Ticket Prices: $20–$40. Occasional half-price tickets are available on Goldstar.com. Dinner, Show-and-Stay or Dinner-and-Show packages are also offered at various levels and prices.

From the Editors: Loudly proclaiming its own fame, Sculler's Jazz Club in Boston generally lives up to the self-hype, featuring world-class acts, such as Tony Bennett, Lou Rawls, George Shearing, Marian McPartland, and Wynton Marsalis, as well a variety of emerging acts. Claiming to have helped launch the U.S. careers of artists like Diana Krall, Jamie Cullum, and Michael Bublé, Sculler's has established itself as one of Boston's foremost jazz venues since opening in 1989. Common complaints include the steep prices and the occasional nose-in-the-air patron, but you absolutely get what you pay for at this club. Recent acts that have passed through include New York Voices, the Brubeck Brothers, Roy Hargrove, and Chuck Mangione.

If you're planning on staying at the hotel, inquiring about the Dinner, Show, and Stay packages may help alleviate the high dinner prices on top of admission (the Dinner/Show package can run anywhere from $60 to $90 and tickets alone are $20–$40 each). Sculler's also offers a Dance Party series featuring live salsa and merengue and organizes annual package vacations to popular jazz destinations around the world (past locations have included jazz festivals in Panama, Montreal, and a jazz cruise in Scandanavia).

WALLY'S CAFÉ JAZZ CLUB
427 Massachusetts Avenue
617-424-1408 • wallyscafe.com

Public Transportation: Good
Handicapped Accessibility: Good
Performances/Programs: Approximately 390 performances are given each year. Jazz is performed seven nights per week. Sets are generally between 9 p.m. and 2 a.m. Weekend jam sessions are 5–7 p.m.
Ticket Prices: No cover.

From the Editors: Beginning its long history in 1947, Wally's Café, formerly Wally's Paradise, weathered the storm of the 20th century to retain its classic charm and great lineup to be one of the longest-lasting and most respected venues for jazz in Boston.

Founded by Joseph Walcott, the first African-American jazz club owner in New England, Wally's was able to keep the jazz hot and the overhead low by bringing in young talent from the music conservatories in the Boston area. That tradition continues today, with three nights a week reserved for the youngest up-and-coming talent, frequently borrowed from the nearby Berklee College of Music.

As with all great jazz hideouts, during the set is not the best time to be chatting with your eight friends about your New Year's Eve plans. Come early (it's *packed* every night of the week), have a few drinks, and prepare for some of the best that Boston has to offer.

BERKLEE BEANTOWN JAZZ FESTIVAL
Berklee Performance Center, 136 Massachusetts Avenue
beantownjazz.org

> **Other Venues:** Several outdoor stages on Columbus Avenue.
> **Public Transportation:** Good
> **Handicapped Accessibility:** Good
> **Performances/Programs:** Approximately 20 performances are presented during the festival, which is held in late September.
> **Ticket Prices:** Free for the outdoor concerts; $30–$40 for performances at the BPC.

From the Editors: The Berklee Beantown Jazz Festival began in 2001 under the direction of Daryl Settles (of the Beehive) and has become one of the biggest yearly attractions in Boston. Held in late September, this not-for-profit festival takes over most of Columbus Ave. for an entire day of great jazz on several different stages, with everything from international stars to up-and-coming local student ensembles. Ticketed portions of the festival take place at the Berklee Performance Center, which hosts special programs apart from the main festival (2008 included an all-star drum summit with some of the most prominent drummers in the nation). Tickets for performances that require them can be purchased through Ticketmaster.com.

BOSTON BALLET
Opera House, 539 Washington Street
617-695-6950 • bostonballet.org

> **Public Transportation:** Yes
> **Handicapped Accessibility:** Excellent
> **Performances/Programs:** Five programs per year, plus the annual *Nutcracker*. Each program runs one to two weeks with four-ten performances. The *Nutcracker* runs regularly throughout the month of December.
> **Ticket Prices:** $25–$120. Children and college students may purchase tickets for $20 beginning two hours before performances. Seniors (65+) may purchase $20 tickets to select performances.
> **Group Discounts:** Groups of 10 or more may receive discounts of up to 50% depending on the performance. Boston Ballet also now offers mini-group discounts for groups of less than 10 people.
> **Other Discounts:** Through the Ballet in the Balcony program, public

schools and non-profit student organizations in the greater Boston area can purchase Friday evening performance tickets for $10 each (non-student tickets are $15).

Subscriptions: Subscriptions are available for three, four, or five shows. Student/youth subscriptions and Flex pass options are also available. All sales are final. Subscribers can exchange tickets for free. Other benefits include first choice seats and discounts on additional ticket purchases.

Membership: Basic donor fees start at $100 and include advance sales, invitations to attend members-only events, a 10% discount on Boston Ballet merchandise, and a subscription to Boston Ballet's online newsletter.

Special Membership for Young Adults: Young Partners of Boston Ballet is a group of dance enthusiasts ages 21 to 45. Membership is $250 annually. Benefits include exclusive members-only receptions, an annual black-tie spring ball, and 10% off all Boston Ballet merchandise.

From the Editors: As Boston's premier ballet company, Boston Ballet offers audiences varied presentations of high-caliber classical, neo-classical, and contemporary choreography. This company's annual *Nutcracker* is a particular local favorite. The month-long show casts many children who train at the Boston Ballet School and often involves one or more choral groups from the greater Boston community. In the past these have included the Boston Jazz Voices and the Merrimack Valley Chorus. Famous Bostonians such as radio announcer (and former Celtics player) Cedric Maxwell and City Council member Sam Yoon have even been known to make occasional cameo appearances in these productions.

The Boston Ballet Center for Dance Education also offers a variety of activities open to the community. Aside from operating the affiliated ballet school, Boston Ballet offers open-lecture series on weekday evenings designed to better acquaint audiences with dance and free pre-curtain discussions with Boston Ballet's choreographers, designers, and guest artists.

Boston Ballet II, which performs primarily for community education purposes, is now in its fourth year of collaborating with the Boston Children's Hospital on programming for children with Down Syndrome.

JOSÉ MATEO BALLET THEATRE
Sanctuary Theatre, 400 Harvard Street, Cambridge
617-354-7467 • ballettheatre.org

    Public Transportation: Good
    Handicapped Accessibility: Good

Performances/Programs: The company presents a fall and spring season, plus the annual *Nutcracker*. Each show runs for about three weeks.

Ticket Prices: $15–$50. Discounts are available for friends and family of cast members. The company also offers a youth concert series and seniors matinée series at discounted prices. Through the Community Ticket Access program, the company provides free tickets to disadvantaged children and adults.

Membership: There is no annual membership program. All individual donors of $175 or more are invited to gala fundraiser events. Junior patrons (under 30) may also attend gala fundraisers with a donation of $100.

SUMMER STAGES DANCE AT CONCORD ACADEMY
Performing Arts Center at Concord Academy
166 Main Street, Concord
978-402-2339 • summerstagesdance.org

Public Transportation: Poor
Handicapped Accessibility: Good
Performances/Programs: Four concerts each summer feature the work of renowned visiting artists, one or two performances each.

Ticket Prices: On average tickets are $25. Discounted $10 tickets are available for students at selected events.

Membership: Individual giving opportunities start at $100. Benefits include recognition on performance programs and the Summer Stages website, an invitation to the Spring Gala Celebration, and a subscription to a biannual newsletter.

BRATTLE THEATRE
40 Brattle Street, Cambridge
617 876-6837 • brattlefilm.org

Public Transportation: Fair
Handicapped Accessibility: Good
Performances/Programs: Classic, foreign, and art-house films.
Ticket Prices: $9.50; members and students $7.50; seniors and children $6.50. No credit cards or passes.

From the Editors: The Brattle is a favorite art-house movie theater of Harvard students, who find it's an easy walk from campus. First-runs, foreign films, and new releases of old classics are all shown here. The non-profit Brattle also has repertory programming that features the oeuvre of a notable director, films on a specially selected subject, or movies of a particular genre.

BOSTON CENTER FOR THE ARTS (BCA)
527-551 Tremont Street
617-426-5000 • bcaonline.org

Public Transportation: Very good
Handicapped Accessibility: Good
Performances/Programs: Performance schedules vary considerably.
Ticket Prices: Ticket prices vary based on show. Some shows available on Goldstar.com.
Subscriptions: Membership starts at $50 ($35 for students, seniors, and artists). Members receive the ArtPass card, good for 10% off tickets to BCA productions, invitations to opening-night receptions and post-show Q&As, and discounts at South End restaurants and shops.

From the Editors: BCA hosts more than 50 productions each year by about 20 different companies. BCA has four theaters: the BCA Plaza Theatre, the BCA Plaza Black Box, and the Calderwood Pavilion at the BCA (which includes the Roberts Studio Theatre and the Wimberly Theatre). Currently, BCA has four resident theater companies: Company One, Pilgrim Theatre, SpeakEasy Stage Company, and the Theatre Offensive.

CITI PERFORMING ARTS CENTER
866-348-9738 • citicenter.org

Venue: Wang Theatre, 270 Tremont Street; Shubert Theatre, 265 Tremont Street.
Public Transportation: Very good
Handicapped Accessibility: Good
Ticket Prices: Vary based on program. Policies on senior and student discounts, as well as Rush tickets, vary per production. Shows sometimes available on Goldstar.com.
Group Discounts: Group discounts are generally available (vary per show).
Subscriptions: Membership to the Club starts at $40. Benefits include

up to a 20% discount on select performances, participation in Club pre-sales, reduced fees on ticket orders, and discounts on participating restaurants and parking garages. Ticket exchanges only available for members at the Patron level or higher.

For information on Portland, Maine, and
Providence, Rhode Island, visit go-artsamerica.com.

CLEVELAND, OHIO

Located on the southern shore of Cleveland, the city is home to almost 500,000 residents and fosters an arts and entertainment culture with something for everyone. In addition to its world-class orchestra, Cleveland also features a lively theater and visual-arts scene.

ARTS INFO AND DISCOUNTS

Cleveland Scene (clevescene.com)—Alternative weekly newspaper with news, arts, and entertainment.

cleveland.com/arts—Arts listings and coverage from the *Cleveland Plain Dealer*.

clevelandnights.com—Cleveland events guide.

ctix.org—30%–50% discounts on performing-arts and theater tickets. Purchase online through the website. Tickets available on the day of performance and some sold in advance as well.

Northern Ohio Live (northernohiolive.com)—Attractive well-organized monthly magazine covering the Cleveland/Akron arts scene.

THE ARTS

CLEVELAND MUSEUM OF ART
11150 East Boulevard
216-421-7340 • clemusart.com

Public Transportation: Fair (the museum is served by the Regional Transit Authority Red Line; bus service is also available, but requires a five- to seven-minute walk).

Handicapped Accessibility: Good (the museum is handicapped accessible, except for the south steps; assisted-listening devices are available for use in the lecture and recital hall for the hearing impaired).

Hours: Tuesday, Thursday, Saturday and Sunday 10 a.m.–5 p.m., Wednesday and Friday 10 a.m.–9 p.m., closed Monday.

Admission: Free (fee for special exhibitions).

Tours: Free for individuals and groups.

Membership: Individual membership is $50, Family/Duo membership is $65. Students ($25) and senior couples ($45) receive significant discounts. Benefits of membership include reciprocal admission to other local and national art institutions.

From the Editors: With more than 40,000 works of art, the Cleveland Museum of Art is best-known for its top-notch Asian, medieval European, and pre-Columbian collections. In addition, it also holds famous masterpieces by Turner, Van Gogh, Picasso, and Monet, as well as the moving *Stag Night at Sharkey's* by George Bellow.

The Armor Court will be a hit with any child and the special exhibitions the museum often provides features a distinctive and interesting twist to the traditional. With a carefully chosen collection of public programs as well, this well-rounded museum, set in serene Wade Park, is both dependable and enjoyable; it's difficult to go wrong at the Cleveland Museum of Art.

CLEVELAND PLAY HOUSE (CPH)
8500 Euclid Avenue (until May 2011; see Note below)
216-795-7000 • clevelandplayhouse.com

Public Transportation: Good
Handicapped Accessibility: Good
Performances/Programs: Shows at various times throughout the week.
Ticket Prices: $39–$48, student tickets available for $10 (for students

under 25), groups eligible for discounts up to 40%.

Subscriptions: Eight-Play Signature series ($258–$390), Four-Play Patron's Choice ($151–$230). Benefits include no-fee ticket exchanges and ticket insurance.

From the Editors: With five theaters and three public performance spaces covering more than 12 acres, the Cleveland Play House is the biggest regional theater complex under one roof in the U.S., as well as one of the oldest. Established as a professional theater in 1915, CPH has presented American and world premieres by Brecht, Pirandello, Tennessee Williams, William Saroyan, Brian Friel, and Arthur Miller. The Play House strives to continue this tradition with the Playwrights' Unit program, which nurtures a select group of Cleveland-area writers with developmental support and productions.

The CPH also brings in exciting productions from around the world through the Full Circle International Theatre Exchange program, which has introduced Clevelanders to companies from Hungary, Russia, and other lands.

Note: As we go to press, it has been announced that CPH will be selling its current three-theater 12-acre home to the nearby Cleveland Clinic and will join Cleveland State University and PlayHouseSquare Foundation in reconfiguring the historic Allen Theatre (located on Euclid Avenue and 14th Street) as a multi-stage venue. The grand opening is scheduled for September 2011.

CLEVELAND PUBLIC THEATRE (CPT)
6415 Detroit Avenue
216-631-2727 • cptonline.org

Public Transportation: Good

Handicapped Accessibility: Poor (CPT contains four performance spaces, and only one of them, the Gordon Square Theatre, is accessible).

Performances/Programs: Schedule is generally Thursday–Sunday, with some special series/events on other days.

Ticket Prices: $10–$18; students and seniors $3 off the regular price. Thursday performances are pay-what-you-can.

Subscriptions: Flex passes available for $72 (six-pack) and $140 (12-pack).

From the Editors: Founded in 1981 by James Levin (lawyer, actor, and director) and modeled after La MaMa, the internationally renowned experimental theater in New York City, CPT is Cleveland's leading stage for experimental theater. CPT has supported innumerable emerging artists, arts organizations, and itinerant theaters. Companies launched or nurtured by CPT include Wishhounds (Theatre Labyrinth), New World Performance Laboratory, Ground Zero, the Repertory Project (now Verb Ballets), and SAFMOD. CPT has also helped develop regionally and internationally recognized projects, such as the Performance Art Festival (1987), Festival of Alternative Theatre (1988), Sonic Disturbance Sound Festival (1990), American Indian Festival (1992), and Women's Voices, Women Dancing (1993).

DOBAMA THEATRE
Karamu House, 2355 East 89th Street
216-932-3396 • dobama.org

Other Venues: Pilgrim Congregational Church, 2592 West 14th Street; Tri-C East Theatre, 4250 Richmond Road, Highland Hills; Cleveland Playhouse-Brooks Theatre, 8500 Euclid Avenue.
Public Transportation: Good
Handicapped Accessibility: Good (all venues)
Performances/Programs: Performance schedule is Thursday through Sunday.
Ticket Prices: $17–$22, students and seniors $15–$20; tickets are $8 on the preview Thursday before opening; first Sunday of the run is pay-what-you-can.
Subscriptions: Full Flex pass $135, eight tickets good for any performance (enough for two people to see each show); single subscription $68, four tickets good for any performance; Thursdays-Only $98, eight tickets good for any Thursday-night performance (for two people); Preview Night $55, eight tickets good only at each Preview performance.

From the Editors: Dobama Theatre has been exposing Cleveland to thought-provoking, daring, and socially and politically relevant plays for 50 years. In addition to the company's yearly mainstage productions (almost exclusively premieres), Dobama has two notable programs that have helped the company cultivate young audiences: the Night Kitchen and the Marilyn Bianchi Kids' Playwriting Festival.

The Night Kitchen is a late-night series that focuses on young adults, both as spectators and performers. The program has evolved over the years, but has included short plays, experimental work, long-form improvisation, and plays by both local and emerging playwrights dealing with contemporary issues.

The Marilyn Bianchi Kids' Playwriting Festival, named for one of Dobama's founders, is a young playwrights festival that began in 1979. Students from the first to twelfth grades in Cuyahoga County are invited to submit original plays on any subject and in any setting they wish. Of the hundreds of submissions that Dobama gets each year, about a dozen are ultimately chosen to receive full productions in the festival. The winning playwrights also receive a savings bond and their scripts are published in Dobama's annual book of festival plays. To make the event as inclusive as possible, most of the performances are free of charge and one performance is signed and audio-described for sight- and hearing-impaired audience members.

GREAT LAKES THEATER FESTIVAL (GTLF)

Hanna Theatre, PlayhouseSquare, 2067 East 14th Street
216-241-6000 • greatlakestheater.org

Public Transportation: Good
Handicapped Accessibility: Good
Performances/Programs: Schedule is generally Wednesday–Sunday, with some Tuesday performances.
Ticket Prices: $15–$69; students $13 for most shows, group discounts available for parties of 10 or more.
Subscriptions: Options include Three-Play, Four-Play, and Five-Play subscriptions $126–$245, senior and family packages $96–$140, young adult (25 or younger) $42–$60, FestPass for six $318, eight $408, and ten $490. Boxes and Banquettes package is premium seating for four people, any date: Three-Play $636, Four-Play $816, and Five-Play $980; Flex options also available. Benefits include discount reserved parking and free ticket exchanges (one per show).

From the Editors: In 1961, the Lakewood Board of Education invited a homeless Shakespeare company to move into the local civic auditorium and the Great Lakes Theater Festival was born. Though the first season of rotating rep was an all-Bard affair, it wasn't long before the GLTF took on other important playwrights, like Sophocles and George Bernard Shaw, going on to broaden its scope to include musicals, light comedies, modern classics, and works inspired by the classics. From the beginning, GLTF has attracted and nurtured top talent, and the company's alumni list includes John Lithgow, Celeste Holm, Tom Hanks, Piper Laurie, Jean Stapleton, Hal Holbrook, and Olympia Dukakis.

The Great Lakes Theater Festival is the largest provider of educational outreach in Ohio. The company reaches out to students through several programs, including matinée performances especially for students, touring productions, in-school residencies, and the Summer Theater Institute. Adults can get a little education, too, from special events like the pre-show discussion program Director Night and the subscriber series Playnotes, in which a guest scholar introduces the play and puts it in context.

The Great Lakes Theater Festival recently moved into a new home, the 550-seat Hanna Theatre. Not only does the Hanna have great sightlines and lots of legroom all around, it also features plush banquettes, club chairs, and historic boxes that provide both a close view and some old-fashioned theatrical glamour.

KARAMU YOUTH PRODUCTIONS
Karamu House, 2355 E. 89th Street
216-795-7077 • karamuhouse.com

Public Transportation: Fair
Performances/Programs: Performance schedule is Thursday–Sunday.
Ticket Prices: $20–$30; preview nights $10–$15, seniors get a $3 discount, student tickets are $15; no senior and student discounts on preview nights.

CLEVELAND ORCHESTRA
Severance Hall, 11001 Euclid Avenue
216-231-7300 • clevelandorch.com

Public Transportation: Fair
Handicapped Accessibility: Good
Performances/Programs: Approximately 185 performances annually.
Ticket Prices: $31–$110. Full-time college and high-school students with valid student IDs may attend select Cleveland Orchestra performances at the following student prices: $10 for tickets purchased prior to one hour before the concert, $15 for tickets purchased within one hour before the concert. Subject to availability.
Group Discounts: Groups of 20 or more enjoy a discount of up to 15% on tickets. Student groups of 20 or more save 50% off single ticket prices for most concerts.
Subscriptions: Subscriptions are available for the normal season and the orchestra's Miami residency. Concert subscribers get free exchanges at any time; other subscribers may exchange subscription tickets for a differ-

ent performance of the same-week's program at any time. Subscribers may also exchange their tickets for another concert up to five days prior to the performance. A discount at the Cleveland Orchestra Store is also offered to subscribers.

Membership: Basic membership begins at $100. Benefits include an invitation to one open rehearsal at Severance Hall and an invitation to one open rehearsal at Blossom Music Center.

Other Benefits: Recordings, discounts at the Cleveland Orchestra store, an invitation to join the orchestra on national tours with priority ticket privileges, and invitations to special events and receptions throughout the year.

From the Editors: Founded in 1918 under the direction of Nikolai Sokolof, the Cleveland Orchestra has a strong history of performance excellence (it's considered by many experts to be the finest orchestra in America, if not the world) and educational outreach.

The Cleveland Orchestra offers many ways for adults and youth alike to learn more about classical music and see performances at a low cost. Children as young as three can begin to learn about the instruments in the orchestra through Musical Rainbows, 30-minute concerts hosted by Maryann Nagel, a local actress and singer. For children a bit older (7+), the Family Concerts series features guest artists, such as young musicians, dancers, and actors, and all are preceded by fun and free learning activities. A free membership to the Student Advantage Program offers students invitations to free open rehearsals, free master classes, and large discounts on tickets to many of the Orchestra's concerts.

For adults interested in learning more about the repertoire and the artists, the Cleveland Orchestra offers Music Study Groups, a series of informal lectures and discussions held in locations throughout the community, and a Meet the Artist series, an interview and luncheon program, where audiences are able to connect with the season's artists.

To make sure that their music is accessible to the entire community, the Cleveland Orchestra offers multiple free concerts throughout the year, including one to commemorate Martin Luther King Jr.'s birthday in January, along with a free Public Square concert each summer.

OPERA CLEVELAND
State Theatre, 1519 Euclid Avenue at Playhouse Square
216-575-0903 • clevelandopera.org

Public Transportation: Very good (easily accessible by multiple public bus lines).

Handicapped Accessibility: Venue is accessible.

Performances/Programs: Four programs per season with multiple performances, plus special events.

Ticket Prices: $25–$130

Group Discounts: Discounts available for groups of 10 or more.

Subscriptions: Available from $60 (Sunday matinée) to $360 (Loge section seats for Friday or Saturday evenings). Subscriber benefits include ticket exchange privileges and lost ticket replacement.

Membership: Available from $50–$10,000+. Based on donation amount, member benefits include program listing, invites to special events, and backstage tour of the State Theatre.

From the Editors: In 2006 Lyric Opera Cleveland joined forces with Cleveland Opera, and today they are known as Opera Cleveland. Opera Cleveland offers a diverse repertoire of classic, contemporary, and light opera, and includes pre-opera talks and post-opera discussions. The company also reaches out to young audiences with special student matinée presentations and a program that helps kids create their own opera.

BROTHERS LOUNGE
11609 Detroit Avenue
216-226-2767 • brotherslounge.com

Public Transportation: Poor

Handicapped Accessibility: Good

Performances/Programs: Approximately 200 performances per year. Jazz open-mic on Monday, jazz or blues on Friday and Saturday. Show times vary.

Ticket Prices: From free to $10.

CLEVELAND BOP STOP
2920 Detroit Avenue
216-771-6551 • clevelandbopstop.com

Public Transportation: Poor

Handicapped Accessibility: Good

Performances/Programs: Approximately 75 performances per year. Live music performed Friday–Saturday at 8:30 pm.

Ticket Prices: $10 cover.

PIER W
12700 Lake Avenue, Lakewood
216-228-2250 • selectrestaurants.com/pier

Public Transportation: Poor
Handicapped Accessibility: Good
Performances/Programs: Approximately 80 performances per year. Live piano jazz is performed Thursday-Saturday.
Ticket Prices: No cover.

THE CEDAR LEE THEATER
2163 Lee Road, Cleveland Heights
440-717-4696 • clevelandcinemas.com

Performances/Programs: Independent and mainstream films, as well as documentaries and classics; frequently screens cult classics like the *Rocky Horror Picture Show*.
Ticket Prices: $8.50; matinées (all shows before 3 p.m.) $6; seniors and children 5–12 are $5.75; children under 5 not admitted at any time.

From the Editors: The Cedar Lee Theater opened in 1925 and has been a favorite cinema for movie fanatics in Greater Cleveland ever since. Originally a single-screen movie house, the Cedar Lee now has a total of four theaters and two screening rooms that it uses to show a number of different types of films. Cult-film favorites from all eras, movies by local filmmakers, independent features, documentaries, and Hollywood releases all fill the schedule. And other specialty offerings include midnight screenings, director's retrospectives, and high-definition broadcasts of opera and ballet productions.

PLAYHOUSESQUARE CENTER
1501 Euclid Avenue
216-771-8403 • playhousesquare.com

Venues: Allen Theatre, Hanna Theatre, Ohio Theatre, State Theatre, Palace Theatre, 14th Street Theatre, and Kennedy's Theatre.
Public Transportation: Very good (easily accessible by bus).
Handicapped Accessibility: Good
Performances/Programs: Performances by numerous resident companies, such as DANCECleveland, Great Lakes Theater Festival, Ohio Ballet,

Opera Cleveland, Tri-C Cultural Arts Series, and Tri-C Jazz Festival are featured. The Cleveland Play House will move there in November 2011.

Ticket Prices: Vary by program. $10 tickets (called Smart Seats) are available for select performances.

Group Discounts: Discounts are available for groups of 20 or more.

Subscriptions: Broadway Series subscriptions cover the big touring shows that come through the Center. The Discovery Theater Series for Families subscriptions start at $48.

BLOSSOM MUSIC FESTIVAL

Blossom Music Center
1145 West Steels Corners Road, Cuyahoga Falls
800-686-1141 • clevelandorch.com

Public Transportation: Poor
Handicapped Accessibility: Good
Performances/Programs: The 10-week Blossom Festival features weekend concerts by the Cleveland Orchestra and other classical and pops artists from late June to Labor Day. Additionally, Live Nation presents concerts by rock, pop, country, and jazz artists at Blossom from May to September. Ticket exchanges are available with 24 hours advance notice. Gates to the Blossom grounds open two and a half hours before performances. Concerts are performed rain or shine and usually last about two hours.

Ticket Prices: Vary by performance. Children 6 through 12 are admitted anytime to the lawn for half the price of an adult lawn ticket. Children 5 and younger are free on the lawn.

Group Discounts: Discounts are available for groups of 20 or more.

From the Editors: Summer home of the Cleveland Orchestra and located about 25 miles south of Cleveland in the 33,000-acre Cuyahoga Valley National Park, the Blossom Music Festival is a 10-week summer series of orchestral and pops concerts. In addition to the festival, the Blossom Pavilion and hillside lawn (which, combined, accommodate nearly 20,000 music lovers) also hosts a series of popular music, country, and jazz concerts presented by Live Nation from May to September.

Pre- and post-concert eats are available at the Blossom Grille, which also provides prepared picnic dinners (call 330-916-6063 to order) for those who prefer to eat on the lawn or in the park's wooded picnic areas. The Blossom grounds are also home to the Porthouse Theatre Company, the Eells art gallery, and permanent sculpture displays.

CAIN PARK
14591 Superior Road at Lee, Cleveland Heights
216-371-3000 • cainpark.com

Public Transportation: Good

Handicapped Accessibility: Good

Performances/Programs: Performances are given June–August (jazz, folk, pop, dance, theater, etc.). Schedule varies, but generally Tuesday–Sunday.

Ticket Prices: Ticket prices vary, mostly $8–$32; $2 discounts are available for students, seniors, children, and Friends of Cain Park; $3 discounts for military and those with Cleveland Heights Recreation IDs (purchasable by residents at the Cleveland Heights Community Center). Special Tuesday events are $2 and many events are free.

Group Discounts: Discounts available for groups of 20 or more.

Subscriptions: One popular subscription option is the Patron series: Buy at least one ticket to any four or more different events and get a 15% discount off the regular price (all four-plus tickets must be purchased at the same time).

For information on Cincinnati and Columbus, Ohio, and
Detroit, Michigan, visit go-artsamerica.com.

DALLAS/FT. WORTH, TEXAS

The Dallas-Ft. Worth area encompasses 12 counties within north-central Texas and is one of the most economically active and populous areas in the United States. Known, recreationally speaking, as a town that's serious about sports (football, especially!), it also boasts an art scene (especially in the area of visual art) commensurate with its size and population.

ARTS INFO AND DISCOUNTS

Quick (blog.quickdfw.com)—Free weekly entertainment paper owned by the Dallas Morning News.

guidelive.com—Arts and entertainment events guide.

ArtsCard (artscard.com)—For a $15 membership ArtsCard holders receive discounts to a variety of museums and theaters in Dallas, Ft. Worth, and Atlanta, Georgia.

THE ARTS

AMON CARTER MUSEUM (THE CARTER)
3501 Camp Bowie Boulevard, Fort Worth
817-738-1933 • cartermuseum.org

Public Transportation: Very good (easily accessible by the #7 bus; the Trinity Railway Express service is also available).

Handicapped Accessibility: Good (also, complimentary assistive-listening devices are available for the hearing- impaired on a first-come first-served basis).

Hours: Tuesday, Wednesday, Friday, Saturday 10 a.m.–5 p.m.; Thursday 10 a.m.–8 p.m.; Sunday noon–5 p.m., closed Monday.

Admission: Free

Tour: Free permanent-collection tours are offered Thursday–Sunday at 2 p.m. and special-exhibition tours are offered Thursday-Sunday at 3:30 p.m. Free scheduled self-guided tours are also available by appointment. Private tours can be scheduled for groups of five or more. Prices vary and reservations are required.

Membership: Individual membership is $50. Benefits include an invitation to purchase two tickets for exclusive members-only exhibition previews, exclusive access to the Members Lounge, a 15% discount in the museum store, a complimentary subscription of the museum's award-winning magazine, *Program,* and recognition in the Carter's *Annual Report.* Dual/Family Membership for $100 annually includes all the benefits above, plus an invitation to purchase four tickets for exclusive members-only exhibition previews and reciprocal admission to and store discounts at more than 100 participating museums.

From the Editors: The Amon features an excellent Western-American art collection, with works by Frederic Remington, Charles Marion Russell, Thomas Eakins, and Grant Wood, among others. Both the original museum and the recent expansion are designed by Philip Johnson.

DALLAS MUSEUM OF ART (THE DMA)
1717 N. Harwood Street, Dallas
214-922-1200 • dallasmuseumofart.org

Public Transportation: Excellent (easily accessible by Light Rail, M-Line Street Car, bus and DART).

Handicapped Accessibility: Good (hearing aids and wheelchairs are also available on a first-come first-served basis).

Hours: Tuesday, Wednesday, Friday, Saturday, Sunday 11 a.m.–5 p.m., Thursday 11 a.m.–9 p.m., closed Monday.

Admission: $10, seniors (65+) $7, students $5, DMA members and children (under 12) are free. Discounts are available for groups of 10 or more.

Free Day: Thursday evenings 5–9 p.m. and the first Tuesday of each month (special ticket prices may apply to exhibitions).

Tours: Guided tours are available for $30 for a group of 15; school tours are also available. To schedule a group tour, call 214-922-1331. Audio tours are free.

Membership: Base membership is $75 annually and covers one person and a guest or two adults and their children. Benefits includes unlimited free admission to the museum and most special exhibitions, free parking during museum hours, invitations to member previews and special events, plus multiple discounts on museum merchandise and admittance to the museum film series.

Other Benefits: Reciprocal membership to more than 100 other museums available with the following memberships; Sustainer ($125), Friend ($250), Advocate ($500), and Contributor ($1,000).

From the Editors: The most notable attribute of the Dallas Museum of Art is its extensive top-notch permanent collection. With heavy-hitters such as Picasso, van Gogh, Monet, O'Keeffe, Pollock, Gauguin, Mondrian, Picasso, and Cézanne, the DMA is a sure thing. A lesser-known but exciting feature is that on the third Friday of every month, the museum is open until midnight and the price for staying late is included in the general admission for that day; so if you fall for its impressive holdings, you can really get your money's worth.

A word to the wise: The DMA is certainly a worthy museum to visit, but you'll be smart to research the special exhibition before dropping your dollar on anything but the varied and valuable permanent collection.

KIMBELL ART MUSEUM (THE KIMBELL)
3333 Camp Bowie Boulevard, Fort Worth
817-332-8451 • kimbellart.org

Public Transportation: Good (see Amon above)

Parking: Free parking is available at the museum, off Arch Adams and Darnell Streets. Additional parking is also available at the Darnell Street Auditorium, across Arch Adams Street from the museum.

Handicapped Accessibility: Good (the Arch Adams Street entrance is handicapped accessible and a limited number of wheelchairs are also available upon request).

Hours: Tuesday, Wednesday, Thursday, Saturday 10 a.m.–5 p.m., Friday noon–8 p.m., Sunday noon–5 p.m., closed Monday.

Admission: Free (There's a charge for special exhibitions, but half-price exhibition admission is offered on Tuesdays all day, and on Fridays from 5 to 8 p.m.)

Basic Tour: Tours are offered Wednesday 2 p.m., and Sunday 3 p.m.

Membership: Individual $65 membership entitles members to unlimited admission for 2 adults to all exhibitions, a 20% discount on museum publications, invitations to purchase two tickets for Patron opening receptions, Patron previews of exhibitions before they open to the public, priority admission to select presentations, and members-only tours. Dual and Family Patron Membership ($100) includes all the above benefits, plus unlimited admission for four adults to all exhibitions, unlimited admission for children under 18 living at same address and an invitation to purchase four tickets for Patron opening receptions. All memberships include previews, free admission to special exhibitions and advance notice of programs and events, and discounts on shopping, programs, and courses.

Other Benefits: Other premium memberships are offered. The Texas Reciprocal membership program is available to all members contributing $250+ per year.

From the Editors: If the Kimbell can be summed up in three words, those words are "quality over quantity." With a collection of fewer than 350 pieces, you might assume that this museum is one that can be missed; however, this is most certainly not the case. Perhaps its small bark and large bite are the most charming aspects of the Kimbell.

Its exterior architecture, the work of American Master Louis Kahn, speaks to the museum as a whole, crafted with care and infused with benchmark and landmark pieces. The careful and delightful exterior reflects care exercised within the interior, as well. Having been open for a relatively short 35 years, the collection is particularly well-known for its holdings of European old- and modern-master paintings and classical Egyptian, Asian, and ancient American art. The museum has an uncanny quality of touching on the high and transitional points of artistic movements, leaving you with the overall feeling of having traveled through a condensed highlighted tour of the world's art.

In short, the Kimbell Art museum is a true treat; adding convenience to quality, it's also located within walking distance of the aforementioned Amon.

MODERN ART MUSEUM OF FORT WORTH (THE MODERN)

3200 Darnell Street, Fort Worth
817-738-9215 • themodern.org

Public Transportation: Poor

Parking: Street and commercial parking facilities are available.

Handicapped Accessibility: Good (also, assistive-listening devices are available upon request on a first-come first-served basis).

Hours: Tuesday–Saturday 10 a.m.–5 p.m.; Sunday 11 a.m.–5 p.m.; closed Monday.

Admission: $10, students and seniors (65+) $4, children (12 and under) and members are free.

Free Day: The museum is free every Wednesday and on the first Sunday of every month.

Tours: Free. Docent-led public tours are offered Tuesday–Saturday 2 p.m. On Wednesdays when gallery admission is free to the public, tours are available from 11 a.m. to 2 p.m. These tours do not require prior arrangements and begin in the museum lobby.

Membership: Basic membership for individuals is $65 and includes unlimited free admission for two adults, a subscription to *At the Modern,* and discounts on museum merchandise and events.

Other Benefits: Reciprocal membership is available on all membership packages at the Associate Level ($125) and above.

From the Editors: One of the largest modern-art Museums in the country, the Modern displays more than 3,000 works, including pieces by Anselm Kiefer, Pablo Picasso, Jackson Pollock, Gerhard Richter, Susan Rothenberg, Richard Serra, Andres Serrano, and Andy Warhol. In 2002, the museum moved into a new building (next door to the Kimbell) designed by the Japanese architect Tadao Ando.

DALLAS THEATER CENTER

Kalita Humphreys Theater
3636 Turtle Creek Boulevard, Dallas
214-522-8499 • dallastheatercenter.org

Public Transportation: Good

Handicapped Accessibility: Good

Performances/Programs: Performance schedule is Tuesday–Sunday.

Ticket Prices: $15–$60; select preview Sunday-evening performances are pay what you can; $12 student Rush tickets sold one hour before performance. Discounts available for groups of 10 or more, corporations, and businesses.

Subscriptions: Subscriptions: Three-Play $48–$168, Four-Play $51–$219, and Five-Play $60–$270; subscribers save up to 25%. Only subscribers can exchange tickets.

From the Editors: The Dallas Theater Center's Kalita Humphreys Theater is one of only three existing theaters that can claim to have been designed by Frank Lloyd Wright. Unfortunately, that doesn't mean the building is without flaws and limitations, so DTC is now expanding into the new state-of-the-art Dee and Charles Wyly Theatre, designed by none other than Pritzker Prize-winner Rem Koolhaas.

As if its embarrassment of architectural riches isn't enough, DTC is also celebrating its 50th year of providing Dallas with high-quality productions of new plays, great musicals, and classics. DTC also has a free play-reading series called Fresh Ink, which allows playwrights across the country the opportunity to work with local talent.

The Creative Adventure backstage tour and workshop is an easy and inexpensive ($5 per person) way for student groups to get the Dallas Theater Center experience; they tour the facilities from dressing rooms to rooftop, then participate in a workshop dedicated to a discipline such as storytelling or movement. If that piques your child's interest, DTC also has theater day camps that delve into creative theater, acting, musical theater, and precollege actor training (financial assistance is available for these programs). One of the Dallas Theater Center's coolest offerings for the younger set is the DaVerse Lounge, a free open-mic night where anyone 21 and under can get up and read a poem or a spoken-word piece.

JUBILEE THEATRE
506 Main Street, Fort Worth
817-338-4411 • jubileetheatre.org

Public Transportation: Good
Handicapped Accessibility: Good
Performances/Programs: Performance schedule is Thursday–Sunday.
Ticket Prices: $14–$25, preview prices $10; students, seniors, KERA Card members, and Arts Card participants get $2 off regular ticket prices. Groups of 10 or more get a $2 per ticket discount. Saturday matinée special: Buy 1 get 1 free. $5 student Rush tickets are sold 15 minutes before curtain. No exchanges or refunds (unless performance is canceled).

Subscriptions: Subscriptions for four ($55–$80) or six ($85–$120) shows available. Subscribers save up to 20%.

KITCHEN DOG THEATER
McKinney Avenue Contemporary (MAC)
3120 McKinney Avenue
214-953-1055 • kitchendogtheater.org

Public Transportation: Good
Handicapped Accessibility : Yes
Performances/Programs: Performance schedule is generally Thursday–Saturday, as well as some Wednesdays and Sundays.
Ticket Prices: $15–$25, $10 to $15 for students, seniors, and KERA/MAC/ARTSCARD/TCG/NNPN members.
Subscriptions: Five-Play season subscriptions are available for $100, Flex pass available for $125. Subscriber benefits include one free guest pass, 12 staged readings, free admission to opening-night cast parties, and free ticket exchanges.

UNDERMAIN THEATRE
3200 Main Street, Dallas
214-747-5515 • undermain.org

Public Transportation: Good
Handicapped Accessibility: Good
Performances/Programs: Performance schedule is Wednesday–Saturday.
Ticket Prices: $15–$25, discounts available for students, seniors, and KERA members. Groups of 10 or more are eligible for a 15% discount; 30 or more get a 20% discount.

WATERTOWER THEATRE
Addison Conference and Theatre Center
15650 Addison Road, Addison
972-450-6232 • watertowertheatre.org

Public Transportation: Fair
Handicapped Accessibility: Good
Performances/Programs: Performance schedule is Wednesday–Sunday.

Ticket Prices: Mainstage $22–$40, Discover series $20–$25, $3 discounts for students and seniors available for Mainstage shows, group discounts available.

Subscriptions: Subscriptions are $75–$150 for Mainstage and $65–$80 for Discover Series, Flex passes available, discounted subscription rate for students and seniors. Subscriber benefits include free ticket exchanges and $3 discount on additional single tickets.

DALLAS SUMMER MUSICALS!
Music Hall at Fair Park, 909 First Avenue, Dallas
214-631-ARTS (2787) • dallassummermusicals.org

Public Transportation: Good
Handicapped Accessibility: Good
Performances/Programs: Performance schedule generally Wednesday–Sunday.
Ticket Prices: Vary per show, but the long range is $11–$124, senior and student discounts occasionally available. Group discounts (usually 20 or more) are available.
Subscriptions: Several subscription packages available, as low as $30 and as high as $231.

DALLAS SYMPHONY ORCHESTRA (DSO)
Meyerson Symphony Center, 2301 Flora Street, Dallas
214-692-0203 • dallassymphony.com

Public Transportation: Very good (convenient to DART rail and bus service) at Pearl and Bryan Streets.
Handicapped Accessibility: Good
Performances/Programs: Approximately 225 annually.
Ticket Prices: Range from $17 to $122; concerts are individually priced with a variety of seating options. $15 student Rush tickets are available for purchase online at least seven days prior to the concert and at the box office at least two hours before the concert. 5%–20% discounts for groups of 10 or more, depending on the concert.
Subscriptions: Classical, Family, Pops, and a Casual Classics Summer series are offered. Also available are Impromptu packages; for a fixed monthly fee, Impromptu patrons may attend unlimited concerts in the Texas Instruments Classical and DSO Pops Series (provided seating is available) and are entitled to one free guest ticket each season. Student subscriptions

are available at a 50% discount. Subscribers enjoy ticket exchanges and donation for resale, as well as lost or misplaced tickets printed at no cost.

Membership: A $50 donor receives a Dallas Symphony newsletter subscription. Higher levels of giving are good for invitations to exclusive events and open rehearsals, discounts at restaurants and the symphony store, complimentary CDs, and invitations to exclusive holiday parties.

From the Editors: The Dallas Symphony Orchestra began in 1900 as a 40-member ensemble under the direction of the German conductor Hans Kreissig, who helped finance the development of the orchestra and led the players for the first five seasons. More than 100 years later, the DSO is still running strong, with more than 200 performances each year.

The DSO has a major commitment to young audiences and performs youth concerts for pre-K through sixth, along with student Rush tickets and student subscriptions at up to 50% off regular prices. In addition, the DSO has a wonderful online musical resource for children, DSOkids.com, a website dedicated to teaching children about classical music.

For adults wishing to learn a bit more about the orchestra's programs, the DSO offers free Performance Preludes one hour before each Classical series performance, where the evening's program is discussed.

For die-hards wanting to see everything or for those who want the freedom of spontaneity are the DSO's Impromptu packages, where for a fixed monthly fee Impromptu patrons may attend unlimited concerts in the Texas Instruments Classical and DSO Pops series.

FORT WORTH SYMPHONY ORCHESTRA (FWSO)
Bass Performance Hall, 525 Commerce Street, Fort Worth
817-665-6000 • fwsymphony.org

Other Venue: Fort Worth Botanic Garden, 3220 Botanic Garden Boulevard, Fort Worth.

Public Transportation: Depends on venue.

Handicapped Accessibility: Good

Performances/Programs: Vary by season and program.

Ticket Prices: $10–$78. Educators, students, and seniors (65+) can purchase discounted tickets in the Parterre Circle, Lower Gallery, and Upper Gallery for Friday and Sunday Symphonic series concerts. Tickets are $8–$39. Discounts are offered on groups of 10 or more.

Subscriptions: Genre-specific packages are offered, including a Symphonic and Pops series, as well as the Great Performances Festival.

Membership: Individual membership begins at $50 and includes a card that provides discounts to local restaurants and retailers, passes to special donor concerts and events, invitations to working rehearsals, and the opportunity to host a private recital in your home.

Activities for Young Adults: ¡Vivace! (a young patrons membership group) offers admission for two to all ¡Vivace! pre-concert receptions, including complimentary hors d'oeuvres and two cocktails per person (concert tickets purchased separately). Also included are discounted tickets to the annual Symphony Gala (¡Vivace! ticket $150, regular ticket $250; ¡Vivace! table $1,500, regular table $2,500) and invitations to FWSO special events. The annual membership fee for ¡Vivace! is $250 per couple, $125 per individual.

TURTLE CREEK CHORALE
Myerson Symphony Center
816-235-6222 • turtlecreek.org

Venues: Meyerson Symphony Center, 2301 Flora, Dallas; Winspear Opera House and Wyly Theatre, Dallas Center for the Performing Arts, 2403 Flora Street, Dallas.

Public Transportation: Good

Handicapped Accessibility: Good

Performances/Programs: Four programs per season, plus special events.

Ticket Prices: $30 - $80

Subscriptions: Three-concert seasons subscription $87–$147.

Membership: Available for annual giving levels of $300–$12,000. Sterling Circle member benefits include program recognition and party invites.

From the Editors: The Turtle Creek Chorale is an all-men's chorus that reaches over 50,000 audience members each year with its annual subscription concert series. The group is comprised of over 200 volunteer members who pay dues and donate their time to the organization. The chorale travels around the country and sometimes even internationally, performing a wide range of choral works. Annually, the Turtle Creek Chorale presents as many as 50 benefit performances in addition to its tours and regular concert series.

THE DALLAS OPERA
Margot and Bill Winspear Opera House (fall 2009), Dallas
214-443-1000 • dallasopera.org

Public Transportation: Good (easily accessible by light rail service).
Handicapped Accessibility: Good
Performances/Programs: Five operas per season with multiple performances of each.
Ticket Prices: $15–$199
Subscriptions: Five-performance subscriptions are $75–$1,875, with prices varying widely based on seat and date choices. Three-performance Flex subscriptions also available, starting at $75. Subscriber benefits include 20% savings, payment plan option, and ticket exchange privileges.
Membership: Dallas Opera Guild memberships $50–$100+.

From the Editors: It's been over 50 years since the Dallas Opera opened with a production starring opera legend Maria Callas, and since then, the company has built a great reputation for itself. Its musical director is Graeme Jenkins, who has over 150 opera productions on his resume, including Billy Budd and Jenufa (Vienna State Opera) and Così Fan Tutte (English National Opera), among many others. Moving from the Music Hall at Fair Park, the Dallas Opera is now taking its place as the resident company at the new state-of-the-art Margot and Bill Winspear Opera House, designed by Pritzker Prize winner Norman Foster.

ALEXANDRE'S
4026 Cedar Springs Road, Dallas
214-559-0720 • alexandres.com

Public Transportation: Poor
Handicapped Accessibility: Good
Performances/Programs: Approximately 300 performances given per year. Regular shows on Thursdays, Fridays, and Sundays at 9 p.m.
Ticket Prices: No cover.

BROOKLYN JAZZ CAFÉ
1701 South Lamar Street, Dallas
214-428-0025 • brooklynjazzcafe.com

Public Transportation: Poor

Handicapped Accessibility: Good
Performances/Programs: Approximately 360 performances per year. Tuesday–Thursday 7 p.m.; Friday–Saturday 8 p.m. and Sunday 11:30 a.m. and 7 p.m.
Ticket Prices: No cover, $30-per-person minimum.

OVATION
6115 Camp Bowie Boulevard, Ft. Worth
817-732-8900 • ovationrestaurant.com

Public Transportation: Poor
Handicapped Accessibility: Good
Performances/Programs: 280 performances are given each year. Live jazz Wednesday–Sunday. Gospel brunch on Sunday morning.
Ticket Prices: No cover.

PEARL AT COMMERCE
2038 Commerce Street, Dallas
214-655-8824 • pearlatcommerce.com

Public Transportation: Poor
Handicapped Accessibility: Good
Performances/Programs: Approximately 280 performances per year. Schedule runs Monday 6:30 p.m., Tuesday and Wednesday 8 p.m., Thursday 9 p.m., Friday and Saturday 9:30 p.m.
Ticket Prices: $5–$15 cover. There are often discounts provided when purchasing tickets online.

SCAT JAZZ LOUNGE
111 W 4th, Suite 11, Fort Worth
817-870-9100 • scatjazzlounge.com

Public Transportation: Poor
Handicapped Accessibility: Good
Performances/Programs: Approximately 280 performances per year. Tuesday-Saturday 8:30 or 9 p.m.; Sunday 8 p.m.
Ticket Prices: $5–$10

JAZZ BY THE BOULEVARD MUSIC AND ARTS FESTIVAL

Will Rogers Memorial Center
3401 W Lancaster Avenue, Ft. Worth
fortworthjazz.com

Public Transportation: Good
Handicapped Accessibility: Good
Performances/Programs: Approximately 25 performances are presented over the course of the three-day mid-September festival.
Ticket Prices: Free admission. $15–$30 for reserved seating.

From the Editors: The Jazz by the Boulevard Music and Arts Festival in Fort Worth showcases the eclectic lifestyles that few outsiders expect from Texans, with an impressive jazz lineup and a great cross section of the blooming cultural center that Dallas-Ft. Worth is becoming. Cultural/heritage exhibits give festival-goers a sense of the rich jazz history in Ft. Worth. Recent headliners have included Randy Brecker, Buddy Guy, Arturo Sandoval, and Spyro Gyra, among others.

The festival features an extensive vendor area with a food and wine selection to rival most of the other big festivals in the country. There are VIP packages available for purchase, but it is just as well to take advantage of the free admission and save your money for the various wine-tasting events. (However, VIP and reserved-seating tickets can be purchased via a form found on the website.)

DALLAS BLACK DANCE THEATRE

Majestic Theatre, 1925 Elm Street, Dallas
214-871-2376 • dbdt.com

Public Transportation: Good
Handicapped Accessibility: Good
Performances/Programs: Five programs a year in Dallas, about two performances each.
Ticket Prices: Approximately $35
Group Discounts: 15% off single-ticket prices for groups of 10 or more; 25% off single-ticket prices for groups of 20 or more; 40% off single-ticket prices for groups of 50 or more.
Subscriptions: Subscribers can choose three- or five-show packages. Subscribers can also add options of VIP seating/box and VIP receptions. Subscribers save 20% off single-ticket prices. Sales directly from the DBDT

box offices are final and incur a $7.50 service fee. Online purchases are subject to Ticketmaster's return policy.

Membership: Membership fees start at $30 and include invitations to special members-only events, a quarterly newsletter, and recognition in DBDT programs.

TEXAS BALLET THEATER
Bass Performance Hall, 525 Commerce Street Fort Worth
877-829-9200 • texasballettheater.org

Other Venues: Majestic Theatre, 1925 Elm Street, Dallas; Music Hall at Fair Park, 909 1st Avenue, Dallas.

Public Transportation: Poor

Handicapped Accessibility: Good

Performances/Programs: Three programs per year, plus the annual *Nutcracker*. Each program is performed three times. The *Nutcracker* runs for most of December.

Ticket Prices: $19–$99; students can purchase tickets for $10 one hour prior to performances.

Group Discounts: Discounts are available for groups of 20 or more. Specific packages are designed on an individual basis.

Subscriptions: Subscriptions are available for two, three, four, or five shows. Venue preference is available as is a Family series option. All sales are final. Tickets may be exchanged for a $10 fee. Benefits include advance purchases, invitations to private parties, free ticket exchanges, and notices about special events and offers.

Membership: Fees start at $250 and include recognition in performance programs, discount coupons for 10% off ticket purchases, and access to the members-only line at the box office. Membership in the Ballet Guild, a volunteer organization, starts at $35 and requires participation on selected committees.

From the Editors: Formerly called the Ft. Worth/Dallas Ballet, the relatively new Texas Ballet Theater is the second largest professional dance company in Texas. It maintains 39 professional dancers and gives more than 50 performances in the Dallas/Ft. Worth area each year.

In 2003 Ben Stevenson, O.B.E., formerly the director of the Houston Ballet, took over the artistic directorship of Texas Ballet Theater and under his watch the caliber of this company's technical performance has risen steadily. In 2006, Texas Ballet Theater also acquired its own school, Dallas Dance Academy. Already a well-regarded independent training ground, this academy now serves as the official Texas Ballet Theater school.

Particularly popular among the fans of Texas Ballet Theater is an organization called Lone Star Adagio. Primarily a volunteer organization, it's dedicated to raising popular awareness of the company and is now generating excitement as Texas Ballet Theater prepares to take up residency in the brand new Winspear Opera House. Members enjoy many social engagements and opportunities to mingle with Texas Ballet Theater artists.

ANGELIKA FILM CENTER
Mockingbird Station
5321 East Mockingbird Lane, Ste. 230
214-841-4713
angelikafilmcenter.com/angelika_index.asp?hID=7915

Public Transportation: Good (accessible by DART Redline and Blueline trains, as well as buses).

Handicapped Accessibility: Good

Performances/Programs: Hollywood blockbusters, independent fare, foreign films, and documentaries

Ticket Prices: $9.25, before 5 p.m. $7, students and seniors $6.50, children under 12 $6.

From the Editors: The Angelika Film Center is an oasis in a desert of mediocre multiplexes. At the Angelika, independent movies and foreign fare are the focus, but high-quality Hollywood flicks sometimes turn up here too. With eight screens, there's plenty of room for variety, including special events like hi-def screenings of awards shows and sporting events, dinner-and-a-movie specials, and weekday "cry-baby" matinées where parents are invited to bring their infants.

Part of the fun of going to the Angelika is that it has a completely different vibe than the average movie theater. The seating is comfortable and roomy and the venue also boasts a cool café with iced drinks, imported beer, and gourmet eats.

For information on Little Rock, Arkansas; Memphis, Tennessee; and Oklahoma City, Oklahoma; visit www.go-artsamerica.com.

DENVER, COLORADO

Offering a blend of urban sophistication and outdoor splendor, the Mile High City boasts an art scene as diverse as its population. Loaded with art galleries, dance companies, museums, clubs, and other exciting propositions for the art lover, Denver doesn't disappoint.

ARTS INFO

Denver Westword (westword.com)—Alternative weekly with arts and entertainment listings and reviews.

Denver Post (denverpost.com)—News and reviews of the Colorado arts, including many summer festivals.

denver.com/arts—Arts links and info.

denver.citysearch.com—Events listings and coverage.

THE ARTS

DENVER ART MUSEUM (THE DAM)
The Civic Center Cultural Complex
100 W 14th Avenue Parkway
720-865-5000 • denverartmuseum.org

Public Transportation: Very good (the Regional Transportation District runs directly in front of the museum; bus service is also available).

Handicapped Accessibility: Good (also, adaptive and interpretive services/sign-language tours are available with one week's notice).

Hours: Tuesday–Thursday 10 a.m.–5 p.m., Friday 10 a.m.–10 p.m., Saturday 10 a.m.–5 p.m., Sunday noon–5 p.m., closed Monday. Note: Collection galleries in the North Building (levels 2–6) close at 5 p.m., except during special events. The museum is closed on major holidays, including Thanksgiving and Christmas. The DAM is, however, open on New Year's Day.

Admission: $10–$13; college students and seniors $8–$10; youth (6–18) $3–$5; members and kids (5 and under) free.

Tours: Free with general admission. Private docent-led tours are available with two weeks' notice. There are additional fees of $2 per person for adult and senior groups when taking these tours. The museum also offers an architecture tour where guests can explore the Daniel Liebeskind-designed Hamilton Building and the 28-sided North Building, designed by Gio Ponti and James Sudler.

Audio Tour: Free

Membership: Individual membership is $50 annually, Family/Dual membership $75. All members receive free general admission for an entire year, invitations to members-only events, free admission to ticketed exhibitions, the ability to purchase additional discounted admissions to ticketed exhibitions, discounted rates and priority registration for studio classes, kids' camps and classes, and film series. Senior/student/teacher memberships are $45.

Other Benefits: To receive reciprocal membership with more than 40 museums nationwide, you must be a Sustaining member ($125) or above.

From the Editors: The Denver Art Museum is world-renowned for its collection of Native American and Asian art. Furthermore, its African Art collection, comprised of approximately 1,000 pieces, is the largest in the Rocky Mountain region. The combination of these unique niches of art history, all available in one place, alone makes the DAM a worthwhile visit.

The DAM is also particularly strong in its emphasis on family atmosphere, offering classes, camps, and family events. Also for the kids is Seymour, the family-programs mascot, a friendly guide to all the treasures the museum has to offer its youngest guests.

A couple of complaints arise from the architecture of the building itself. While aesthetically compelling from the outside, slanted walls on the inside have been known to distract the viewer from the actual pieces of art.

COLORADO SHAKESPEARE FESTIVAL

303-492-0554 • coloradoshakes.org

Venues: The Mary Rippon Outdoor Theatre and the University Theatre, University of Colorado, Boulder
Public Transportation: Good
Handicapped Accessibility: Good (both)
Performances/Programs: Performance schedule is Tuesday–Sunday.
Ticket Prices: $14–$54 single tickets, preview tickets half-price, $5 discount for students, seniors, and university faculty/staff. Half-price tickets for 13–17 year olds (no previews), tickets for kids 5–12 years old are $5, 25% discounts available for groups of 10 or more.
Subscriptions: Season subscriptions (or Five-Flex Pak) are $64–$204. Five-Flex Pak benefits include 2-for-1 vouchers for Curious Theatre Company, Boulder Philharmonic, Central City Opera, and the Colorado Music Festival; subscribers save up to 28%.

THEATREWORKS

719-262-3232 • theatreworkscs.org

Venues: The Dusty Loo Bon Vivant Theater and the Osborne Studio, University of Colorado, Colorado Springs.
Public Transportation: Good
Handicapped Accessibility: Good
Performances/Programs: Performance schedule is Thursday–Sunday.
Ticket Prices: $22, tickets for children under 16 $12.
Subscriptions: Eight-Show subscription is $160–$176. Benefits include a free pass for a friend, free drinks and snacks in the VIP Zone, and invites to special events and lectures.

COLORADO SYMPHONY ORCHESTRA (CSO)
Boettcher Concert Hall, Denver Performing Arts Complex
1000 14th Street
303-MAESTRO (303-623-7876) • coloradosymphony.org

Performances/Programs: Approximately 175 annually.

Ticket Prices: Admission prices start at $15.

Group Discounts: Discounts of up to 20% off for groups of 10 or more; students and children may receive up to 50% off.

Subscriptions: An extensive array of subscription options are offered, including the Masterworks series, CSO Presents Pops, CSO Presents Chase Family series, CSO Presents Holiday series, CSO Special Performances, and custom-designed packages specially tailored to the subscribers' preferences, consisting of 7 to 15 concerts. Benefits include a free Performing Arts companion pass, free Summer Music Festival companion pass, and free ticket exchanges.

Membership: $5 gets you a subscription to the *Highnotes* symphony newsletter. At higher levels, benefits include invitations to open rehearsals, post-concert receptions, exclusive season-preview events, and more.

Educational/Community Outreach: The CSO offers Youth and Children's Concerts for students ages 8–13 for $6 per ticket; Petite Musique is the orchestra's program for toddlers and children up to 7 years old and tickets for these concerts are $5 for children, $7 for adults. Admission to CSO Open Rehearsals, geared for grades 9–12, are $5 per ticket.

From the Editors: A young and emerging orchestra, the Colorado Symphony Orchestra was established in 1989 as the successor to the Denver Symphony. The CSO is the only resident full-time professional symphonic orchestra in Colorado. The orchestra's musicians are actively involved advising in the management of the orchestra and participate on the Board of Trustees and other committees.

The CSO offers further education for concert-goers through free pre-concert lectures for the Masterworks series and Talk-backs, informal post-concert discussions held after select concerts. Five-dollar tickets are available to the orchestra's Open Rehearsals, where high-school students are invited to experience the inner workings of the orchestra. Petite Musique (for toddler-7 years old) and Youth and Children's Concerts (grades 3–8) offer musical experiences tailored for the young. With tickets beginning as low as $15 for most concerts and discounts up to 30% off for subscriptions, the Colorado Symphony Orchestra is accessible to all ages and incomes.

CENTRAL CITY OPERA
Central City Opera House, 124 Eureka Street, Central City
303-292-6700 • centralcityopera.org

Public Transportation: Poor
Handicapped Accessibility: Good
Performances/Programs: Three shows per season with multiple performances of each, plus special events like Family Matinée performances of operas and Opera House screenings of classic and silent films.
Ticket Prices: $50–$99
Group Discounts: Groups get a 15% discount.
Subscriptions: Two-opera subscriptions are $95–$183. Subscribers save 10% over single ticket prices, and they are permitted to get free ticket exchanges.
Membership: Central City Opera House Association Guild memberships available from $30–$255. Benefits include 15% discount on single Opera tickets, one free admission to the Denver Antiques Show & Sale, and invites to social events.

From the Editors: A product of Gold Rush-era prosperity, the Central City Opera House was built in 1878 and is the jewel of the Central City / Black Hawk National Landmark Historic District. Under the leadership of General/Artistic director Pelham G. Pearce, the Central City Opera annually produces a terrific summer season, giving music-loving Coloradoans an excuse to travel out to this mountain town (located about an hour away from both Denver and Boulder) to take in an opera and to explore the historical and cultural offerings of the area.

OPERA COLORADO
Ellie Caulkins Opera House, 950 13th Street
303-778-1500 • operacolorado.org

Public Transportation: Good (accessible by RTD Light Rail)
Handicapped Accessibility: Good
Performances/Programs: Three productions per season with multiple performances of each.
Ticket Prices: $30–$160, with prices varying by date, time and performance selected. Join E-Mail Club to find out about special ticket offers.
Group Discounts: Groups of 10 or more get a 20% discount and don't pay ticketing fees.
Subscriptions: Three-opera subscriptions are $87–$399, depending on

seat and date selection. Subscriber benefits include ticket exchanges and 15% discount on additional single tickets.

Membership: Donations from $50–$50,000 and up are welcome. Donor benefits include program recognition, dress rehearsal tickets, and invites to special events, depending on donation amount.

From the Editors: Opera Colorado has established a tradition that includes singers of the highest level, such as Grammy-winning lyric soprano Renee Fleming, Denyce Graves, and tenor Ben Heppner. Dedicated to bringing opera to young audiences, Opera Colorado's Outreach program brings chamber opera to schools in the area. Meet the Artists, Student Dress Rehearsal Tickets, and the DU Enrichment course, a partner program with the University of Denver, offer audience members additional opportunities to learn more about the operas and productions.

DAZZLE
930 Lincoln Street
303-839-5100 • dazzlejazz.com

Public Transportation: Poor
Handicapped Accessibility: Good
Performances/Programs: Live music nightly; most shows at 8 or 10:30 p.m.
Ticket Prices: $5–$10
Subscriptions: Dazzle offers multiple types of subscriptions: $200 gets you a 20% discount on the 10-Performance series, no cover on late-night shows, and two free tickets to the show of your choice; $800 gets all of the above with no cover for any performance in the year. This results in a saving of from 20%-100%, depending on subscription level.

LANNIE'S CLOCKTOWER CABARET (LANNIE'S)
1601 Arapahoe Street
303-293-0075 • lannies.com

Public Transportation: Poor
Handicapped Accessibility: Good
Performances/Programs: Shows are scheduled Tuesday–Saturday, 8 p.m. during the week and 11 p.m. Friday and Saturday.
Ticket Prices: $5–$20

BALLET NOUVEAU COLORADO (BNC)
Pinnacle Events Center, 1001 W. 84th Avenue
303-466-5685 • bncdance.com

Other Venue: Lakewood Cultural Center, 470 S. Allison Parkway, Lakewood.

Public Transportation: Poor

Handicapped Accessibility: Good

Performances/Programs: Five programs per year: two fall programs, two spring programs, and the annual *Nutcracker*.

Ticket Prices: $26, $22 for students, seniors, and children. The Pinnacle Events Center sometimes offers Five-Buck Fridays ($5).

Subscriptions: Season packages can be custom-made to include two, three, four, or five performances. Subscribers to three or more shows receive exchange privileges. Subscribers to four or more shows receive an additional 5% off single ticket prices. Subscribers to five shows receive a special invitation to a company rehearsal. All subscribers also receive 10% off tickets to the company gala event and buy-one get-one-free ticket offers from the Curious Theatre Company, in addition to ticket-exchange privileges up to 48 hours before a performance.

Membership: BNC accepts tax-deductible annual contributions beginning at $30. Contributors receive email updates on BNC programs and plans. Larger contributions include extra benefits.

CLEO PARKER ROBINSON DANCE
Cleo Parker Robinson Dance Theatre, 119 Park Avenue West
303-295-1759 • cleoparkerdance.org

Public Transportation: Poor

Handicapped Accessibility: Good

Performances/Programs: The company usually presents a Fall, Winter and Spring Concert in Denver.

Ticket Prices: Tickets are handled by Ticketmaster and tend to run $20–$30. Discounts for students and seniors are sometimes available. Ticketmaster generally cannot exchange or refund tickets once purchased.

COLORADO BALLET
Ellie Caulkins Opera House, Denver Performing Arts Complex
14th and Curtis Streets
303-339-1723 • coloradoballet.org

Public Transportation: Good
Handicapped Accessibility: Good
Performances/Programs: Four programs per year, plus the annual *Nutcracker*. Each program runs for two or three weeks with anywhere from six to 12 performances. The *Nutcracker* runs for the entire month of December.
Ticket Prices: $19–$149. Students/school groups can purchase $7 tickets to final dress rehearsals.
Group Discounts: Groups of 10 or more receive discounted tickets. Packages are designed on an individual basis. Call to arrange.
Subscriptions: Subscriptions are available for three, four, or five shows on opening-night and Wednesday-night performances. Benefits include priority seating, discounts on additional ticket purchases and merchandise at the Boutique, free admission to a Patron performance, convenient ticket exchanges, ticket insurance, invitations to an annual open house and a seminar with Colorado Ballet's artistic director.
Membership: Basic membership fees start at $100 and include a 10% discount on any single ticket purchase and name recognition in performance programs.

From the Editors: This regional ballet company was born out of a small Denver dance school established over 50 years ago. Founders Lillian Covillo and the late Freidann Parker trained ballet students for 10 years before deciding to establish the Colorado Concert Ballet. They wanted to create a professional company so that their talented students wouldn't have to go to other cities for jobs.

Colorado Ballet now employs 32 professional dancers hailing from all corners of the world and is a thriving arts presence in Colorado. Colorado Ballet is especially proud to have received a 2009 Colorado Masterpieces Grant from the Colorado Council on the Arts. Each year, this prestigious award funds one statewide tour of an exhibit or performance that focuses on the state's cultural and artistic legacy. Selected partly on the basis of its excellent educational outreach programs, this grant will enable Colorado Ballet to tour the state with a special show including works by Colorado choreographers and Agnes de Mille's classic Western-inspired ballet, *Rodeo*. This show will tour the cities of Denver, Greeley, Sterling, Pueblo, and Colorado Springs beginning in fall 2009.

DENVER FILM SOCIETY AT THE STARZ FILM CENTRE
900 Auraria Parkway (on Auraria Campus)
303-595-3456, ext. 250 • denverfilm.org/about

Public Transportation: Good (accessible by light rail and bus).
Handicapped Accessibility: Good
Performances/Programs: Mostly art-house and independent films, both domestic and foreign.
Ticket Prices: $9.50, members $6, students and seniors $7, first show of the day $7.50; different prices for special programming.

From the Editors: Developing ways for diverse audiences to encounter film via creative and thought-provoking experiences is the mission of the Denver Film Society, which presents a lively weekly program of new exclusives, revivals of American and foreign films, and documentaries (totaling more than 600 films per year!). A multitude of special series and symposia are also featured at the Starz FilmCenter and the DFS puts together the noted annual festival Film on the Rocks, a concert and film series held at the Red Rocks Amphitheatre all summer long. The society's efforts culminate each November in the Starz Denver Film Festival, an 11-day celebration of cinema that includes red-carpet premieres, international screenings, and awards ceremonies. Among the awards handed out at the event are the John Cassavettes Award and the Maysles Brothers Award for Best Documentary.

MAYAN THEATRE
110 Broadway Boulevard
303-352-1992
landmarktheatres.com/Market/Denver/MayanTheatre.htm

Public Transportation: Unknown
Handicapped Accessibility: Fair (first-floor screening room is accessible; call in advance to arrange accommodations at 303-744-6799).
Performances/Programs: Mainstream, independent, documentary, and foreign films.
Ticket Prices: $9.75, seniors and children $7.25.

From the Editors: Built in 1930 and carefully restored in the 1980s, the Mayan Theatre is one of just three theaters left in the country that were done in the Art Deco Mayan Revival style. The theater's central Denver location means that there are plenty of art galleries, vintage clothing shops, antique stores, and restaurants nearby to visit before or after the movie. The Mayan's three screens show foreign films, daring independent features, and other art-house flicks.

DENVER CENTER FOR THE PERFORMING ARTS
Denver Center for the Performing Arts Complex
1101 13ᵗʰ Street
303-893-4100 • denvercenter.org

Public Transportation: Very good (easily accessible by light rail).
Handicapped Accessibility: Good
Performances/Programs: The Denver Center for the Performing Arts Complex is a four-block 12-acre complex containing 11 performance venues. The Denver Center for the Performing Arts is the primary user of the facilities, but the Colorado Symphony, Opera Colorado, and Colorado Ballet also use the theaters.
Ticket Prices: Vary by program. Join E-mail Club to find out about special discounts and ticket offers.
Group Discounts: Discounts are typically available for groups of 10–20 or more, depending on the production.
Subscriptions/Membership: Subscriptions and memberships are available for some of the individual companies at the complex, such as the Denver Center Theatre Company and Denver Center Attractions (which brings in the Broadway touring shows).
Educational/Community Outreach: Educational programs at the center include onsite classes for people of all ages, school tours, professional-development opportunities, and the National Theatre Conservatory, a degree-granting institution. The Complex also houses the National Center for Voice and Speech, a research, clinical, and teaching organization.

For information on Salt Lake City, Utah,
visit go-artsamerica.com.

HARTFORD/NEW HAVEN, CONNECTICUT

A s home to Yale University, New Haven offers a wealth of artistic and cultural resources. New Haven, as well as nearby Hartford, is home to many business commuters who work in nearby New York City. These same commuters, however, need not stray far from home to enjoy a terrific evening at theater or a world-class museum. They can find these venues easily (and plentifully) in Hartford/New Haven.

ARTS INFO AND DISCOUNTS

Hartford Advocate (hartfordadvocate.com)—Alternative paper with good arts and entertainment coverage.

Hartford Courant (courant.com)—Good coverage of the southern New England arts scene.

New Haven Register (nhregister.com)—Local newspaper.

letsgoarts.org—Listings, courtesy of the Greater Hartford Arts Council.

infonewhaven.com/arts—Guide to the New Haven arts scene.

hartfordartstix.org—Half-price tickets and other discounts.

THE ARTS

THE BRUCE MUSEUM
One Museum Drive, Greenwich
203-869-0376 • brucemuseum.org

> **Public Transportation:** Good (Metro North to Greenwich Station)
> **Handicapped Accessibility:** Good
> **Hours:** Tuesday–Saturday 10 a.m.–5 p.m.; Sunday 1–5 p.m.; closed Mondays and major holidays.
> **Ticket Prices:** $7, students (5–22 w/valid ID) $6, seniors (65+) $6, museum members and children under 5 free.
> **Free Days:** Free admission on Tuesdays.
> **Groups:** Adult and school groups of eight or more require advance reservations and are subject to a special group fee.
> **Educational/Community Outreach:** Museum-based school programs are available Tuesday through Friday at 10 and 11:15 a.m. and 1 p.m. After-school museum-based programs are available Tuesday through Friday.
> **Membership:** $50 individual ($70 family), $30 students with ID to age 22, $35 for seniors (65+), $55 senior couple. Benefits include free admission for one year, invitations to two exhibition openings, a 10% discount in the museum store, a bi-monthly newsletter subscription, and discounts on museum programs and events.

> **From the Editors:** The Bruce Museum was originally bequeathed in 1906 by its first owner, Richard Moffat Bruce, as a natural history, historical, and art museum, "for the use and benefit of the public." Its current director, Peter Sutton, a world-class scholar of northern and Dutch paintings, has put the Bruce on the map, with major exhibitions that travel to other acclaimed world art venues, like the National Gallery in London.
> The current exhibition originating at the museum (which will travel to New York's Jewish Museum in 2009) is of rarely seen Old Masters' works and other paintings: Reclaimed: Paintings from the Collection of Jacques Goudstikker.

NEW BRITAIN MUSEUM OF AMERICAN ART (NBMAA)
58 Lexington Street, New Britain
860-229-0257 • nbmaa.org

> **Public Transportation:** Poor
> **Handicapped Accessibility:** Good

Hours: Tuesday, Wednesday, Friday 11 a.m.–5 p.m., Thursday 11 a.m.–8 p.m., Saturday 10 a.m.–5 p.m., closed Monday.

Admission: $9, seniors $8, children under 12 free.

Free Day: Saturdays (10 a.m.-noon)

Tours: Docent-led tours are $10 person.

Audio Tours: Free. You may choose among 36 art objects for up to a full one-hour tour of the highlights of the museum's permanent collection, or from three family tours, all of which are available in numerous languages.

Membership: Individual membership is $45 and provides unlimited free general admission, invitations to openings, lectures, concerts, and gallery talks; discounts on lectures, adult classes, and workshops, plus unlimited free membership to 11 New England museums, including Mattatuck Museum Arts and History Center, Lyman Allyn Art Museum, Newport Art Museum and Art Association, Cape Cod Museum of Art, Provincetown Art Association and Museum, Danforth Museum of Art, Fruitlands Museums, Fitchburg Art Museum, Bennington Museum, and Farnsworth Art Museum. Discounted memberships are available for seniors ($40), as well as educators and students ($35). Household membership ($75) provides admission for entire families, all benefits included.

From the Editors: Founded in 1903, the New Britain Museum of American Art was and remains the first institution to be designated strictly as a holding for American art in the U.S. Although it remains a relatively small collection at approximately 5,000 pieces, its choices are strong, particularly in the painting and sculpture areas, with works from Winslow Homer, John Quidor, William Sidney Mount, Thomas Eakins, Mary Cassett, and John Singer Sargent.

Coupled with these American heavy-hitters is the excellent setting in which the museum itself is located. Set in Walnut Hill Park, the grounds are picturesque and reflect some of the inspiration to the landscape pieces within.

An insider's tip: The nearby Angelo's Deli on West Main St., just off of Lexington (where the museum itself is located), is a true Italian deli, providing a great lunch (or the makings of a picnic) after taking in the art New Britain has to offer.

WADSWORTH ATHENAEUM MUSEUM OF ART
600 Main Street, Hartford
860-278-2670 • wadsworthatheneum.org

Public Transportation: Good (easily accessible by Connecticut Transit bus).

Handicapped Accessibility: Good (ASL interpreters are also available for hearing-impaired visitors, but must be pre-arranged).

Hours: Sunday 10 a.m.–5 p.m., Tuesday–Friday 11 a.m.–5 p.m., Saturday 10 a.m.–5 p.m., closed Monday. Note: The first Thursday of every month, the museum's hours are 11 a.m.–8 p.m.

Admission: $10, seniors $8, students (13-college) $5, members and children under 12 free, First Thursdays admission (5–8 p.m.) is $5. Group discounts are available.

Free Day: There are four community open-house days per year.

Tours: Free with general admission. Museum Highlights tours are given on the following schedule: Tuesdays and Wednesdays 1 p.m., Saturdays and Sundays 2:30 p.m. Art in Focus tours are given on Thursdays and the second Sunday of every month at noon.

Membership: Individual membership is $45 annually and includes free unlimited gallery previews and events, unlimited museum admission for one, early invitations to exhibitions, and unique travel opportunities. Household membership ($60) offers the same benefits for two adults and their children.

Other Benefits: Reciprocal privileges at 14 museums nationwide are offered at the Reciprocal membership level ($170).

From the Editors: The Wadsworth Athenaeum not only offers a fabulous collection of art, but has a fascinating history that ought to drive any art enthusiast to its doors. The country's first permanent gallery of fine art, its main building's castle-like architecture is a nod to the Gothic Revival style of Hartford's Christ Church (1828), which founder Daniel Wadsworth admired.

The Wadsworth is well-known for its fine and extensive collection of Hudson River School 19th-century wilderness paintings. It was also one of the first museums in the U.S. to acquire surrealist masterpieces from artists like Dali and de Chico, in addition to Renaissance art by Caravaggio. Now housing other heavy-hitters, like Picasso, Miro, Warhol, Hopper, Klimt, and Matisse, the permanent collection is varied and hugely valuable.

The Wadsworth Athenaeum continues to evolve in progressive ways. The museum now offers a program called Access Art, which provides transportation to and from the museum and accommodates up to 20 passengers (for more information, call 860-278-2760 ext. 3046; fees apply).

YALE CENTER FOR BRITISH ART (YCBA)
1080 Chapel Street, New Haven
203-432-2800 • ycba.yale.edu

Public Transportation: Fair (reachable via Metro-North or Amtrak; requires taxi or bus Service to reach museum).

Handicapped Accessibility: Good

Hours: Tuesday–Saturday 10 a.m.–5 p.m., Sunday noon–5 p.m., closed Mondays and holidays. Reference Library hours: Tuesday–Friday 10 a.m.–4:30 p.m.; when Yale College is in session: Wednesday 10 a.m.–8 p.m., Saturday 10 a.m.–4:30 p.m., Sunday noon–4:30 p.m. Study Room hours (for viewing prints, drawings, and rare books): Tuesday–Friday 10 a.m.–4:30 p.m. Museum Shop: Tuesday–Saturday 10 a.m.–5 p.m., Sunday noon–5 p.m.

Admission: Free

Tours: Free. Introductory and special-exhibition tours are given on a regular basis, though not daily.

Membership: Individual membership is $50 and all members enjoy unlimited visits at both the Yale University Art Gallery and the Yale Center for British Art, a membership card entitling members to various discounts and benefits, invitations to exhibition openings, members-only events at both museums, and reciprocal membership at more than 20 other art museums. Dual/family ($75) and student ($15) memberships are also offered.

From the Editors: Donated to Yale by Paul Mellon, this collection of paintings, sculpture, drawings, prints, rare books, and manuscripts is the largest and most comprehensive collection of British art outside the United Kingdom.

YALE UNIVERSITY ART GALLERY
1111 Chapel Street (at York Street), New Haven
203-432-0600 • artgallery.yale.edu

Public Transportation: Fair (Amtrak, Metro-North, and Shore Line East all operate through New Haven's Union Station; from the station, it's a five-minute trip via taxi, bus, or car to the gallery).

Handicapped Accessibility: Good

Hours: Tuesday–Saturday 10 a.m.–5 p.m., Thursday until 8 p.m. (Sept.–June), Sunday 1–6 p.m., closed Mondays and major holidays.

Admission: Free

Tours: Tours are available for both adult and student groups.

Membership: Individual membership is $50 and all members enjoy un-limited visits at both the Yale University Art Gallery and the Yale Center for British Art, a membership card entitling members to various discounts and benefits, invitations to exhibition openings, members-only events at both museums and reciprocal membership at more than 20 other art museums. Dual/ Family ($75) and Student ($15) memberships are also offered.

From the Editors: This comprehensive museum originally opened in 1832 when Yale's president arranged to buy paintings and miniatures from John Trumbull. Since then, the collection has grown primarily due to generous gifts from prosperous alumni. Well-known for this American collection, the museum also has several pre- and post-Impressionist paint-ings (including Van Gogh's *The Night Café*) and a collection of modern (as in 1913-1929) art donated by arts patroness Katherine Dreier.

CONNECTICUT REPERTORY THEATRE (CRT)
The Harriet Jorgensen Theatre
University of Connecticut, Storrs
860-486-4226 • crt.uconn.edu

Other Venues: The Nafe Katter Theatre and the Studio/Mobius The-atre, University of Connecticut, Storrs.
Public Transportation: Poor
Handicapped Accessibility: Good (all venues)
Performances/Programs: Schedule is Wednesday–Sunday, with occa-sional Tuesday shows.
Ticket Prices: $26–$35, preview performances $17–$20, discounts available for students and seniors. Student pass $24 for four coupons (each can be redeemed for a ticket to any CRT mainstage performance; available to currently enrolled UConn students only).
Subscriptions: Subscribers save 25%. Benefits include priority seating, unlimited ticket exchanges (with 48 hours notice), ticket insurance, and two 50%-discount coupons.

GOODSPEED MUSICALS
Goodspeed Opera House, 6 Main Street, East Haddam
860-873-8668 • goodspeed.org

Other Venue: The Norma Terris Theatre, 33 North Main Street, Chester

Public Transportation: Poor (MetroNorth and Amtrak train to Old Saybrook, then get a taxi—very expensive).

Handicapped Accessibility: Good

Performances/Programs: Performance schedule is Wednesday–Sunday.

Ticket Prices: $26–$63, discounts available for groups, $25 tickets for people 25 and under for Friday-night performances (except opening nights). Student Rush tickets sold for $10 starting at 10 a.m. for Wednesday, Thursday, Friday, or Sunday evening performances (can be purchased by phone or at box office); $10 tickets for children 5–18 on selected kids and teen nights (when adult purchases full-price ticket). Seniors can get $25 tickets for Wednesday-night performances.

Subscriptions: Three-Show subscriptions, regular and flex, $78–$177. Benefits include ticket exchanges and priority seating.

HARTFORD STAGE
50 Church Street
860-527-5151 • hartfordstage.org

Public Transportation: Fair

Handicapped Accessibility: Good

Performances/Programs: Performance schedule is Tuesday–Sunday.

Ticket Prices: $23–$64. Half-price Rush tickets are sold two hours prior to the show; seniors can purchase tickets for half-price on the day of performance; discounts available for groups of 10 or more (up to 30% off); join e-Club for special offers. EZ Ticket Prices: Four-pack of tickets that can be used for any show for $186.

Subscriptions: Four-Play $86–$252 and Six-Play $126–$348 subscriptions available. Senior subscription prices are $102–$227 for Four-Play, and $144–$313 for Six-Play. Benefits include free ticket replacement and exchanges. Only subscribers can exchange tickets.

From the Editors: The Hartford Stage's very first venue was a grocery-store warehouse where the company produced Shakespeare and Moliere, as well as 20th-century masters like Beckett and Genet. The Tennessee Williams Marathon, introduced in 1999, has seen to it that one of the most influential American playwrights of that century is annually celebrated in an event that includes readings, film screenings, discussion panels, and even premieres of forgotten Williams plays. But Hartford Stage is just as notable for its dedication to new plays and each year it does at least one world or

American premiere, including works by Edward Albee, Horton Foote, Eve Ensler, Richard Foreman, A.R. Gurney, and Derek Walcott.

HARTBEAT ENSEMBLE
555 Asylum Avenue, Studio #101, Hartford
888-548-9144 • hartbeatensemble.org

Performances/Programs: Performance schedule varies, but generally Thursday–Sunday.

Ticket Prices: $10–$20, discounts available for students, seniors, Charter Oak, and Let's Go members.

LONG WHARF THEATRE
222 Sargent Drive, New Haven
203-787-4282 • longwharf.org

Public Transportation: Fair (New Haven train station, then 5-minute cab ride to theater).

Handicapped Accessibility: Good

Performances/Programs: Performance schedule is Tuesday–Sunday.

Ticket Prices: $42–$67. Preview tickets $32–$42; seniors can get tickets for $20, students and people under 30 can get $20 tickets; usually one pay-what-you-will performance for each show (tickets must be purchased at the box office on the day of performance in cash). Groups of 10 or more get a discount (savings of up to 35%); AAA members eligible for discounts.

Subscriptions: Six-Play $180–$330, Five-Play $155–$285, and Four-Play $128–$228; seniors get a small discount on subscription packages. Benefits include a newsletter subscription, free ticket exchanges (24 hours notice and you're allowed to see a show a second time for free).

From the Editors: The Long Wharf Theatre, named for a port on the New Haven harbor and not actually located on a wharf (in case you were wondering), is one of the most respected theaters in the Northeast. Though the company has done its fair share of classics since opening with *The Crucible* in 1965, the Long Wharf is most notable for launching new work. Its productions of *Wit* (starring Kathleen Chalfant), *American Buffalo*, *The Gin Game* (with Hume Cronyn and Jessica Tandy), and *Requiem for a Heavyweight* all transferred to New York.

Long Wharf holds many of the interesting pre- and post-show discussions that have become a staple of the bigger regional theaters, but one of its more unusual offerings is Backstage with the Technical Staff. This is a pre-show panel where the audience gets to learn the details of the physical creation of the show (costumes, sets, lights, etc.) from the people who make it happen.

Long Wharf also boasts several educational initiatives, including in-school residencies and specially priced student matinée performances. The Long Wharf Theatre Studio gets students involved in the arts through workshops in playwriting, Shakespeare, improvisational acting, scene work, and creative play. The theater's newest initiative, the Educator's Laboratory, helps teachers understand how they can use the arts as a tool for teaching the general curriculum.

SEVEN ANGELS THEATRE

Hamilton Park Pavilion, 1 Plank Road, Waterbury
203-757-4676 • sevenangelstheatre.org

Public Transportation: Fair
Handicapped Accessibility: Good
Ticket Prices: $29–$48, discounts available for groups of 12 or more.
Subscriptions: Season subscriptions start at $139. Benefits include $5 discount on all extra single tickets.

SPIRIT OF BROADWAY THEATER

24 Chestnut Street, Norwich
860-886-2378 • spiritofbroadway.org

Public Transportation: Poor
Handicapped Accessibility: Good
Performances/Programs: Performance schedule is Wednesday–Sunday.
Ticket Prices: $30, students and seniors $25, group discounts available.

THEATERWORKS

233 Pearl Street, Hartford
860-527-7838 • theaterworkshartford.org

Public Transportation: Fair
Handicapped Accessibility: Good

Performances/Programs: Performance schedule is Tuesday–Sunday.

Ticket Prices: $37–$47 (for $11 extra, you get center reserved seats). Rush tickets for college students are $10 (available at show time), some free tickets available for high-school students, occasionally free tickets also available to downtown Hartford residents. Group discounts for parties of 11 or more.

Subscriptions: Five-Play subscription is $123.23. Subscribers save 30% –45%. Benefits include "credit seats" (if you miss a play, you can request to bring friends to see the next show for free).

WESTPORT COUNTRY PLAYHOUSE
25 Powers Court, Westport
203-227-4177 • westportplayhouse.org

Public Transportation: Fair (Metro North to Westport station, then taxi to theater).

Handicapped Accessibility: Good

Performances/Programs: Performance schedule is Tuesday–Sunday, with occasional Monday shows.

Ticket Prices: $30–$55, discounts available for groups of 10 or more.

Subscriptions: Packages include Six-Play $192-$360, Five-Play $160–$300, and Four-Play ($160–$260).

Subscription Alternatives: Flex pass, $45 per ticket, six-ticket minimum; Family Pack, 10 tickets for $260; Business Class, six tickets for $378; and Ultra Pass, $45 per ticket, eight-ticket minimum). Subscribers save an average of $75 over single ticket buyers. Benefits include special discounts for guest tickets, special events, and easy ticket exchanges.

From the Editors: Ever since its birth in a big red barn in 1930, Westport Country Playhouse has embodied the perfect blend of theatrical professionalism and rustic New England charm. Some of the greatest performers of the 20th century—Bert Lahr, Laurette Taylor, Paul Robeson, Helen Hayes, Ethel Barrymore, and Jose Ferrer, to name a few—have trod those boards. In 1946, Thornton Wilder appeared as the stage manager in his own play, *Our Town*, and in 2002 famed Westport resident Paul Newman played the part in a production that later transferred to Broadway. Newman's wife, actress Joanne Woodward, has had a key role in the development of the Playhouse since 2000, when she took on the role of artistic director.

Given its beautiful location, just an hour outside of New York City, Westport Country Playhouse markets itself as a travel destination, complete with specialty and tour packages that allow travelers to enjoy Westport restaurants, inns, and historic attractions. The Playhouse's entertainment goes beyond its top-notch productions, such as concerts, Selected Shorts short-story readings, and other seasonal offerings.

Few regional theaters offer the kind of intensive hands-on instruction that Westport does. The Woodward Internship Program gives aspiring theater professionals the chance to train in any number of disciplines, including stage management, scenic construction, painting, administration, and marketing, while earning college credit. And the Woodward Apprentice Program allows high-school students (as well as some adults) to get their feet wet through firsthand experience working with production staff and through classes and workshops.

YALE REPERTORY THEATRE

University Theatre, 222 York Street
203-432-1234 • yale.edu/yalerep

Other Venues: Yale Repertory Theatre, 1120 Chapel Street, and New Theater, Holcombe T. Green, Jr. Hall, 1156 Chapel Street, both in New Haven.

Public Transportation: Fair

Handicapped Accessibility: Good

Performances/Programs: Performance schedule is Tuesday–Saturday, with an occasional Monday.

Ticket Prices: $35–$58, senior and student discounts available. Groups of 10 or more save up to 20%.

Subscriptions: Six-Play subscriptions $170–$260; senior Six-Play subscription $145–$220. Yale Pass $160 (for Yale faculty, staff, and emeriti); Four-Ticket Pass $190; Six-Ticket Pass $260; student Four-Ticket Pass $50; student Six-Ticket Pass $60. Benefits include discounted parking and free ticket exchanges.

CONCORA CONNECTICUT CHORAL ARTISTS

860-224-7500 • concora.org

Venues: Immanuel Congregational Church, Hartford; Center Church, Hartford; First Church of Christ, New Britain; South Church, New Britain; and various other locations.

Public Transportation: Depends on venue.

Handicapped Accessibility: Most venues accessible, contact venue management for more details.

Performances/Programs: Four concerts per season, plus special events like Wine & Jazz and recitals.

Ticket Prices: students $10; $20–$45 for others (tickets are cheaper if you buy early).

Group Discounts: Discounts available for groups of 8 or more.

Subscriptions: Subscription may be available; contact for details.

Membership: Friends of Bach memberships start at $100, but any donation is accepted and greatly appreciated.

ARCH STREET TAVERN
85 Arch Street, Hartford
860-246-7610 • archstreettavern.com

Public Transportation: Poor

Handicapped Accessibility: Good

Performances/Programs: Approximately 55 performances are presented annually. The Hartford Jazz Orchestra plays every Monday night at 8 p.m.

Ticket Prices: No cover.

FIREHOUSE 12
45 Crown Street, New Haven
203-785-0468 • firehouse12.com

Public Transportation: Poor

Handicapped Accessibility: Poor

Performances/Programs: Approximately 30 performances are given per year, including fall and spring jazz series. Shows are on Fridays at 8:30 and 10 p.m.

Ticket Prices: $15 for 8:30 p.m. set, $10 at 10 p.m.

Subscriptions: Season tickets for the fall and spring jazz series are available for $150. Tickets are valid for most performances in the series. The approximate discount for subscribing is $150.

From the Editors: With New York City just a car (or train) ride away, it's hard to imagine a need for great performance spaces in New Haven-Hartford area. However, Firehouse 12 in New Haven saw an opportunity and has jumped on it. Originally a recording space, Firehouse 12 has transformed itself into a multi-faceted entertainment venture, combining a recording studio, a record label, a performance space, and a full-service bar. The performance room doubles as the tracking space for the recording studio, creating an intimate acoustically engineered listening room with space for 75.

Every Friday, the seasonal jazz series features well-known and up-and-coming musicians, many of whom have worked around the venue in the studio or with the label. The chic bar is perfect for relaxing before or after a set of hot jazz and it attracts a young, local, jazz-loving clientele.

SZECHUAN TOKYO
1245 New Britain Avenue, West Hartford
860-561-0180 • asianfusion.net

Public Transportation: Poor
Handicapped Accessibility: Good
Performances/Programs: Approximately 380 performances per year, every Thursday 7:30 p.m., and Friday 8 p.m.
Ticket Prices: No cover, $10 drink minimum.

CINESTUDIO
300 Summit Street, Trinity College campus, Hartford
860-297-2544 • cinestudio.org

Public Transportation: Good (campus is served by two bus routes).
Handicapped Accessibility: Good
Performances/Programs: Artistically significant American and international film.

From the Editors: Cinestudio is a gorgeous re-creation of a 1930s movie house, recalling a time when attending the cinema wasn't just two hours of entertainment, but an entire experience. Classics and independents are regularly shown at Cinestudio and Hartford movie fans will find this the finest place in town to catch a film.

Cinestudio also takes special care of its disabled patrons. For those who are hard of hearing, the theater offers infrared assisted-listening devices that can be picked up at the box office, and wheelchair-bound visitors can enter through the lower door of the Chemistry building.

WADSWORTH ATHENAEUM MUSEUM OF ART (FILM PROGRAM)
The Aetna Theater, 600 Main Street, Hartford
860-278-2670 • wadsworthatheneum.org

Public Transportation: Good (see museum information).
Handicapped Accessibility: Good
Performances/Programs: Independent and art films.
Ticket Prices: General admission $9, students and seniors $8, museum members $7, Film Buff members $3.50, Film Star members free.
Hours: Tuesday–Friday 11 a.m.–5 p.m., Saturday and Sunday 10 a.m.–5 p.m., closed Monday. First Thursdays 11 a.m.–8 p.m.

From the Editors: Don't miss out on this gem, America's oldest public-art museum, which also screens the best in independent and art films. At the Aetna, you'll find yourself in a magnificent Art Deco theater, first built to house George Balanchine's Ballets Russes. This locale is a winner for anyone with a taste of the artistic and the offbeat. Wine, beer, and snacks are available before showtime in the theater's Loctite Lobby. Film discussions take place after each film screening.

THE BUSHNELL
166 Capitol Avenue, Hartford
888-824-2874 • bushnell.org

Public Transportation: Fair
Handicapped Accessibility: Good
Performances/Programs: The Bushnell hosts over 350 events annually, including Broadway tours, symphony orchestras, family shows, films, concerts, cabaret, and comedy.
Ticket Prices: Vary by program. Join Email Club for discount offers.
Group Discounts: Discounts available for groups of 10–20 or more.
Subscriptions/Membership: Membership begins at $50, with significant benefits starting at the $250+ level (priority ticket purchasing) and $500+ level (10% discount on single tickets).

INTERNATIONAL FESTIVAL OF ARTS AND IDEAS
195 Church Street, New Haven
888-ART-IDEA (278-4332)

Public Transportation: Very good (easily accessible by CT Transit, Amtrak and Metro North).

Handicapped Accessibility: Good

Performances/Programs: Hundreds of events (music, dance, theater, discussions, etc.) are offered each June. Performance schedule Tuesday through Sunday.

Ticket Prices: $10–$48, 10% discounts available for students and seniors, 30% discounts for children 17 and under. Rush tickets at a 50% discount are available in a limited quantity for select Festival events, by walk-up purchase only, at the Shubert Theater box office from 10 a.m. to noon on the day of performance.

Group Discounts: Group discounts for parties of 10 or more (available for most performances).

Membership: Memberships start at $125. Members get priority ticket purchase privileges, discounts at local stores and restaurants, and other benefits.

Subscriptions: Multiple options include See Everything package $399, International Flavor package (three shows) $75, Courtyard Concert series (three concerts) $75, Global Scenes (three readings) $40.

Educational/Community Outreach: Educational activities include master classes and the Big Read.

HOUSTON, TEXAS

Houston boasts a population of more than two million people, one of the largest and most populous cities in America. As a major center for energy and shipping, this sprawling Texas metropolis also prides itself on its ever-growing arts scene, which includes several acclaimed theater companies and a first-class selection of museums.

ARTS INFO & DISCOUNTS

Houston Press (houstonpress.com)—Houston news and entertainment weekly.

artshound.com—Excellent arts directory from the Houston Arts Alliance, with occasional discounts.

Houston Chronicle (chron.com)—First-rate arts coverage, especially on their innovative website.

houstontheaterdistrict.org—Information on shows and arts events and a place to sign up for a special promotions and e-mail offers. Also a half-price section, but mostly applies to restaurants and hotels.

THE ARTS

MENIL COLLECTION
1515 Sul Ross Street
713-525-9400 • menil.org

Public Transportation: Poor

Handicapped Accessibility: Fair (the main area is completely accessible, but accessing other buildings, like the Rothko Chapel or the Byzantine Fresco Chapel Museum, can be difficult).

Hours: Wednesday–Sunday, 11 a.m.–7 p.m.

Admission: Free

Tours: None (due to environment of the collection).

Membership: Contributor membership ($100) includes invitations to all exhibition previews for a household, announcements of public lectures and programs, 10% discounts in the Menil Collection bookstore, and a subscription to Menil (the membership bulletin). Student membership is available for $25.

Other Benefits: A Menil Contemporaries membership includes all the benefits of membership corresponding to contribution amount, plus special educational events, gallery talks, and an invitation to participate in the unique annual weekend trip. Cost for this program is per individual and varies based on age of member.

From the Editors: With nearly 15,000 pieces, the Menil collection excels with its wide array of antiquities, including Byzantine, medieval, and tribal art, as well as multiple works from 20th-century Masters (with an emphasis on surrealism). The museum has a unique feel. In opposition to most modern-day museums, the Menil's holdings are selective rather than encyclopedic, offering depth to specific areas and artists. With a collection that clearly echoes the range of interests of the Menils and their curators, the focus and specialty of the museum is its ability to present pieces in an intimate, stripped-down manner—as if one were alone, experiencing them in a private setting.

With a later emphasis on sacred pieces and the construction of the non-denominational Rothko Chapel (which holds 14 of the master's works within its walls), an experience at the Menil is both thought-provoking and calming. As one of the foremost collections of art in the world (including only one of two 13th-century Byzantine frescos in the entire Western Hemisphere), the Menil is a must-see.

MUSEUM OF FINE ARTS, HOUSTON (MFAH)
1001 Bisonnet Street
713-639-7300 • mfah.org

Public Transportation: Excellent (the museum is accessible via Metro's Light Rail, which delivers you directly to the front door).

Handicapped Accessibility: Good (the museum's galleries and grounds are all fully handicapped accessible).

Hours: Tuesday–Wednesday 10 a.m.–5 p.m., Thursday 10 a.m.–9 p.m., Friday–Saturday 10 a.m.–7 p.m., Sunday 12:15–7p.m., closed Mondays (except some holidays).

Admission: $7, seniors and youth $3.50, members and children under 5 are free. Discounts for groups of 10 or more are available. (Other discount offers available. Check with museum office for more details.)

Free Day: Thursday

Tours: Free. The museum offers a wealth of tours, including Explore the MFAH, an hour-long overview of the museum's permanent collection; Exhibition Tour, a 45-minute tour highlighting a specific current exhibition; and Art 101, a tour that discusses art from the ancient world and lasts approximately an hour. Group tours are offered Tuesday through Saturday for 10 or more guests.

Membership: Individual membership is $50 and includes free unlimited general admission for one, free admission to museum lectures and programs for adults, discounted admission at Bayou Bend and Rienzi, invitations to selected preview parties, the annual fall party, and discounts at the MFAH Shops and on Films Program tickets. Student ($40) and Dual ($65) memberships are also offered.

Other Benefits: Membership in the Texas Museum Reciprocal Program is offered at the Patron Level ($150).

From the Editors: Known for its Impressionist and Post-Impressionist art, the Museum of Fine Arts of Houston is the largest museum in the U.S. south of Chicago, west of Washington, D.C., and east of Los Angeles. Other specific areas of strength include Baroque, Renaissance, and African Tribal art.

The museum grounds also include a sculpture garden, teaching wing, and a special section for top Texas artists and students to display their work—certainly a unique feature not found in other large museums.

An insider's scoop for those with families: The museum offers a particularly great range and volume of programs for kids, with a weekly Creation Station (where children gather to create their next masterpieces), Sketching in the Gallery on Sundays, as well as Story-Time Hours and Target Free

Sundays. Another example of the MFAH's academic outreach is the Glassell School, an institution that offers a full selection of courses for adults and children.

ALLEY THEATRE
615 Texas Avenue
713-220-5700 • alleytheatre.org

> **Public Transportation:** Good
> **Handicapped Accessibility:** Good
> **Performances/Programs:** Performance schedule is Tuesday–Sunday.
> **Ticket Prices:** $21–$39; $21 Cheap Thrills tickets available for Tuesday and Sunday evening performances, Rush tickets available for some performances, student Rush tickets sold one hour before curtain on weeknights or matinées, senior discounts available for most performances, select performances designated as pay what you can (minimum $6, max two tickets). Group discounts are available.
> **Subscriptions:** Eight Play $225–$340 and Five Play $130–$250. Subscriber benefits include free ticket exchanges with one week's notice and ticket insurance. Only subscribers can exchange tickets.

From the Editors: Its name couldn't be less appropriate. The Alley Theatre actually looks like a squat castle with towers, terraces, and a spiral staircase. On the verge of its 50th anniversary, the Alley was awarded the 1996 Regional Theatre Tony in honor of its commitment to creating high-quality theater for Houston and it has continued to fulfill that mission to this day.

The company's annual season of 11 shows is presented on two stages: the 824-seat Hubbard mainstage and the 310-seat Neuhaus (great sight-lines in both). In each new season, there's usually a mix of the new, the classic, and the re-discovered; shows that recently enjoyed runs in New York are often on the bill, too. Several notable plays and musicals have premiered here, including *The Effect of Gamma Rays on Man-in-the-Moon Marigolds*, Paula Vogel's *The Baltimore Waltz*, and the Frank Wildhorn musicals *Jekyll & Hyde* and *The Civil War*. The Alley is proud to have its own acting company and it keeps a team of designers and craftspeople busy year-round.

Education and the involvement of young people are obviously at the top of the Alley Theatre's priority list. Discounts like student Rush and Cheap Thrills tickets ($21 tickets for people under 30 on Tuesday and Sunday nights) help make theater affordable for the younger set. 1st Act is a special subscription program that provides young professionals with social and networking events, along with great seats to the Alley's season. The Houston Young Playwright Exchange (HYPE) helps teen playwrights develop their work and the Young Performers Studio (YPS) introduces kids of all ages to theater and performance. Aspiring theater professionals at the college and graduate level can benefit from the Alley's considerable resources by joining its Internship Program as a production intern (specialties include light and sound, scenery, and costumes) or in PR, marketing, development, or education.

A.D. PLAYERS THEATER

Grace Theater, 2710 W. Alabama
713-526-2721 • adplayers.org

> **Other Venue:** Children's Theater, 3471 Westheimer
> **Public Transportation:** Good
> **Handicapped Accessibility:** Good
> **Performances/Programs:** Performance schedule is Wednesday–Sunday.
> **Ticket Prices:** $28–$37, discounts available for students, seniors, and groups of 10 or more; children's show tickets are $11.
> **Subscriptions:** Silver Spotlight package, three plays, $90; benefits include discounts to special events. Gold Spotlighter package, five plays, $135; benefits include the above, plus free tickets for you and a guest to special events and 15% discount on guest tickets. Subscribers save up to 25%. Other options include Children's Theater package ($30 for all four shows) and Flex Pass package (six passes for $216).

ENSEMBLE THEATRE

3535 Main Street
713-807-4300 • ensemblehouston.com

> **Public Transportation:** Very good
> **Handicapped Accessibility:** Good
> **Performances/Programs:** Performance schedule is Wednesday–Sunday.
> **Ticket Prices:** $12–$30, discounts available for students and seniors at most performances, discounts available for groups of 10 or more.
> **Subscriptions:** Triple Play, three flex tix for $75; senior/student package, one ticket for all six mainstage shows, $90; Silver subscription, one ticket for all six shows $150; Gold subscription, one ticket to opening night

of each mainstage show $225; Platinum subscription, tickets to each opening night and VIP reception, plus tickets to annual black tie gala and all other benefits, $1,000.

MAIN STREET THEATER
Rice Village, 2540 Times Boulevard
713-524-6706 • mainstreettheater.com

Other Venue: Main Street Theater, Chelsea Market, 4617 Montrose Boulevard.
Public Transportation: Good
Handicapped Accessibility: Good
Performances/Programs: Performance schedule is Thursday–Sunday.
Ticket Prices: $20–$36, student and senior tickets $16–$28, preview tickets $10, half-price Rush tickets available on selected seats 90 minutes before curtain, $10 tickets for any student with a valid School ID, pay-what-you-can performance the first Sunday after opening night ($5 minimum). Youth Theater tickets are $10–$12. Discounts available for groups of 10 or more.
Subscriptions: Six-Play $47–$105, Preview Six-Play $54, Season Pass $160, and Student Pass (buy one adult sub and get extra $36 sub for accompanying teenager); students and seniors eligible for discounted subscription prices. Subscribers can exchange tickets for free; non-subs pay $5 fee.

STAGES REPERTORY THEATRE
Houston Center for the Arts, 3201 Allen Parkway
713-527-0123 • stagestheatre.com

Public Transportation: Good
Handicapped Accessibility: Good
Performances/Programs: Performance schedule is Wednesday–Sunday.
Ticket Prices: $30, discounts available for students, seniors, educators, and groups.
Subscriptions: Six-Play subscription is $150 (choose fixed or flexible seating).

THEATRE UNDER THE STARS (TUTS)
Hobby Center for the Performing Arts, 800 Bagby Street
713-558-TUTS (8887) • tuts.com

Other Venue: Miller Outdoor Theatre, Hermann Park, 100 Concert Drive.
Public Transportation: Good
Handicapped Accessibility: Good
Performances/Programs: Performance schedule is Tuesday–Sunday.
Ticket Prices: $29–$93, student and senior discounts usually available. Groups of 15 or more are eligible for 20% discount.
Subscriptions: Four-Show and Six-Show subscriptions $142–$454; seniors and full-time students can get discounts for subscription tickets in rear orchestra and rear mezzanine. Benefits include the ability to transfer your tickets to someone else if you can't use them, ticket exchanges ($2.50 fee), and ticket insurance. Only subscribers can exchange tickets.

HOUSTON CHAMBER CHOIR
713-224-5566 • houstonchamberchoir.org

Venues: Various locations in and around Houston area.
Public Transportation: Depends on venue.
Handicapped Accessibility: Most venues accessible; contact venue management for more details.
Performances/Programs: Several classical, jazz, and holiday concerts per season, plus special events.
Ticket Prices: $25–$35
Subscriptions: Full season subscription is $150. Subscriber benefits include premium reserved seating, lost ticket replacement, and invites to exclusive receptions.

HOUSTON SYMPHONY
Jones Hall, 615 Louisiana Street
713-224-7575 • houstonsymphony.org

Public Transportation: Good
Handicapped Accessibility: Good
Performances/Programs: Over 170 performances are given per year.
Ticket Prices: $20–$107, depending on dates and seats. Subject to availability, specially discounted tickets may be offered to students and

seniors (65+) for Classical and Pops subscription concerts. Rush tickets for Classical concerts cost $11. Rush tickets for Cynthia Woods Mitchell Pops are $15. Rush tickets can be purchased starting at noon on the day of the performance. Discounts are provided for groups of 10 or more.

Subscriptions: Subscriptions are available for the Classical and Pops series. Six- or nine-concert Classical subscribers may exchange tickets for any other regularly scheduled Classical concert, subject to availability. Special concerts are not exchangeable.

Membership: Individual membership begins at $50 with a subscription to the Symphony Notes newsletter.

From the Editors: The Houston Symphony, founded in 1913, is one of the oldest performing arts organizations in the U.S. Maestro Hans Graf, the Symphony's 15th music director, follows in a long line of distinguished leaders, such as Sir John Barbirolli, Christoph Eschenbach, and Andre Previn.

The Symphony fosters education through special events, such as the Weatherfold Family Concerts, with pre- and post-concert fun for children; free pre-concert discussions beginning 50 minutes before each Classical series concert; and the free Sounds Like Fun! concert series for children. College students wishing to attend more concerts can take advantage of a College Classics subscription: great orchestra seats for only $9 per concert and the subscription comes with the same benefits that full subscribers receive.

In the summer, the HSO offers a series of free concerts for the community, Target Summer Symphony Nights, at the Miller Outdoor Theater.

HOUSTON GRAND OPERA
Wortham Theater Center, 501 Texas Street
713-228-6737 • houstongrandopera.com

Public Transportation: Fair
Handicapped Accessibility: Good
Performances/Programs: Six full productions with multiple performances, plus special events such as the Opera Ball, concerts, and free public performances of operas.
Ticket Prices: Single tickets start at $20.
Group Discounts: Discounts available for groups of 10 or more.
Subscriptions: Full six-opera subscriptions available for $78–$1,498.50. Build your own Opera to order three- four- and five-opera subscriptions for $19–$248 per show. Subscriber benefits include free ticket exchanges, free

lost ticket replacement, invites to special events, and 10% discount on additional single tickets.

Membership: Membership beginning at $100 includes special discounts, guild membership and other privileges such as dress rehearsal tickets and invitations to special events. The Young Patrons Circle is a special membership group for individuals and couples ages 21–39. Annual dues are $1,500, and membership includes invitations to special members-only events, along with discounts and priority ticket purchasing options.

From the Editors: Houston Grand Opera opened in 1955 with a performance of Salome, and has gone on to become one of the world's leading opera companies, bringing in top performers of national and international renown and presenting dozens of world premiere productions. HGO's free pre-curtain lectures, which begin approximately 45 minutes before each performance, help make opera more accessible to the audience. Other notable educational programs at HGO include Storybook Opera for kids pre-K to second grade, 45-minute Opera to Go! touring productions, the High School Voice Studio, Opera Camps, and the "Song of Houston" series of original works.

CÉZANNE
4100 Montrose Boulevard
713-522-9621 • blacklabradorpub.com

Public Transportation: Poor
Handicapped Accessibility: No
Performances/Programs: Approximately 100 performances are presented annually. Shows start at 9 p.m. Friday–Saturday.
Ticket Prices: $10–$15 cover

RED CAT JAZZ CAFÉ
924 Congress Street
713-226-7870 • redcatjazzcafe.com

Public Transportation: Poor
Handicapped Accessibility: Good
Performances/Programs: Approximately 400 performances are given per year. Shows start at 7 p.m. Monday and Wednesday, 8 p.m. Sunday and Tuesday, and 8:30/9 p.m. Thursday, Friday, and Saturday.
Ticket Prices: $10–$20 cover

SAMBUCA
909 Texas Avenue
713-224-5299 • sambucarestaurant.com

Public Transportation: Poor
Handicapped Accessibility: Good
Performances/Programs: Approximately 350 performances are presented per year. Many genres are represented, with jazz showcased at least one night a week.
Ticket Prices: $1 added to dinner bill to cover music costs.

TOMMY'S SEAFOOD & STEAKHOUSE
11660 Ste, 129 Westheimer
281-679-1112 • tommys.com

Public Transportation: Poor
Handicapped Accessibility: Good
Performances/Programs: Approximately 200 performances per year. Shows Wednesday–Saturday at 8 and 10 p.m.
Ticket Prices: No cover.

HOUSTON BALLET
Wortham Theater Center, 501 Texas Avenue
713-227-2787 • houstonballet.org

Public Transportation: Poor
Handicapped Accessibility: Good
Performances/Programs: Four different programs per year, plus the annual *Nutcracker*. Each program runs about two weeks with six performances.
Ticket Prices: $17–$136. On select nights, students and seniors may purchase discounted tickets 90 minutes prior to the performance. Student tickets are $10; senior (65+) tickets are $17 or $30.50, depending on seating. Available dates are published on the Houston Ballet website.
Group Discounts: Groups of 10 or more can receive up to 50% off ticket purchases.
Subscriptions: Subscriptions are available for the Spring series shows, a select-your-own series of four, five, or six shows, or a maximum flexibility option of six passes to use any way you like. Benefits include two free upgrade certificates, free exchange privileges, 10% discount on additional tickets, and a one-year subscription to *Houston Ballet News*.

Membership: Donor fees start at $40 and include a quarterly newsletter. Donors of $500 or more receive recognition in playbills.

Special Membership for Young Adults: Junior Patrons is a membership program for children ages 3 through 13. Membership is $50 and includes special seating at matinée performances, private receptions, backstage tours, and photos.

From the Editors: Houston Ballet has enjoyed excellent artistic leadership since its inception, beginning in 1969 with Nina Popova, a former dancer with both the Ballets Russes de Monte Carlo and American Ballet Theatre. Throughout the 1970s and '80s, Ben Stevenson, O.B.E., led the company to nationally respected standing by putting together a strong core group of permanent choreographers, including Sir Kenneth MacMillan and Christopher Bruce. MacMillan worked with Houston Ballet until his death in 1992 and Bruce remains an associate choreographer with the company. Acclaimed Australian ballet choreographer Stanton Welch now heads up the company of 54 dancers, the fourth largest in the country.

Each year, Houston Ballet kicks off the holiday season with its Nutcracker Market. Modeled after European and Latin American street markets, this extravagant four-day shopping event draws more than 300 merchants to booths at the Reliant Center and offers specialty items for everyone in the family. Tickets are generally $10 and children under 6 may enter for free. Proceeds are put toward funding the Houston Ballet training academy and scholarship programs.

AURORA PICTURE SHOW
1524 Sul Ross
713-868-2101 • aurorapictureshow.org

Public Transportation: Poor
Handicapped Accessibility: Good
Performances/Programs: Unconventional and experimental films and videos.
Ticket Prices: $6–$7

From the Editors: The non-profit Aurora Picture Show devotes itself to noncommercial film, video, and media, screening both features and shorts in a variety of genres. The Aurora's programming falls into such categories such as Documentary, Historical, and Texas-Focus, and it presents many screenings in non-traditional venues.

WORLDFEST-HOUSTON INTERNATIONAL FILM AND VIDEO FESTIVAL
PO Box 56566, Houston
713-965-9955 • worldfest.org

Performances/Programs: Every April. Check website for details and locations.

From the Editors: The WorldFest-Houston International Film and Video Festival truly embodies the traditional film-festival spirit, dedicating itself exclusively to independent cinema from the U.S. and abroad and not accepting entries from major studios. Every April this festival presents approximately 55 new features and 100 new short films, each introduced by its director before the screening. Professional seminars, workshops, and other events are offered during the 10-day festival and all events and screenings are open to the public.

More than 30,000 audience members and 500 filmmakers attend WorldFest-Houston International Film and Video Festival each year, which distinguishes itself further by being the only film fest that presents a stunning regatta as its signature event, held at the Houston Yacht Club on the last day of the festival.

For information on Austin and San Antonio, Texas,
visit go-artsamerica.com.

KANSAS CITY, MISSOURI

Nicknamed the "Paris of the Plains" and located on the banks of the Mississippi River, Kansas City is home to some of the most beautiful public fountains and parks in the nation. The city offers a unique mix of old-world beauty and down-home soul, as well as plentiful music, theater, and visual art.

ARTS INFO

The Pitch (pitch.com)—Weekly paper that includes comprehensive arts and nightlife coverage.

artslinks.org—Arts news and events from the Arts Council of Metropolitan Kansas City.

visitkc.com—Kansas City events guide.

kansascity.com/entertainment—Arts and entertainment coverage from the *Kansas City Star*.

THE ARTS

NELSON-ATKINS MUSEUM OF ART (THE NELSON)
4525 Oak Street
816-751-1ART (1278) • nelson-atkins.org

Public Transportation: Good (the closest stop on the Kansas City Max route is at 45th and Main Streets, approximately two blocks west of the Nelson-Atkins).

Handicapped Accessibility: Good (the museum is fully accessible, with an accessible entrance in the parking garage).

Hours: Wednesday 10 a.m.–4 p.m., Thursday, Friday 10 a.m.–9 p.m., Saturday 10 a.m.–5 p.m., Sunday noon–5 p.m., closed Monday–Tuesday.

Admission: Free

Tours: Free and available any day the museum is open to the public.

Audio Tour: Free

Membership: Individual membership is $60. Dual ($90) and Family ($100) memberships are also offered.

Other Benefits: Reciprocal membership to 32 other museums is available starting at the Associate Friend of Art level ($250).

From the Editors: A world-class museum located in the heart of Kansas City, the Nelson-Atkins Museum of Art offers art lovers a fabulous opportunity to view a great collection of pieces from basically every major art movement possible. The best part? It's all free, including tours (both docent-led and audio). For those interested in Asian art, the Nelson is particularly well-stocked. Another strength of the museum is the variety of activities and amenities offered to those traveling with children. Complete with the world's largest shuttlecocks, the Henry Moore Sculpture Garden is a favorite for the younger crowd.

Other events on the premises include occasional musical performances at Kirkwood Hall and an avant-garde film series (check online for dates, times, and particular showings.) Special exhibitions are also very inexpensive (generally ranging from complimentary to $5). Overall, with its complimentary admission and terrific offerings, the Nelson-Atkins Museum of Art is more than worth a visit.

COTERIE THEATRE
Crown Center, 2450 Grand Boulevard
816-474-6552 • coterietheatre.org

Public Transportation: Good
Handicapped Accessibility: Good
Ticket Prices: $14; tickets for full-time students, seniors, and anyone under 18 are $9. Tickets are $5–$6 for groups of 20 or more. 2-for-1 tickets for Saturday matinées.
Subscriptions: Tickets to three shows for $8 each. Benefits include free parking with ticket stub, easy ticket exchanges, and invites to special events.

KANSAS CITY REPERTORY THEATRE
Copaken Stage, One H&R Block Way
816-235-2700 • kcrep.org

Other Venue: Spencer Theatre, James C. Olsen Performing Arts Center, University of Missouri-Kansas City, 4949 Cherry Street.
Public Transportation: Good
Handicapped Accessibility: Good
Performances/Programs: Performance schedule is Tuesday–Sunday.
Ticket Prices: $29–$60; students under 18 pay $15–$20, discounts available for groups of 10 or more.
Subscriptions: Full-Season $134–$225, Full-Season student $84, Spencer Theatre $108–$176, Spencer Theatre student $48, Copaken Stage series $74–$110, Copaken Stage student $36. Flex passes: Three-Play $114, student $36; Four-Play $152, student $48; Five-Play $185, student $60, Six-Play $222, student $72; and Seven-Play $231, student $84. Benefits include $10 rebates to help pay babysitter expenses and free tickets to other university productions.

From the Editors: Originally created as an arm of the University of Missouri-Kansas City (UMKC) and known as the Missouri Repertory Theatre for most of its 45-year history, the newly dubbed Kansas City Repertory Theatre has actually been independent from the university for most of that time, but the two organizations maintain a close relationship. KC Rep's 630-seat Spencer Theatre (recently renovated to add extra leg room, to everyone's delight) is located in UMKC's James C. Olsen Performing Arts Center. The company has also established a new performing space, the state-of-the-art Copaken Stage, located in downtown Kansas City (the Rep warns patrons to plan to arrive early on nights when there's a show at the nearby Spring Center because of the traffic).

Though the Kansas City Rep's annual season often includes classics and recent Off-Broadway plays, more often the KC Rep's chooses works that reflect the richness of the American experience past and present. August Wilson dramas, bio-musicals that celebrate the life and music of Hank Williams and Woody Guthrie, and stage adaptations of American literary favorites like Harper Lee's *To Kill a Mockingbird* and Louisa May Alcott's *Little Women* are just a few. KC Rep also tries to make its shows more accessible by offering sign-interpreted performances and even a Spanish-interpreted performance of the annual production of *A Christmas Carol*.

UNICORN THEATRE
3828 Main Street
816-531-PLAY (7529) • unicorntheatre.org

Public Transportation: Good
Handicapped Accessibility: Good
Performances/Programs: Performance schedule is Tuesday–Sunday.
Ticket Prices: $20–$30, $5 discount for seniors and full-time students, $7 student Rush tickets available five minutes before curtain, discounts for groups of 10 or more.
Subscriptions: Five-Show $95–$140, Six-Show $114–$162, Seven-Show $133–$189, and Eight-Show $144–$208 packages available. Subscriber benefits include one free ticket exchange per show, 10% off extra tickets, and a complimentary Kansas City Performing Arts Cooperative Discount card that allows members to receive a one-time discount for two-for-one tickets at eight other participating arts organizations.

KANSAS CITY CHORALE
816-235-6222 • kcchorale.org

Venues: Various locations.
Public Transportation: Depends on venue.
Handicapped Accessibility: Most venues accessible; call venue management for more details.
Performances/Programs: Four per season with multiple performances of each.
Ticket Prices: $13 for students, $23–$33 for others.

KANSAS CITY SYMPHONY (KCS)
The Lyric Theatre, 1029 Central (11ᵗʰ & Central)
816-471-0400 • kcsymphony.org

Other Venues: Yardley Hall at Johnson County Community College, College Blvd. and Quivira Road, Overland Park; Church of the Resurrection, 5001 W. 137ᵗʰ Street, Leawood.

Public Transportation: Depends on venue.

Handicapped Accessibility: Good

Performances/Programs: Approximately 135 performances are given per season.

Ticket Prices: $15–$65. Student discounts are offered on all concerts and frequently Rush tickets are available to students two hours prior to all concerts not previously sold out. Rush-ticket prices begin at $8 per student for Classical series concerts and $10 per student for Pops series concerts.

Group Discounts: Discounts available for groups of 10 or more.

Subscriptions: Subscriptions are pre-selected packages tailored to specific musical tastes; subscribers choose the concerts they want to see. Classical, Masterworks, Bravo, Ovation, or Pops series subscriptions are available. Subscribers receive significant discounts on ticket prices and children are free with the purchase of an adult subscription. Tickets can be exchanged for any other Classical, Pops, or Family concert up until the day before a performance.

Membership: Begins at Associate membership for $100. Benefits include recognition in the annual Contributors' Concert program book, an invitation to the special Kansas City Symphony annual Contributors' Concert in May, and a subscription to the Kansas City Symphony newsletter.

Other Benefits: Donors at higher levels receive complimentary tickets to special events, open invitations to the Symphony Suite at the Lyric Theatre, and dinner with guest artists after the concert.

From the Editors: Founded in 1982 as the successor to the Kansas City Philharmonic, the Kansas City Symphony serves the metropolitan area with a 42-week season and 80 full-time musicians. The KCS offers many educational and outreach performances in addition to its regular subscription concerts and performances with the Lyric Opera of Kansas City and the Kansas City Ballet.

In efforts to promote the learning of young musicians, the KCS offers two educational series for children: KinderKonzerts, for kindergarten and first grade, which introduce basic music principles and instruments; and Young People's Concerts for fourth-eighth grades, which combine music with other disciplines of learning. This year's Young People's Concert, *How the West Was Won*, takes the children on a musical journey from Missouri to California following the trail of Old West settlers. Students a bit older (grades 6–12 and above) will appreciate KCS's open dress rehearsals (only $3/person), where they're able to see a rehearsal in progress and are given the opportunity to ask the musicians questions. All of KCS's events are listed in their free monthly online newsletter, *E-Notes*.

LYRIC OPERA OF KANSAS CITY
The Lyric Theater, Kansas City
877-673-7252 • kcopera.org

Handicapped Accessibility: Good
Performances/Programs: Four productions and 16 performances
Ticket Prices: Prices vary by date, time, and performance; contact for more details. Student tickets are available one hour prior to each performance for $10.
Membership: The Lyric Opera Guild and Bohemians (for ages 21–40) are membership groups that actively support the opera in a variety of different programs. Members are invited to participate in special opera trips, lectures, and other events throughout the year. For more information about joining the Guild or the Bohemians, please call 816-471-4933, ext. 120.

From the Editors: The Lyric Opera of Kansas City has established itself as a notable opera company that continues to grow. The Lyric Opera offers quality performances and a variety of operatic repertoire from standard to contemporary, performed in the original language with subtitles.

THE BLUE ROOM
1616 18th Street
816-474-8463 • americanjazzmuseum.com

Public Transportation: Poor
Handicapped Accessibility: Good
Performances/Programs: Live jazz is presented Monday and Thursday at 7 p.m., Friday and Saturday at 8:30 p.m.
Ticket Prices: $10 cover on Friday and Saturday; no cover on Monday and Thursday.

MAJESTIC STEAKHOUSE
931 Broadway
816-471-8484 • kansascitymenus.com/majesticsteakhouse

Public Transportation: Poor
Handicapped Accessibility: No
Performances/Programs: Jazz is performed seven nights a week. Performances are: 6:30 p.m. during the week; 7 p.m. Friday and Saturday; 5 p.m. on Sunday. Also, a Saturday afternoon performance plays at 4 p.m.
Ticket Prices: No Cover

KANSAS CITY BALLET (KCB)
Lyric Theatre, 11th Street and Central Street
kcballet.org

Other Venue: Music Hall, 301 W. 13th Street (13th & Central).
Public Transportation: Poor
Handicapped Accessibility: Good
Performances/Programs: Three programs each year, plus the annual *Nutcracker*. Each program runs for one week. The *Nutcracker* is performed regularly throughout December.
Ticket Prices: $20–$75. Students and seniors may purchase $12 tickets to repertory concerts beginning two hours before the performance.
Group Discounts: Groups of 15 or more may receive up to a 30% discount on ticket purchases.
Subscriptions: Subscriptions are available for the entire season (all three shows) or for two shows (winter and spring). Benefits include tickets exchanges, discounted pre-paid parking, discounts on additional single-ticket purchases, and discounts at other local arts organizations.
Membership: The basic donor fee is any amount up to $99 and includes a letter of acknowledgement and a subscription to the company e-newsletter.
Special Membership for Young Adults: Kansas City Ballet BARRE is a membership group aimed at young professionals over 21. Membership is $70 and includes Friday-night season tickets, invitations to special events, and other special offers.
Educational/Community Outreach: Through extensive community-outreach programs, KCB also affirms its commitment to "nourishing the community through dance." It offers free pre-curtain talks by artists and dance scholars, providing opportunities for audiences to learn more about dance. KCB performs special matinées for school groups, conducts residen-

cies in local public schools, and holds master classes for community members. The KCB School also offers open classes designed for students ages 13 to 65. A one-time class fee is $15. 10 and 20 class cards are available.

From the Editors: Kansas City Ballet is made up of 25 professional dancers who perform the richly varied programs conceived by Artistic Director William Whitener. The repertoire includes the requisite Romantic classics, as well as key works from the 20th century, such as Ailey's *Feast of Ashes*, Balanchine's *Agon*, Tharp's *Deuce Coupe*, and Cunningham's *Duets*.

Having grown steadily since its founding in 1957, KCB now excitedly awaits two new developments in the next couple of years. In 2009 the old Union Station Power House will be renovated and reopened as the Todd Bolender Center for Dance and Creativity, giving KCB a new permanent home; and in 2010, the new Kauffman Center for the Performing Arts will become the company's resident performance theater. With this new facility, KCB will be able to increase its number of performances and the length of the annual season.

MAINSTREET THEATER
1400 Main Street
888-262-4386 · amctheatres.com/theatres/domestic/mainstreet

Public Transportation: Very good
Handicapped Accessibility: Good
Performances/Programs: Six-screen all-digital movie theater, restaurant and bar.
Ticket Prices: Adults $10

From the Editors: The Mainstreet, first opened its doors in 1921, was completely renovated by AMC and re-opened in 2009 as a six-screen AMC movie house, complete with the latest in digital technology. Among the theaters are three Cinema Suites featuring Seat-Side Service, with special amenities like plush reclining seats and a custom food menu from the Mainstreet's on-site restaurant. Most of the movies shown are standard multiplex fare.

For information on St. Louis, Missouri,; Tulsa, Oklahoma;
and Wichita, Kansas; visit go-artsamerica.com

MIAMI/FT.LAUDERDALE, FLORIDA

Miami may be synonymous with sizzling beaches and spicy nightlife, but in addition to the balmy climate and party atmosphere the city's cultural offerings are tremendous. The Miami/Ft. Lauderdale area boasts many outstanding museums, acclaimed dance companies, and cutting-edge theater.

ARTS INFO AND DISCOUNTS

Miami New Times (miaminewtimes.com)—Great arts and entertainment coverage.

miamiandbeaches.com/visitors/arts_culture.asp—Miami arts and cultural guide.

miami.com—Miami Herald's events guide.

theatermania.com/florida/discount-tickets—Worth checking for occasional discounts.

THE ARTS

BASS MUSEUM
2121 Park Avenue, Miami Beach
305-673-7530 • bassmuseum.org

Public Transportation: Good (accessible via the 103, 107, 108, 111, 112, 113, 119, and 246 bus lines).
Handicapped Accessibility: Good
Hours: Wednesday–Sunday noon–5 p.m., closed on Monday, Tuesday, and some holidays.
Admission: $8, students (w/ID) $6, members and children under 6 free.
Basic Tour: Free with paid admission and available upon request.
Membership: Individual membership begins at $50 and includes a card for unlimited free admission to the museum, free or reduced admission to special programs and activities, a subscription to the members' calendar of events, invitations to private previews, special receptions and events, a 10% discount in the museum shop, an invitation to the member-appreciation event and volunteer opportunities. Student ($25) and Family/Dual memberships ($75) are also available. Donors at the Sustaining Level ($150) and above receive reciprocal museum membership at more than 70 museums nationwide.

From the Editors: Based on the 1963 donation of 500 works of European art and an endowment to the city of Miami Beach by John and Johanna Bass, the core collection includes European works on paper by Rembrandt, Dürer, and Toulouse-Lautrec, as well as Japanese, Chinese, Korean, and Afro-Brazilian art. The renovated and expanded museum reopened in 2001.

LOWE ART MUSEUM
University of Miami, 1301 Stanford Drive, Coral Gables
305-284-3535 • lowemuseum.org

Public Transportation: Good (accessible via Metrorail and U. of M. shuttle bus).
Handicapped Accessibility: Good
Hours: Tuesday–Saturday 10 a.m.–4 p.m., Sunday noon–4 p.m., closed Monday.
Admission: $10; students, seniors and adult group tours (10+) $5; school

and college Group Tours (10+) $3; Lowe Lectures for non-member adults $10; opening receptions for non-members $10. Museum members, children under 12 and University of Miami students, faculty and staff w/ID are admitted to the museum free of charge. Lowe Lectures are free for members and U. of M. students w/ID; opening receptions are also free to members.

Basic Tour: Docent-led and self-guided tours are available for groups of 10+ and must be planned three weeks in advance. The cost is $5 for adults and $3 for students (kindergarten through college); tours are free for University of Miami students.

Audio Tour: Not available.

Membership: Individual membership starts at $50. Members receive admission to the museum for one year, admission to all lectures and special events, invitations to exclusive exhibitions previews, receptions, and other museum programs, special members-only events, travel opportunities, the Lowe newsletter with annual recognition of members, eligibility to join the Volunteer Docent Guild, a 10% discount at the museum store and admission to the Lowe Dean happy hour. Membership at the Barton level ($100 and above) makes members eligible for reciprocal membership at numerous other museums throughout the country.

From the Editors: The small but encyclopedic museum (oldest in Miami) has more than 9,000 objects arranged chronologically, including a large donation from the Samuel H. Kress foundation. The Native North American collection is especially interesting.

THE MUSEUM OF CONTEMPORARY ART, NORTH MIAMI (MOCA)
The Joan Lehman Building, 770 NE 125th Street, North Miami
305-893-6211 • mocanomi.org

Public Transportation: Good (easily accessible by Miami-Dade Transit buses 9, 10, 16, and 75).

Handicapped Accessibility: Good

Hours: Tuesday, Thursday, Friday, and Saturday 11 a.m.–5 p.m., Wednesday 1 p.m.–9 p.m., Sunday noon–5 p.m., closed Monday. Jazz at MOCA is presented the last Friday of each month 7–10 p.m.

Admission: $5; students and seniors w/ID $3; children, North Miami residents, and city employees free. Admission is by donation every Tuesday.

Basic Tour: Available on a daily basis and complimentary with admission.

Membership: Individual membership starts at $50 and includes unlimited free membership to MOCA Galleries, members-only exhibition previews and receptions, invitations to MOCA educational and public programs, a members-only breakfast at MOCA programs (private tours of MOCA exhibitions), members-only discounts on educational programs, a subscription to the MOCA newsletter and members' e-newsletter, and a 10% discount in the MOCA shop. An artist/student/educator membership ($30) and additional custom membership options are also available.

NORTON MUSEUM OF ART (THE NMA)
1451 S. Olive Avenue, West Palm Beach
561-659-4689 • norton.org

Public Transportation: Poor
Handicapped Accessibility: Good
Hours: Tuesday–Saturday 10 a.m.–5 p.m., Sunday 1–5 p.m., closed Mondays and major holidays.
Admission: $8, children (13–21) $5, children (under 13) free; special exhibits are slightly more expensive with regular tickets at $12 and children (13–21) at $5. Groups of 15 or more may schedule two weeks in advance for private, discounted, docent-led tours. Palm Beach residents are admitted free to the Norton collection every Saturday.
Tours: Free guided docent-led tours of the museum's collection and certain exhibitions are offered daily 2–3 p.m. Lunchtime Lecture tours, docent-led themed tours, are offered Monday–Friday 12:30–1 p.m. October through May.
Membership: Individual membership is $70 and provides basic benefits for one, including free unlimited year-round admission, complimentary tickets to selected special events, invitations to members-only exhibition previews, and an express admission line. Household membership is offered for $100.
Other Benefits: Reciprocal membership to more than 50 museums is available at the Contributor membership level ($250) and above.

From the Editors: If you're a fan of Gauguin, Matisse, Miró, Monet, Picasso, Hassam, Hopper, Manship, O'Keeffe, Pollock, or Sheeler, you won't be disappointed by the NMA. With a collection of this caliber, as well as beautiful architecture, an ocean-side location, and a friendly staff, the NMA is an international destination for art appreciation.

Particularly noteworthy is the NMA's Chinese art collection, one of the most impressive collections of its kind in the U.S. Another lesser-known aspect of the museum is its focus on provenance research (the goal being traceability of a particular piece from its creation to present day). This research puts many of the pieces in the collection into a fascinating historical and social context and adds tremendously to the overall accessibility and meaning of the holdings. Also adding to the museum's cachet is an extensive selection of programs and tours geared toward children (the museum is particularly known for its docent-led tours catering to school groups).

ACTORS' PLAYHOUSE AT THE MIRACLE THEATRE

280 Miracle Mile, Coral Gables
305-444-9293 • actorsplayhouse.org

> **Public Transportation:** Fair
> **Handicapped Accessibility:** Good
> **Performances/Programs:** Performance schedule is Wednesday–Sunday.
> **Ticket Prices:** $33–$46, 10% discount for seniors, $15 tickets for students 22 or younger (sold 15 minutes before curtain), discounts available for groups of 15 or more.
> **Subscriptions:** Subscriptions are $174–$270; student subscriptions are $102. Benefits include free admission to play readings, ticket exchanges, lost-ticket insurance, and savings on classes and workshops.

CALDWELL THEATRE COMPANY

Count de Hoernle Theatre
7901 N. Federal Highway, Boca Raton
561-241-7432 • caldwelltheatre.com

> **Public Transportation:** Good
> **Handicapped Accessibility:** Good
> **Performances/Programs:** Performance schedule is Tuesday–Sunday.
> **Ticket Prices:** $36–$42, $10 student Rush tickets available for full-time students (sold 15 minutes before curtain), group discounts available for parties of 15 or more.
> **Subscriptions:** Subscriptions are $100–$140.

FLORIDA STAGE

Plaza del Mar, 262 South Ocean Boulevard, Manalapan
800-514-3837 • floridastage.org

> **Public Transportation:** Good
> **Handicapped Accessibility:** Good

Performances/Programs: Performance schedule is Wednesday–Sunday.

Ticket Prices: $35–$45, discounts for groups of 10 or more.

Subscriptions: Four-Play ($140–$168) and Five-Play ($175–$205); for opening nights, Four-Play is $280 and Five-Play $350; Three-Play Samplers available for $117–$126.

From the Editors: Florida Stage is the only theater in the Southeast exclusively committed to producing and developing new work, which it does annually through its five-play season and the 1st Stage New Works Festival. Steven Dietz, Nilo Cruz, and Lee Blessing are among the many noted writers whose plays have had their world premieres here; Florida Stage has also premiered several musicals (with an emphasis on shows built around a particular composer/band's catalogue, such as the recent *Dream a Little Dream: The Nearly True Story of The Mamas and The Papas*).

Florida Stage nurtures young talent as well, through several creative programs, like the Young Playwrights Festival, the Young Voices Monologue Festival, and the G-Star School of the Arts International Collaborative.

Several more intimate events at Florida Stage are for adults, but these will cost you. Tea with the Artist invites patrons who have contributed at least $500 to the theater's annual campaign to enjoy a reception with a visiting actor, writer, director, or designer.

The Theatre Club of Florida Stage hosts regular presentations (always followed by a discussion and refreshments), which explore some aspect of the current production through a lecture or a one-on-one interview with a special guest. Theatre Club membership costs $150 and members can bring additional guests for a fee of $50 per person.

GABLESTAGE AT THE BILTMORE
The Biltmore Hotel, 1200 Anastasia Avenue, Coral Gables
305-446-1116 • gablestage.org

Public Transportation: Good

Handicapped Accessibility: Good

Performances/Programs: Performance schedule is Thursday–Sunday.

Ticket Prices: $37.50–$42.50, discounts available for groups of 20 or more.

Subscriptions: $200 membership gets you tickets to all six shows for the season. Members save $75.

MALTZ JUPITER THEATRE
1001 East Indiantown Road, Jupiter
800-445-1666 • jupitertheatre.org

> **Public Transportation:** Poor
> **Handicapped Accessibility:** Good
> **Performances/Programs:** Performance schedule is Tuesday–Sunday.
> **Ticket Prices:** $20–$45, discounts available for groups and full-time students; sign up with E-Club for special offers.
> **Subscriptions:** Four-Play $118–$198, Five-Play $133–$229.

From the Editors: It's not every theater that can claim it was built by Burt Reynolds, but the Maltz Jupiter Theatre (long before it acquired this new name) did in fact begin as Mr. Reynolds' brainchild back in 1978. The actor created the Burt Reynolds Dinner Theatre as a place where he could flex his muscles as a director and a teacher. He eventually sold the venue, which re-opened under its current name in 2004, following a renovation that transformed it from a dinner theater to a state-of-the-art regional theater.

The Jupiter Theatre remains committed to education, demonstrated through its many student workshops, master classes, arts camps, internships, and school-based initiatives. With the Conservatory of Performing Arts (COPA), Jupiter Theatre also provides instruction for kids and teens in all aspects of performance, including acting, voice, musical theater, ballet, and jazz (scholarships are available).

NEW THEATRE
4120 Laguna Street, Coral Gables
305-443-5909 • new-theatre.org

> **Public Transportation:** Fair (requires combination of Metrorail, trolley, and walking a few blocks, or bus).
> **Handicapped Accessibility:** Good
> **Performances/Programs:** Performance schedule is Thursday–Sunday.
> **Ticket Prices:** $35–$40, student Rush tickets (full-time students under 25) are $15. Group discounts are available for parties of 15 or more.
> **Subscriptions:** Five-Play Flex pass is $150. Benefits include $10 off ticket price when you bring a friend and ticket exchanges; you can also see each show a second time for free.

PALM BEACH DRAMAWORKS
322 Banyan Boulevard, Palm Beach
561-514-4042 • palmbeachdramaworks.org

Public Transportation: Fair
Handicapped Accessibility: Good
Performances/Programs: Performance schedule is Wednesday–Sunday.
Ticket Prices: $40–$42. Group discounts available for parties of 20 or more.
Subscriptions: Three-Play $96–$150, Four-Play $128–$192. Benefits include free ticket exchanges and lost-ticket protection.

RIVERSIDE THEATRE
3250 Riverside Park Drive, Vero Beach
800-445-6745 • riversidetheatre.com

Performances/Programs: Performance schedules vary, but generally Wednesday–Sunday for mainstage and Tuesday–Sunday for second stage.
Subscriptions: Four-Show $118–$173 and Five-Show $146–$214. Benefits include ticket exchange privileges, discounts on additional tickets, and lost-ticket insurance. Subscribers save up to 27%.

TEATRO AVANTE
744 S.W. 8th Street, 2nd Floor, Miami
305-445-1301 • teatroavante.com

Public Transportation: Good
Handicapped Accessibility: No
Performances/Programs: Varies. Teatro tours its productions to other venues in the area (including ones that are handicapped accessible) and internationally. Teatro hosts the annual International Hispanic Theatre Festival in its own venue and others in the area in June and July.
Ticket Prices: $25; $20 tickets for seniors, handicapped, students, and groups of 10 or more.

NEW WORLD SYMPHONY (NWS)
Lincoln Theatre, 541 Lincoln Road, Miami Beach
305-673-3331 • nws.edu

Public Transportation: Good
Performances/Programs: 65 given per season.
Ticket Prices: $10–$161.
Subscriptions: Offered for Friday–Sunday concerts and other themed series. Selections include Symphony with a Splash, Concerts for Kids, Chamber Music, and Sounds of the Times. There may also be discounts on purchases of four performances or more. Subscriber benefits include preferred seating, a 20% discount on most additional single tickets, and ticket-exchange privileges.
Membership: Friends of New World Symphony membership begins at $250 and benefits include access for two people to six private events, a 10% discount on select NWS concerts, and complimentary tickets to music forums.
Activities for children: At selected children's concerts, kids can come early and meet the musicians at the Instrument Petting Zoo, where children can see and play the instruments.

From the Editors: Established in 1987 under the artistic direction of Michael Tilson Thomas, this unique educational initiative prepares gifted graduates of distinguished music programs for leadership positions in orchestras and ensembles around the world. Since its inaugural concert on February 4, 1988, the New World Symphony has been heard in such prestigious venues as New York's Carnegie Hall and Avery Fisher Hall, London's Barbican Centre, Paris's Bastille Opera, and Argentina's Teatro Colon.

FLORIDA GRAND OPERA
Adrienne Arsht Center for the Performing Arts
1300 Biscayne Boulevard
800-741-1010 • fgo.org

Other Venue: Broward Center for the Performing Arts, 201 SW 5th Avenue, Fort Lauderdale.
Public Transportation: Good
Handicapped Accessibility: Good
Performances/Programs: Five productions per season, each with multiple performances.
Ticket Prices: $10–$250
Subscriptions: Four-show subscriptions start as low as $32.

Membership: Donations beginning at $25 are recognized in season program book; higher level donation benefits include priority seating and invitations to dress rehearsals and special events.

From the Editors: Florida Grand Opera has a rich tradition of operatic excellence spanning almost 70 years. In 1965, Luciano Pavarotti made his American debut at FGO in their production of Lucia di Lammermoor. Many of the greatest internationally acclaimed operatic artists have performed with FGO, and the company's expansive repertoire includes both standard operas and newly commissioned works.

PALM BEACH OPERA
The Kravis Center for the Performing Arts
801 Okeechobee Boulevard, West Palm Beach
561-833-7888 • pbopera.org

Public Transportation: Good (accessible by Trolley, Palm Tran and Tri-Rail Routes).
Handicapped Accessibility: Good
Performances/Programs: Three full opera productions with multiple performances of each, plus special concert events.
Ticket Prices: $23–$175 for single tickets. Tickets for college students are $12.
Group Discounts: Discounts available for groups of 10 or more.
Subscriptions: Season subscriptions start at $60.
Membership: Membership begins at $100 and may include such benefits as priority seating and ticket exchange, invitations to dress rehearsals, opening night dinners, and other special events. Young Friends is a special membership program for young professionals ages 25–49. Membership is $125 for an individual and $225 per couple, and includes special priced opera tickets, along with invitations to cocktail receptions and a special invitation to an opera production cast party.

From the Editors: Palm Beach Opera brings seasoned opera stars of international acclaim together with young up-and-coming singers. The PBO Resident Artist Program and PBO annual Vocal Competition bring fresh talent from around the country to study and perform with the Palm Beach Opera. Resident artists are featured in the One Opera in One Hour series, allowing the PBO audience to see the next generation in operatic talent. A variety of educational programs bring PBO into the local schools, giving students direct contact with the company.

THE GLOBE CAFÉ AND BAR
377 Alhambra Circle, Coral Gables
305-445-3555 • theglobecafe.com

Public Transportation: Poor
Handicapped Accessibility: Good
Performances/Programs: Saturday-night jazz at 9 p.m.
Ticket Prices: No cover.

JAZZIZ BISTRO
5751 Seminole Way, Hollywood
954-583-8335 • jazzizbistro.com

Public Transportation: Poor
Handicapped Accessibility: Good
Performances/Programs: Live music is performed Friday–Saturday at 8 p.m., Sunday at 7:30 p.m.
Ticket Prices: $5–$10 cover.

O'HARA'S JAZZ AND BLUES CAFÉ
722 E. Las Olas Boulevard, Ft. Lauderdale
954-524-1764 • oharasjazzcafe.com

Public Transportation: Poor
Handicapped Accessibility: Good
Performances/Programs: Live music is performed nightly, Monday–Friday 9 p.m., Friday–Saturday 9:30 p.m., Sunday 3 and 9 p.m.
Ticket Prices: No cover

VAN DYKE CAFÉ
846 Lincoln Road, Miami Beach
305-534-3600 • thevandykecafe.com

Public Transportation: Poor
Handicapped Accessibility: Good
Performances/Programs: About 350 performances per year. Show-times are 9 p.m.–1 a.m.
Ticket Prices: $5–$20 cover.

BALLET FLORIDA
Duncan Theater, Palm Beach Community College
4200 Congress Avenue, Lake Worth
561-659-2000 • balletflorida.com

Other Venues: Eissey Campus Theatre, Palm Beach Community College (North Campus), 3160 PGA Boulevard Palm Beach Gardens; Kravis Center for the Performing Arts, 701 Okeechobee Boulevard, West Palm Beach

Public Transportation: Good (Kravis Center), other venues vary.

Handicapped Accessibility: Good (all venues)

Performances/Programs: Six programs per year, plus the annual *Nutcracker*.

Ticket Prices: $15–$75. Students may purchase half-price tickets beginning three days before opening nights.

Group Discounts: Groups of 15 or more can save 25% to 30% on tickets. One complimentary ticket is offered for every 20 tickets bought.

Other Discounts: WXEL, WPBT, and JCC of the Palm Beaches members may purchase one ticket and get one free, beginning three days before opening night. Police officers and firefighters receive 20% off tickets beginning three days before opening night.

Subscriptions: A subscription series may be purchased for all performances at one of three venues. All sales are final. Benefits include priority seating, free ticket exchanges, and discounts on additional ticket purchases.

Membership: Donor fees start at $100 and include recognition in Ballet Florida performance programs.

Educational/Community Outreach: The Academy of Ballet Florida is the company's official school. It offers curriculum training as well as open classes in various dance styles, such as ballet, jazz, modern, tap, cardio fitness, and toddler classes. It also offers an annual Master Class series. Since its beginning in 1998, this program has given students and community members a chance to learn from the international guest artists that come to work with Ballet Florida's dancers. These classes are open to academy students, as well as the general public.

From the Editors: Ballet Florida is home to 22 professional dancers originating from nine different countries. Founded more than 20 years ago, this company is now the largest arts-producing organization in Palm Beach County. Each season, Ballet Florida brings a distinctive repertoire to its audiences, which combines traditional classical works with pieces by contemporary artists, such as Trey McIntyre. The company has a strong local fan base, many of whom are members of the Golden Circle and are privy to year-round social events. Highlights include the post-performance receptions on opening nights where meeting and mingling with the talented artists of Ballet Florida is encouraged.

BOCA BALLET THEATRE (BBT)

Florida Atlantic University, Griswold Theater
777 Glades Road, Boca Raton
561-995-0709 • bocaballet.org

Public Transportation: Poor
Handicapped Accessibility: Good
Performances/Programs: Four different programs per year, two or three performances each.
Ticket Prices: $35; special events $45, children under 17 and seniors can purchase tickets for $25.
Group Discounts: Group rates are available on special request.
Subscriptions: A subscription includes one performance of each season program (four performances). Subscribers receive $10 off individual ticket prices. All sales final.
Membership: Basic membership $25. Benefits include a quarterly newsletter, invitations to special events, acknowledgement in performance programs, and priority ticket handling.

MIAMI CITY BALLET (MCB)

Adrienne Arsht Center, 1300 NE Biscayne Boulevard
305-929-7010 • miamicityballet.org

Other Venues: Broward Center for the Performing Arts, 201 SW Fifth Avenue, Ft. Lauderdale; Kravis Center for the Performing Arts, 701 Okeechobee Boulevard, West Palm Beach.
Public Transportation: Good
Handicapped Accessibility: Good
Performances/Programs: Four programs each year, plus the annual *Nutcracker*. Each show generally runs for one weekend at each of their three regular venues.
Ticket Prices: $19–$175. Students receive approximately 50% off single-ticket prices. Student groups of 10 or more also receive additional discounts on *Nutcracker* tickets. Some additional offers may be available through Ticketmaster.
Group Discounts: Groups of 20 or more receive a 15% discount.
Subscriptions: Subscription packages are available for two or four

shows at one of three venues.

Membership: Membership opportunities start at $250 and include recognition in MCB's playbills, a subscription to MCB's newsletter, and invitations to special events.

From the Editors: Miami City Ballet comprises 55 professional dancers, many of whom come from some of the most prestigious ballet training centers in the world. The company serves the counties of Broward, Miami-Dade, and Palm Beach, and Collier on Florida's west coast. Having danced for 18 years with George Balanchine at New York City Ballet and originated many lead roles, founding artistic director Edward Villella has made the Balanchine style and repertory the foundation of this company. Yet, the repertory is rounded out with more traditional classics, as well as with works by notable choreographers of the late 20th and early 21st centuries.

In 2009, Miami City Ballet will launch a new artistic partnership with the Cleveland Orchestra. The project was initiated after a successful residency program with the Cleveland Orchestra in 2007 and the establishment of a Musical Arts Association network of supporters across Miami. With a history of working with internationally renowned ballet companies, there are high hopes for the partnership with Cleveland to bring a new vibrancy to ballet performances, as well as generate future collaborative projects.

CINEMA PARADISO
503 SE 6th Street, Fort Lauderdale
954-525-FILM (3456) • fliff.com/cinemaparadiso.asp

Public Transportation: Good (accessible by bus)
Handicapped Accessibility: Good (enter from building's west side).
Performances/Programs: Home to the Fort Lauderdale International Film Festival, this venue is known for screening foreign, independent, and locally produced features, with many making their regional premieres.
Ticket Prices: General admission $9, students and seniors $7, FLIFF members $5.

From the Editors: In conjunction with Emerging Pictures, Fort Lauderdale's Cinema Paradiso screens first runs of independent and foreign pictures. The theater's programming also frequently includes South Florida premieres and special events, as well as the monthly Cinema Verite, a film and discussion series that features an eclectic mix of indie films. Opera buffs also love Cinema Pardiso for its screenings of high-definition broadcasts from Milan's La Scala Opera.

COLONY THEATER
1040 Lincoln Road, Miami Beach
305-674-1040 • miami.com/colony-theater

Public Transportation: Good (within walking distance of multiple local buses).
Handicapped Accessibility: Good
Performances/Programs: Mostly live theater, but the occasional film is screened here.

From the Editors: The stunning Colony Theater is fully deserving of its status as a landmark in the National Register of Historic Places, as anyone who spots it along Lincoln Road in Miami Beach can attest. Designed in the distinctive Art Deco style and opened in 1934 as a Paramount Pictures movie house, the Colony has functioned primarily as a live-performance space since 1986. However, motion pictures are sometimes screened here and cinema enthusiasts will delight in visiting the beautiful Colony on those occasions: The theater was renovated recently, resulting in an en-larged state-of-the-art interior and a restoration of the façade and lobby's original Art Deco grandeur.

COSFORD CINEMA
University of Miami, Memorial Building
1111 Memorial Drive, Coral Gables
305-284-4861 • com.miami.edu/cosford/

Public Transportation: Fair (bus service is available, but requires a walk to access venue).
Performances/Programs: New releases, independent films, classics, and foreign cinema.
Ticket Prices: Free for University of Miami students, $8 for adults, $6 for students and seniors from other universities.

From the Editors: Named by the *Miami New Times* as the best art cinema, Cosford Cinema screens international and independent movies, student film festivals, and special programs. The Cosford, located on the University of Miami's Coral Gables campus, is frequently used for lecture series and events that have brought in renowned guest speakers like Kevin Spacey, John Landis, Richard Gere, and UM alum Ray Liotta.

The Bill Cosford Cinema is a 240-seat state-of-the-art facility capable of showing all traditional film formats, electronic video formats, and high-def.

The Cosford is also home to the Raymond J. Regis Motion Picture Archives, a collection that includes thousands of rare original prints of theatrical motion pictures.

GUSMAN THEATER
Gusman Center, 174 Flagler Street, Miami
305-374-2444 • gusmancenter.org

Public Transportation: Good (accessible by bus)
Handicapped Accessibility: Good
Performances/Programs: Mostly presents live theater, but film screenings are occasionally hosted here.
Ticket Prices: Varies based on program.

From the Editors: First opened in 1926, the Gusman Theater was originally a silent-movie palace. Nowadays, the handsome Miami venue primarily plays host to live theatricals, but the Gusman does still screen films on occasion.

MIAMI BEACH CINEMATHEQUE
512 Espanola Way, Miami Beach
305-673-4567 • mbcinema.com

Public Transportation: Fair
Performances/Programs: Frequently hosts film festivals and series, as well as a regular program of independent, art-house, and classic movies.
Ticket Prices: Non-members $10, $6 members and students.

From the Editors: The Miami Beach Cinematheque, located on Española Way, is the home of the Miami Beach Film Society, an organization dedicated to providing an alternative to the mainstream movie-going experience. The society hosts screenings of an array of festivals and film series at the Cinematheque, which contains a wonderful library, allowing patrons to sit back and enjoy a good book before or after movie showings. There is also a coffee bar, behind which you just may find Film Society founder Dana Keith, creating his own unique beverages. The Miami Beach Cinematheque recently teamed up with Emerging Pictures; it can now screen first-run indie pictures and art films in high-definition.

TOWER THEATER
1508 SW 8th Street, Miami
305-643-8706 • mdc.edu/IAC/towertheater/aboutUs.asp

Public Transportation: Yes (accessible by bus)
Handicapped Accessibility: Good
Performances/Programs: The theater hosts both live educational lectures and screenings of English and Spanish language films.
Ticket Prices: Vary based on program.

From the Editors: The Tower Theater began as a silent-movie house in 1926, but is now under the auspices of Miami Dade College. Located on Calle Ocho in Little Havana, the Tower supports the arts and the community with film screenings, exhibitions, performances, and free lectures from Miami-Dade faculty and other local scholars. Many of the films shown at the Tower Theater are in Spanish, or English-language movies with Spanish subtitles.

ADRIENNE ARSHT CENTER FOR THE PERFORMING ARTS OF MIAMI-DADE COUNTY
1300 NE Biscanye Blvd., Miami
305-949-6722 · arshtcenter.org

Venues: Sanford and Dolores Ziff Ballet Opera House, John S. and James L. Knight Concert Hall, Carnival Studio Theater.
Public Transportation: Excellent
Handicapped Accessibility: Good
Performances/Programs: Programming includes Broadway in Miami, Miami City Ballet, Florida Grand Opera, City Jazz Roots, and a three-week residency by the Cleveland Orchestra.
Membership: Begins at $65 and includes exclusive access to member-only events, invitation to special events and lectures, and discounts to local hotels and restaurants.

For information on Jacksonville and
Tampa/St. Petersburg, Florida, visit go-artsamerica.com.

MINNEAPOLIS/ST. PAUL, MINNESOTA

Minneapolis has long been a theater-lover's paradise, with more theater per capita (second only to New York) than any other city in the nation. The people of Minneapolis (as well as neighboring St. Paul) have a long-standing tradition of encouraging the performing and literary arts, and this tradition is well-represented by the offerings below.

ARTS INFO

City Pages (citypages.com)—Alternative weekly with comprehensive arts and entertainment coverage.

Star Tribune (startribune.com)—The biggest newspaper in Minnesota.

twincities.com—Operated by the daily *Pioneer Press*.

vita.mn—Twin Cities events guide.

minneapolis-art.com—Info and links for Minneapolis arts organizations.

THE ARTS

MINNEAPOLIS INSTITUTE OF ARTS (THE MIA)
2400 3rd Avenue S, Minneapolis
612- 870-3131 • artsmia.org

Public Transportation: Good (the MIA is readily accessible via Metro bus and Light Rail).

Handicapped Accessibility: Good (to reserve a wheelchair or electric scooter in advance, call 612-870 -3091).

Hours: Tuesday–Wednesday, Friday–Saturday 10 a.m.–5 p.m., Thursday 10 a.m.–9 p.m.; Sunday 11 a.m.–5 p.m., and some holidays.

Admission: Free

Basic Tour: Daily public tours are available 1–2 p.m. daily.

Audio Tours: Yes, tours are available for seniors, students, and children for $4; $5 for non-members; free for members.

Membership: Individual membership starts at $45 and includes unlimited free passes to all special exhibitions and priority ticketing for events, a subscription to *Arts* magazine, invitations to the MIA's large annual events, members-only special exhibition preview days, invitations to special members appreciation weekend, 10% discount at the museum shop and D'Amico and Sons' Arts Café and Arts Break restaurants; discounts on selected performances and classes at the Children's Theatre Company and the Minneapolis College of Art and Design, monthly special at the museum shop, free audio guide rentals and orientation tours. Reciprocal membership to other museums nationwide is available at the Reciprocal level ($250) and above.

From the Editors: The MIA has an encyclopedic collection with a strong emphasis on European, American, African, and Judaic art. The extensive Asian art collection is housed in 22 different galleries. The museum is also strong in ancient art and has several period rooms, including a Chinese reception hall, study, and garden.

WALKER ART CENTER
1750 Hennepin Avenue, Minneapolis
612-375-7600 • walkerart.org

Public Transportation: Very good (The Walker is accessible via Metro Transit Bus Lines 4, 6, 12, and 25).

Handicapped Accessibility: Good

Hours: The Galleries are open Tuesday–Sunday 11 a.m.–5 p.m., Thursday 11 a.m.–9 p.m., closed Monday and holidays. Minneapolis Sculpture Garden is open daily from 6 a.m.–midnight, free. The Cowles Conservatory is Tuesday–Saturday 10 a.m.–8 p.m., Sunday 10 a.m.–5 p.m., closed Monday.

Admission: $10, seniors (65+) $8, students and teens $6, members and children (12 and under) free.

Free Day: Thursday evenings 5–9 p.m. and the first Saturday of every month 10 a.m.–5 p.m.

Tours: Free tours are offered Tuesday–Sunday at 2 p.m. and include explorations of the gallery, architecture, and garden of the museum.

Audio Tours: Free

Membership: Individual membership is $50 and includes free gallery admission, up to 50% off event tickets, invitations to special exhibitions, as well as discounts on select local arts events and multiple art and design magazines. Dual/Household membership is offered at $60. Students, seniors, and non-resident memberships are $40.

Other Benefits: Reciprocal membership to more than 200 museums is available at the Friend Level ($150) and above.

From the Editors: Although a few old masters can be found in the collection, the Walker concentrates on 20th-century art, especially Pop Art, with works by Warhol, Lichtenstein, Rauschenberg, and Jasper Johns in a very flexible and accessible space. The adjacent 11-acre Minneapolis Sculpture Garden is an attraction all own, for no other reason than the giant *Spoonbridge and Cherry* by Claes Oldenburg and Coosje van Bruggen.

Adjoining the Guthrie Theater, the Walker maintains a very active performance program presenting music, theater, dance, films, and other events.

WEISMAN ART MUSEUM
University of Minnesota's Twin Cities Campus
333 East River Road, Minneapolis
612-625-9494 • weisman.umn.edu

Public Transportation: Very good (easily accessible by both bus and Metro lines).

Handicapped Accessibility: Good

Hours: Tuesday, Wednesday, Friday 10 a.m.–5 p.m., Thursday 10 a.m.–8 p.m., Saturday and Sunday 11 a.m.–5 p.m., closed Monday and holidays.

Admission: Free

Tours: Free public tours are offered every Saturday and Sunday at 1 p.m.

Membership: Individual membership ($40–$59) includes invitations to special events and openings, a subscription to WAM newsletter, discounts on events and classes, and reciprocal benefits at select organizations. Discounted membership is available for students ($30–$39).

From the Editors: Designed by Frank Gehry, the Weisman (a.k.a. "Baby Bilbao") is a steel-clad collection of curves and angles reflecting everything around it, including the nearby Mississippi River. Inside is a modern American art collection primarily focusing on the first half of the 20th century, including a portrait of founder Frederick Weisman by Andy Warhol.

BEDLAM THEATRE
West Bank Theatre, 1501 S. 6th Street, Minneapolis
612-341-1038 • www.bedlamtheatre.org

Public Transportation: Excellent (easily accessible by Cedar/Riverside LRT and bus).

Performances/Programs: Performance schedule varies, but often Wednesday–Sunday (some pay-what-you-can Monday performances).

Ticket Prices: Tickets usually $10–$20, $5 discounts for students, seniors, artists, and low-income, and $2 additional rebate if you arrive by some form of sustainable transportation.

THE CHILDREN'S THEATRE COMPANY
2400 Third Avenue South, Minneapolis
612-874-0400 • childrenstheatre.org

Handicapped Accessibility: Good

Performances/Programs: Performance schedule is Tuesday–Sunday.

Ticket Prices: Single adult tickets are $16–$35, discounts available for children, teens, students, and seniors, Rush tickets sold 15 minutes before each performance, group discounts available

Subscriptions: Total Flex pass (eight vouchers) is $250, Five-Play (adults $76–$133, children/students/seniors $54–$110), Three-Play (adults $51–$90, children/students/seniors $36–$74). Benefits include discounts on additional tickets, free ticket exchanges, lost-ticket insurance, and free parking.

GUTHRIE THEATER
818 South 2nd Street, Minneapolis
877-44-STAGE (78243) • guthrietheater.org

Public Transportation: Very good
Handicapped Accessibility: Good
Performances/Programs: Performance schedule is Tuesday–Sunday.
Ticket Prices: $24–$65, $15–$25 Rush tickets sold 10 minutes before each performance, discounts available for groups of 20 or more, discounts sometimes available on TheaterMania.
Subscriptions: Four-Play $62–$269, Six-Play $91–$397 and Eight-Play $111–$519, discount packages available for students and seniors. Benefits include free ticket exchanges and discounts on classes at the Guthrie Learning Center.

From the Editors: Opened in 2006, the new Guthrie Theatre was reimagined by artistic director Joe Dowling and architect Jean Nouvel as a gathering place for the community. Minnesotans who have yet to sample the Guthrie's eclectic offerings (it's not every theater that has an Arthur Miller play, a new musical version of *Little House on the Prairie*, and a Dar Williams concert in the space of a couple days) can still tell you about fine dining at the Cue or enthuse over the Mississippi River views from the Guthrie's Endless Bridge lobby. The public is encouraged to enjoy the building's restaurants, lounge, and atmosphere—folks are even welcome to hang out in one of the lobbies and take advantage of the free wi-fi.

The theater hosts regular In Conversation Q&As with thesps like Patrick Stewart and Neil Simon, and annually brings in a special speaker for the Global Voice forum (Chilean writer Isabel Allende, Irish poet Seamus Heaney, and Russian dancer Mikhail Baryshnikov are past guests).

The place is also rife with educational programs: Shakespeare Classic introduces kids ages 8–15 to the Bard through performances and events; $15 Sampler Classes allow adults to try out a class in writing or even tap dancing. The Guthrie even teaches corporate professionals how they can use performance skills to enhance their working life and helps attorneys meet continuing education requirements with custom CLE programs that are actually enjoyable.

HISTORY THEATRE
30 E Tenth Street, St. Paul
651-292-4323 • historytheatre.com

Public Transportation: Good
Handicapped Accessibility: Good
Performances/Programs: Performance schedule is Thursday–Sunday (occasional Mondays).
Ticket Prices: $25–$32, discounts available for students and seniors.
Subscriptions: Premium pass is $125, Buddy pass (i.e., flex pass) and Friday-Night passes are $100, students and seniors get $10 discount on Premium and Buddy passes.

JUNGLE THEATER
2951 Lyndale Avenue South, Minneapolis
612-822-7063 • jungletheater.com

Public Transportation: Excellent (bus stop right in front of theater).
Handicapped Accessibility: Good
Performances/Programs: Performance schedule is Tuesday–Sunday.
Ticket Prices: $26–$36, discounts for students and seniors available, Rush tickets sold 30 minutes prior to every performance, group discounts available.
Subscriptions: Four-Show Flex pass $100, Six-Show Flex pass ($150).

MIXED BLOOD THEATRE
1501 South 4th Street, Minneapolis
612-338-6131 • mixedblood.com

Public Transportation: Good (easily accessible by Light Rail).
Handicapped Accessibility: Good
Performances/Programs: Performance schedule is Wednesday–Sunday.
Ticket Prices: $10–$30.
Subscriptions: Regular Five-Show subscriptions are $50–$105, Flex pass ($112) gets one voucher per show,

From the Editors: Ethno Metro pass ($126) gets all five shows, plus tickets to a select show at other area theaters (Ordway Center, Children's Theatre Company, Mu Performing Arts and Stages Theatre Co., and Interact Center).

MINNESOTA JEWISH THEATRE
Hillcrest Center Theater, 1978 Ford Parkway, St. Paul
651-647-4315 • mnjewishtheatre.org

Public Transportation: Good
Handicapped Accessibility: Good
Performances/Programs: Performance schedule varies a bit, but generally Wednesday through Sunday.
   Ticket Prices: $17–$35, student Rush tickets $12, discounts available for groups of 10 or more.
   Subscriptions: Three-Show subscriptions are $50–$72. Benefits include ticket exchanges.

PARK SQUARE THEATER
Historic Hamm Building, 20 W. 7th Place, St. Paul
651-291-7005 • parksquaretheatre.org

Public Transportation: Easily accessible by bus.
Handicapped Accessibility: Good
Performances/Programs: Performance schedule is Wednesday–Sunday.
   Ticket Prices: $15–$45, discounts for groups of 10 or more.
   Subscriptions: Six-Play series $180–$201; Five-Play series $145–$169; Four-Play series $116–$143; and Three-Play series $87–$110. Subscriber benefits include 25% savings on extra tickets, ticket insurance, free ticket exchanges, parking discounts, and see the show again for free when you bring new friends.

PENUMBRA THEATRE COMPANY
270 North Kent Street, St. Paul
651-224-3180 • penumbratheatre.org

Public Transportation: Good
Handicapped Accessibility: Good
Performances/Programs: Performance schedule is Wednesday–Sunday, with some Tuesday performances.
   Ticket Prices: $38, student tickets are $18, 2-for-1 discounts available for selected performances, group discounts available.
   Subscriptions: Four-Play $120 and Flex package (three vouchers $90) available. Benefits include complimentary beverages, lost-ticket replacement, and free ticket exchanges.

STEPPINGSTONE THEATER
55 Victoria Street N, St. Paul
651-225-9265 • steppingstonetheatre.org

Public Transportation: Good
Handicapped Accessibility: Good
Performances/Programs: Performance schedule is Tuesday–Sunday.
Ticket Prices: $11, children and seniors discounts, members of MERSC (Minnesota Employee Recreation and Services Council) eligible for discounts.
Subscriptions: Six-Show pass $50; Family Flex pass ($75) gives you 10 admissions.

EXULTATE CHAMBER CHOIR & ORCHESTRA
651-707-0727 • exultate.org

Venues: Various locations throughout the Minneapolis/St. Paul area.
Public Transportation: Depends on venue.
Handicapped Accessibility: Most venues accessible, call management for details.
Program/Performances: Four programs per season, with multiple performances of each.
Ticket Prices: Adults $18–$20, seniors (65+) and students (under 16) $15.
Subscriptions: Save $15 when you purchase one ticket for each of the four concerts in the season.
Membership: Contact for details

CANTUS
612-435-0046 • cantusonline.org

Venues: Various locations in and around Minneapolis/St. Paul.
Public Transportation: Depends on venue.
Handicapped Accessibility: Good
Performances/Programs: Five programs with multiple performances, plus other performances nationwide.
Ticket Prices: General admission $25, kids (12 and under) $12.50, and student Rush for season concerts $10; other events vary. Serve as a volunteer to get free tickets.
Subscriptions: Not listed, contact for details.
Membership: Donations from $25–$5,000+ are very welcome.

MINNESOTA CHORALE
612-333-4866 • mnchorale.org

Venues: Various locations around Minneapolis/St. Paul.
Public Transportation: Depends on venue.
Handicapped Accessibility: Good
Performances/Programs: Several performances (the group is regularly contracted by the Minnesota Orchestra).
Ticket Prices: Varies by program and venue.
Subscriptions: Contact for more information.
Membership: Donations are accepted and greatly appreciated.

MINNESOTA ORCHESTRA
Orchestra Hall, 1111 Nicollet Mall, Minneapolis
612-371-5656 • minnesotaorchestra.org

Public Transportation: Good (the MTC website provides information regarding routes convenient to Orchestra Hall; also, the Minnesota orchestra offers a free Coffee Concert coach bus service from area shopping malls to Orchestra Hall for 11 a.m. Thursday morning Coffee Concerts).
Handicapped Accessibility: Good
Performances/Programs: 215 per year.
Ticket Prices: $13–$83. Students can purchase student e-tickets online in advance for $10. Public Rush tickets are priced at $25. High-school and college-student Rush tickets are $15, with a current valid student ID. University of Minnesota students, faculty, and staff are also eligible for special discounts on tickets.
Group Discounts: Groups of 10 or more save up to 20% on Minnesota Orchestra tickets. Special corporate discounts are also available.
Subscriptions: Offered in pre-arranged series by genre: Classical, Inside the Classics, Chamber, Quartet, Pop Stars!, Sunday Brunch, and Family. You can also create-your-own package by choosing three or more concerts from a broad selection. With create-your-own Family Package, families can choose from a selection of programs tailored to young listeners. Tickets are just $25 for adults and $10 for kids when you purchase a package of three or more concerts. College students may attend the three concerts of the Inside the Classics for only $30. Subscribers receive up to 50% off regular ticket prices, discounts on additional tickets, priority seating, and ticket exchanges.
Membership: Patron membership begins at $100. Benefits include an invitation for two to the annual Guarantors' Concert, an invitation for two

to the annual meeting and reception, and a complimentary subscription to *Orchestra Times*, the orchestra's quarterly newsletter.

From the Editors: Founded in 1903, the Minnesota Orchestra has demonstrated leadership in performance, recordings, and programming. An innovative ensemble, the orchestra was among the first to be recorded and heard on the radio. Friday-night performances are still broadcast live by Minnesota Public Radio and many concerts are featured on such programs as "SymphonyCast" and "Performance Today."

An advocate for new works, the ensemble has premiered and commissioned nearly 200 compositions since its founding. It has received multiple awards for adventurous programming from ASCAP, including the Leonard Bernstein Awards for Education Programming (2005–2007) and the John S. Edwards Award for Strongest Commitment to New American Music (2008).

With a strong dedication to young people, the orchestra offers free family-focused concerts, along with Young People's Concerts for elementary-age school groups, and WAMSO Kinder Konzerts (48 each year!), designed to help introduce pre-school children to the joys of the Minnesota Orchestra. Rush tickets are available for students ($15) and the public ($25). Young patrons are invited to join the Crescendo Project, where they receive additional discounts on tickets and subscriptions, along with invitations to private events and receptions.

THE ROSE ENSEMBLE
651-225-4340 • roseensemble.com

Venues: Various venues in and around Minneapolis/St. Paul and locations around the country.

Public Transportation: Depends on venue.

Handicapped Accessibility: All venues are accessible.

Performances/Programs: Four per season, but the group may be hired out and performs other events as well.

Ticket Prices: Depending on venue, prices are either $23 for all seats, or $17–$35 for various seating. $3 discounts for students and seniors, $2 discount for Minnesota Public Radio members. Children 10 and under are free. Buy two or more tickets to select concerts and receive a third for free.

Group Discounts: Discounts available for groups of 8 or more.

Subscriptions: Contact for more information.

Membership: Available from $1–$5,000+. Higher level donors receive benefits such as invites to private receptions and dinners, free Rose Ensemble CDs, and season passes.

ST. PAUL CHAMBER ORCHESTRA (SPCO)
Benson Great Hall, 3900 Bethel Drive, St. Paul
651-291-1144 • thespco.org

Other Venues: Bigelow Chapel, United Theological Seminary, 3000 Fifth Street Northwest, New Brighton; Ordway Center for the Performing Arts, 345 Washington Street, St. Paul; Ted Mann Concert Hall, University of Minnesota, 2128 Fourth Street South, Minneapolis.

Public Transportation: Depends on venue.

Handicapped Accessibility: Good

Performances/Programs: 150 plus performances per season.

Ticket Prices: $10–$59. Discounts are offered for seniors and student Rush tickets are $10 each one hour prior to performances. Children 6–17 are $5 with the purchase of an adult ticket.

Group Discounts: Groups of 10 or more can receive up to 30% discounts.

Subscriptions: Subscriptions can be ordered based on city and day of the week, and by repertoire. Subscribers save up to 33% at SPCO. Additional subscription discounts are available for seniors on the following series and price sections: SPCO at Ordway Center, Sections 2, 3 and 4; Ted Mann Sunday Matinée, Sections 1, 2 and 3; and Ordway Friday-Morning Coffee, Sections 1, 2 and 3. Benefits include ticket exchanges up to two hours prior to the concert and pre-paid parking.

Membership: A gift of $1000 or more gives you membership in the Conductors Circle, with access to exclusive events.

Activities for Young Adults: Club 20/30 allows 20- and 30-year-olds to purchase concert tickets for $10 with no membership fee.

From the Editors: This is the nation's only full-time professional chamber orchestra. Working in collaboration with five highly regarded Artistic Partners (Dawn Upshaw, Pierre-Laurent Aimard, Roberto Abbado, Douglas Boyd, and Nicholas McGegan), SPCO presents more than 150 concerts and educational programs each year.

With a clear dedication to keeping its performances accessible to all audiences, SPCO offers many free programs and discounts on tickets. Seats begin as low as $10, children's tickets (6–17) are available for $5 for all concerts with the purchase of an adult ticket. Start the Music!, for children 3–6; xplorchestra!, for 6–12; and Family Concerts at Ordway Center are all free.

For those who like to mix their classical intake with other musical styles, SPCO offers Jazzed-Up Fridays, where the first half of the concert features classical music. Post-intermission, you have the choice to stay for some more chamber music or go to the lobby for some jazz or world music.

VOCALESSENCE
612-547-1451 • vocalessence.com

Venues: Various locations throughout Minneapolis/St. Paul.
Public Transportation: Depends on venue.
Handicapped Accessibility: Most venues accessible; contact venue management for details.
Performances/Programs: Seven season programs, various tours and special events.
Ticket Prices: $20–$40.
Subscriptions: Three- ($115), four- ($145), five- ($175) and six-concert ($200) subscriptions available. Subscriber benefits include ticket exchanges and discounts on additional tickets.
Membership: Not available, but donations accepted and greatly appreciated.

From the Editors: VocalEssence was founded in 1969 as the Plymouth Music Series by Phillip Brunelle. The organization presents concerts featuring both the full 130-voice chorus and the 32-voice professional mixed chorus. To date, VocalEssence has preformed over 115 commissioned works and has also performed Midwest, United States, and World premieres. The group's name was changed in 2002 to VocalEssence to capture its goal of exploring the human voice, from spoken word to song.

THE MINNESOTA OPERA
Ordway Center, 345 Washington Street, St. Paul
612-333-6669 • mnopera.org

Public Transportation: Good (accessible to nearby bus service).
Handicapped Accessibility: Good, Ordway Center is accessible
Performances/Programs: Five productions per season with multiple performances of each.
Ticket Prices: $20–$200, with prices varying depending on date and seats selected. Students and seniors may qualify for additional discounts; call for information.
Group Discounts: Discounts available for groups of 10 or more.
Subscriptions: Full Five-opera subscriptions available for $135–$755. Create your own Three- and Four-opera subscriptions also available. Subscriber benefits include flexible ticket exchanges, discounted tickets for family and friends, free lost ticket replacement, free season preview CD, discounts on education classes.

Membership: Available from $50–$20,000+. Based on donation amount, member benefits include rehearsal passes, program recognition, personal tours of the Opera, complimentary parking, Opera News subscription, copies of libretti for the season's productions, and invites to special events.

From the Editors: The Minnesota Opera began as an "alternative" opera company in the 1960s but eventually altered its experimental nature in the '80s to include more standard repertoire. Now dedicated to offering a broad range of operas, Minnesota Opera maintains a strong commitment to the values defined within the Bel Canto philosophy and offers at least one opera from the Bel Canto period each season.

ARTIST'S QUARTER
408 St. Peter Street, St. Paul
651-292-1359

Public Transportation: Poor
Handicapped Accessibility: Good
Performances/Programs: Approximately 350 performances per year. Shows nightly at 8 or 9 p.m..
Ticket Prices: $5–$25. Generally no cover charge on Monday.

DAKOTA JAZZ CLUB AND RESTAURANT
1010 Nicollet Mall, Minneapolis
612-332-1010 • dakotacooks.com

Public Transportation: Poor
Handicapped Accessibility: Good
Performances/Programs: Live jazz is presented seven nights a week: Sunday–Thursday 7 p.m., Friday–Saturday 8 and 11:30 p.m.
Ticket Prices: $5–$50
Membership: Membership levels are offered for $200, $400, $1,000, and $2,000.

From the Editors: One of the gems of the growing jazz culture in the Twin Cities is Dakota Jazz Club and Restaurant. Hosting mostly local acts and a smattering of the finest national touring acts, Dakota has seen the likes of Roy Hargrove, John Pizzarelli, and Amel Larrieux. For most of the acts, the cover charge is probably less than the cost of your martini, but for bigger names, expect to pay big name prices ($40–$50).

Dakota promotes jazz education, hosting competitions for local high-school musicians. Check out the sponsorship packages on the website for several discounts, including free cover for all local acts, discounted tickets for national acts, and several different levels of discounted dining. Pick the right night and you may just find yourself appearing on the next Grammy-nominated jazz album, as many national acts have recorded live albums at Dakota.

JAMES SEWELL BALLET

The O'Shaughnessy Theater, College of St. Catherine
2004 Randolph Avenue, St. Paul
612-672-0480 • jsballet.org

Other Venue: Southern Theater, 1420 Washington Avenue South, Minneapolis.

Public Transportation: Good

Handicapped Accessibility: Good

Performances/Programs: Fall, winter, and spring programs in Minneapolis, each with four–five performances.

Ticket Prices: $30. Small discounts are available to CSC alumni, faculty, and staff. Half-price tickets for students and children 12 and under; the First Chance Dance program is short informal performances for $10.

Group Discounts: For groups of 10 or more, individual ticket prices are discounted to $19 each.

MINNESOTA DANCE THEATRE AND DANCE INSTITUTE (MDT)

Lab Theater, 700 North First Street, Minneapolis
612-338-0627 • mndance.org

Other Venue: The State Theatre, 805 Hennepin Ave., Minneapolis.

Public Transportation: Good (easily accessible via Light Rail or bus).

Handicapped Accessibility: Good

Performances/Programs: Two programs: one in the fall and one in the spring, three performances each. MDT also does a week-long run of the annual *Nutcracker* ballet.

Ticket Prices: About $30. *Nutcracker* performances are slightly more expensive, ranging from $25 up to about $50. Student discounts are available through season packages.

Subscriptions: Two packages are available. Package A includes the fall and spring programs and the *Nutcracker*. Program B includes only the fall and spring programs. Adult and student packages are available. Subscribers get free ticket exchanges up to 24 hours prior to performance. Other benefits include priority seating, 20% off all additional singe tickets, invitations to MDT/DI Up-Close and Personals, 20% off on MDT/DI merchandise, and invitations to opening night post-performance receptions.

ZENON DANCE COMPANY AND SCHOOL
Southern Theater
1420 Washington Avenue South, Minneapolis
612-338-1101 • zenondance.org

> **Public Transportation:** Poor
> **Handicapped Accessibility:** Good
> **Performances/Programs:** Zenon performs a two-week season at the Southern Theater every year. Performances are Thursday through Sunday.
> **Ticket Prices:** Around $30. Southern Theater members can purchase $12 tickets on opening nights; $5 discount for all other performances. Student Rush tickets are $10 (when available). Students, seniors, and low-income patrons receive a $2-per-ticket discount. Children under 12 are half off the regular highest ticket price.
> **Group Discounts:** Groups of 10 or more at the Southern Theater get a $4 discount off each ticket.

OAK STREET CINEMA
309 Oak Street SE, Minneapolis
612-331-3134 • mnfilmarts.org/oakstreet

> **Public Transportation:** Very good (easily accessible by several local bus lines).
> **Handicapped Accessibility:** Good
> **Performances/Programs:** Independent, foreign, and classic films.
> **Ticket Prices:** General admission $7, seniors and children $5, members and students $4.

From the Editors: The Oak Street Cinema was known simply as the Oak when it was first built in 1916 near the University of Minnesota campus. The theater was remodeled in the Art Deco style in 1935 and could accommodate about 400 moviegoers in its lovely auditorium. It was known as the Campus Theater for years thereafter, serving as a favorite spot for U.

of M. film buffs, until it closed down in 1989. After briefly getting some use as a live-performance venue, the theater was renovated and opened as a movie house again in 1995 with the name Oak Street Cinema.

Now one of the best art-film theaters in the Twin Cities, the Oak Street screens classics, indies, foreign flicks, and film festivals, and it remains closely allied to its neighbor, the University of Minnesota.

HENNEPIN THEATRE DISTRICT

The State, Orpheum, and Pantages Theaters
710–910 Hennepin Avenue, Minneapolis
612-339-7007 • hennepintheatredistrict.org

> **Public Transportation:** Very good (easily accessible by bus or LRT).
> **Handicapped Accessibility:** Good
> **Performances/Programs:** Programming includes Broadway touring shows, concerts, comedy, family shows, dance, theater, and literary events.
> **Ticket Prices:** Vary by program. Family discounts available for selected shows. Many productions offer student Rush tickets.
> **Group Discounts:** Group discounts are available (usually for groups of 20 or more).
> **Subscription/Membership:** Broadway subscriptions allow subscribers to pick three or more shows to attend per season. Hennepin Theatre Trust membership at the $150 level or higher includes the following benefits: the opportunity to purchase two tickets per Broadway production prior to public, concierge ticketing, and invites to special events.

PHILADELPHIA, PENNSYLVANIA

Philadelphia holds a hallowed place in American history. From Independence Hall to the Liberty Bell, the city fairly bursts with historical landmarks. The City of Brotherly Love is also home to a wonderful selection of artistic destinations. With a vibrant visual-art scene (featuring numerous outdoor murals and public installations), including varied musical and theatrical offerings, Philadelphia is a can't-miss destination for serious art lovers.

ARTS INFO AND DISCOUNTS

City Paper (citypaper.net)—Weekly news and entertainment paper.
gophila.com—Philly events guide.
philadelphiaweekly.com—Online version of popular alternative weekly.
phila.gov/visitors/arts.html—Links and info on Philly's arts and cultural institutions.
philly.com—Extensive coverage of the diverse local scene on the site of *The Philadelphia Inquirer* and *Daily News*.
theatermania.com/philadelphia/discount-tickets—Worth checking for occasional discounts.

THE ARTS

THE BARNES FOUNDATION
300 N. Latch's Lane, Merion
610-667-0290 • barnesfoundation.org

Public Transportation: Good (accessible via SEPTA bus and train lines).

Handicapped Accessibility: Good

Hours: Advance reservations required. September–June the Barnes is open on Friday–Sunday 9:30 a.m.–5 p.m. July–August, the museum is open Wednesday–Sunday 9:30 a.m.–5 p.m.

Admission: $12

Basic Tour: Docent-led tours of the Gallery are held three times per day, on a first-come first-served basis. Visitors may not reserve tours in advance and groups are not permitted to participate. The schedule of tours is as follows: September–June Friday-Sunday at 10 a.m. and 1 and 2 p.m. July–August Wednesday–Sunday at 10 a.m. and 1 and 2 p.m. Guided Tours of the Arboretum are offered September–October and April–June Friday–Sunday at 11:15 a.m.; July–August Wednesday-Sunday at 11:15 a.m.

Audio Tour: $7

Membership: Public membership begins at the Family level ($120) and includes complimentary tickets to the Gallery and Arboretum, access to tickets reserved exclusively for members, 10% discounts in the gallery shop, discounts on special events including lectures, private tours, and workshops, exclusive volunteer opportunities, and recognition in the annual donor report. Discounted memberships are available at the student ($35) and student/alumni level ($75).

From the Editors: Assembled by Dr. Albert Barnes, this can't-miss stop for Impressionist fans has more than 180 Renoirs, 70 Cézannes, two dozen Picassos, and lots of other works by all the great masters of the late 19th century. The museum is set in an attractive twelve-acre arboretum.

THE PENNSYLVANIA ACADEMY OF THE ARTS (THE PAFA)
118 North Broad Street
215-972-7600 • pafa.org

Other Venue: The Samuel M.V. Hamilton Building, 128 Broad Street.

Public Transportation: Good (Race-Vine and 15th Street SEPTA subway stops are just around the corner from the museum).

Handicapped Accessibility: Good (accessible entrance located at Cherry and Burns Streets; the Burns Street elevator provides access to the gallery floor).

Hours: Tuesday–Saturday 10 a.m.–5 p.m., Sunday 11 a.m–5 p.m., closed Mondays and holidays.

Admission: $10, students and seniors with ID $8, youth (5–18) $6. Special exhibitions $15, students and seniors with ID $12, youth (5–18) $6. Admission for all exhibitions is free for members and children under 5. Admission to the Morris Gallery and the ground floor of the Historic Landmark Building is always free.

Basic Tour: Free with admission; tours are given between 11:30 a.m. and 1:15 p.m. on weekdays and 1 p.m. and 2:45 p.m. on weekends. Guided tours are also available for people with physical or mental disabilities upon request and sign-language interpreters are available for all programs with prior arrangements.

Membership: All members at the Individual level ($50) and above enjoy unlimited free admission to the Academy, a 10% discount at the Academy Café, a 10% discount at the museum store, two free admission tickets to *USArtists: American Fine Art Show*, invitations to members-only tours, events, and exhibition preview receptions, *Preview*, the museum's quarterly in-house periodical, plus free admission to the museum's Art-at-Lunch series. Discount memberships for students ($20) are also offered. A Young Friends membership ($60) is available for people 21–40, which includes regular individual benefits plus invitations to Young Friends events and Academy programs. Reciprocal membership is available to more than 250 museums throughout the country at the Friend Level ($150) and above.

From the Editors: Founded in 1805, the PaFA is the nation's first and oldest art museum. Located in one of the best examples of Victorian Gothic architecture in the United States, each of the museum's galleries are devoted to a specific aspect of American art.

THE PHILADELPHIA MUSEUM OF ART (THE PMA)
26th Street and Benjamin Franklin Parkway
215-763-8100 • philamuseum.org

Other Venue: Perelman Building, Fairmount and Pennsylvania Avenues.

Public Transportation: Very good (both SEPTA and the Phlash shuttle provide convenient access to the museum).

Handicapped Accessibility: Good

Hours: Main museum Tuesday–Sunday 10 a.m.–5 p.m., Fridays 10 a.m. –8:45 p.m., closed Mondays and holidays. Perelman Building Tuesday–Sunday 10 a.m.–5 p.m., closed Mondays and holidays.

Admission: Main museum $16, seniors (65+) $14, students and children (13–18) $12, members and children (12 and under) free; Perelman Building $9, seniors (65+) $7, students and children (13–18) $6, members and children (12 and under) free. Sundays are pay what you wish for both. Additional fees for some exhibits are required.

Tours: Free introductory walks, a broad overview of the museum's collections, are offered daily at 11 a.m. and 2 p.m. For collection and special-exhibition tours, prices, times, and dates vary.

Audio Tour: $5

Membership: Individual membership costs $65 and includes free unlimited general admission for a year, free admission to Art After 5, one free ticket to special exhibits of your choice, free admission to the Rodin Museum, and members-only discounts on concerts and art-history courses. Discounted student ($40) and household ($100) memberships are also offered.

Other Benefits: Reciprocal admission at more than 50 museums available for each level of membership.

Note: Shuttles run between the Perelman Building and the museum's main building every 10–15 minutes Tuesday–Sunday 10 a.m.–5 p.m.

From the Editors: Situated at the end of Benjamin Franklin Parkway in the heart of Philadelphia, the infamous *Rocky*-run location of this museum alone ought to be enough to wrangle any visual enthusiast. However, with holdings that range from treasures of the Middle Ages to modern masterpieces, the geographic location of the building is certainly not the only worthy attribute of the Philadelphia Museum of Art.

With an interesting and easy-to-follow layout, the museum takes special care to guide its visitors historically through its holdings. Special exhibitions are extremely popular here and often require advance planning. Friday evenings tend to be a great time to visit, as crowds are usually at their minimum; the coat/bag check is free (but compulsory); absolutely no photography is allowed in special exhibits and no flash photography is permitted in the permanent collections.

1812 PRODUCTIONS
215-592-9560 • 1812productions.org

Venues: 1812 Productions has no permanent home, so they use various venues, including the Tin Angel, 20 South 2nd Street; Plays and Players Theatre, 1714 Delancey Street; and Adrienne Theatre, 2030 Sansom Street.

Public Transportation: Very good (all venues accessible via SEPTA).

Handicapped Accessibility : Yes (all venues).

Performances/Programs: Performance schedule is Tuesday–Sunday.

Ticket Prices: $17–$35

Subscriptions: Four-Show subscriptions are $60–$100.

ARDEN THEATRE COMPANY
40 N. 2nd Street
215-922-1122 • ardentheater.org

Public Transportation: Excellent (easily accessible via SEPTA buses and subways, Amtrak, and NJ PATCO).

Handicapped Accessibility: Good

Performances/Programs: Performance schedule is Tuesday–Sunday.

Ticket Prices: $27–$45; seniors, full-time students, military, and educators get a $2 discount; discounts for groups of 10 or more.

Subscriptions: Five-Show $105–$195 and Three-Show $69–$129, small subscription discounts available for students and seniors; Arden Children's Theatre Two-Play prices are $40–$50/adults, $38–$48/seniors (62+), $32–$40/teens (13–17), and $26–$30/kids (12 and under). Benefits include ticket exchanges, parking discounts, and free ticket insurance.

From the Editors: Arden Theatre Company loves to tell a good story and its stories come from many sources. Fairy tales, Sondheim musicals, Irish plays, stage adaptations of everything from *Arabian Nights* to *Crime and Punishment*, and August Wilson dramas are the sorts of things you can expect to see on the Arden's stages. The company has produced numerous world premieres and develops new work with its Independence Foundation New Play Showcase program.

Founded in 1988, the Old City-dwelling Arden is one of history-rich Philadelphia's younger troupes, yet it has already earned dozens of Barrymore Awards and numerous other accolades and honors for its top-quality productions. For the kids, Arden has theater training camps and workshops where children and teens can take classes taught by theater professionals.

INTERACT THEATRE COMPANY
The Adrienne, 2030 Sansom Street
215-568-8079 • interacttheater.org

Public Transportation: Good
Handicapped Accessibility: Good
Performances/Programs: Performance schedule is Tuesday–Sunday.
Ticket Prices: $15–$27, discounts available for full-time students and seniors, $10 student Rush tickets sold 10 minutes before the show, group discounts available for parties of 10 or more.
Subscriptions: Four-Show subscriptions $86–$101, Preview subscription $54, senior subscriptions $76–$86, student subscriptions $61–$68. Benefits include free ticket exchanges, free admission to InterAct staged readings, and discounts to other arts organizations in Philadelphia.

LANTERN THEATER COMPANY
St. Stephen's Theater, 10th and Ludlow Streets
215-829-0395 • lanterntheater.org

Public Transportation: Excellent (easily accessible by way of SEPTA buses, subways, trains, and NJ PATCO).
Handicapped Accessibility: Fair/Poor (not wheelchair accessible, but can accommodate other special needs).
Performances/Programs: Performance schedule is Wednesday–Sunday.
Ticket Prices: $20–$50, $20–$40 for seniors and full-time students, group discounts available for parties of 12 or more.
Subscriptions: $72–$160, students and seniors $72–$120. A La Carte (four-ticket flex package) is $128, $120 for students and seniors. Benefits include unlimited ticket exchanges, ticket discounts for friends, and free ticket insurance.

PEOPLE'S LIGHT AND THEATRE COMPANY
39 Conestoga Road, Malvern
610-644-3500 • peopleslight.org

Public Transportation: Fair (a few miles from Malvern and Paoli train stations, cab needed).
Handicapped Accessibility : Yes
Performances/Programs: Performance schedule is Tuesday–Sunday.

Ticket Prices: $29–$48, discounts available for students and seniors, group discounts available for parties of 10 or more.

Subscriptions: Six-Play series $132–$240; Pick Four $92–$164; Family series $80–$86 adult, $50–$56 youth; People's Pass six passes $186–$258.

From the Editors: The People's Light and Theatre Company is a professional company with a distinctly community feel. The productions are performed in two black-box spaces, and guest artists are housed and fed in a renovated 18th-century farmhouse that includes the on-site restaurant Places!

People's Light reaches out to the community through countless educational initiatives, among them adult and youth classes, school residencies and tours, summer programs, community workshops, and the New Voices Ensemble for teens.

The company's onstage offerings include both classical and experimental theater, literary adaptations, family shows, many world premieres of new plays, pieces with an international flavor, and even comic pantomime.

PHILADELPHIA THEATRE COMPANY

Suzanne Roberts Theatre
480 S. Broad Street (Broad and Lombard)
866-985-0420 • philadelphiatheatrecompany.org

Public Transportation: Excellent (easily accessible by SEPTA and PAT-CO).

Handicapped Accessibility: Good

Performances/Programs: Performance schedule is Tuesday–Sunday.

Ticket Prices: $46–$58, $10 student Rush tickets, $25 rear-mezzanine tickets for students, discounts for seniors available, occasional pay-what-you-can performances offered, discounts for groups of 10 or more.

Subscriptions: Four-Show $132–$192 and Four-Pass Flex $136–$196; Young Flex (for 25 and younger) $60. Benefits include free ticket exchanges, free ticket insurance, and discounts for parking, restaurants, shopping, and cultural institutions

From the Editors: When the Philadelphia Theatre Company isn't presenting world premieres by distinguished playwrights and artists like Terrence McNally, David Ives, and Bill Irwin, it's producing the Philly premieres of plays and musicals by equally distinguished writers like Wendy Wasserstein and William Finn, as well as work by emerging talents such as Lynn

Nottage and Gina Gionfriddo. PTC's allegiance is to the American play-wright and it helps to give them voice through the STAGES New Play Reading Series, which has already helped develop over 80 new pieces (some of which were eventually produced on the Philadelphia Theatre stage.) Also at PTC, the Career Development Initiative gives aspiring theater profession-als on-the-job training in production, administration, and other facets of the production process through internships and high-school independent-study projects.

PTC attends to its audience through events, like the LGBT pre-show Night OUT! receptions and Meet-the-Artist panels. A special program known as NEXT: Young Patrons of Philadelphia Theatre Company brings together young professionals aged 26–40 who share a love of the arts and are looking for opportunities to socialize with other PTC supporters (mem-bership to NEXT is $150, which includes a Four-pass Flex subscription). Meanwhile the Community Audience Program, in conjunction with various local social-service organizations, gives people who wouldn't normally be able to go to the theater a chance to enjoy the entire season as a subscriber.

PRINCE MUSIC THEATER
1412 Chestnut Street
215-569-9700 • princemusictheater.org

Public Transportation: Very good
Handicapped Accessibility: Good
Performances/Programs: Performance schedule is generally Tuesday–Sunday.
Ticket Prices: $30–$60, discounts for students, seniors, and groups available.
Subscriptions: Season subscriptions and Flex passes are $90–$250, Four-Show Cabaret season subscriptions $110–$210.

From the Editors: The Prince Music Theater is a cultural district unto itself. Its musicals include faithful revivals of classics and daring new works by brilliant up-and-comers. The Prince also hosts notable film events, such as the Philadelphia International Film Festival and Philly's own Gay and Lesbian Film Festival. Many of the country's finest singers and entertainers come to serenade audiences at Morgan's Cabaret. There's even a kind of amateur hour called Open Stage@the Prince, which allows regular folks to demonstrate their talents both onstage and off.

Founded in 1984 as the American Music Theater Festival, AMTF took over an old movie house in 1999 and opened under the new name, in honor of a titan of American theater, Harold Prince. Prince's own lifelong dedication to working with smart young theater writers and educating aspiring artists is reflected in the theater's programming and through educational initiatives. The Rainbow Connection, for instance, is a program that teaches at-risk middle schoolers to express themselves through the arts and helps them to write their own musical, while the Prince Summer Studio focuses on performance, coaching teens of all levels of experience in singing and dancing during one-week sessions that culminate in a live performance recorded on CD for the participants.

SOCIETY HILL PLAYHOUSE
507 South 8th Street
215-923-0210 • societyhillplayhouse.org

Public Transportation: Fair (11-minute walk from Lombard South Station).
Handicapped Accessibility: No
Performances/Programs: Performance schedule varies, but mainly Wednesday–Sunday for mainstage.
Ticket Prices: Vary, since different types of productions play here, but around $45 for mainstage and $20 for Red Room shows; group rates available.

WALNUT STREET THEATRE
825 Walnut Street (corner of 9th and Walnut)
215-574-3550 • walnutstreettheater.org

Public Transportation: Very good
Handicapped Accessibility: Good
Performances/Programs: Performance schedule is Tuesday–Sunday.
Ticket Prices: $10–$70, day-of-show tickets $35–$40 for all mainstage production, $10 and $30 standby tickets also available, discounts for people 24 or younger, military, and members of the entertainment industry, discounts available for groups of 15 or more.
Subscriptions: Five-Play subscriptions $85–$195, $130–$330 for opening night, $90–$130 for seniors and anyone 24 or younger.

WILMA THEATRE
265 South Broad Street
215-546-7824 • wilmatheater.org

Public Transportation: Very good
Handicapped Accessibility: Good
Performances/Programs: Performance schedule is Tuesday–Sunday.
Ticket Prices: $39–$60, half-price Rush tickets sold 30 minutes before curtain, $10 student Rush tickets sold on day of performance, discounts available for seniors.
Subscriptions: Four-Show $116–$178, Four-Show Flex $148 (for 35-and-under patrons $108). Subscription discounts available for students, seniors, and educators. Benefits include free ticket exchanges and ticket insurance. Subscribers save over 25%.

From the Editors: The Wilma Theater is thoroughly unpredictable. Headed by the dynamic duo Blanka and Jiri Zizka, the Wilma isn't interested in doing things the easy way (i.e., producing the latest four-person kitchen-sink drama that played to acclaim in New York). This theater's mission is to present theater as an art form, but that doesn't mean it's all pretentious and academic. The same season that sports a pair of Caryl Churchill plays (one new, one old) also has a Ken Ludwig farce; in another season, a fascinating Tom Stoppard play is followed by one of Sarah Ruhl's whimsical bittersweet works. New plays and original multimedia-heavy pieces are mixed in with dramas by guys like Arthur Miller, Athol Fugard, and Bertolt Brecht.

CHORAL ARTS SOCIETY
215-240-6417 • choralarts.com

Venues: Various locations in and around the Philadelphia area.
Public Transportation: Depends on venue.
Handicapped Accessibility: Most venues are accessible; call venue management for details.
Performances/Programs: Three programs per season, some with multiple performances.
Ticket Prices: General admission $25, students $12.
Membership: Not available but donations are accepted and greatly appreciated.

PHILADELPHIA ORCHESTRA
The Kimmel Center for the Performing Arts
Broad and Spruce Streets
215-893-1999 • philorch.org

Other Venue: The Mann Center for the Performing Arts, 5201 Parkside Avenue.

Public Transportation: Yes (both the Kimmel Center and the Mann are accessible via subway, PATCO, and SEPTA bus lines).

Performances/ Programs: Approximately 110 per season.

Ticket Prices: $10–$153; $10 student understudy tickets are available online and $8 student Rush tickets can be purchased at the box office.

Group Discounts: Groups of 10 or more get group discounts and all processing fees are waived.

Other Discounts: The Philadelphia Orchestra makes PECO Power Hour seats available for $10 at the Kimmel Center box office 5:30–6:30 p.m. the day of each subscription concert (11:30 a.m.–12:30 p.m. for 2 p.m. performances).

Subscriptions: Themed collections include Masterworks, Connoisseur, Odyssey, Celebrations, Weekday, Weekend, and Matinée. There are also Access, Monumental Works, Great Pianists, Chamber Music, and Family. The Create Your Own collection allows subscribers to choose six or more concerts. Subscribers are eligible for unlimited ticket exchanges. The Orchestra also offers its patrons the opportunity to join the eZseat Club, which allows members to buy as many concerts as they wish and receive a 25% discount off single tickets; full subscriber benefits are included in this club, including online exchanges. eZseat costs $50 for basic membership, $75 for premium; it's $25 for students.

Membership: Friends Circle membership begins at $75. Benefits include two open rehearsal tickets, a Philadelphia Orchestra membership card, and 10% discounts at Applause, the gift shop at the Kimmel Center. Members also receive discounts to many nearby shops and restaurants, as well as pre-paid discount parking.

Activities for Children: Hosted by award-winning storyteller Charlotte Blake Alston and featuring Philadelphia Orchestra musicians, Sound All Around concerts are a fun interactive way to introduce your three- to five-year-old to the instruments of the orchestra. Named as *Philadelphia* magazine's Best of Philly Best Music Program in 2007.

From the Editors: Founded in 1900, the Philadelphia Orchestra is regarded as one of the leading orchestras in the world. Its newly appointed chief conductor and artistic adviser Charles Dutoit follows in a rich tradition of excellent musical advisors including Fritz Scheel, Carl Pohlig, Leopold Stokowski, Eugene Ormandy, Riccardo Muti, Wolfgang Sawallisch, and Christoph Eschenbach. In addition to the regular series, the Philadelphia Orchestra also offers chamber music and family concerts suitable for children ages 6–12. Subscribers to Family concerts receive *The Eighth Note* newsletter, filled with information and activities to help prepare for each concert, including special listening sections, interviews with guest artists and musicians, games, and puzzles.

Before every classical subscription concert are free pre-concert Conversations, where various artists discuss the evening's program. In addition, after many subscription concerts are free Postlude concerts, which feature orchestra members or guest artists. Multiple free concerts are also given throughout the year by the Philadelphia Orchestra through the Free Neighborhood Concert Program.

PHILADELPHIA SINGERS
215-751-9494 • philadelphiasingers.org

Venues: Various locations in and around the Philadelphia area.
Public Transportation: Depends on venue.
Handicapped Accessibility: Most venues are accessible; call venue management for details.
Performances/Programs: Four concerts per season.
Ticket Prices: Varies by program and concert venue.
Subscriptions: Available in three or four concert seasons $80–$156.
Membership: Available from $50–$10,000+. Depending upon donation amount, member benefits include program listing, rehearsal and pre-concert lecture passes, and invites to dinners and receptions.

From the Editors: Founded by the late Michael Korn in 1972, The Philadelphia Singers is now under the musical direction of David Hayes. In addition to its performances each season (which have included Philly premieres of works by major composers like Poulenc, Britten, Gershwin, Steve Reich, and John Adams), the Singers are also involved with musical education programs and frequently commissions new work. The ensemble holds the belief that art can advance individuals and communities and has made it its mission to provide Philadelphia with quality classical choral performances. Annually, the chorus reaches over 40,000 people through its live concerts.

OPERA COMPANY OF PHILADELPHIA
The Academy of Music, 240 South Broad Street
215-732-8400 • operaphilly.com

Other Venue: The Perelman Theater, 260 S. Broad Street
Public Transportation: Very good (easily accessible by Metro and PATCO service).
Handicapped Accessibility: Good (both venues).
Performances/Programs: Five-six productions per season with multiple performances of each.
Ticket Prices: Prices vary depending on date, time, performances, and seats.

From the Editors: The Philadelphia Opera Company has been this city's primary opera company since its founding in 1975. The Company seeks to blend the traditional with the contemporary and to create new traditions in the opera world. The Opera has a serious commitment to producing new American operas and tries to premiere as many American works as possible.

The Philadelphia Opera Company has long understood that young opera talent should be nurtured and given opportunities to perform, and has cast these bright young stars along with internationally recognized opera stars.

CHRIS' JAZZ CAFÉ
1421 Sansom Street
215-568-3131 • chrisjazzcafe.com

Public Transportation: Good
Handicapped Accessibility: Good
Performances/Programs: Approximately 500 performances per year. Live music played Monday–Saturday, often several performances per night.
Ticket Prices: $2–$10. Students often receive discounted admission for the 10 p.m. sets.

ORTLIEB'S JAZZ HAUS
847 N 3rd Street
215-922-1035 • ortliebsjazzhaus.com

Public Transportation: Poor
Handicapped Accessibility: No
Performances/Programs: Approximately 250 performances per year.
Live music performed Tuesday–Sunday.
Ticket Prices: $5–$20 on Friday and Saturday.

GERALD VEASLEY'S JAZZ BASE
Sheraton Reading Crown Hotel
1741 Papermill Road, Reading
610-777-2310 • geraldveasleysjazzbase.com

Public Transportation: Poor
Handicapped Accessibility: Good
Performances/Programs: Approximately 50 performances given per
year.
Ticket Prices: $8–$30

THE PHILADELPHIA CLEF CLUB OF THE PERFORMING ARTS
736–38 South Broad Street
215-893-9912 • clefclub.org

Public Transportation: Poor
Handicapped Accessibility: Good
Performances/Programs: Approximately 50 performances and programs per year.
Ticket Prices: $10–$50. Many shows feature discounts for children under 12.
Educational/Community Outreach: The Clef Club provides a number
of educational opportunities for children and adults with summer camps
and master classes throughout the year.

From the Editors: Philadelphia has a long and storied history when it
comes to jazz. Many of the great players of the 20th century cut their teeth in
Philly's numerous gritty clubs, many of which haven't existed for 20 years.
One of the surviving venues from this era that thrives today is the Clef Club
of Jazz and Performing Arts. The Clef Club was founded in 1966 by black

members of AF of M, the musicians union, who had been denied membership to the segregated Local #77. The local union became the longest surviving Black Musician's Union in the U.S., with members including the likes of Nina Simone, John Coltrane, Grover Washington, Jr., and Dizzy Gillespie. The Clef Club was conceived as the local social club for the union, but quickly gained a wild popularity with local jazz fans clamoring to see the big celebrities who often graced the place. The union even created a B membership for out-of-town musicians and the locals who simply loved jazz.

After moving locations and redefining its mission, the Clef Club has become an important center of education for jazz in the U.S., collecting a plethora of jazz relics and oral histories for the benefit of generations of jazz lovers. The Club still hosts a variety of concerts that highlight not only the great history of jazz in Philadelphia, but also the impact that jazz has had on a variety of other disciplines.

KORESH DANCE COMPANY
Suzanne Roberts Theater, 480 S. Broad Street
215-751-0959 • koreshdance.org

Public Transportation: Good (accessible by SEPTA Route C bus, Broad Street Subway or PATCO).

Handicapped Accessibility: Good

Performances/Programs: Koresh is usually on tour throughout the country, but generally performs one or two programs a year in Philadelphia. Each program runs about four performances.

Ticket Prices: Tickets are handled directly by presenting venues. Prices generally range from $40 to $60. The Suzanne Roberts Theater offers happy-hour student Rush tickets for $10.

Group Discounts: The Roberts Theater also offers discounts to groups of 10 or more.

Membership: Basic annual donor fees start at $25. This includes a subscription to the Koresh online newsletter, recognition in company performance programs, and invitations to special company events.

PENNSYLVANIA BALLET
Philadelphia Academy of Music, 260 South Broad Street
215-551-7000 • paballet.org

Other Venues: Merriam Theater at the University of the Arts (located next to the Academy of Music).

Public Transportation: Good

Handicapped Accessibility: Good

Performances/Programs: Five programs a year, plus the annual *Nutcracker*. Each program runs one week with about six performances. The *Nutcracker* runs for about three weeks.

Ticket Prices: $20–$100; student Rush tickets available for $15 one hour prior to all performances except the *Nutcracker*.

Group Discounts: Groups of 10 or more may save up to 50% off ticket prices depending on the size of the group.

Subscriptions: Subscriptions are available for all five programs or can be customized to include only three or four programs. Discounted series prices are available to seniors 65 and older, as well as college and graduate students. A Family Matinée series is also available. Tickets are nonrefundable. Subscribers may exchange tickets. Other benefits include free replacement tickets, priority seat selection, discounts at local businesses, invitations to parties, and admission to the ballet's lecture series.

Membership: Donor fees start at $75 and include admission for two to a dress rehearsal and a copy of the company newsletter.

Educational/Community Outreach: Always active in the local communities, Pennsylvania Ballet has put significant resources into creative programming initiatives to draw more audiences into the ballet. The company's pre-professional company, Pennsylvania Ballet II, is an especially active component of these programs. This eight-dancer group is led by a former Pennsylvania Ballet principal dancer and schedules 25–30 free performances each year in schools, senior centers, and community arts centers.

From the Editors: Pennsylvania Ballet was founded in 1963 with the help of a Ford Foundation initiative to set up and develop professional regional ballet companies. Enjoying immediate success both in New York and on national tour, it became the first ballet company in the country to offer year-round employment to its dancers. Pennsylvania Ballet has continued to enjoy critical success as it has grown to a total of 40 full-time performers serving audiences throughout the tri-state region.

For regular audience members, the Family Matinée performances include fun-filled afternoon activities for children and opportunities to get company dancers' autographs. Kids 4–12 can also become a member of Kidz Corps. Membership is $40 and includes a membership card, T-shirt, a birthday card signed by a company dancer, and three specially planned events throughout the year. Adults may also enjoy an additional subscription to the Prologue Lecture series for $150 on Tuesday evenings which includes a light dinner buffet.

RITZ AT THE BOURSE
400 Ranstead Street
215-925-7900
landmarktheaters.com/market/Philadelphia/RitzatBourse.htm

Public Transportation: Yes (accessible by 2nd and 5th Street subway stops).

Handicapped Accessibility: Good

Performances/Programs: A blend of mainstream Hollywood and art-house films.

Ticket Prices: Monday–Friday all shows before 5 p.m. are $6. Monday, Tuesday, and Thursday all shows after 5 p.m. are $8.50; Friday shows after 5 p.m. are $9. Saturday, Sunday, and holidays, it's $9 for all shows after the first matinée show ($6.75); Wednesday all shows are $6. Seniors (65+) are $6 any time except Saturdays and holidays. Students are $6.75 any time except Saturdays and holidays.

PHILADELPHIA LIVE ARTS FESTIVAL AND PHILLY FRINGE
215-413-1318 • livearts-fringe.org

Venues: Various public venues throughout Philadelphia.

Public Transportation: Good (accessible via Amtrak, NJ Transit, SEPTA rail, subway and buses).

Handicapped Accessibility: Good

Performances/Programs: This annual festival, held at the end of the summer in various venues throughout Philly, is actually two festivals in one: the Live Arts, in which dance and theater companies from all over are invited to participate; and the unfiltered Philly Fringe, in which all local groups are welcome to participate.

Ticket Prices: $10–$25. Many events are free. Receive a discount when you buy tickets to two or more different shows at one time. Discounts are available for students and people 25 and under.

Group Discounts: Groups of 10 or more are eligible for discounts.

Subscriptions: The most popular option is the All-Access Pass ($650), which gets you and a friend admission to every show.

PITTSBURGH, PENNSYLVANIA

Steeltown, U.S.A, has long enjoyed the educational and cultural patronage of wealthy industrialists, such as Andrew Carnegie, and the city's visual and performing arts reflect this tradition. Although heavy industry is no longer a part of everyday life here, the city boasts a large number of working professionals who also greatly contribute to the city's artistic life.

ARTS INFO

Pittsburgh City Paper (pittsburghcitypaper.ws)—Alternative weekly arts paper with comprehensive arts and entertainment coverage.

Pittsburgh Post-Gazette (post-gazette.com)—Pittsburgh's major daily newspaper has a strong commitment to local arts.

pgharts.org—The Pittsburgh Cultural Trust.

pittsburghlive.com—Pittsburgh events guide and coverage operated by the *Pittsburgh Tribune*.

proartstickets.org—Info and ticketing for arts events in Pittsburgh.

THE ARTS

THE CARNEGIE MUSEUM OF ART (THE CMOA)
4400 Forbes Avenue
412-622-3131 • cmoa.org

Public Transportation: Poor
Handicapped Accessibility: Good
Hours: Tuesday, Wednesday, Friday–Saturday 10 a.m.–5 p.m., Thursday 10 a.m.–8 p.m., Sunday noon–5 p.m., closed Monday and major holidays.
Admission: $15, seniors (65+) $12, students and children (3–18) $11, members and children under 3 free.
Tours: Docent-led tours, ranging from one to two hours in length, and self-guided tours are available for an additional charge.
Membership: Individual membership is $75 and includes unlimited general admission for one year at Carnegie Museum of Art, Carnegie Museum of Natural History, the Andy Warhol Museum, and Carnegie Science Center (including SportsWorks and laser shows). Also included are general-admission privileges to more than 260 participating science centers worldwide, invitations to members-only events and exhibition previews, and discounts on classes, camps, standard IMAX films, lectures, and social events. Senior membership ($50) and Dual/Family memberships (prices vary) are also available.
Other Benefits: Premium membership ($200) includes all benefits listed above, plus reciprocal privileges at select art and natural history museums.

From the Editors: The Heinz Architectural Center underscores the CMOA's bent toward the collection, study, and exhibition of architectural drawings and sculpture. The Center itself provides a reason for those with architectural interests to visit; the edifice combines Classicism and Modernism, alluding to the Carnegie Institute without mirroring it. It also houses its own galleries and a study room.

The Hall of Architecture holds the largest collection of plaster casts of architectural masterpieces in America and is one of the three largest collections of its kind in the world. Other areas of distinction include: contemporary art and multimedia; American art from the 19th century; European and American decorative art; and French Impressionist and Post-Impressionist paintings.

ANDY WARHOL MUSEUM (THE WARHOL)
117 Sandusky Street
412-237-8300 • warhol.org

Public Transportation: Very good (easily accessible via Port Authority).
Handicapped Accessibility: Good
Hours: Sunday, Tuesday–Thursday, Saturday 10 a.m.–5 p.m., Friday 10 a.m.–10 p.m., closed Monday.
Admission: $15, seniors (55+) $9, students and children (3–18) $8, children under 3 and members of the Carnegie Museums of Pittsburgh Free; Fridays are half-price 5–10 p.m.
Tours: One-hour tours are available on a regular basis and offer an introduction to the art and life of Andy Warhol.
Membership: Individual membership is $75 and includes unlimited general admission for one year at Carnegie Museum of Art, Carnegie Museum of Natural History, the Andy Warhol Museum, and Carnegie Science Center (including SportsWorks and laser shows). Also included are general-admission privileges to more than 260 participating science centers worldwide, invitations to members-only events and exhibition previews, and discounts on classes, camps, standard IMAX films, lectures, and social events. Senior membership ($50) and Dual/Family memberships (prices vary) are also available.

From the Editors: Warhol was a Pittsburgh native who participated in almost every art form and was highly eccentric. His avant-garde social life was legion, but as a practicing Catholic, he lived with his mother until her death. The eclectic Warhol Museum surveys all his work: paintings, silkscreens, cartoons, photographs made in photo booths, and films, including all the celebrities encompassed therein. Every Friday night is Good Friday with half-price admission, dances, lectures, and concerts, plus a cash bar. On weekends there are special activities for children.

CITY THEATRE
1300 Bingham Street
412-431-CITY (2489) • citytheatrecompany.org

Public Transportation: Good
Handicapped Accessibility: Good
Performances/Programs: Performance schedule is Tuesday–Sunday.
Ticket Prices: $35–$40, students $15 and $20, senior discounts available.

Subscriptions: Six-Play $96–$252, Flex passes: Eight-Pack $248, Six-Pack $198.

From the Editors: City Theatre is the place to go for contemporary plays by writers new, established, and just plain hip. Everything from the edgy and odd (*Night of the Living Dead: The Opera*) to the traditional and heartwarming (*Tuesdays with Morrie*) has been seen on City's two stages. Christopher Durang, Jeffrey Hatcher, and Adam Rapp have all had premieres here, and City Theatre is developing more new work through its MOMENTUM festival, which features play readings along with writers' panels and workshops. Budding writers are nurtured through the comprehensive Young Playwrights program, which includes teacher training, in-school workshops, a contest, and a festival. City Theatre also gets kids involved in writing through its Playmakers program, which recently has been teaching students to create their own radio plays.

PITTSBURGH CIVIC LIGHT OPERA (PITTSBURGH CLO)
The Benedum Center, Liberty and 7th Street
412-281-3973 • pittsburghclo.org

Public Transportation: Excellent
Handicapped Accessibility: Good
Performances/ Programs: Performance schedule is Tuesday–Sunday.
Ticket Prices: $20–$60, college students $12, college faculty/staff $14.
Group Discounts: Discounts available for groups of 10 or more.
Subscriptions: Six-Show $111–$327; Three-Show $55.50–$163.50, CLO Cabaret $100–$220. Benefits include free exchanges, reserved parking, ticket insurance, discounts to local restaurants, discounts on additional CLO tickets for family and friends, and a subscriber standby policy: If you can't make a show, you can take your unused ticket to a future performance a half-hour before the show to get any available second-tier seat.

PITTSBURGH IRISH AND CLASSICAL THEATRE
Charity Randall and Henry Heymann Theatres in the
Stephen Foster Memorial, 4301 Forbes Avenue
412-561-6000 • picttheatre.org

Public Transportation: Good
Handicapped Accessibility: Good

Performances/Programs: Performance schedule is Tuesday–Sunday.

Ticket Prices: $33–$47, $17 tickets for anyone 25 and under, discounts available for seniors.

Subscriptions: Season subscriptions are $180–$240.

PITTSBURGH MUSICAL THEATER
327 South Main Street
412-456-6666 • pittsburghmusicals.com

Other Venues: Byham Theater, 101 Sixth Street; New Hazlett Theater, Allegheny Square E.

Public Transportation: Good (easily accessible by bus).

Handicapped Accessibility: Good

Performances/Programs: Performance schedule is Thursday–Sunday.

Ticket Prices: $23–$39, half-price student tickets available, discounts available for groups of 10 or more, New Hazlett Theater Series single tickets $10–$20.

Subscriptions: Byham Theater Four-Show $60–$99, students/kids $30; New Hazlett Theater $30, students/kids $15.

PITTSBURGH PUBLIC THEATER
O'Reilly Theater, 621 Penn Avenue
412-316-1600 • ppt.org

Public Transportation: Very good

Handicapped Accessibility: Good

Performances/Programs: Performance schedule is Tuesday–Sunday.

Ticket Prices: $30–$60, $15 tickets available for full-time students or anyone 26 and younger, seniors get tickets for half-price one hour before the show, discounts available for groups of 10 or more, no ticket exchanges for non-subscribers.

Subscriptions: Six-Show $126–$267, Six-voucher Flex plans $258–$309. Benefits include ticket exchanges and dining/shopping discounts.

MENDELSSOHN CHOIR
Heinz Hall, 600 Penn Avenue
412-926-2488 • themendelssohn.org

Public Transportation: Varies by venue.
Handicapped Accessibility: Most venues accessible; contact venue management for details.
Performances/Programs: Three-four subscriber programs, plus numerous appearances with the Pittsburgh Symphony and nationwide.
Ticket Prices: Varies by venue and program.
Subscriptions: Not listed, contact via website for details.
Membership: Available from $100–$10,000+.

THE PITTSBURGH CAMERATA
412-421-5884 • pittsburghcamerata.org

Venues: Sixth Presbyterian Church, 1688 Murray Ave.; St. Andrew's Episcopal Church, 5801 Hampton Street, Highland Park; Mt. Lebanon United Lutheran Church, 975 Washington Rd., Mt. Lebanon
Public Transportation: Varies by venue.
Handicapped Accessibility: Most venues accessible, contact venue management for details.
Performances/Programs: Three programs per season, multiple performances of each.
Ticket Prices: Adults $20, students $10; kids attend all concerts free.
Subscriptions: Students $20, seniors $40, and adults $50.
Membership: Not available, but donations are accepted and greatly appreciated.

PITTSBURGH SYMPHONY (PSO)
Heinz Hall, 600 Penn Avenue
412-392-4900 • pittsburghsymphony.org

Handicapped Accessibility: Good
Performances/Programs: 162 per season
Ticket Prices: Prices range from $15–$122.50. Student and senior Rush tickets are available two hours before most performances.
Group Discounts: Groups of 10 or more receive up to 25% off regular ticket prices for Bank of New York Mellon Grand Classics and PNC Pittsburgh Symphony Pops performances.

Subscriptions: Subscriptions are based on location and repertoire, beginning with the four-performance Grand Classic series and expanding to include packages with up to 22 concerts. Classic, Pops, Chamber Music, and Family subscriptions are among the PSO's most popular offerings. Student subscriptions are available and cost only $12 per concert. Senior Sunday-matinée subscriptions are offered at 50% off the regular ticket price.

Membership: An Orchestra Club membership ($50) entitles members to receive *Noteworthy,* the PSO's patron newsletter with the latest on orchestral programs, current donor events, behind-the-scenes information, a limited-edition donor CD featuring the Pittsburgh Symphony Orchestra and an invitation to the Equitable Resources Donor Appreciation and Community Side-by-Side Concert.

Other Benefits: At higher donation levels, benefits include one private music lesson with a PSO musician, as well as the opportunity to attend a private salon event featuring the PSO Composer of the Year (for 2008: John Adams).

From the Editors: The Pittsburgh Symphony began in 1898 under the direction of Victor Herbert. Herbert, well-known for his hugely popular comic operas, was the perfect director for an orchestra that intended to forge a connection with a varied audience of diverse music lovers, and continues to do so to this day.

Throughout the season, the Pittsburgh Symphony offers not just stellar performances, but also vibrant learning opportunities for the community. Teaming with public libraries in the area, Unlocking the Classics lectures are held throughout the year at various locations in the community to discuss the symphony and upcoming performance repertoire. Fiddlesticks Family Concerts, hosted by a "fiddlin' feline," is a fun way for young children (3–8) to experience classical music. The Symphony keeps its concerts accessible with great student and senior subscription rates (seniors 50% off; students $12/concert). As an extra convenience, local university students, staff, and faculty are able to purchase their tickets on campus.

PITTSBURGH OPERA
The Benedum Center, 7th Street and Penn Avenue
412-281-0912 • pittsburghopera.org

Public Transportation: Excellent
Handicapped Accessibility: Good
Performances/Programs: Five productions per season with multiple performances of each.

Ticket Prices: $10–$140. Half price student Rush tickets available. Deeply discounted CheapSeats available for students, faculty, and staff at selected local colleges.

Group Discounts: Discounts available for groups of 6 or more.

Subscriptions: Five-opera ($64.50–$584.50), Four-opera ($42–$562), and Three-opera ($31.50–$421.50) subscriptions available, with prices varying depending on seats selected. Subscriber benefits include free ticket exchanges and 15% discount on additional single tickets.

Membership: Available from $50–$50,000+. Depending on donation amount, donor benefits include program listing, drink vouchers, dress rehearsal passes, ticket discounts, and party invites.

From the Editors: The Pittsburgh Opera was founded in 1939, and throughout its history, the company has featured such legends as Luciano Pavarotti, Beverly Sills, and Joan Sutherland in its productions. And with the well-respected Pittsburgh Opera Resident Artist Program, the Opera is seeing to it that new generations of singers are being trained to become the stars of tomorrow. The Pittsburgh Opera also runs a number of other educational programs, such as High School Apprentices (career discussions and coaching sessions for young opera hopefuls) and Opera Opportunity reduced-price tickets for students.

PITTSBURGH JAZZ SOCIETY
Rhythm House Café, 3020 Washington Pike, Bridgeville
412-343-9555 • pittsburghjazz.org

Public Transportation: Poor
Handicapped Accessibility: Good
Performances/Programs: Approximately 60 performances per year. Sunday Night Jazz Concerts at Rhythm House Café are at 7 p.m.
Ticket Prices: No cover

MCG JAZZ
1815 Metropolitan Street
412-322-0800 • mcgjazz.org

Public Transportation: Poor
Handicapped Accessibility: Good
Performances/Programs: Approximately 10–15 performances per season. (Sept.–March)

Ticket Prices: From $30–$50. Student snd senior discounts apply for certain shows.

Subscriptions: Subscriptions can be purchased for specific days in groups of 4 or 8 concerts for any number of tickets per concert. Returns can be made through the box office depending on availability of seats.

Membership: Membership at MCG provides members with discounts on CDs and special invitations to MCG member events.

From the Editors: MCG Jazz, a subsidiary of the arts foundation Manchester Craftsmen's Guild, has been working for more than 20 years to provide a forum for world-class entertainment focusing on the incredible wealth of jazz history in the United States. The Guild was originally conceived by Bill Strickland and the caliber of talent that MCG brings in rivals any international venue. Many of the recordings made at the venue have been nominated for or won Grammys. In the 2008–2009 season alone, the headliners included Chuck Mangione, Toshiko Akiyoshi, Spyro Gyra, Take 6, and Kurt Elling.

PITTSBURGH BALLET THEATRE (PBT)
Benedum Center for the Performing Arts
719 Liberty Avenue
412-281-0360 • pbt.org

Other Venue: Byham Theater, 101 Sixth Street.

Public Transportation: Poor

Handicapped Accessibility: Good

Performances/Programs: Four programs each year, plus the annual *Nutcracker*. Each program has three performances over one weekend. The *Nutcracker* runs for about two weeks in December.

Ticket Prices: $20–$90. Students can buy $10 tickets to student matinées. University students can also purchase discounted tickets through drop boxes on select campuses.

Group Discounts: Groups of 10 or more receive a 20% discount. Groups of 50 or more receive up to a 30% discount. Motor coach and college groups receive up to a 30% discount.

Subscriptions: Subscriptions are available for three, four, or five shows. Prices vary according to seating area selection. Benefits include guaranteed parking at Theater Square Garage and advance ticket sales notice.

Membership: Donor fees start at $50 and include a 10% discount at the PBT Boutique.

From the Editors: Pittsburgh Ballet Theatre began over 30 years ago as a small theater-playhouse company. As it's grown, it has toured the country extensively, as well as Canada, Puerto Rico, and the Dominican Republic. It's home to a reputable company of 30 professional dancers and a nationally recognized training school.

Pittsburgh Ballet Theatre offers ample opportunity for audiences to connect and learn more about the work it's presenting. These include Insights, informal talks with guest artists held prior to performances, and Afterthoughts, post-performance discussions with company staff and artists. Subscribers may be interested in Talks with Terry on Sunday afternoons at 1 p.m., informal conversations held in the theater (just prior to subscriber matinées) and hosted by Artistic Director Terrence Orr. For families, the Family Pointe is a pre-performance program built to entertain children ages 5 to 14. Additionally, Pittsburgh Ballet holds occasional open rehearsals on Wednesday evenings with cocktails, hors d'oeuvres, and a chance to interact with the company's artists. See the website for dates and times.

HARRIS THEATER
809 Liberty Avenue
412-682-4111 • pghfilmmakers.org/about/harris.html

Public Transportation: Good (accessible by Wood Street Light Rail stop).
Handicapped Accessibility: Good
Performances/Programs: An eclectic mix of foreign and American independent cinema, as well as programs of themed films.
Ticket Prices: Vary based on program.

From the Editors: The Harris Theater, the first Pittsburgh movie theater to show art films, is owned by the Pittsburgh Cultural Trust and has been operated by the non-profit Pittsburgh Filmmakers for nearly 15 years. Located on Liberty Avenue in the historic district, the 200-seat Harris is open seven days a week.

REGENT SQUARE THEATER
1035 South Braddock Avenue, Swissvale
412-682-4111 • pghfilmmakers.org

Public Transportation: Good (accessible by public bus lines)
Handicapped Accessibility: Good

Performances/Programs: In addition to independent film from around the world, the Regent is known for hosting a Sunday-night series of classic films.

Ticket Prices: Vary based on program.

From the Editors: Like the Harris Theater, the Regent Square Theater is also run by the Pittsburgh Filmmakers. One of those rare, large, single-screen venues, the Regent Square shows a mix of independent films, classics, and foreign movies.

For information on Buffalo, New York,
visit go-artsamerica.com.

SAN DIEGO, CALIFORNIA

California's second largest city, San Diego is well-known for its temperate climate, geographical variety, and plentiful pristine beaches. San Diego's arts and culture community is equally vibrant and boasts terrific museums, regional theaters and music venues.

ARTS INFO AND DISCOUNTS

San Diego CityBeat (sdcitybeat.com)—Alternative weekly paper.

entertainment.signonsandiego.com—San Diego arts and entertainment guide from the *San Diego Union Tribune*.

sandiegoartandsol.com—San Diego's official guide to arts and culture.

sandiegoperforms.com/ARTSTIX—Half-price tickets for San Diego arts events.

goldstar.com—Excellent choice for both info and discounts.

THE ARTS

MUSEUM OF CONTEMPORARY ART, SAN DIEGO (MCSAD)
1100 and 1001 Kettner Boulevard
858-454-3541 • mcasd.org

Other Venue: Museum of Contemporary Art, La Jolla

Public Transportation: Good (downtown locations can be reached on the Blue Line; La Jolla is easily accessible via SD Bus Route 30).

Handicapped Accessibility: Good

Hours: Thursday–Tuesday 11 a.m.–5 p.m., closed Wednesday. Open the third Thursday of each month 11 a.m.–7 p.m.

Admission: General admission $10, seniors and military $5, MCASD members and visitors under 25 free. Admission is valid for seven days at all MCASD locations. Free museum admission is on the third Thursday from 5 to 7 p.m.

Basic Tour: Public tours are free at all MCASD locations on the third Thursday of the month at 6 p.m. and on weekends at 2 p.m.

Membership: Active (Dual/Household) memberships range from $75 to $149 and include personalized membership cards for two; free unlimited admission to all MCASD locations including the Jacobs Building, 1001 Kettner, and La Jolla; preview mailings, exclusive invitations, and free or reduced admission to all museum events throughout the year; 15% discounts at both museum stores; 10% discounts at the Museum Café in La Jolla; and a subscription to *VIEW*, MCASD's award-winning quarterly newsletter. Members also enjoy reciprocal membership at numerous museums nationwide. Membership is entirely tax deductible and discounted senior, military, artist, student, and educator memberships are offered for just $35.

From the Editors: One museum at two locations reflects all angles and edges of contemporary art. The original museum (in La Jolla) began in a community art center in 1941 and now the museum has a permanent endowment fund of more than $40 million, with an operating budget of $6 million. Besides being filled with innovative engaging art, both the downtown and La Jolla museum buildings themselves are worth a visit.

SAN DIEGO MUSEUM OF ART (SDMART)
1450 El Prado, Balboa Park
619-232-7931 • sdmart.org

Public Transportation: Good
Handicapped Accessibility: Good
Hours: Tuesday, Thursday–Saturday 10 a.m.–5 p.m., Wednesday noon–5 p.m., Sunday 1–5 p.m.
Admission: $12, senior and military $9, students $8, youths (6–17) $4.50, members and children under 5 free. During the month of February, pick up a free Museum Month Pass at any San Diego County Macy's and receive half-off admission at 33 participating San Diego County museums, including SDMA.
Tours: Daily tours are available; schedules are located in the rotunda. When not previously scheduled for a group tour, docents may be available to give tours of the museum's collections and special exhibitions. In addition, tours led by Teen Art Guides (aka TAGGERs) are available for certain special exhibitions.
Membership: Individual membership is $45. All members receive free unlimited admission; four guest passes (valid year-round, except Art Alive); discounts on classes, concerts, lectures, and films; use of the Art Reference Library; the opportunity to join specific organizations; participation in the museum's international-travel program; free admission to Culture & Cocktails; and an invitation to members-only annual director's lecture. Student/educator and senior discounts are also available.
Other Benefits: Reciprocal membership to other art institutions is available at the Friend level ($175) or above.

From the Editors: Situated in downtown's Balboa Park (the home of the 1915–1916 Panama-Pacific Exhibition), the San Diego Museum of Art is the fortunate recipient of the largesse of several local families, most notably the Timkens, who put up the funds for the original building, and the Putnum sisters (Irene, Anne, and Amy), who donated more than two-thirds of the museum's vast European collection. On the walls are paintings by Spanish artists Murillo, Zurbarán, Cotán, Ribera, and El Greco; Italian masters Giorgione, Giotto, Veronese, Luini, and Canaletto; as well as Rubens, Hals, and van Dyck from the Northern European School. Besides many exciting visiting exhibitions, there is also a large Southern Asian collection and many drawings by the 19th-century Parisian giant Toulouse-Lautrec.

TIMKEN MUSEUM OF ART
1500 El Prado, Balboa Park
619-239-5548 • timkenmuseum.org

Public Transportation: Very good (the Metropolitan Transit bus takes you within walking distance).

Handicapped Accessibility: Good

Hours: Tuesday–Saturday 10 a.m.–4:30 p.m., Sunday 1:30–4 p.m., closed Monday and the month of September.

Admission: Free

Basic Tour: Docent-led tours are offered Tuesday–Thursday 10 a.m.–noon, and every third Tuesday 1–3 p.m. Tours are 30–60 minutes in length.

Membership: Colleague membership ($250–$499) is the ground-level membership at the Timken and includes the museum newsletter, invitations to members' previews and Timken special events, 15% discounts on all Timken merchandise, and access to the Balboa Arts Conservation Center.

From the Editors: Another Balboa Park art museum built with Timken money and filled with European art by the Putnum sisters, here you'll see masterpieces by many 16th- 19th-century Spanish, Dutch, Flemish, French, and Italian artists, as well as some American art and Russian icons.

CYGNET THEATRE COMPANY
Rolando/College Theatre, 6663 El Cajon Boulevard, Suite N
619-337-1525 • cygnettheatre.com

Other Venue: Old Town Theatre, 4040 Twiggs St.

Public Transportation: Good

Handicapped Accessibility: Good

Performances/Programs: Performance schedule is Wednesday–Sunday.

Ticket Prices: $22–$48, $4 discounts available for seniors, students, and military, shows occasionally available on Goldstar.com.

Subscriptions: Six-Play $84–$150, Five-Play $75–$135, Four-Play $68–$120, and Flex $126–$150, subscription discounts available for seniors and military.

DIVERSIONARY THEATRE
4545 Park Boulevard #101
619-220-0097 • diversionary.org

Public Transportation: Good
Handicapped Accessibility: Good
Performances/Programs: Performance schedule is Thursday–Monday.
Ticket Prices: $20–$35, $4 discounts for seniors, students, and military, $10 student Rush tickets sold one hour before curtain, some discounts available for Pride Pass holders, discounts available for groups of 10 or more, shows available on Goldstar.com.
Subscriptions: Season subscriptions $116–$230, discounted for seniors.

LA JOLLA PLAYHOUSE
2910 La Jolla Village Drive, La Jolla
858-550-1010 • lajollaplayhouse.org

Public Transportation: Good
Handicapped Accessibility: Good
Performances/Programs: Performance schedule is Tuesday–Sunday.
Ticket Prices: $25–$75, $3 discounts for students, seniors, and military, $15–$20 Rush tickets for full-time students and seniors, one pay-what-you-can performance designated for each show (minimum $1 payment), discounts available for groups of 10 or more.
Subscriptions: Three-Show $79–$148. Benefits include ticket exchanges, discounts on summer theater programs for kids, and half-price youth tickets (when you bring someone 17 or younger with you to your performance).

From the Editors: Innovative new plays, unexpected adaptations, experimental theater pieces, and classics are on display on every La Jolla Playhouse season schedule. In addition, La Jolla Playhouse has become a Broadway breeding ground of sorts with *Jersey Boys*, *Thoroughly Modern Millie*, *Cry-Baby*, *I Am My Own Wife*, *The Farnsworth Invention*, and Billy Crystal's *700 Sundays* all having begun at this theater.

The Playhouse has also done something extraordinary in establishing the Performance Outreach Program, an initiative that each year puts top-notch playwrights to the task of crafting an original play for young audiences (not just the same old fairy-tale adaptations), which then tours schools, libraries, and community centers everywhere.

The La Jolla Playhouse hosts many special events that add to the experience of seeing one of its productions. The Out and About series brings GLBT Playhouse patrons together for a catered Sunday brunch and matinée. Play and Party gets teens involved by combining a performance with a post-show dance party (even the cast and crew join in), while Performance and Cocktails events cater to the 21-and-over set who want to drink and mingle before the show. For people in need of an affordable way to view Playhouse productions, pay-what-you-can performances have 100 tickets set aside to be sold from 11 a.m. to noon on the day of show for as little as $1 (cash only, two per person, arrive early!).

LAMB'S PLAYERS THEATRE

Horton Grand Theatre, 444 Fourth Avenue
619-437-0600 • lambsplayers.org

Other Venue: Coronado Resident Theatre, Spreckels Building, 1142 Orange Avenue, Coronado.
Public Transportation: Good
Handicapped Accessibility: Good
Performances/Programs: Performance schedule is Tuesday–Sunday.
Ticket Prices: $20–$56, discounts available for seniors, military, and youth (5–29), groups of 10 or more eligible for discounts, shows sometimes available on Goldstar.com.
Subscriptions: Season subscription $65–$255.

MO'OLELO PERFORMING ARTS COMPANY

619-342-7395 • electrictemple.net

Venue: No fixed venue, but regularly performs at La Jolla Playhouse, 2910 La Jolla Village Drive, La Jolla.
Public Transportation: Good (La Jolla venue)
Handicapped Accessibility: Good (La Jolla venue)
Performances/Programs: Performance schedule is Wednesday–Sunday.
Ticket Prices: $18–$35, groups of 10 or more, students, seniors, and members of Actors Equity or Actors Alliance receive discounts. Green discount: Bring proof of carpooling, driving a hybrid, bicycling, or taking public transportation to this show and get a $5 discount for the next Mo`olelo production. You can find others looking for and sharing rides to Mo`olelo

at GoLoco; $5 fee for ticket exchanges (fee is waived for anyone who has donated $100 or more to the theater in the last 12 months).

THE OLD GLOBE

The Old Globe Theater, 1363 Old Globe Way, Balboa Park
619-23-GLOBE (234-5623) • oldglobe.org

Public Transportation: Good
Handicapped Accessibility: Good
Performances/Programs: Performance schedule is Tuesday–Sunday.
Ticket Prices: $56–$64, limited number of $29 tickets available for most performances, discounts available for students, seniors, and military for most performances, discounts available for groups of 15 or more.
Subscriptions: Four-Play $141–$273, Eight-Play $242–$472. Subscription discounts available for full-time students, seniors, and military. Benefits include free ticket exchanges and discounts to the gift shop and area restaurants.

From the Editors: There's a little bit of England nestled in beautiful Balboa Park, where you'll find the Old Globe Theatre, originally built in 1935 for the California Pacific International Exposition and modeled after Shakespeare's own Globe Theater. However, it's in the outdoor Lowell Davies Festival Theatre where the Old Globe does its three Shakespeare productions under the stars each summer. The other dozen shows that fill out the season (musicals, new plays, older favorites, the annual Dr. Seuss' *How the Grinch Stole Christmas!* musical) are done in the 580-seat Old Globe Theatre or the smaller Arena Stage.

To get a preview of what's on the Old Globe's stages from the comfort of home, look for the behind-the-scenes series "Backstage at the Globe" airing on UCSD-TV. Some pre-show events offered by the Old Globe include the Wine Lovers Night tasting, the Thank Globe, It's Friday bash with appetizers and live music from a local artist, and the Out At The Globe mixer for GLBT theater fans.

One of the Old Globe's few, but significant, defects is that its events and shows seem a little out of reach for low-income theatergoers. Tickets start at $56 and if you aren't a student or senior, the only option is to try for the limited number of $29 tickets sold at each show.

SAN DIEGO REPERTORY THEATRE (SAN DIEGO REP)
San Diego Rep at The Lyceum, 79 Horton Plaza
619-544-1000 • sandiegorep.com

Public Transportation: Very good
Handicapped Accessibility: Good
Performances/Programs: Performance schedule is Thursday–Sunday.
Ticket Prices: $29–$53, senior and military discounts $25–$43, student tickets $18, discounts for groups of 10 or more, shows available on Goldstar.com.
Subscriptions: Five-Play $125–$211, Three-Play $72–$123, and six-voucher pass $252–$282. Subscription discounts for seniors, full-time students, and active military. Benefits include free ticket exchanges and free indoor parking.

STARLIGHT THEATRE
Starlight Bowl at Balboa Park, 2005 Pan American Plaza
619-544-STAR (7827) • starlighttheatre.org

Public Transportation: Good
Performances/Programs: Performance schedule is Thursday–Sunday.
Ticket Prices: $10–$75, discounts available for students, seniors, and military.
Kids Free Program: Children 12 years and younger can attend for free when accompanied by paying adult on Thursdays and Sundays. Shows available on Goldstar.com.

SAN DIEGO SYMPHONY
Copley Symphony Hall, 750 B Street
619-235-0804 • sandiegosymphony.com

Public Transportation: Good
Handicapped Accessibility: Good
Performances/Programs: More than 100 performances given annually.
Ticket Prices: $20–$93, depending on seat location. Last-minute student tickets (one hour before performance) are $10 cash.
Group Discounts: Groups of 15 or more may receive discounts up to 15%; student and senior group rates are also available.
Membership: Friends of the Symphony membership begins at $100.

Benefits include a Symphony schedule magnet. At significantly higher levels, such as the Symphony Stars membership ($1,100 annually), benefits include at least three members-only daytime functions (luncheons, private recitals, etc.), festive evening parties, the opportunity to host a musical event in the members' home or place of business, plus full access to the Revelle Room and VIP Tent during Masterworks and Summer Pops intermissions.

From the Editors: Formed in 1910, the San Diego Symphony is committed to providing quality musical experiences for the greater San Diego community. The symphony offers many educational programs for all ages. Its Young People's Concerts are specially designed for grades 4–8, featuring narration from the stage and addressing music and other subjects. The Junior Maestro's Club (annual family membership fee is $75 for the first two children) offers a special invitation to Meet the Artist with Maestro Philip Mann and to attend the Symphony Side-by-Side Concert, where Symphony musicians and local students perform together. University Nights allow full-time students to purchase $10 tickets in advance for the first Saturday night Jacobs' Masterworks concert of each month. After the concert is a special reception at Renditions Restaurant, where students can mingle with the musicians and enjoy drink specials. For those wishing to study ahead for an upcoming concert, program notes and audio clips are available online for each Masterworks concert. Also online is a multimedia archive, with videos of select performances.

SAN DIEGO OPERA
San Diego Civic Theater, 1100 Third Avenue
619-533-7000 • sdopera.com

Public Transportation: Good
Handicapped Accessibility: Good
Performances/Programs: Four–six productions per season with multiple performances of each.
Ticket Prices: $30–$210. Student Rush tickets may be available.
Group Discounts: Discounts available for groups of 10 or more.
Subscriptions: Three-opera ($90–$630) and Four-opera ($120–$840) subscriptions available, with prices varying depending on seats selected. Senior subscription discounts available. Subscriber benefits include free ticket exchanges and special offers.
Membership: Available from $100–$10,000+. Based on donation amount, member benefits include seat upgrades, event invites, dining certificates, program recognition, and Subscription Upgrade Points.

From the Editors: Cited by Opera America as one of the top 10 opera companies in the U.S., the San Diego Opera is the city's primary source for world-class opera and is internationally recognized as a vital member of the opera community. The company, founded in 1950, has been lauded for its Operation: Opera program, which brings opera to 100,000 school-aged children in San Diego and Northern Mexico.

ANTHOLOGY
1330 India Street
619-595-0300 • anthologysd.com

   Public Transportation: Poor
   Handicapped Accessibility: Good
   Performances/Programs: 240 performances per year. Live music Tuesday–Saturday at 7:30 p.m.
   Ticket Prices: Range from $5–$30.

CROCE'S RESTAURANT AND JAZZ BAR
802 5th Avenue
619-233-4355 • croces.com

   Public Transportation: Poor
   Handicapped Accessibility: Good
   Performances/Programs: Approximately 350 performances presented per year. Live music played nightly at 8 p.m. (8:30 p.m. on Friday and Saturday); Jazz Brunch on Sunday at 11:30 a.m.
   Ticket Prices: $5–$20, but the fee is often waived if you're eating at the restaurant.

DIZZY'S
San Diego Wine and Culinary Ctr., 2nd and J Street
858-270-7467 • dizzyssandiego.com

   Public Transportation: Good
   Handicapped Accessibility: Good
   Performances/Programs: Approximately 50 performances per year. Live music generally played Wednesday–Sunday at 7 or 8 p.m.
   Ticket Prices: $10–$30 cover.

SOUTH PARK BAR AND GRILL
1946 Fern Street
619-696-0096 • southparkbarandgrill.com

Public Transportation: Poor
Handicapped Accessibility: Good
Performances/Programs: Approximately 160 performances are presented per year. Show times are Wednesday–Saturday at 7 and 9 p.m., Sunday at 6 p.m.
Ticket Prices: No cover.

CALIFORNIA BALLET
Balboa Theatre, 868 Fourth Avenue
858-560-5676 • californiaballet.org

Other Venue: Civic Theatre, 1100 Third Ave (at 3rd and B).
Public Transportation: Poor
Handicapped Accessibility: Good
Performances/Programs: Four different programs per year with two-four performances each.
Ticket Prices: $25–$80. Tickets for children 12 and under are $25. Discounts are available to students for selected performances directly through the performance venues. California Ballet's Scout Ticketing Program offers discounts for selected performances to Scout troops.
Group Discounts: For groups of 15 or more, individual tickets are discounted 25%.
Subscriptions: A subscription includes all four shows. The Gold Rope series includes special premium seating for all four shows. Subscribers save up to 25% off individual ticket prices (excluding Gold Rope).
Membership: Membership is available at any financial level, starting as low as $1. Members receive advance notice of performances, special discounts on tickets, a regular newsletter on dance, invitations to special functions, backstage tours, invitations to rehearsal, and, on occasion, complimentary tickets.

LANDMARK KEN CINEMA
4061 Adams Avenue
619-819-0236
landmarktheatres.com/market/SanDiego/KenCinema.htm

Public Transportation: Good (accessible by public bus).
Performances/Programs: Obscure rarely screened gems, as well as independent and documentary features.
Ticket Prices: Vary based on program.

From the Editors: San Diego's Landmark Ken Cinema is a welcome rarity—an old-style neighborhood movie house that has one screen and includes balcony seating. You never know what to expect at the Ken, which alternately screens independent films, classics, foreign flicks, and documentaries.

For information on Phoenix and Tucson, Arizona, and Santa Fe, New Mexico, visit go-artsamerica.com.

SEATTLE, WASHINGTON

In addition to possessing a wealth of natural beauty (not to mention the world-famous Space Needle), Seattle has been at the forefront of American popular culture more than any other city in the Pacific Northwest. From grunge rock to Starbucks coffee, Seattle is a true original and has a creative vitality that translates into a superb cultural landscape for tourists and residents to savor.

ARTS INFO

The Stranger (thestranger.com)—Alternative weekly newspaper.

Seattle Times (seattletimes.nwsource.com)—Largest newspaper in Washington state.

seattlepi.com—a k a *Seattle Post-Intelligencer*, the city's daily online newspaper.

seattle.gov/Arts—Office of Arts and Cultural Affairs.

seattle.net/entertainment—Seattle arts and entertainment guide.

seattleonthefringe.com—Off-beat arts, entertainment, and activities guide.

THE ARTS

FRYE ART MUSEUM
704 Terry Avenue
206-622-9250 • fryemuseum.org

Public Transportation: Good (accessible via Metro Transit routes 3, 4, or 12 from downtown).
Handicapped Accessibility: Good
Hours: Tuesday–Wednesday, Friday–Saturday 10 a.m.–5 p.m., Thursday 10 a.m.–8 p.m., Sunday noon–5 p.m., closed Monday.
Admission: Free
Tours: Public Tours are available Wednesday-Sunday at 1:30 p.m.
Membership: Individual membership is $50. All members enjoy invitations to members-only events and exclusive exhibition opening receptions, lectures, films, and music with free or discounted tickets, and the opportunity to reserve tickets in advance. Discounts for students ($25) and seniors ($30) are also offered.

From the Editors: This small museum focuses on American, French, and German artists from the 19th and 20th centuries, including the largest collection of the 1870–1900 Munich School (Friedrich von Kaulbach, Gabriel Max) in the United States.

HENRY ART GALLERY
University of Washington, 15th Avenue NE and NE 41st
206-543-2280 • henryart.org

Public Transportation: Good (easily accessible by bus).
Handicapped Accessibility: Good
Hours: Thursday–Sunday 11 a.m.–9 p.m., closed Monday–Wednesday.
Admission: $10, seniors $6, members, high-school, and college students free.
Free Day: Thursday
Tours: The museum regularly offers 50-minute tours to student and community groups. To schedule a group tour, email tours@henryart.org.
Membership: Individual membership is $45 and includes unlimited free admission to all exhibitions, discounts on education programs, lectures, and films, invitations to Henry's events and exhibition openings, and discounts and perks from the Henry's merchant partners. Discounted

memberships for students $25, and seniors $30 are also available.

Other Benefits: Henry members at the Sustaining level ($125) and above have the added benefit of reciprocal membership privileges to more than 300 museums through the North American Reciprocal Membership Program (NARM).

From the Editors: The oldest museum in Washington state, founded by Horace Henry in 1890, focuses on American art. Thanks to subsequent donations, the collection now has more than 23,500 objects displayed in 46,000 square feet.

SEATTLE ART MUSEUM (SAM)

1300 1ˢᵗ Avenue
206-654-3100 • seattleartmuseum.org

Public Transportation: Very good (easily accessible via the Metro bus).
Handicapped Accessibility: Good
Hours: Tuesday–Sunday 10 a.m.–5 p.m., Thursday–Friday 10 a.m.–9 p.m., closed Monday.
Admission: $15, seniors (62+) $12, students and teens (13–17) $9, members and children under 12 free. The preceding are suggested fees and include the cost of special exhibitions.
Free Day: First Thursday of every month free, first Friday of every month free to seniors (62+), second Friday of every month free to teens (13–19) 5–9 p.m.

From the Editors: Once you get inside the recently expanded SAM (past Jonathon Borofsky's 48-foot-tall *Hammering Man*), be prepared to see one of the most extensive Northwest Coast Native American art collections in existence, as well as an equally excellent collection of African art. You'll also find a strong selection of European and American art from across the centuries, including a first-rate Northwest contemporary collection.

SEATTLE ASIAN ART MUSEUM (SAAM)

1400 East Prospect Street, Volunteer Park
206-654-3100 • seattleartmuseum.org/visit/visitSAAM.asp

Public Transportation: Very good (easily accessible via the Metro bus 10).
Handicapped Accessibility: Good.

Hours: Tuesday–Sunday 10 a.m.–5 p.m., Thursday–Friday 10 a.m.–9 p.m., closed Monday.

Admission: $13, seniors (62+) $10, students and teens (13–17) $7, members and children under 12 free. Note: The preceding are suggested fees and include the cost of special exhibitions.

Free Day: First Thursday of every month is free, first Friday of every month is free to seniors (62+), first Saturday of every month is free to families.

From the Editors: Located in the 1933 Art Moderne building that was originally home to the Seattle Art Museum's main collection, SAAM exhibits works from all Asian countries and cultures, with a special emphasis on Chinese and Japanese art.

A CONTEMPORARY THEATRE (ACT)

ACT Theatre, Kreielsheimer Place, 700 Union Street
206-292-7676 • acttheatre.org

Public Transportation: Good
Handicapped Accessibility: Good
Performances/Programs: Performance schedule is Tuesday–Sunday.
Ticket Prices: $37–$55, discounts sometimes available for people using wheelchairs and their companion, 25% off advance tickets for seniors; half-price on day of show $10 tickets for full-time students, $15 tickets for anyone 25 and under, Rush and $15 day of show tickets available for members of Theatre Puget Sound, Theatre Communications Group, SAG, and Actors Equity, discounts available for groups of 20 or more.
Subscriptions: Three-Show $99. Benefits include free ticket exchanges, low-priced parking, and free replacement tickets.

From the Editors: People sometimes complain that the parking can be a bit confusing and that the seating is a tad too cozy, but you don't hear many complaints about the quality of work at A Contemporary Theatre. Each weighty season includes new plays, a premiere, one or two classics, and maybe a lesser-known gem. The Hansberry Project, ACT's own in-house professional black theater company, produces a mainstage show each season, in addition to running workshops and community events that further the exploration of African-American life through theater. The Central Heating Lab program, which helps artists develop new work, goes beyond standard play development to include projects in dance, music, cabaret, and even film and visual art. This enthusiasm for art in all its forms even extends to the gift shop; StageCraft is ACT's theatrical artisan bazaar, where an interdisciplinary variety of Seattle theater artists sell handmade crafts, scarves, jewelry, cookbooks, and more.

5th AVENUE THEATRE

The 5th Avenue Theatre, 1308 5th Avenue
888-5 TH-4TIX (584-4849) • 5thavenue.org

Public Transportation: Very good (accessible by bus, streetcar, and ferry).

Handicapped Accessibility : Yes

Performances/Programs: Performance schedule is Tuesday–Sunday.

Ticket Prices: $22–$90, at select performances, tickets for people 25 and younger $20, discounts available for groups of 10 or more, no ticket exchanges for non-subscribers.

Subscriptions: Four-Show $85–$293, Five-Show $103–$363, and Six-Seven-Show $119–$434, discounts for 30-and-unders. Benefits include free parking, free ticket exchanges, and lost-ticket replacement.

INTIMAN THEATRE

201 Mercer Street, Seattle Center
206-269-1900 • intiman.org

Public Transportation: Excellent (easily accessible by bus and mono-rail).

Handicapped Accessibility: Good

Performances/Programs: Performance schedule is Tuesday–Sunday.

Ticket Prices: $34–$51, $5 discounts for seniors in advance, half-off if purchased on the day of performance, $10 tickets for 25-and-unders, one pay-what-you-can performance for each show, $20 Rush tickets sold 15 minutes before performance, discounts for groups of 10 or more, non-subscribers permitted to exchange tickets with 24 hours advance notice and a $5 fee.

Subscriptions: Five-Play $182–$252, Four-Play $152–$204, and Three-Play $114–$156. Flex passes: four vouchers $204, five vouchers $252, and six vouchers $300. Subscription discounts available for seniors, 25-and-unders, educators, and groups. Benefits include free ticket exchanges, dining discounts, and additional tickets at a discount.

From the Editors: Originally founded as a company devoted to international dramatic literature, the Intiman (Swedish for "the intimate") has been producing plays by the likes of Shaw, Sophocles, Shakespeare, Strindberg, Chekhov, and Oscar Wilde for most of its 36-year history. Eventually, the theater began including more American drama—a Eugene O'Neill here, a Tennessee Williams there—and especially in recent years, the Intiman has taken on more contemporary work, producing several new plays, a few one-man shows, and even its very first musical, *The Light in the Piazza*, in 2003. The theater recently completed a five-year project known as The American Cycle, which brought productions of the thoroughly American tales *Our Town*, *All the King's Men*, *To Kill a Mockingbird*, *Native Son*, and *The Grapes of Wrath* to the Intiman stage.

The Intiman Theatre has certainly not lost its taste for Great Drama, though, and continues its commitment to producing great historic international plays. This mission is evident in local classrooms, too, where Intiman's teaching artists bring the Living History program to students, using classic texts as a starting point for thinking about the big questions that still face us today. The Intiman also makes it easy and affordable for students to see these great plays live onstage by offering $5 tickets through the Teen-Tix program (seattlecenter.com/teentix).

SEATTLE REPERTORY THEATRE
155 Mercer Street
877- 900-9285 • seattlerep.org

Public Transportation: Good
Handicapped Accessibility: Good
Performances/Programs: Performance schedule is Tuesday–Sunday.
Ticket Prices: $15–$42, $10 tickets for people 25 and under, $20 Rush tickets sold a half-hour before curtain, $15 standby tickets, pay-what-you-can performances (minimum $1). Discounts are available for seniors and groups of 10 or more.
Subscriptions: Four-Show $147–$198, Five-Show $85–$285, Six-Show $210–$288, Seven-Show $129–$359, and Nine-Show $185–$439. Also offered are the Players Pack of six vouchers for $297 and subscription discounts for seniors and 25-and-unders. Subscription benefits include free ticket exchanges, free lost-ticket replacement, and free beverage coupons.

VILLAGE THEATRE

Francis J. Gaudette Theatre, 303 Front Street North, Issaquah
425-392-2202 • villagetheatre.org

Other Venue: Everett Performing Arts Center, 2710 Wetmore Avenue, Everett.

Handicapped Accessibility: Good (both venues)

Performances/Programs: Performance schedule is Tuesday–Sunday.

Ticket Prices: $34–$58, FlexPass $200–$230, senior and youth discounts for some performances, student and military Rush 30 minutes before curtain. Students under 21 and military may purchase half-price Rush tickets. See a show a second time for half-price by bringing paid ticket stub. Discounts are available for groups of 10 or more.

Subscriptions: Season subscriptions $175–$230, subscription discounts for youth under 21 and seniors. Benefits include free ticket exchanges and lost-ticket insurance. The Gaudette location has a family room where parents can leave their young children while they attend the show.

SEATTLE SYMPHONY ORCHESTRA

Benaroya Hall, 200 University Street
206-215-4747 • seattlesymphony.org

Public Transportation: Good (Benaroya Hall is served by numerous bus routes).

Handicapped Accessibility: Good

Performances/Programs: About 220 annually.

Ticket Prices: $10–$97. Campus Club, a free service of the SSO, allows college students to purchase tickets for $10.

Group Discounts: Discounts for groups of 10 or more.

Subscriptions: Subscription options include the UBS Masterworks Series, available for weeknights, weekends, or matinées in packages of 4, 7, 10, 13, or 22 concerts; Seattle Pops, five concerts, you select a single day of the week and time; Musically Speaking, six concerts, matinées, music, and a lecture series; Basically Baroque, three concerts; and Mainly Mozart, four concerts on Thursdays or Saturdays; among many many others. Benefits include passes to Meet the Musicians events, a free ticket for your birthday, and ticket exchanges (with at least 24 hours notice).

Membership: Basic membership begins at $75 and benefits include a Symphony membership card entitling you to a 15% discount at a variety of area restaurants and businesses.

Other Benefits: At significantly higher giving levels, members can enjoy a customized symphony experience to suit their personal interests, invitations to exclusive Stradivarius Salon dinners with guest artists, and a private one-on-one dinner with Maestro Gerard Schwarz.

From the Editors: The Seattle Symphony, under the direction of Gerard Schwarz since 1983, has experienced great artistic growth, developing a reputation for innovative and adventurous programming. In 1998, the Symphony moved to its new home, Benaroya Hall, and three years later, Soundbridge Seattle Symphony Music Discovery Center was opened. Soundbridge is a place where all ages come to explore symphonic music through exhibits, classes, and live-music presentations.

The Symphony's education and community programs bring classical music to nearly 90,000 people, including students at 190 schools in the Pacific Northwest. The Symphony offers many events specially designed for children: Tiny Tots (from birth up to 5 years old), Discover Music! concerts (5–12), and Discover Music! enhancement classes. For young adults, the Campus Club offers $10 tickets with a free membership and the Wolfgang membership for adults in their 20s and 30s offers discounted membership and special events. Throughout the year, the Seattle Symphony also gives free community concerts, featuring young artists and local high-school orchestras.

SEATTLE MEN'S CHORUS

Benaroya Hall, 200 University Street
206-388-1400 • flyinghouse.org/smc

Other Venues: McCaw Hall and Meany Theater
Public Transportation: Good
Handicapped Accessibility: Most venues accessible; contact venue management for details.
Performance/Productions: Three concerts per season, plus special events.
Ticket Prices: $39–$52
Subscriptions: Three-show subscription $58.50–$167.50. Subscriber benefits include discounts for family and friends, free ticket exchanges, priority seating, and lost ticket insurance.
Membership: Available from up to $25–$25,000+.

From the Editors: One of America's premier all-male gay choruses, the Seattle Men's Chorus was founded in 1979 and has grown to include over 300 singers. The Chorus, which is under the musical directorship of

Dennis Coleman, has performed many commissioned works, as well as concerts featuring many celebrities and noted musicians. The group has also launched the very successful Seattle Women's Chorus, along with two smaller ensembles: Captain Smartypants and Sensible Shoes, both of which specialize in pop and vocal jazz.

OLYMPIC MUSIC FESTIVAL

Olympic Music Festival Barn, 7360 Center Road, Quilcene
360-732-4800 • olympicmusicfestival.org

Public Transportation: Not given
Handicapped Accessibility: Good
Performance/Productions: 10–12 productions per season with multiple performances of each.
Ticket Prices: $12–$30
Subscriptions: $250 for a festival-long Flex pass.

From the Editors: The Olympic Music Festival, which had its first season in 1984, runs from June to early September and provides the Washington artistic community with chamber-music performances. The venue is outdoors and suitable for bringing a picnic lunch and enjoying an afternoon outside. The performances are broadcast locally on KING-FM and nationally on National Public Radio's "Performance Today."

SEATTLE OPERA

Marion Oliver McCaw Hall, 321 Mercer Street
800-426-1619 • seattleopera.org

Public Transportation: Good
Handicapped Accessibility: Good
Performances/Programs: Four productions per season with multiple performances of each.
Ticket Prices: Prices vary depending on date, time, performances and seats selected.
Group Discounts: Discounts available for groups of 10 or more.
Subscriptions: Three- and Four-opera subscription packages available, with rates starting at $130. Subscriber benefits include free-fee ticket exchanges.
Membership: Available from $75–$250,000+. Friends of Seattle Opera benefits include program recognition, a subscription to *Seattle Opera*

Magazine, opportunity for advance single ticket purchase, and much more at higher donation levels.

From the Editors: The Seattle Opera is recognized as America's premiere presenter of Wagner operas. The company is also renowned for producing a large number of lesser-known operas and for performing many newer works. The Seattle Opera boasts the highest per capita attendance of the major opera companies in the United States through its mainstage performances, and the Opera serves thousands more through community and outreach programs.

DIMITRIOU'S JAZZ ALLEY
2033 6th Avenue
206-441-9729 • jazzalley.com

Public Transportation: Poor

Handicapped Accessibility: Good

Performances/Programs: Approximately 280 performances per year. Generally, shows are Thursday–Sunday, with occasional Wednesday shows. See calendar for times.

Ticket Prices: $5–$30, 20% discounts for seniors on Wednesday and Sunday. Half-price admission for students on Wednesday and the second set on Thursday.

From the Editors: Opened nearly 30 years ago, Jazz Alley has carved out its niche as one of the premier jazz venues on the West Coast. Almost every big-name contemporary jazz act has passed through the club, including Oscar Peterson, Nancy Wilson, Taj Mahal, and McCoy Tyner.

The club is situated in Seattle's University District, placing it at a distinct advantage in drawing college crowds and jazz aficionados. With a fully revamped sound system, the world-class acoustics seem almost too sophisticated for the intimate setting (100 seats).

With both senior and student discounts, Jazz Alley proves its dedication to jazz lovers in Seattle (children under 12 are free). If you're traveling with a big party, be sure to book in advance.

EGAN'S BALLARD JAM HOUSE
1707 NW Market Street
206-789-1621 • ballardjamhouse.com

Public Transportation: Poor
Handicapped Accessibility: Good
Performances/Programs: Approximately 400 performances per year. Live music Wednesday–Saturday. Start times are generally at 7, 9 and 11 p.m.
Ticket Prices: $5–$10.

GRAZIE
16943 South Center Parkway, Tukwila
206-575-1606 • grazierestaurant.com

Public Transportation: Poor
Handicapped Accessibility: Good
Performances/Programs: Approximately 100 performances per year. Live music Friday–Saturday at 7:30 p.m.
Ticket Prices: No cover.

JAZZ IN JANUARY/EMP PROJECT
325 5th Avenue, North
877-EMP-SFM1 (367-7361) • empsfm.com

Public Transportation: Poor
Handicapped Accessibility: Good
Performances/Programs: 10 performances given each year in January.
Ticket Prices: $5–$15. Many concerts are free for EMP members. See website for details.

SEATTLE JAZZ VESPERS
Seattle First Baptist, 1111 Harvard Avenue
206-325-6052 • seattlefirstbaptist.org

Public Transportation: Poor
Handicapped Accessibility: Good
Performances/Programs: Approximately 12–15 annually. These performances generally take place on the first Sunday of every month at 6 p.m.
Ticket Prices: No charge.

SERAFINA
2043 Eastlake Avenue, East
206-323-0807 • serafinaseattle.com

> **Public Transportation:** Poor
> **Handicapped Accessibility:** Good
> **Performances/Programs:** Approximately 180 performances per year.

Live music Friday–Sunday at 9 p.m. Sunday Jazz Brunch at 11 a.m.

> **Ticket Prices:** No cover.

STREET CLOUDS
1131 34th Avenue
206-726-1522 • stclouds.com

> **Public Transportation:** Poor
> **Handicapped Accessibility:** Good
> **Performances/Programs:** Approximately 180 performances. Live mu-

sic performed Monday and Thursday–Saturday at 8 or 9 p.m.

> **Ticket Prices:** No cover

TULA'S
2214 2nd Avenue
206-443-4221 • tulas.com

> **Public Transportation:** Poor
> **Handicapped Accessibility:** Good
> **Performances/Programs:** Approximately 360 performances per year.

Jazz nightly at 7 or 8 p.m.

> **Ticket Prices:** $5–$15. Occasionally $5 discounts are offered with din-

ner reservations.

PACIFIC NORTHWEST BALLET (PNB)
Marion Oliver McCaw Hall, 321 Mercer Street
206.441.2424 • pnb.org

> **Public Transportation:** Good
> **Handicapped Accessibility:** Good
> **Performances/ Programs:** Six programs each year. Each show runs for

two weeks with about eight performances.

Ticket Prices: $25–$155. Half-price tickets are available to students and seniors beginning 90 minutes prior to performances.

Group Discounts: Groups of 10 or more can save up to 20% on tickets.

Other Discounts: For select Friday-evening shows, patrons under 25 can get single tickets for $15 or two tickets for $25. Youths 13–18 can also purchase $5 tickets to PNB performances by joining Seattle Center's Teen Tix program.

Subscriptions: Full-season subscriptions for all six shows or mini-season subscriptions for four or five shows are available. Subscribers save up to 20%. Sales are final. Subscribers can exchange tickets for free up to 24 hours prior to a performance. Benefits include discounts at nearby restaurants, free upgrade seating vouchers, discounts on additional single tickets, free ticket exchanges, prepaid reserved parking, and pre-performance lectures.

Membership: Annual membership starts at $100 and includes an invitation to a dress rehearsal, recognition in PNB's annual report, admission to PNB's annual meeting, and priority season-ticket purchases. Backstage Pass is the membership organization for young people in their 20s and 30s. Benefits for members in Backstage Pass include subscription discounts and social/educational events throughout the year.

From the Editors: As ballet companies go, PNB is certainly one of the best, and best-regarded, in the United States. It features a sundry collection of work by some of the biggest names in dance, including William Forsythe, Mark Morris, Twyla Tharp, and Christopher Wheeldon.

More recently this company has really taken advantage of the Internet and its various resources to bring itself to audiences via YouTube, MySpace, and the dancers' self-created website, PNB Unleashed. The site, managed by four PNB company members, reveals some of the interesting inner workings of the company, as well as the dancers' day-to-day process in preparation for performance. Additionally, it offers a blog maintained exclusively by PNB artistic director Peter Boal, personal interviews with company dancers, and invitations for web readers to send questions and/or commentary. For the more local Seattle community, PNB has developed materials for teachers to incorporate into school classrooms and has initiated a variety of lecture-type series for interested audience members.

NORTHWEST FILM FORUM
1515 12th Avenue
206-329-2629 • nwfilmforum.org

Public Transportation: Good (accessible by city bus lines).

Handicapped Accessibility: Good (the entrance, cinemas, and restrooms of Northwest Film Forum are fully wheelchair accessible; the workshop space isn't fully accessible, but with two weeks written notice, workshops can be moved to accommodate students).

Ticket Prices: General admission $9; seniors and children under 12 $6.50; members $6.

Membership: The non-profit Northwest Film Forum is a member-driven organization. In addition to receiving huge discounts on movies and production services/equipment, members have the ability to shape the future of the organization.

From the Editors: The Seattle-based Northwest Film Forum, which has nearly 1,000 members, is a non-profit center dedicated to the film arts. The NWFF facilitates both film production and exhibition with its two intimate cinemas, a film vault loaded with more than 1,000 movies, production and post-production equipment and facilities, offices for filmmakers, educational workshop space, and a filmmaking library.

Each year the Northwest Film Forum helps 250 filmmakers produce approximately 80 movies, some of which have gone on to appear in renowned festivals like Sundance. The NWFF hosts classes, lectures, workshops, and distinguished visiting artists, and it screens fine independent and international films almost every day of the year.

THE PARAMOUNT THEATRE
Paramount Theatre, 911 Pine Street
206-467-5510 • theparamount.com

Other Venue: Moore Theatre, 1932 Second Avenue

Public Transportation: Good (accessible by bus).

Handicapped Accessibility: Good

Performances/Programs: The Seattle Theatre Group (STG) operates the historic Paramount and Moore theaters. Programming includes Broadway touring shows, concerts, dance, jazz, comedy, family shows, and silent-film presentations.

Ticket Prices: Vary based on presentation. Discount offerings and group discounts vary from show to show. No ticket exchanges for non-subscribers.

Subscriptions: Several subscription series are available, including a Build-Your-Own option. Benefits include lost-ticket insurance and additional ticket discounts (some subscriptions also include free ticket exchanges).

BUMBERSHOOT: SEATTLE'S MUSIC AND ARTS FESTIVAL
Seattle Center, 305 Harrison Street
206-816-6444 • bumbershoot.org

Public Transportation: Good

Handicapped Accessibility: Good

Performances/Programs: A three-day annual festival that takes place over Labor Day weekend and includes hundreds of music, film, comedy, spoken-word, dance, visual arts, and theater performances in 20 indoor and outdoor venues all over the 74-acre Seattle Center. Performance schedule is throughout the day and evening Saturday, Sunday, and Monday.

Ticket Prices: A one-day pass is $35–$40; standard three-day pass $80–$100. $15 tickets are available for kids, seniors, and those with disabilities. Sign up for free online to be a BumberFan and receive ticket savings and discounts on Festival merchandise.

For information on Portland, Oregon,
visit go-artsamerica.com.

SUMMER FESTIVALS

"Hot town, summer in the city/Back of my neck getting dirty and gritty/ Been down, isn't it a pity/Doesn't seem to be a shadow in the city."

Thankfully, things have changed a lot since John Sebastian of the Lovin' Spoonful penned that line more than 40 years ago. Temperatures may be the same (or even warmer), but almost all major cities now offer extensive and well-attended summer arts activities and festivals. We list many of them in each city's section.

Summer is still a great time, however, to get out of the city and re-learn what having green below and blue above is like, and for arts buffs, few activities are more enjoyable and complete than a good theater, music, or multi-art summer festival. You're surrounded by fellow enthusiasts; prices, especially if you book early or become a member, can be inexpensive; and you can frequently walk from one event to another, as well as to local restaurants and wherever you're staying. The only trick is figuring out how to get to the festival, as many of them are in relatively remote rural locations. Usually, a call to the festival office or local tourist bureau can get you an answer to that question, as well as others, such as, "Where's a nice reasonably priced B&B or self-catering cottage?"

If any of these festivals interest you, go to the website and sign-up for email updates, which is the best way to find out about discount tickets.

❀ MULTI-ART FESTIVALS ❀

BONNAROO MUSIC AND ARTS FESTIVAL
Bonnaroo Manchester Farm, Manchester, Tennessee
bonnaroo.com

Public Transportation: Good (shuttles available from the Nashville airport; Greyhound bus stops within a mile of the event).

Handicapped Accessibility: Good

Performances/Programs: This four-day multi-stage festival is held every June and features numerous performances (mostly music acts and comedians) throughout the day at different venues around the festival area.

Ticket Prices: Ticket prices are roughly $150–$250 and around $1,000 for VIP tickets.

CHAUTAUQUA INSTITUTION
One Ames Avenue, Chautauqua, New York
716-357-6200 • ciweb.org

Venues: Performances and events are held in numerous venues and locations around the Chautauqua grounds.

Performances/Programs: The Chautauqua Institution summer resort provides nine weeks of music, performance, arts, lectures, classes, sports, workshops, religious services, and educational programs from June to August each year. Events occur daily from late June– mid-August; performance schedule varies.

Public Transportation: Buses, Amtrak, and nearby airport, with taxi and car services also available; complimentary shuttle buses and trams for transport around the Chautauqua Institution grounds, which are also walkable.

Handicapped Accessibility: Good

Ticket Prices: Vary depending on type of event. Daily, weekend, and season-pass options available.

Group Discounts: Discounts available for groups of 20 or more.

Educational/Community Outreach: Educational opportunities include workshops, classes, lectures, programs for both kids and adults, contemporary-issues forums, and reenactments of historical events.

From the Editors: A National Historic Landmark, the Chautauqua Institution was founded in the 19th century as a training program for Sunday-school teachers, and religious education remains a key part of the programming each season in the form of worship and sacred-song services, fellowship groups, and interfaith lectures and discussions. The Chautauqua summer festival's commitment to providing spiritual renewal for its visitors is also realized through the arts, represented by theatrical productions, operas, concerts, dance, and other performances.

The institution's beautiful lakeside setting provides ample inspiration and the environment can be enjoyed while taking part in recreational activities like tennis, golf, volleyball, boating, and much more. You can get the most out of the Chautauqua experience by making it a weekend or a week (or more) vacation and procuring accommodations on the grounds; visit the website to see all the options available.

COACHELLA VALLEY MUSIC AND ARTS FESTIVAL
Empire Polo Field, 81–800 Avenue 51, Indio, California
coachella.com

Venues: Coachella Stage, Outdoor Theater, Gobi Tent, Mojave Tent, Sahara Tent, The Dome.
Performances/Programs: Coachella is a three-day April festival that hosts well over 100 music acts (alternative rock, folk, hip-hop, and more) and features art exhibitions. Dozens of bands/musicians perform each day.
Public Transportation: Bus/train stops three miles from grounds; taxis available to take visitors to the grounds.
Handicapped Accessibility: Good
Ticket Prices: $120 for One-Day pass, $269 for Three-Day pass.
Group Discounts: None available
Educational/Community Outreach: Increases environmental awareness through programs like the filtered-water program and the Energy-FACTory, and helps youth by donating money from ticket sales to the Indio Youth Task Force.

From the Editors: Coachella Valley Music and Arts Festival, usually just called Coachella, is much more about the music than the art, though interactive installations and sculptural art can be found on the grounds. Now in its 10th year, the annual California festival has expanded to three days and features an impressive slate of bands and musicians that will leave any alternative music fan drooling. The 2009 festival hosted indie-music icons Conor Oberst and TV On the Radio, old-school legends Leonard Cohen, Morrissey, the Cure, Henry Rollins (doing spoken word!), and Lollapalooza founder Perry Farrell, popular modern artists Joss Stone, Franz Ferdinand, the Killers, the Yeah Yeah Yeahs, wild-cards M.I.A. and the Brian Jonestown Massacre, and pop music pioneer Paul McCartney. Coachella invites on-site camping and offers luxury lodging facilities.

RIVERFEST ARKANSAS
Riverfest Amphitheatre, 100 E. LA Harpe, Little Rock, Arkansas
501-255-FEST • riverfestarkansas.com

Performances/Programs: Riverfest Arkansas is a three-day arts and music festival held in May. Performance schedule is Friday through Sunday.

Ticket Prices: $20 at the gate and online, which includes all three days and all performances and are good for people 7 and up. $10 in advance at area Harvest Foods stores and Central Arkansas Big Red stores. This presale ticket is good for all three days for people 7 years old and up. Children 6 and under get in free, while children 7–10 are admitted for a daily price of $5 at the gate. See the festival for free by volunteering.

SPOLETO FESTIVAL USA
Performances are held in several venues
throughout Charleston, South Carolina
843-579-3100 • spoletousa.org

Performances/Programs: Spoleto is a 17-day festival of opera, music, dance, and theater held late May/early June, presenting more than 120 performances.

Public Transportation: Varies based on venue.

Handicapped Accessibility: Good.

Ticket Prices: $10–$150. Tickets may be exchanged subject to availability and fees.

Group Discounts: Discounts available for groups of 15 or more.

Educational/Community Outreach: Educational opportunities include workshops, classes, and teaching partnerships.

From the Editors: Devised as an American counterpart to Italy's Spoleto Festival dei Due Mondi, the Spoleto Festival USA is an annual celebration of art at its finest. During the 17-day event, opera, ballet, modern dance, theater, classical-music, and jazz performances are held in churches, theaters, recital halls, and other venues throughout historic Charleston, South Carolina. Spoleto USA has premiered works by legends like Arthur

Miller, Laurie Anderson, Steve Reich, Philip Glass, and Allen Ginsberg, while also featuring many emerging artists. Spoleto attendees in their 20s and 30s can make the festival experience extra fun by getting a SCENE membership ($75–$125), which includes invites to soirees, VIP parties, dress rehearsals, and more.

TANGLEWOOD MUSIC FESTIVAL
297 West Street, Lenox, Massachusetts
888-266-1200 • bso.org

Public Transportation: Good (Tanglewood Express motorcoach service is available for many performances at a cost of $30 roundtrip).

Handicapped Accessibility: Good

Performances/Programs: This summer music festival features the Boston Symphony Orchestra in residence, as well as many other musicians and music groups. Performance schedule varies.

Ticket Prices: $18–$89. A 50% discount on Friday-evening lawn tickets is available for students 13 or older. Lawn free for children under 12.

Group Discounts: Group discounts are available for parties of 25 or more.

Subscriptions: Lawn Pass Books, featuring tickets for lawn seating at 11 performances, cost $170–$180. Open-rehearsal subscriptions allow subscribers to attend four ($64) or eight rehearsals ($128).

Educational/Community Outreach: Education is a major component of Tanglewood and includes a summer academy for advanced musical study, concerts for kids, and conversations with artists. Music seminars are offered for $100–$150, with one additional seminar offered free of charge.

From the Editors: A Berkshires estate that serves as the summer home for the Boston Symphony Orchestra, Tanglewood welcomes 350,000 musicians and music lovers annually for a wealth of concerts, seminars, and other events. Tanglewood audiences have enjoyed the American premieres of compositions by Shostakovich, Britten, and Pierre Boulez, and the festival continues to showcase the greatest talents of the classical-music world, as well as a few popular music notables.

The jewel of the festival is the Tanglewood Music Center, founded by BSO music director and beloved teacher Serge Koussevitzky in 1940. The Center has educated approximately 20% of the musicians currently playing in America's major symphony orchestras and TMC alumni include some of the most distinguished conductors, composers, singers, and musicians of the 20th and 21st centuries. Notable among them are Leonard Bernstein, Zubin Mehta, Seiji Ozawa, Michael Tilson Thomas, Lorin Maazel, Ned Rorem, Lukas Foss, Leontyne Price, and Dawn Upshaw.

THEATER FESTIVALS

ALABAMA SHAKESPEARE FESTIVAL
1 Festival Drive, Montgomery, Alabama
801-841-4273 • asf.net

Public Transportation: Poor
Handicapped Accessibility: Good
Performances/Programs: Alabama Shakespeare Festival produces approximately 14 shows per year with four shows running in repertory in April/May. The performance schedule is generally Tuesday–Sunday.
Ticket Prices: $25–$42. Discounts are offered for patrons for 25 and under.
Group Ticket Prices: Discounts for groups of 10 or more.
Subscriptions: Multiple subscriptions are offered. The most popular options include the Create Your Own pass (four, five, or six vouchers) $144–$216; Ultimate Musical Pass (all three musicals) $152; Premium $291; and Festival Pass $168.
Educational/Community Outreach: Alabama Shakespeare Festival offers numerous educational programs (camps, classes, seminars, student matinées, etc.). Some require a fee, while others are free.

From the Editors: From humble beginnings as a summer festival of classical theater held in a stuffy high-school auditorium, the Alabama Shakespeare Festival has become a year-round feast of new plays and musicals, revues, revivals, and, yes, Shakespeare, performed in a two-theater complex situated in the English-style Blount Cultural Park, overlooking a beautiful lake. The Southern Writers' Project: Festival of New Plays keeps the Montgomery-based ASF true to its heritage by developing the work of Southern dramatists and culminates each year in a three-day event that includes food, fun, and the world-premiere production of a new play.

But the event atmosphere doesn't stop there. ASF has interesting programs throughout the season, such as Saturday Theatre in the Mind lectures that delve into the background of ASF's plays, Stage Side Chats with ASF staff, and pre-show Bard Talks with the resident dramaturg about ASF's Shakespeare productions (all free).

Attend opening-night receptions if you'd like to mingle with the cast post-show, or if you prefer something more informal, just sit back and listen to the live music in the lobby before each performance. And to really make your festival experience complete, providing the weather is good, reserve a gourmet picnic basket through the box office, then enjoy a wonderful meal in the park before your show (be sure to order at least three days in advance).

AMERICAN PLAYERS THEATRE
5950 Golf Course Road, Spring Green, Wisconsin
608-588-7401 • playinthewoods.org

Public Transportation: Good (shuttle service is available to and from amphitheater).

Handicapped Accessibility: Good

Performances/Programs: The American Players Theater produces five productions per year and gives about 116 performances from June to early October. The performance schedule is generally Tuesday through Sunday.

Ticket Prices: $36–$58

Group Ticket Prices: Discounts may be available for groups of 20 or more.

Educational/Community Outreach: Educational programs include student matinées, workshops, camps, tours, and residencies (some programs are free).

AMERICAN SHAKESPEARE CENTER
Blackfriars Playhouse, 10 South Market Street, Staunton, Virginia
1-877-MUCH-ADO • americanshakespearecenter.com

Public Transportation: Good

Performances/Programs: Plays are produced in rep throughout the year—about 14 productions in all. Performance schedule is Wednesday–Sunday and some Mondays.

Ticket Prices: $20–$40, students, seniors, and children discounts available. Pay-what-you-will performances are offered for each show.

Group Ticket Prices: Discounts are available for groups of 15 or more.

Educational/Community Outreach: Educational programs include workshops, actor training, student matinées, youth camps, readings, lectures, and discussions.

CONTEMPORARY AMERICAN THEATER FESTIVAL
Shepherd University, Shepherdstown, West Virginia
800-999-CATF (2283) • catf.org

Public Transportation: Poor
Handicapped Accessibility: Good
Performances/Programs: Five plays are presented in rotating rep each season July–August. Performance schedule is Wednesday through Sunday.
Ticket Prices: $30–$36. Discounts are available for students and seniors. Each show has a pay-what-you-can performance during previews.
Subscriptions: A CATCard four-show subscription costs $100–$120. A CATCard Plus subscription featuring tickets to all five shows costs $125–$145. Special student and senior rates for CATCards are available.

BERKSHIRE THEATRE FESTIVAL
6 E. Main Street, Stockbridge, Massachusetts
413-298-5576 • berkshiretheatre.org

Public Transportation: Poor
Handicapped Accessibility: Good
Performances/Programs: Twelve productions are presented each year; the mainstage season is June through early September, while the Unicorn Theatre season goes from May to December. Performance schedule is Sunday–Saturday.
Ticket Prices: $39–$68. Theatre for Young Audiences single tickets $7–$39.
Group Ticket Prices: Group discounts are available.
Subscriptions: Full-season subscriptions cost $137–$272.
Educational/Community Outreach: Educational programs include apprenticeships ($3,000 plus), Theatre for Young Audiences ($7–$10), and internships (college credit for participants).

HUDSON VALLEY SHAKESPEARE FESTIVAL
Boscobel Restoration, 1601 Route 9D, Garrison, New York
845-265-9575 • hvshakespeare.org

Public Transportation: Good (easily accessible by Metro North train and special Bard Bus that operates between train station and theater).
Handicapped Accessibility: Good
Performances/Programs: Three productions are presented from June to early September. Performance schedule is Tuesday–Sunday.

Ticket Prices: $28–$44. A 15% discount for students and seniors (excluding Saturday nights) is available. Half-price tickets for children 12 and under (excluding Saturday nights) are also offered. On Family Nights, tickets for a family of four cost just $80.

Group Ticket Prices: Discounts available for groups of 10 or more on most dates.

Educational/Community Outreach: Educational programs include touring productions, artists-in-residence program, summer apprentice program, and an institute for teaching Shakespeare.

OREGON SHAKESPEARE FESTIVAL
15 S. Pioneer Street, Ashland, Oregon
800-219-8161 • osfashland.org

Public Transportation: Fair (taxi/shuttle services are available and a bus runs during the day).

Handicapped Accessibility: Good

Performances/Programs: The theater produces 11 shows each season from mid-February through October, totaling 750–800 performances. Performance schedule is Tuesday–Sunday.

Ticket Prices: $20–$81. Half-price tickets for people ages 6 to 17. Ticket exchanges are available with $2 fee and seven days notice (some exceptions made for additional $5 fee).

Group Ticket Prices: Discounts are available for groups of 15 or more.

Membership: Memberships start at $60. Benefits include priority ticket ordering, gift-shop discounts, reduced ticket prices, access to the member's lounge, free post-matinée discussions, free publications, and free ticket exchanges.

Educational/Community Outreach: Educational opportunities include classes for adults and students, seminars, pre-show talks ($5), lectures ($6), and free Q&As.

From the Editors: Theater lovers by the thousands descend on the little mountain town of Ashland every year to take in the Oregon Shakespeare Festival, one of the longest-running and most respected of the nation's many tributes to the Bard. Winner of the 1983 Regional Tony Award, the OSF has dedicated itself to presenting the finest productions of Shakespeare's work (the entire canon has already been produced three times since OSF's birth in 1935), plus productions of new plays, revivals, classics of the Western world, and works that reflect the theatrical traditions of other parts of the globe.

The Festival operates from February to October, utilizing three theaters: the outdoor Elizabethan, the 600-seat Angus Bowmer (named for the OSF's founder), and the smallest space, the New Theatre. To get the most authentic Oregon Shakespeare Festival experience, you'll want to come in the warmer months (but avoid the sweltering ones), when you can see Shakespeare in the Elizabethan Theatre, relax in Lithia Park's Japanese garden, and appreciate the full beauty of Ashland by trying outdoor activities like hiking, kayaking, and white-water rafting.

Of course, the less adventurous are welcome to skip the kayaking in favor of visiting an art museum or two, reveling in the ambience of one of the local bed-and-breakfasts, and going on OSF's excellent backstage tour. If trekking to Ashland seems like a pretty big trip just to see a few plays, the regulars who visit from all over the country yearly insist it's worth the effort and that once you go, it's likely to become a habit.

SHAW FESTIVAL
Shaw Festival Theatre, 10 Queen's Parade
Niagara-on-the-Lake, Ontario, Canada
800-511-7429 • shawfest.com

Public Transportation: Good (bus, rail, and shuttle options are available).

Handicapped Accessibility: Good

Performances/Programs: 10–12 plays are produced each year April–October, with more than 800 performances. Performance schedule is generally Tuesday–Sunday.

Ticket Prices: Ticket prices are $45–$105. Reading-series $18. Lunchtime one-act $27. Special discounts on regular and matinée performances are available for students and seniors. The $30 Under 30 program allows patrons between 19 and 29 years old to enjoy regularly priced performances at all three theatres for just $30. Ticket exchanges available with 24 hours notice and $4 fee.

Group Ticket Prices: Discounts are available for groups of 10 or more.

Subscriptions: Several options are offered, including the Triple Play Flex Pass for $165, which allows subscribers to save up to 25% on three shows during the 2008 season; the Theatre Lovers Flex Pass offers subscribers four shows for $196 (save up to $104).

Educational/Community Outreach: Educational programs include Teacher Days, Career Days, tours, workshops, and pre- and post-show chats.

From the Editors: There are many many Shakespeares out there, but there's only one Shaw Festival. Located at gorgeous Niagara-on-the-Lake, the Shaw Festival is inspired by the work of the brilliant dramatist George Bernard Shaw. His writings are the focus of this annual Ontario theater festival, which is also dedicated to producing plays by Shaw's contemporaries, as well as modern works set during the period of his long life, which lasted from 1856 to 1950. Only at the Shaw Festival will you see authentic spare-no-expense productions of Victorian dramas, rediscovered classics, and Canadian plays that otherwise go unproduced, either because they've been unjustly forgotten over the years or because most theater companies don't have the resources necessary to put them on stage.

Though the chief joy of the Shaw Festival is seeing wonderful plays performed by its extraordinary acting ensemble in three handsome theaters, there are many other things to do when not taking in a show. Free Sunday concerts and educational seminars are offered as a part of the festival and Niagara itself has lots to enjoy, including markets and wineries, fishing and golfing, and historical sites such as Fort George.

STRATFORD FESTIVAL OF CANADA
Festival Theatre, 55 Queen Street, Stratford, Ontario, Canada
800-567-1600 • stratfordfestival.on.ca

Other Venues: Avon Theatre, 99 Downie Street; Tom Patterson Theatre, 111 Lakeside Drive; Studio Theatre, 34 George Street East.

Handicapped Accessibility: Good, all theaters.

Public Transportation: Fair (somewhat accessible by bus and rail).

Performances/Programs: Performance schedule is generally Tuesday–Sunday from April–October.

Ticket Prices: Ticket prices are $29–$109. The Play On program provides $20 tickets for people 16–29. The Play Encore program offers discounts of up to 50% off for people 30–35. Sixty $20 tickets available in the balcony for every performance. Senior, student, and youth discounts also available. Half-price Rush sold two hours before each show, if available.

Group Ticket Prices: Discount rates available for groups of 15 or more.

Memberships: Memberships start at $75. Benefits include priority ticket ordering, access to the best seats, discounts, special offers, the member newsletter, and behind-the-scenes events.

Educational/Community Outreach: Educational programs include Birmingham Conservatory for Classical Theatre, courses, teacher's conferences, student workshops, scavenger hunts, and tours.

From the Editors: While not to be confused with the place of William

Shakespeare's birth, Stratford, Ontario, has nonetheless made the most of its name by birthing Canada's most celebrated annual festival, the Stratford Shakespeare Festival. Stratford presents plays by the Bard, dramas from Euripides to Beckett, classic musicals, and new plays in rep from April to November each year, with workshops, discussion groups, lectures, and concerts adding to the festive atmosphere.

The Stratford Festival attracts many of the world's finest actors, and luminaries like Christopher Plummer, Peter Ustinov, and Jessica Tandy have all graced its stages. Modern-day groundlings worried that they won't be able to afford the ticket prices for Stratford's high-quality productions needn't fear; discount options abound.

TEXAS SHAKESPEARE FESTIVAL
Kilgore College, Kilgore, Texas
903-983-8601 • texasshakespeare.com

Performances/Programs: Five productions are performed for four weeks in rep each summer in late June and July. Performance schedule is Thursday–Sunday.

Ticket Prices: $20–$25. Children's show $6.

Group Ticket Prices: Discounts are offered for groups of 25 or more.

Subscriptions: Season packages start at $75.

Educational/Community Outreach: Educational opportunities include acting and stage-combat workshops.

UTAH SHAKESPEAREAN FESTIVAL
300 West Street, Cedar City, Utah
800-PLAYTIX • bard.org

Public Transportation: Fair (there's a bus, but with limited service).

Handicapped Accessibility: Good

Performances/Programs: The six-show summer festival runs from mid-June to early September; there's also a three-show season in the fall. Performance schedule is Monday–Saturday

Ticket Prices: $23–$66. Sixty-six tickets for partially obscured view-gallery bench seat are available for $17–$21 at 10 a.m. each morning for the performance that day (for shows in the Adams Shakespearean Theater). Additional discounts are available for seniors, youth, military, AAA members, and those making early-ticket purchases.

Group Ticket Prices: Group discounts available.

Subscriptions: A Six Pack subscription allows patrons to buy tickets to all six summer productions in any order and save. You can choose any days and seating sections. The only requirement is that you purchase all six shows when you place your order. The All for Fall subscription allows patrons to buy a ticket to all three fall productions and save $3 per ticket. Ticket exchanges available with 24 hours notice and $5 fee (fee waived for members).

Membership: Memberships start at $50 and include invites to special events, complimentary drinks and seat cushions, etc., depending on membership level.

Educational/Community Outreach: Educational programs include classes, workshops, free literary seminars, and the Elementary Shakespeare Showcase (free shortened productions).

From the Editors: In addition to providing wonderful productions of plays by the Bard in the Tudor-inspired Adams Shakespearean Theatre, dramas by other greats at the Randall L. Jones Theatre and free readings of new work, the Utah Shakespearean Festival has a host of other activities. There are seminars on theatrical subjects ranging from props to acting, pre-show play talks, scholarly symposia, backstage tours, free access to the Braithwaite Fine Arts Gallery—and, of course, all of Utah's breathtaking natural wonders on view in the local resorts and state parks.

An Elizabethan-themed entertainment full of food, music, singing, storytelling, and juggling known as the Greenshow is held on the courtyard at the Adams Theatre each night before showtime and it's absolutely free. A post-show entertainment option, from 11 p.m. to midnight, is the Grind Coffee House (19 North Main Street) cabaret that features festival performers looking to let off a little artistic steam; the cost is $10.

WILLIAMSTOWN THEATRE FESTIVAL
Williams College, 1000 Main Street (Route 2)
Williamstown, Massachusetts
413-597-3400 • wtfestival.org

Public Transportation: Poor

Performances/Programs: Performance schedule is Wednesday–Sunday. Over 200 performances are presented from June until August.

Ticket Prices: Generally $25–$69. General Rush $15 for plays and $25 for musicals, and are available for the Thursday-evening performances of all mainstage productions, beginning at 6 p.m. on the day of the performance. Student Rush $15 for plays, $25 for musicals, and are available with a valid student ID beginning two hours prior to curtain for every performance, except Saturday evenings. The festival also offers a Kids' Night where children under 18 can attend the first Friday performance of each mainstage production free of charge when accompanied by an adult with a full-priced ticket. The Festival also has a few designated free performances. Ticket exchanges are available with 48 hours advance and a $3 fee.

Educational/Community Outreach: Educational initiatives include training programs for young theater professionals and the Greylock Theatre Project outreach program for disadvantaged youth.

CLASSICAL MUSIC FESTIVALS

ASPEN MUSIC FESTIVAL AND SCHOOL
2 Music School Road, Aspen, Colorado
970-925-9042 • aspenmusicfestival.com

Public Transportation: Very good (easily accessible via RFTA buses).

Performances/Programs: A classical-music festival held in Aspen, Colo., annually featuring 350 events during a nine-week season from June–August.

Ticket Prices: Vary. Regular performances can cost up to $80 a ticket, while others are offered free of charge. Lawn seats are always free.

Subscriptions: The Aspen Music Festival offers the following subscription options: the Gold Season Pass ($1,250), which includes entrée to all regularly scheduled events and validation by phone on day of event; the Kickoff Pass ($185), which is good for all regular events through July 3; and the Full Season Pass ($975), which offers unlimited access to the festival's 350-plus regular events throughout the summer. Children 17 and under are eligible for the $50 Youth Season Picture Pass. Passes are good for all regularly scheduled events except operas, special events, benefits, and films.

Educational/Community Outreach: The Aspen Music Festival and School is a major training ground for young musicians with programs in performance and composition.

BERKSHIRE CHORAL FESTIVAL
245 North Undermountain Road, Sheffield, Massachusetts
413-229-1999 • choralfest.org

Handicapped Accessibility: Good
Performances/Programs: An annual summer festival that takes place for five weeks in July/August in Sheffield, and continues several weeks more abroad. Performances in Sheffield are given on Saturday.
Ticket Prices: $15–$45
Educational/Community Outreach: Educational offerings include Berkshire Scholar Program (full scholarship given) and an Apprentice Program (includes room, board and stipend).

CARMEL BACH FESTIVAL
Throughout Carmel, California
831-624-2046 • bachfestival.org

Public Transportation: Fair (accessible by Amtrak and Greyhound, but a taxi from the station will be required).
Handicapped Accessibility: Varies by venue.
Performances/Programs: Annual three-week summer festival takes place in numerous venues throughout Carmel and other towns in California in July to August; more than 150 events are scheduled. Performance schedule varies.
Ticket Prices: $25–$60, $20 tickets available for students and active military to most performances. Some events are free.
Group Discounts: Discounts are available for groups of 10 or more.
Subscriptions: Several subscriptions are offered by the festival, including the Sunset Theater package (all six main concerts) for $270–$380 and the Intermezzo Concert package (consisting of seven recital tickets) for $125.
Educational/Community Outreach: Educational initiatives include pre-concert talks and youth music programs.

BRAVO! VAIL VALLEY MUSIC FESTIVAL
Gerald R. Ford Amphitheater, 530 S Frontage Road E, Vail
877-812-5700 • vailmusicfestival.org

Other Venues: Vilar Center for the Arts, 68 Avondale Lane, Beaver Creek, Colorado.

Public Transportation: Good

Handicapped Accessibility: Good

Performances/Programs: The festival runs from late June to early August and features renowned orchestras, soloists, and chamber musicians. Performance schedule varies.

Ticket Prices: $23–$84. One or two free performances are also offered.

Group Discounts: Discounts available for groups of 15 or more.

Subscriptions: Several subscription packages are offered. The Amphitheater subscription consists of reserved or premium-reserved tickets to every Bravo orchestra performance at the Gerald R. Ford Amphitheater for 10% off the total price. The Complete Classics package allows subscribers to purchase regular-reserved or premium-reserved tickets to every classical Bravo performance (11 total) and receive a 10% discount. The Club Bravo! pass ($139–$169) provides subscribers with lawn seating to all Amphitheater concerts. Other subscription options, including a Teen pass for young music aficionados ($39), are also available.

Educational/Community Outreach: Music Matters is the festival's free community music-education program.

FESTIVAL DEL SOLE-NAPA VALLEY
Various locations throughout Napa Valley, California
707-226-8742 • festivaldelsole.com/napavalley

Performances/Programs: A festival held in July celebrating music, food, wine, and art. It's usually 7–10 days long and consists of approximately 50 events.

Ticket Prices: $45–$125.

CRESTED BUTTE MUSIC FESTIVAL
308 3rd Street, Crested Butte, Colorado
970-349-0619 • crestedbuttemusicfestival.com

Public Transportation: Good (Most venues accessible to public transportation).

Handicapped Accessibility: Good

Performances/Programs: This summer festival of classical music, opera, and dance takes place in July. Performances held in a variety of venues. Performance schedule varies, but there are shows almost every night and also daytime performances.

Ticket Prices: $25–$50; fundraising performances are $100–$150. Some free events are also presented. Discounts are available for students and children.

Subscriptions: Season passes available.

Educational/Community Outreach: Educational opportunities include the Opera Young Artist program and free Young People's concerts.

GRAND CANYON MUSIC FESTIVAL
Shrine of the Ages, Grand Canyon, Arizona
800-997-8285 • grandcanyonmusicfest.org

Public Transportation: Poor

Handicapped Accessibility: Good

Performances/Programs: Concerts are offered on three consecutive weekends each September. Performance schedule varies. Several performances are offered free of charge.

Ticket Prices: $15, $8 children. Discounts available for residents of Tusayan and Grand Canyon Village.

Group Discounts: Group rates available.

Subscriptions: A season-ticket package is offered for $100 that includes admission to all seven concerts in the festival series.

Educational/Community Outreach: Educational initiatives include the Native American Composers Apprenticeship Project.

GRAND TETON MUSIC FESTIVAL
Walk Festival Hall, Teton Village, West Virginia
307-733-3050 • gtmf.org

Public Transportation: Good (easily accessible via START bus).

Handicapped Accessibility: Good

Performances/Programs: A summer music festival taking place in July and August each year. Performance schedule varies, but mostly Tuesday–Saturday.

Ticket Prices: $20–$50, student tickets $5–$10.

Group Discounts: Discounts available for groups of 12 or more.

Subscriptions: The following subscription options are offered: Full Season subscriptions are $600 and guarantee seating for the complete season; a Weekend Orchestra subscription is $260 and consists of seven weekend orchestra concerts; the 4-of-a-Kind Mini Series costs $125–$150 and allows subscribers the ability to select tickets to any four concerts; Buy 3, Get 1 Free allows subscribers to choose any three concerts during the Festival season and receive a fourth concert free. Benefits include priority seating, ticket-exchange privileges, and lost-ticket replacement.

Educational/Community Outreach: Educational programs include free family concerts, Tune-Up! music lessons, the Orchestra Mentorship program, and free pre-concert lectures.

MOAB MUSIC FESTIVAL
Moab Music Festival Box Office, 58 East 300 South, Moab, Utah
435-259-7003 • moabmusicfest.org

Public Transportation: Good
Handicapped Accessibility: Most venues are accessible.
Ticket Prices: $15–$25. Benefit concert $50–$200, $5 student tickets available for many performances. See concerts for free by volunteering.
Performances/Programs: The Moab Music Festival is a three-week chamber music festival. September performances take place in several different venues. Performance schedule varies.
Subscriptions: A season ticket package of seven concerts is offered for $125. A weekend ticket package is available for $30–$55.
Educational/Community Outreach: The festival sometimes offers music-education programs.

NEWPORT MUSIC FESTIVAL
Festival Box Office, 850 Aquidneck Avenue, Middletown, Rhode Island
401-849-0700 • newportmusic.org

Public Transportation: Good (most venues accessible via RIPTA trolley service).
Handicapped Accessibility: Good
Performances/Programs: A 17-day music festival held in July, featuring approximately 60 concerts. Performances are held in several different venues, with most concerts taking place in the Newport Mansions. Several performances are given every day of the festival.

Ticket Prices: $25–$45, $10 student Rush tickets available on day of concert.

Group Discounts: Discounts are available for groups of 20 or more.

From the Editors: The Newport Music Festival turns the idea of the summer festival on its head by moving it from the sunny lawn to the great indoors. The massive 19th century mansions of Newport, Rhode Island, built as summer "cottages" for the rich and famous of the Gilded Age, serve as venues for the festival's 60-odd concerts, held morning, noon, and night (and occasionally midnight) for a few weeks each July. Watching the festival's many guest artists and international acts perform in the beautiful sprawling rooms of mansions like the Breakers (once owned by the Vanderbilt family), festival attendees experience chamber music in the same intimate and luxurious fashion as the kings and aristocrats for whom it was originally performed.

OREGON FESTIVAL OF AMERICAN MUSIC
Hult Center for the Performing Arts, One Eugene Center, Eugene, Oregon
541-434-7000 • ofam.org

Other Venue: John G. Shedd Institute for the Arts, 285 E. Broadway, Eugene, Oregon.

Public Transportation: Good

Handicapped Accessibility: Good

Performances/Programs: This festival is usually held in late July/early August for one–three weeks and each year focuses on a different composer or artist influential in the history of American music. The performance schedule is Tuesday through Sunday.

Ticket Prices: $18–$50. Many free events are also presented at the festival.

Educational/Community Outreach: The Shedd Institute for the Arts, which produces the festival, has educational programs like music classes and camps.

🎷 JAZZ FESTIVALS 🎷

GEORGE WEIN'S JAZZ FESTIVAL 55
Fort Adams State Park, 1 Lincoln Drive, Newport, Rhode Island
jazzfestival55.com

Public Transportation: Good (easily accessible by water taxi service).
Handicapped Accessibility: Good

From the Editors: The original Newport Festival was *the* place to be for jazz musicians in the latter half of the last century. The festival takes place over two-three days in August and continues to play host to some of the most influential and talented performers in the medium. As Newport is less equipped to handle the large crowds that flock to the festival than places like New York or Chicago might be, it's best to book accommodations months in advance or be willing to drive to the festival site from another more convenient location (though, keep in mind that parking can be very limited at Fort Adams). As we went to press, several changes were announced for the 2009 season, due to the withdrawal of its major sponsor, JVC.

MONTEREY JAZZ FESTIVAL (MJF)
Monterey Fairgrounds, 2004 Fairground Road, Del Rey Oaks, California
montereyjazzfestival.org

Public Transportation: Okay
Handicapped Accessibility: Good
Performances/Programs: Approximately 80 performances over three days in nine different venues—all in September.
Ticket Prices: $35–$45 for single-day tickets, $110 for entire weekend. Youth under 18, $15 admission to all three days. Half-price available on Goldstar.com for certain performances.

From the Editors: The Monterey Jazz Festival is the longest continuously running festival of its kind in the country, having played host to some of America's greatest musicians since 1958. The inaugural festival had performers like Billie Holiday, Louis Armstrong, Sonny Rollins, and Dizzy Gillespie. Every year since then, the performers that have graced the stage at MJF have been unparalleled in their fame and talent. Having relocated to the Monterey Fairgrounds, the event is now able to draw an audience of more than 40,000.

Tickets can be purchased online well in advance (as early as early summer in most cases). Be sure to scout out hotels/camping as early as possible, as the festival continues to bring in more and more jazz lovers every year, selling out most accommodations months ahead of time. Throughout the rest of the year, MJF has an extensive jazz education program with a variety of camps, workshops, and clinics for jazz enthusiasts of all ages.

MT. HOOD FESTIVAL OF JAZZ
Mt. Hood Community College, 26000 SE Stark Street, Gresham, Oregon
503-661-2700 • mthoodjazz.org

Public Transportation: Poor
Handicapped Accessibility: Good
Performances/Programs: Approximately 15 performances are presented over three days.
Ticket Prices: $30 per day or $50 for two-night package. Portions of the festival are free and open to the public. See schedule for details. $20 student tickets also frequently available.

From the Editors: Between the Mt. Hood Festival of Jazz and the Portland Jazz Festival, the Pacific Northwest has placed itself as a sort of jazz oasis in what the rest of the world considers cowboy country. Since 1982, Mt. Hood Community College has hosted one of the West's most prestigious events, with headliners like Sonny Rollins, Buddy Rich, Jon Hendricks, and the New York Voices. The majority of the festival focuses on acts that are no strangers to the Portland/Seattle scene and even some of the local student groups (the MHCC jazz program is rated very highly by *Downbeat* magazine).

Many of the daytime events are free and open to the public and the evening concert is generally affordably priced ($20–$30). Tickets can be purchased beginning in May/June from the website or from the MHCC box office. There are also a variety of other events during the festival, including wine tastings, film screenings, readings, and art installations that are all open to the public.

NEW ORLEANS JAZZ & HERITAGE FESTIVAL
Fairgrounds Race Course, 1751 Gentilly Boulevard
nojazzfest.com

Public Transportation: Poor
Handicapped Accessibility: Good
Performances/Programs: More than 500 different performers over two weekends—late April/early May.
Ticket Prices: Single-day passes $40 in advance, $50 at the gate. Children (2–11) $5.
Other Discounts: Discount packages are available for the weekends at $35 per day ($105 for each three-day weekend). Packages are only available early on (this offer expired at the end of February for the 2009 festival).

From the Editors: The New Orleans Jazz & Heritage has been one of the premier events in the U.S. for jazz and popular music for 40 years. The idea for the festival arose out of a spontaneous parade with Mahalia Jackson, Duke Ellington, and the Eureka Brass Band. Virtually every notable jazz artist (and many a superstar popular act) has graced the festival stage, far too many to list here. The 40th anniversary festival in 2009 featured the likes of Tony Bennett, James Taylor, Dave Matthews Band, Neil Young, Wynton Marsalis, Joe Cocker, Etta James, Earth, Wind & Fire, Bonnie Raitt, and literally hundreds of others.

Purchase weekend ticket packages well in advance for good discounts (approximately $50 off of regular single-day ticket price). Tickets can be purchased through Ticketmaster or at the New Orleans Superdome and the New Orleans Arena. Parking is very limited at the Fairgrounds Race Course, but some hotels offer a shuttle service during the festival.

DANCE FESTIVALS

AMERICAN DANCE FESTIVAL (ADF)
715 Broad Street, Durham, North Carolina
919-684-6402 • americandancefestival.org

Public Transportation: Poor
Handicapped Accessibility: Good
Performances/Programs: A six-week June/July summer festival of modern dance based at the Duke University Campus.

Ticket Prices: $25–$41, half-price student Rush tickets sold one hour prior to performance, $3 discount for seniors, 15% off single tickets for Duke employees with a valid Duke ID.

Group Discounts: Discounts available for groups of 10 or more.

Subscriptions: Save 25% when you pick four-six shows; save 35% when you pick seven-plus shows. Benefits include the best seats in the house, easy ticket exchange, ticket insurance, a subscriber coupon book, and 25% off ADF merchandise.

Educational/Community Outreach: The ADF School offers four- and six-week classes, a dance-professionals workshop, and degree programs.

BATES DANCE FESTIVAL
The Schaeffer Theatre at Bates College
365 College Street, Lewiston, Maine
207-786-6161 • batesdancefestival.org

Public Transportation: Good (Greyhound and other shuttles offer transportation to Lewiston and Bates College from the Portland jetport).

Handicapped Accessibility: Good

Performances/Programs: A five-week festival held on the Bates College campus from July through early August that features performances, panel discussions, films, and lectures. Performance schedule varies.

Ticket Prices: $20, discounts available for children 12 and under, seniors, and students, faculty, and staff of Bates College.

Group Discounts: Group discounts available for parties of 15 or more.

Subscriptions: 10% discount for anyone who orders five or more shows.

Educational/Community Outreach: Education programs are integral to the festival; there's the two-week Young Dancers Workshop, the three-week Professional Training Program, and the Community Dance Program (occurring on alternate years), which invites local residents to work with festival artists.

JACOB'S PILLOW DANCE
358 George Carter Road, Becket, Massachusetts
413-243-9919 • jacobspillow.org

Public Transportation: Fair (somewhat accessible via Peter Pan or Bonanza bus service and taxi).

Handicapped Accessibility: Good

Performances/Programs: A summer festival that runs from June to August and celebrates dance of all forms; over 200 free events offered during the season. Performance schedule is Wednesday–Sunday.

Ticket Prices: $29–$58, but many free performances are also a part of the festival; $10 youth tickets offered for some performances. Discounts are available for seniors, college students, and children (ages 8–16). Join E-mail Club to be considered for special offers and ticket giveaways.

Group Discounts: Discounts are available for groups of 20 or more.

Subscriptions: A full-season subscription provides the subscriber with the same seat for all 10 shows in the Ted Shawn Theatre, and/or all eight shows in the Doris Duke Studio Theatre. A Flex 5+ subscription allows subscribers to create a unique season by picking five or more shows, any day, any time. Also available is the Youth Matinée series, $10 youth tickets for designated matinée shows that may be more accessible to the whole family. Choose five Youth Matinées for $50. Children must be accompanied by an adult. Benefits include free ticket exchanges, lost-ticket replacement, and discounts on additional tickets.

Educational/Community Outreach: Educational initiatives include the School at Jacob's Pillow, which offers classes, coaching, master classes, talks, exhibitions, study assignments, and more; and community programs like low-cost dance classes during the festival and dance residencies in area public schools.

From the Editors: The only dance institution to ever be declared a National Historic Landmark, Jacob's Pillow is a mecca for dancers and those who love dance. Located on an old mountaintop farm in the Berkshires, the Pillow is full of history, having once been a stop on the Underground Railroad. It's also a great keeper of dance history, housing the impressive Jacob's Pillow Archives, a collection of multimedia, correspondence, programs, and costumes.

Attendees of the 75-year old Jacob's Pillow Dance Festival have been present at the launch of Martha Graham's career, seen world-premiere works from Merce Cunningham and Paul Taylor, watched greats like Margot Fonteyn and Mikhail Baryshnikov perform, and have taken morning dance class with Bill T. Jones. Rising stars, established troupes, and enthusiastic novices all continue to make the pilgrimage to Jacob's Pillow each summer to watch, learn, and perform dance of all styles.

NEW YORK DANCE FESTIVAL
New York Institute of Dance and Education
93 North Street, Auburn, New York
315-252-4420 • nyide.com

Public Transportation: Good (chosen venues are always accessible to public transportation).

Handicapped Accessibility: Good

Performances/Programs: A three-week festival beginning the second week of July each year, which includes performances, lectures, and dance-related educational intensives. Most of the educational intensives are held in the Institute building above, but concert venues rotate between some of NY's major cities, including Rochester, Ithaca, Saratoga, and NYC.

Ticket Prices: World-Class Concert series $15–$25. Opening gala $75–$100.

Educational/Community Outreach: The main part of the festival is its educational component. Educational programs include the NY Summer Dance Intensive, the NY Musical Theatre Project, and the NY Drum Festival (scholarships available, no prior experience or audition necessary to participate).

VAIL INTERNATIONAL DANCE FESTIVAL
Gerald R. Ford Amphitheater, 530 S Frontage Road East, Vail, Colorado
888-920-2787 • vaildance.org

Other Venue: Vilar Center for the Arts, 68 Avondale Lane, Beaver Creek, Colorado.

Public Transportation: Good

Handicapped Accessibility: Good

Performances/Programs: Performances almost every night of the late July/early August festival.

Ticket Prices: $17–$85.

Subscriptions: Multiple packages are available, including Performance Plus pass $75, which includes one lawn ticket to each performance held at Ford Amphitheater, plus $10 off a bottle of wine each night (seven shows total); Student Performance Plus pass $50, good for one lawn ticket to each performance held at Ford Amphitheater (must present valid student ID, seven shows total); Student Spotlight pass $150, which includes one ticket to each performance at Vilar Performing Arts Center (must present valid student ID, four shows total); and Center Stage pass $575, which includes one premium-reserved seat to each performance (11 shows total).

CITIZENS OF THE ARTS

Glenn Schaeffer defies every stereotype of a gaming executive . Formerly President and Chief Financial Officer for the Mandalay Resort Group, a public corporation operating 16 casino properties nationwide, Schaeffer has also had a lifelong affair with literature.

Schaeffer graduated summa cum laude in English Literature from UC Irvine, then went on to receive a Master's degree from UC Irvine and an MFA from the Iowa Writers' Workshop (now home to the Glenn Schaeffer Library and Archives). He sits on the board of the National Poetry Series and was instrumental in creating the Black Mountain Institute, an international literary center dedicated to promoting discourse on today's most pressing issues.

Located on the UNLV campus in Las Vegas, the Black Mountain Institute provides an environment where thinkers and writers from all segments of global society can fight against entrenched perspectives, whatever their political or cultural source. Activities include "readings, lectures, and debates by public intellectuals whose work embodies BMI's mission; the administration of a fellowship program that supports the creation of internationally focused writing for an educated lay audience; the administration of a safe haven for writers of conscience from countries in which such freedoms are curtailed or endangered; the publication of a nationally recognized literary journal; and the translation into English of major literary works from traditionally under-translated languages."

Inspired by the life and special interests of their son Graham, who died at 15 in January 2006, Bob "Dixie" Johnson, his wife Elizabeth, and their family and friends formed the Graham Johnson Cultural Arts Endowment "to enrich the lives of the members of our community through the enjoyment of cultural and performing arts."

Centered in and around Wake Forest, North Carolina, the Foundation's goals "are to help those who have skill sets, but may lack the confidence to perform, and assist in the development of not only the skills, but more importantly build self-confidence in that individual." Among the activities they sponsor and support are Irishfest, Festive Fridays, and a Battle of the Bands, as well as visits to local schools by artists and writers. According to Johnson, "We broadly define arts, so we can achieve the greater goal, that of gaining self-confidence and recognition of those individuals for the talents they have. Arts are a primary tool for development of the greater personal goals of our citizens."

IMPROVING THE ARTS IN YOUR HOMETOWN

Whatever your hometown is—New York City, Tulsa, or Brecksville, Ohio—there are many things you can do to improve your cultural life, as well as that of your friends and neighbors. If you can't give money, you can give time, and if you can't give time, you can give your passion. All contributions no matter how large or small benefit the arts in America.

MAKE NEARBY CULTURAL INSTITUTIONS PART OF YOUR LIFE

An Ohio friend recently went to New York to check out a special exhibition at the Metropolitan Museum of Art and noticed that the three works he liked the most were loaned from the Toledo Museum of Art. Although 20 minutes from his house, he'd never visited the museum, because "I figured that there couldn't be any great art in Toledo, Ohio."

Ten years ago the Las Vegas Little Theatre seemed to be a center for uninspired Neil Simon re-runs. Today it offers challenging well-acted productions that any theater would be proud to put on its stage and is a sterling example of how interested citizens working with an existing small local-arts organization can create a valuable community asset.

You live near great or potentially great cultural institutions, which will only become better with your help. Schedule a visit (or purchase a ticket to their next performance) now! If you like what you see (even if all you see is potential), consider becoming a member or patron.

PARTICIPATE IN AN ART

Participation can be an excellent teacher of the arts. In addition, side benefits include exercise and an expanded social network. Learn to dance, sing in a choir, or develop your painting skills by helping the local theater build sets. Everyone has a talent. William Compton, Sr., (Jeffrey's father) is seriously tone-deaf and has always been a bit clumsy, but put a pencil or crayons in his hand (even at age 92) and you will see art.

ASSIST YOUR LOCAL SCHOOLS EFFORTS IN THE ARTS

Shrinking school budgets always attack the arts first; many public schools have wisely turned to arts-minded members of the community for donated time and money to keep these programs going. If your efforts help a grade-school student appreciate the humor and beauty of poetry or create an unforgettable experience for 100 kids putting on a musical, your donation hasn't just benefited, it's blossomed.

WATCH AND SUPPORT PUBLIC TELEVISION

While the overall quality of TV arts programming has improved over the years (especially on the A&E, Ovation, and Discovery channels), nothing compares with PBS. It's the American birthplace of the legendary arts documentaries from Kenneth Clark and Ken Burns to Sister Wendy. *Live at Lincoln Center*, *An Evening at Pops*, *Great Performances*, and the like take you to the crème of American performing arts—at no admission charge. "Charlie Rose" and the "Newshour with Jim Lehrer" consistently devote time to important developments in the arts world. Watch PBS, and better yet, become a member of your local station. You help guarantee the continued development of excellent arts programming, plus you get a lot of side benefits and discounts, including a tax deduction.

LISTEN TO AND SUPPORT PUBLIC RADIO

In many cities, National Public Radio (NPR) is the only place to go for classical music and jazz programming—not to mention informative local and national arts coverage, especially on "Morning Edition," "All Things Considered," and "Fresh Air." Trying to find an NPR station in a strange town? Tune the dial from 88.0 to 92.0—where most public radio stations can be located.

READ

Few things can stretch your mind like a good book: fiction, non-fiction, even '50s' pulp novels have their benefits. When you can, read aloud to your kids or grandkids or nieces and nephews (or volunteer to read aloud at your local library or bookstore). Your listeners will enjoy, learn, and bond—both with books and with you.

USING YOUR PUBLIC LIBRARY BY BOB DANCER

(Note: Bob Dancer, a professional gambler and the country's leading expert in video poker, reads more than 100 library books a year, although he could easily afford to buy them all at Barnes & Noble or on Amazon. com. Of course, one of the reasons he can afford to buy the books is because he doesn't. By Bob's own estimate, his wealth is more than $50,000 greater today because he uses the library.)

Many people live and/or work near a public library. If this includes you, this is a tremendous resource if you regularly read books or magazines. And if you don't own a computer to send email or search the web, these services are often available at libraries as well.

The two major advantages of a library are that almost all its services are free and once you've read a book, you can return it, instead of cluttering your living space with stacks and stacks of books, many of which you'll never read again.

The three major disadvantages of a library are that you're reading books with other people's cooties on them, the 14-day or 21-day return policy can be restrictive, and you can't always depend on the exact title you want being available when you want it.

There are workarounds to each of these disadvantages. You can wear gloves when you read a library book if you're obsessive about germs. Usually, books may be renewed (frequently online without making a second trip to the library) to extend the time you can have them. And most library systems allow you to place a hold on a book, so your turn will eventually come around. In the meantime, other books are available that you'd enjoy reading. Remember, any book you haven't read is a new book.

If you're planning on rereading a book over and over again, or must have a particular title now, buying that book makes sense. But if you're only planning on reading it once, the library can be the best alternative.

What about library fines (a frequent sore spot between teenagers and their parents)? I average about $40 a year in overdue fines (or to buy the occasional lost book). While I try to avoid these fees, it comes out to 40¢ per book, which is still quite reasonable. Sometimes I'm "almost through" with a book when it becomes due and for some reason isn't renewable. Paying a few days of late fees is an inexpensive alternative to either not being able to finish the book or having to go out and buy a copy.

go-artsamerica.com

Appearing Now!

- ✔ *Arts America* Updates
- ✔ Arts Info from 30 additional cities;

   Anchorage to Detroit to Tampa to Wichita

- ✔ Breaking Arts News
- ✔ Editors' Blogs
- ✔ Reader Comments
- ✔ Travel Information

Coming soon!

   Blogs from all fifty cities (RSS/Atom updates)

   Special Admission, Ticket and Travel Discounts

INDEX

ABOUT THE ARTS AMERICA TEAM

Jeffrey Compton & Norma Foote met in a high-school English class. Jeffrey was sitting at one of the desks; Norma was the teacher. Norma taught Jeffrey a skill that has given him tremendous joy for more than 40 years.

Seven years ago, Jeff contacted Norma to help teach members of his consulting-company staff that same skill and during the course of the project, they discovered a mutual love of the arts and a mutual sense of adventure. These discoveries led directly to the *Arts America* project. In the time between adventures with Jeffrey, Norma taught English at Brecksville High School for 30 years and served as English Department Chair for 25 of those years. In the mid-1980s she took over full teaching responsibility (former-ly taught by four teachers) for the school's poorly subscribed Humanities course and within one year had to schedule an additional section due to over-registration. Among her many honors were Presidential Scholars Awards, Commended Teacher from the State of Ohio, and Teacher of the Year from the Brecksville School System.

Jeffrey ran a small manufacturing company in Cleveland and a marketing consult-ing firm in Las Vegas, founded an equity theater group, served on the boards of Chorus America (winner Michael Korn Corporate Award 1989), the Cleveland State University Foundation, the Robert Page Singers, the Casino Management Association, and Cauli-flower Alley.

John Broughton is a writer living in Alexandria, Virginia, with his wife and two cats. Most of his career has involved computers and (more recently) the Internet; his interest in those began in 1969 with a National Science Foundation summer program. He was the Y2K Campus Coordinator for the University of California at Berkeley and is the author of the 2008 book *Wikipedia: The Missing Manual* (O'Reilly Media/Pogue Press).

Sean Kent is an author and playwright who has been fascinated by the performing arts since childhood. Sean began writing almost a decade ago and has since seen his plays produced at multiple venues throughout New York City. In 2005, Sean's first full-length work, *The Salacious Uncle Baldrick*, was produced at fringeNYC to much critical acclaim. Most recently, he was a writer and content producer for the primetime re-launch of the CBS primetime game show "Million Dollar Password." As a graduate of the acting programs of both the Baltimore School for the Arts and the North Carolina School of the Arts, Sean has also worked extensively as an actor in projects such as the feature film *School Ties* and the critically acclaimed television series, *Homicide: Life on the Street*. Sean is also an original core company member of Sonnet Repertory Theatre, a New York-based not-for-profit theater company dedicated to the production of new and classic works. Sean currently lives in the "sixth borough," Weehawken, NJ, with his wife, Katrina Kent.

Brooke Pierce graduated in 2002 from New York University where she double majored in Dramatic Writing and Religious Studies and served as Theatre Editor of the NYU paper. She has written for *TheaterMania*, *New England Entertainment Digest*, *Stage Directions* magazine, *Show Business Weekly*, and *Go2 Mobile*, and was a contributing author to *The TheaterMania Guide to Musical Theater Recordings* and the *Moon Metro New York City* guidebook. Staged readings of Brooke's plays and musical-theater projects have been held at Stage One Theater in Louisville, New Jersey Dramatists and The Waterfront Ensemble in Teaneck and Jersey City, Orlando-UCF Shakespeare Festival's PlayFest 2005 in Orlando, and at both Ensemble Studio Theatre and the American Theatre of Actors in NYC. Brooke wrote the book for the musical *Sympathy Jones* (music and lyrics by Masi Asare), which was produced at the New York Musical Theatre Festival in 2007. Her latest play, *Beneath the Banyan Tree*, recently had a reading at the Snapple Theater, produced by eyeBlink Entertainment. Brooke is co-director of the new London-based theater company This Stage Limited and she's a member of the Drama Desk and the Dramatists Guild of America.

Kathleya Afanador is a choreographer, researcher, and writer. She graduated summa cum laude from Cornell University, majoring in Auditory and Visual Cognition and in Dance, with a concentration in Computing in the Arts. Upon receiving a NSF IGERT Fellowship in 2006, she moved to Phoenix for two years, balancing her time between ASU's Arts, Media, and Engineering program and graduate study in cognitive psychology. Subsequently she relocated to London, UK, to pursue choreography at Trinity Laban Conservatoire. Her choreography has been presented in various cities across the United States, as well as internationally in Italy and the UK. She has presented research on cross-modal perception at the 2006 Congress on Research in Dance Conference and the 2007 International Computer Music Conference. She is a co-founder and the choreographer for Armadillo Dance Project (armadillodanceproject.com), an ongoing collaboration that uses computer-interactive technology to create theatrical performances and new-media installations.

Patrick Allen was born in Arlington, VA, where he still lives today. He developed a passion for music, which he has exercised by joining various musical groups and supporting the arts since first learning to play drums in the fifth grade. Patrick believes that the connection between the arts and politics is extremely fascinating and is currently working various arts-related jobs, attempting to find ways in which arts and politics can be successfully linked together to the benefit of both communities in and around the Washington, D.C., area. Patrick attended Christopher Newport University (2004-2008), where he received a B.A. in political science.

Tiffany Du Mouchelle is a soprano recognized for her fearlessness in exploring new and challenging repertoire. She performs a wide range of musical styles in more than 15 different languages. A resident of New York City, Ms. Du Mouchelle performs as a soloist, chamber musician, and opera singer in New York's most prestigious venues. She made her Lincoln Center solo debut in 2006 as the winner of the Mannes College of Music Concerto Competition and has performed with the Chamber Music Society of

Lincoln Center, Center for Contemporary Opera, and American Composer's Alliance. In 2005, she co-founded Aurora Borealis, a duo with percussionist Stephen Solook. Their primary focus being a composer-performer collaboration, they frequently commission, premiere, and collaborate on new works with composers from all over the world. Ms. Du Mouchelle is a performing member of Cultures in Harmony, a musical diplomacy organization whose aim is to promote cultural dialogue through music. Recent trips have included workshops with youth in Egypt, musical collaborations and concerts with musicians from Alexandria, and musical workshops for youth in the Yoro Village of Papua New Guinea. Ms. Du Mouchelle is a graduate of Mannes College of Music, where she received her BM and MM degrees.

Kara Mason is an editor at the Solomon R. Guggenheim Museum, New York. Formerly an editor at Archipelago Books (Brooklyn) and Welcome Books (New York), she has edited illustrated books such as *Novalis* (with drawings by Paul Klee), *Henri Michaux's Stroke by Stroke*, and *The Oxford Project* by Peter Feldstein, as well as several travel guides, including *Tuscan Country: A Photographer's Journey and Paris: Wish You Were Here*. At the Guggenheim she has edited recent exhibition catalogues, including *Catherine Opie: American Photographer* and *The Third Mind: American Artists Contemplate Asia, 1860–1989*. She's a graduate of Skidmore College, where she once performed with a company member of the postmodern Trisha Brown Dance Company in the Frances Young Tang Teaching Museum. Her writing has been published in *Artful Dodge* and *American Book Review*. She lives in Brooklyn, New York.

Alex Riccomini works as a freelance writer, specializing in writing for the arts. She is a graduate of Boston University with a degree in English, magna cum laude, and is currently enrolled in the 2010 class at the University of Sydney for a Master of Arts by Research in English, en route (hopefully) to a Ph.D. in English. A regular writer for TOMS Shoes and Meta Mehling & Associates, she has also edited for *New American Paintings* magazine and HarperCollins Australia. She's currently based in San Francisco.

Mark Sanderlin, a native Oregonian, hails from a diverse musical background, having shared the bill with various pop and jazz acts, such as Michael Allen Harrison, Peter Eldridge, Lion of Ido, This Condition, and Julianne Johnson. Classical credits include *Carmen* and *La Boheme* with the Portland Opera and various recitals and performances in the greater Portland area and on and around Long Island, NY. As a solo performer, Mark has appeared at many notable NYC venues, including Caffe Vivaldi, the Waltz-Astoria, and the National Underground. He's currently finishing a degree in Music Business at Hofstra University and has two albums of original music available on iTunes and Amazon.com. The original song, "Rain," was a nominee in the Best Miscellaneous Mp3 category for the 2007 IACmusic Golden Kayak Awards. Aside from this project, Mark is also a frequent contributor of reviews and feature articles for *Amplifier* magazine (amplifiermagazine.com) and maintains his own music review blog (marksanderlin.blogspot.com).

Melissa Somosky developed her love for film at an early age, sometimes staying up all night to watch her favorite movies twice in a row. She was fortunate enough to live all over the country and experience cinema in a variety of locales. After attending high school in the great state of Colorado, Melissa continued her education on film in a more formal setting, at the College of William and Mary, where she participated in the Williamsburg Women's Film Festival and the Williamsburg Documentary Project. Some of her favorite classes focused on literary adaptations for the screen. After graduating with a B.A. in English Literature and American Studies, Melissa migrated up the East Coast, taking time to work for such media outlets as the National Geographic Channel and A&E Television.